COUNSELING THEORIES

A Simple Explanation and Biblical Evaluation

G. Michael Cocoris

COUNSELING THEORIES

A Simple Explanation and Biblical Evaluation

G. Michael Cocoris

© 2009, 2019, 2024 by G. Michael Cocoris

All rights reserved. This publication may not be reproduced *for sale* (in whole or in part, edited, or revised) in any way, form, or means including, but not limited to, electronic, mechanical, photocopying, recording, or any kind of storage and retrieval system, except for brief quotations in printed reviews, without the written permission of G. Michael Cocoris, 2016 Euclid #20, Santa Monica, CA 90405, michaelcocoris@gmail.com, or his appointed representatives. Permission is hereby granted, however, for the reproduction of the whole or parts of the whole without changing the content in any way for *free distribution,* provided all copies contain this copyright notice in its entirety. Permission is also granted to charge for the cost of copying. Unless otherwise indicated, all Scripture quotations are taken from the New King James Version ®, Copyright © 1979, 1980, 1982 by Thomas Nelson, Inc. Used by permission. All rights reserved.

Cover design and internal layout by John T. Cocoris.

TABLE OF CONTENTS

PREFACE   1

CHAPTER 1   **INTRODUCTION**   5

CHAPTER 2   **THE STANDARD OF EVALUATION**   7

CHAPTER 3   **A BRIEF HISTORY OF PSYCHOLOGY**   29

CHAPTER 4   **PSYCHOANALYSIS**   45

CHAPTER 5   **ANALYTICAL PSYCHOTHERAPY**   71

CHAPTER 6   **PSYCHODYNAMIC PSYCHOTHERAPIES**   107

CHAPTER 7   **ADLERIAN THERAPY**   123

CHAPTER 8   **BEHAVIOR THERAPY**   135

CHAPTER 9   **RATIONAL-EMOTIVE THERAPY**   145

CHAPTER 10   **COGNITIVE THERAPY**   157

CHAPTER 11   **REALITY THERAPY**   171

CHAPTER 12   **MULTIMODAL THERAPY**   183

CHAPTER 13   **EXISTENTIAL THERAPY**   191

CHAPTER 13	EXISTENTIAL THERAPY	191
CHAPTER 14	PERSON-CENTERED THERAPY	211
CHAPTER 15	GESTALT THERAPY	223
CHAPTER 16	TRANSACTIONAL ANALYSIS	233
CHAPTER 17	FAMILY THERAPY	247
CHAPTER 18	NOUTHETIC COUNSELING	257
CHAPTER 19	OTHER CHRISTIAN RESPONSES	293
CHAPTER 20	SUMMARY	309
CHAPTER 21	CONCLUSION	335
APPENDIX:	PSYCHOTHERAPIES CHART	351
BIBLIOGRAPHY		353
ABOUT THE AUTHOR		357

PREFACE

For as long as I can remember, I have wanted to help people. My mother, the Boy Scouts, and various service clubs in high school were molding influences in that direction. Becoming a Christian at age eighteen only intensified that desire.

When I entered college, I intended to major in psychology and enter the ministry. My first (and last) class in psychology discouraged the pursuit of a psychology major. The faculty of the psychology department, not the subject, changed my mind. I ended up majoring in English with minors in history and philosophy.

In seminary, I had one class in Pastoral Counseling, which was very helpful. At the time (the 1960s), very few counseling books were written from a Christian perspective. My major in seminary was Bible exposition. Thus, my formal training is in Bible exposition, not psychology or counseling.

Since seminary, I have listened to and tried to help people for thousands of hours, but I have spent most of my time expounding one biblical book after another. To understand and biblically evaluate "counseling," I have read books, attended lectures, and talked to professionals.

When Jay Adams published his book Competent to Counsel (1970), I read it and was greatly impressed. It seemed to me that it was the most biblical approach to counseling I had seen. For the next several years, I practiced Adams's basic approach, being a directive counselor telling people what the Bible said they should do.

Larry Crabb Jr.'s *Basic Principles of Biblical Counseling* (1975) and his *Effective Biblical Counseling* (1977) changed my thinking. Those books made me more of a cognitive counselor. After all, we are transformed by renewing our minds (Rom. 12:2).

In the last half of the 1970s, I taught evangelism at Dallas Theological Seminary, my alma mater. Doctors Paul Meier and Frank Minirth, Christian psychiatrists, taught in the same Pastoral Ministries department. Conversations with them, especially Dr. Meier, introduced me to a more psychodynamic understanding of counseling.

After I had become Pastor of the Church of the Open Door in Los Angeles (1979), I became acquainted with Dr. Bruce Narramore, Professor of Psychology at Rosemead School of Psychology. One semester, we team-taught a course at Rosemead that was an attempt to integrate theology and psychology. He taught the course; I provided some theological input. My interaction with Dr. Narramore was another exposure to a Christian version of the psychodynamic approach, as were several significant conversations with Linda Mason, a therapist in Pennsylvania, whom I had led to Christ many years ago. Based on three books, I wrote my summary of the various theories of psychotherapy. That material was lost when my briefcase was stolen on a trip to China. In the mid-1990s, I redid the material on the various views of psychotherapy and taught it in a course on "A Theological Evaluation of Psychological Systems" at a small theological seminary.

In 2003, a small group of people at my church and I watched thirty videos on Christian counseling and I taught "A Theological Evaluation of Psychological Systems" to them. In preparation for the class, I attended lectures at the C. G. Jungian Institute of Los Angeles and, during the class at church, some of us took a seminar in the home of William Glasser, taught by his wife and for one day by him.

Along the way, I attended other lectures, including one by Albert Ellis (at Cal State Fullerton) and a seminar by Larry Crabb, and read other books. The result is the material that follows. As is apparent, I have gleaned a great deal from the volumes by Jones and Butman, Corey, and Corsini and Wedding. I am particularly indebted to the work of Jones and Butman. It has provided me with many helpful insights, especially in evaluating the various psychotherapy methods from a Christian point of view.

Initially, I did this study solely for myself, with no thought of anyone else reading what I wrote. I began with the three books by Corsini and Wedding, Corey, and Jones and Butman. Since, at that point, I aimed to summarize the various concepts briefly so I could think through them when I wrote, I was not concerned with quotation marks or documentation. In some places, I noted the reference, usually in parentheses at the end of the paragraph. Since then, I have added many more references from those three volumes but may have missed some. In other words, I may have quoted or virtually quoted those three books without proper annotation because of how this material evolved. Beyond the three primary sources, all other materials are appropriately acknowledged.

The purpose of this material is to explain and biblically evaluate the theories of psychotherapies. The aim is educational. This is not a practical "how to" manual on counseling. Understanding the <u>theories</u> of psychotherapies and <u>practicing therapy</u> are two very different things.

Originally, Kathleen McCray served as a proofreader, but since she read this material, a number of changes and many additions have been made. Teresa Rogers

Preface

proofread this edition and gave me a number of helpful suggestions.

    Hopefully, this explanation and biblical evaluation of psychotherapies will give you an understanding of the theories of psychotherapies and a biblical perspective concerning counseling.

G. Michael Cocoris
Santa Monica, California

Chapter 1

INTRODUCTION

Obviously, something is radically wrong with the human race. A simple example is that throughout recorded history, human beings have had conflicts with each other on a family level (Cain killed Abel), on a tribal level, and on a national level. In a sense, the history of the world is the history of war. There has been one war right after another. In recorded human history, there have been relatively few years when there was no war somewhere on the planet. Conflict is a characteristic of human creatures. On a more personal level, individuals struggle with a myriad of "problems," such as anxiety and depression, as well as bizarre behavior.

What is wrong with people? For centuries, people have tried to answer that perplexing question. They have speculated, theorized, and studied human beings to determine the cause and cure of human difficulties. Until relatively recently, the people grappling with this issue were the religious, the philosophers, and the medical doctors. However, psychotherapy was created and developed at the end of the 19th century and throughout the 20th century.

As many as 260 different schools of psychotherapy have been identified (Jones and Butman, p. 11). Not all of these are well-known or widely used. There are only about nine (Corey) to twelve (Jones and Butman) major psychotherapies, which can be categorized into three general categories: psychodynamic, behavioral/cognitive, and humanistic (Jones and Butman say there are four; they add family systems; Jones and Butman, p. 15).

The psychodynamic category includes classic psychoanalysis begun by Sigmund Freud in Vienna and revisions and extensions of his theories. The approaches within this classification believe that humans have an unconscious mind, that early childhood dynamics affect peoples' behavior as adults, and that the personality needs to be reconstructed.

The behavioral/cognitive category includes several distinct theories. To a great extent, Alfred Adler, also from Vienna, pioneered many cognitive therapies. The behaviorist within this classification puts a premium on doing, while the cognitive branch emphasizes thinking.

The humanistic category also includes a variety of explanations, all of which stress concern for what it means to be fully human in the present. These approaches are not a unified school of therapy with a standard theory or set of techniques. Instead, they are a philosophy of therapy that focuses on the person's subjective world.

It is interesting to note that Vienna is where the three major categories of psychotherapy originated. Freud and Adler were from Vienna and so was Frankl, who developed Logotherapy, one of the humanistic schools of thought. In the preface to Viktor Frankl's book *Man's Search for Meaning*, Gordon Allport calls Frankl's Logotherapy the "Third Viennese School of Psychotherapy" (Allport in *Man's Search for Meaning*, p. 12).

Be that as it may, the problem with these various theories of psychotherapy is that they contradict one another. The question becomes, "Which theory of psychotherapy is right?" How would one determine the answer to that question? What standard determines what is right and what is not right in psychotherapy?

Those who believe the Bible is the Word of God would say that the Bible provides the standard by which such things should be evaluated. After all, the Scriptures describe God, people, the relationship between God and people, and the relationships of people with each other. As one Christian author has pointed out, "Christians have been thinking about and practicing psychology for centuries. Believing that God has revealed the most important truth about human beings in the Bible, they learned there that God created the world and human beings were specially created in his image. But they also learned that something was terribly wrong with human beings—they were sinners and needed to be rescued from their plight, for which they bore responsibility. Because humans were created in God's image, they were endowed with reason, so they can apprehend truth in the Bible and in the created order. In the Bible, they found God's norms for human beings and his design for the forcing of human life in the salvation obtained through faith in Christ on the basis of his life, death, and resurrection" (Johnson, p. 14).

Granted, the Bible is not a book on psychotherapy in the modern sense of the term. Yet it is filled with psychology in the sense that it is about God, people, the relationship between God and people, and the relationship of people with each other. Besides, "God created man and therefore knows more about human nature than any psychologist could ever discover experientially" (Gordon H. Clark. *Faith and Saving Faith*, p. 29).

Assuming that the Bible is the standard by which psychotherapies are to be evaluated, the next question is, "Exactly how is that done?" That is the subject of the next chapter.

Chapter 2

THE STANDARD OF EVALUATION

One way to use the Bible to evaluate the various psychotherapies is to start with the categories of psychotherapy. In their book *Modern Psychotherapies*, Jones and Butman do that. The categories they evaluate are 1) philosophical assumptions, 2) the model of personality, 3) the model of abnormality, 4) the model of health, and 5) the model of psychotherapy (Jones and Butman, pp. 30-35). Jones and Butman's five categories will be used to evaluate the various theories of psychotherapy.

This approach fits the nature of therapy better than using theology. If a person seeks therapy, there is a "problem." By the nature of the case, any therapy claims to have a treatment to help relieve the problem. Thus, all theories of psychotherapy have at least a theory of pathology (the problem) and a method of therapy. Some approaches articulate no more than these two elements. They are "micro-theories" of specific phenomena. Their goal is to do nothing more than develop well-articulated, small-scale theories about a particular phenomenon, such as depression (Jones and Butman, p. 198).

Nevertheless, a theory of pathology and a method of therapy at least imply an opinion about "health." If nothing else, it is the opposite of the problem. Although not always delineated, all theories also involve a view of people, which implies philosophical assumptions.

Therefore, an evaluation of any psychotherapy consists of five parts: philosophical assumptions (all the way to ultimate reality), a view of people, a theory of pathology, the nature of health, and a method of therapy. What does the Bible say about these five issues?

Philosophical Assumptions

Special Revelation The Bible declares there is a God who has revealed truth in the Bible about Himself and human beings. From a biblical point of view, only a fool says, "There is no God" (Ps. 14:1). Not all the truth about people is in the Scripture, but what is recorded is true. Solomon says that people ought to learn things from nature to apply to themselves (Prov. 6:6). The fact that the Bible quotes secular sources indicates that it recognizes there are other sources of accurate information (2 Sam. 1:18; 1 Kings 11:41; 14:19, 14:29; 15:7; 2 Kings 18:18). Paul quotes a secular source to describe a group of people (Titus 1:12). Peter says husbands ought to live with their wives according to knowledge, which means that a husband must learn things about his particular wife (1 Pet. 3:7).

Truth can be discovered from experience, observation, logic, and experiments. Scientists have studied the stars. Sailors have charted the oceans. Farmers have learned about the land and psychologists have acquired knowledge about humans.

Much of what is in psychological theory is nothing more than observations about people. For example, it is obvious that the two extremes of human relationships are isolation from all humans and intimacy. Eric Berne has analyzed the levels between these two extremes and given them names (Eric Berne, *Games People Play*; see Jones and Butman, p. 328). Is not that exactly the kind of thing God commanded? He created human beings to have dominion (Gen. 1:26) "over every living thing that moves on the earth" (Gen. 1:28). The first thing the first man did was name what he saw (Gen. 2:19)!

The point is truth about people can be gained from the information in the Bible and sources outside the Bible. "All truth is God's truth, wherever it is found" (Carter and Narramore, p. 13). God is the source of all truth, which He reveals through the Bible and nature (Collins, pp. 115-132). No truth outside the Bible contradicts a truth in the Bible. "If we believe that God is the source of all truth, we assume that there is no inherent conflict between the facts of psychology and the data of Scripture" (Carter and Narramore, p. 22).

Some psychology theories, however, contradict the teachings of the Scripture and, therefore, must be rejected. Parts of a theory may be compatible, and if so, those parts can be integrated into a biblical approach, but no theory or treatment that contradicts the Scripture is acceptable.

View of People

The Bible has a great deal to say about people, but just because believers in Jesus Christ have a Bible in their hands and the Holy Spirit in their hearts does

The Standard of Evaluation

not mean they have a thorough understanding of the make-up of people. Humans are complex creatures. While people know themselves, at least to some degree (1 Cor. 2:11), not even the Apostle Paul, who authored inspired Scripture, completely understood himself (Rom. 7:15; 1 Cor. 4:4; see also Ps. 139:23-24; Jer. 17:9)! As long as we are in this life, "we see in a mirror dimly" (1 Cor. 13:12). So, we do not completely even understand ourselves, much less people in general. Nevertheless, the Bible has many things to say about people we should and can comprehend.

The Make-up of People Three biblical concepts, namely, the material/immaterial nature of people, the image of God in people, and the sinful nature of people, explain the make-up of people.

1. The Bible says Adam, the first human being, was created from the "dust of the ground" and made a living creature (Gen. 2:7). The first human was made from the earth (1 Cor. 15:47). Then, into this lifeless, material body, God breathed "the breath of life." Therefore, Genesis 2 says there are two parts to humans: a material part, namely, a body made from the dust of the ground, and an immaterial part.

Throughout the Bible, various words are used for both aspects of people. For example, the Bible calls the material part "body, flesh, tent," etc. and the immaterial part "heart, soul, spirit," etc. Each word used of the immaterial part has multiple meanings in the Scripture.

Heart is used of the material and immaterial parts of people. In some passages, the word "heart" refers to the body (Gen. 18:5; Judg. 19:5; Acts 14:17) and in other passages, it means everything in a person but the body (1 Sam. 16:7)! The heart can stand for the person as a whole. The heart is said to think (Prov. 23:7; Mt. 13:15). It experiences emotions (Ps. 4:7; Eccl. 2:20; Rom. 1:24; Jn. 16:6). It can also make choices (Rom. 6:17; 2 Cor. 9:7). Heart is even used of the conscience (Job 27:6; 1 Jn. 3:19-21). It is capable of being desperately wicked (Jer. 17:9; Mt. 15:19), yet when God takes up residence in a person, He is said to dwell there (2 Cor. 1:22; Eph. 3:17) and He can shed love abroad in the heart (Rom. 5:5).

Soul is also a many-sided word, which basically means "life" and is often translated "life" (Prov. 7:23; 8:35-36). (The Greek word translated "soul" is *psyche* from which comes the English word "psychology.") It is used of the body (Ps. 107:5, 9; Prov. 27:7; Mt. 6:25, where *psyche* is translated "life") and of the entire person (Jos. 10: 28, 30, 32, 35, 37, 39, where it is translated "people;" in this sense, the soul is the self). Soul designates desires (Ps. 42:2-3; Prov. 21:10), thinking (Ps. 13:2), feelings (Ps. 35:9; Mt. 26:38), choice (Ps. 62:1), etc. At death, the soul is not dissolved (Mt.

10:28), but it is disembodied (Acts 2:27, 31).

Spirit is a difficult word to define. It means "wind, breath, spirit" and is used of God (Job 4:24), angels (Heb. 1:4), evil spirits (Mt. 12:43), and the immaterial part of people (2 Cor. 7:1). It is also used of various functions within the immaterial part of people such as insight (Mk. 2:8), feeling (Lk. 1:47), and choice (Acts 19:21).

The Scripture also refers to the person as "I" (Rom. 7:15-20; Gal 2:20). The Greek word translated "I" is *ego*. Perhaps the immaterial part, the "self," the "I" (the *ego*), should be called the persona, a word which simply means person.

Thus, there are two parts in the make-up of humans: a material part and an immaterial part. Nevertheless, even though people are made up of several parts, they are simultaneously unitary beings. People are not like a chemical mixture in which the atoms of each element retain their distinctive characteristics (oil and water). Instead, people's "parts" are more like a chemical compound. The atoms of all the elements become a new combination to form molecules. The resultant molecule has characteristics unlike the elements, which unite to compose them.

For example, in the chemical compound sodium chloride (table salt), the two elements of sodium and chloride lose their characteristics; these qualities cannot be detected in the new compound. Yet, it is possible to break up the compound with the result that each element will again have its original distinctive characteristics. Likewise, people are made up of material and immaterial parts, which form a unity that will be broken at death (the compound will be dissolved at death). In the meantime, the unity has its own characteristics (see Erickson, pp. 536-37).

The unity of the material and immaterial parts means that what affects one will affect the other. What affects the body can and does affect the mind and emotions and what affects the mind and emotions can and does affect a person's physical frame. They catch each other's diseases. To say the same thing another way, human beings are psychological/physical creatures. Psychosomatic conditions affect both the soul and the body. Psychosomatic comes from the Greek words *psyche*, meaning "soul" and *soma*, meaning "body." "A sound heart *is* life to the body, but envy *is* rottenness to the bones" (Prov. 14:30). Psychosomatic illness is a reality.

2. The Bible also says Adam was created in the image of God (Gen. 1:26-27). The image of God is usually said to be intelligence, emotion, and will (Erickson, p. 154). Two New Testament passages support this view. Colossians 3:10 says after regeneration, the new man is created with knowledge after the image of God who created him. This verse seems to say that at least part of the image of God is the ability

to know. Adam had sufficient intelligence to name all the animals (Gen. 2:19-20). He could think, reason, and speak. Ephesians 4:24 says that, after regeneration, the new man is created after God in righteousness and true holiness. The capacity for righteousness and holiness implies the ability to love God, understand His Word, and obey His commands. Therefore, perhaps it could be inferred that, originally, the image included the capacity to feel, think, and choose, including the ability to make moral choices.

Thus, the image could be said to consist of personhood, that is, God is a person (a being with the capacity to think, feel, and choose). Thus, because Adam was created in His image, he had intellectual power, natural affection, and moral freedom. The Bible and virtually all psychotherapies agree that people have a mind, emotions, and a will.

As a result of the image of God in people, they can have relationships and accomplish a task. The statement "Let Us make man" indicates some sort of relationship within the Godhead and the statement "male and female He created them" also demonstrates that the image enables people to have relationships. Also, the statement "Let Us make man in Our image" immediately followed by "Let them have dominion" indicated the people can work. Human beings have purpose; they are made to do something. Adam was a gardener (Gen. 2:8). Abel was a "keeper of sheep" (Gen. 4:2) and Cain was a "tiller of the ground" (Gen. 4:2). Others became musicians (Gen. 4:21), teachers (Gen. 4:22), and craftsmen (Gen. 4:22). Is having a talent or a gift a part of having dominion?

To sum up the concept of the image of God in people, people are psychological beings, meaning they have intellectual power, natural affection, and moral freedom. Their psychological makeup *makes it possible* for them to have a relationship with God and others and *enables* them to have dominion. People are spiritual, social, psychological (mind, emotions, and will), and functional (purposeful) beings.

Thus, humans are physical (material/body) and psychological (the image of God/ mind, emotional, and will) beings who have the capacity to have a relationship with God and others and have dominion (work). In other words, humans are spiritual, social, psychological (mind, emotions, and will), purposeful (work), and physical beings. In short, humans are a persona united to a body.

3. In addition, Scripture teaches that humans are sinful. Eve sinned out of deception (Gen. 3:1-6; 1 Tim. 2:14) and Adam sinned out of deliberate disobedience (Gen. 3:6; Rom. 5:19). After Adam had sinned, the image of God was defaced, but not erased

(Ryrie, p. 192). At least to some degree, the image of God remained in the human race (see Gen. 9:6; Jas. 3:9). Nevertheless, since Adam's fall, humans have become sinful creatures. What does that mean?

Paul says, "For all have sinned and fall short of the glory of God" (Rom. 3:23). The glory of God is a reflection of His character (see Ryrie, p. 212). So, sin is anything contrary to the character of God (Rom. 3:23). It is not just an external act but an internal condition (Mt. 5:21-30; 15:19-20). In disposition, attitudes, speech, and acts, humans miss the mark of conformity to God Himself.

Because of Adam's disobedience, sin and death (separation) entered the world (Rom. 5:12, 18-19). Sin alienated people from God (Gen. 3:8-10). Separated from the God of heaven, humans fell under the sway of the god of this world, Satan (1 Jn. 5:19; 2 Cor. 4:4). Moreover, sinful creatures living in a community apart from God produced a system that leaves God out of everything. In the Bible, that is called the "world," a system that leaves God out (Jas. 4:4; 1 Jn. 2:15, 16). Sin separated people from each other (Gen. 3:7). After Adam, all humans are born with a sin nature (Eph. 2:3). Sin also fragmented people within themselves (Jas. 1:8; 4:1) and affected every part of their person (see the next paragraph.). Sin affected the whole creation (Gen. 3:17-19; Rom. 8:20).

Thus, the human condition consists of being born estranged from God, being under the sway of the Devil (Jas. 3:15), and living in the world (consisting of creation under the curse of sin as well as systems that leave God out), and in the flesh (the sin nature). Sin has affected everything! It has even affected creation. Regarding people, it has affected their relationship with God and others and their relationship with themselves. People are *separated* from God, others, and within themselves. Sin has affected people's bodies, minds, emotions, wills, and consciences.

The creation is decaying	Romans 8:21
The spirit is dead (separation from God)	Ephesians 4:18 (2:1)
The mind is darkened (deceived)	Ephesians 4:18 (2 Cor. 4:4)
The emotions are degraded	Ephesians 4:19
The will is depraved	Ephesians 4:19
The conscience is devoid	Ephesians 4:19
The body is diseased	1 Corinthians 15:53 (Eccl. 12:1-5)
Relationships are dysfunctional	Titus 3:3

The Standard of Evaluation

What the Bible says about human beings can be itemized as follows.

1. Humans are *spiritual* beings. They were made to have a relationship with God, but all have a law of sin in their members (Rom. 7:23).
2. Humans are social beings. They were made to have a relationship with others.
3. Humans are *rational* beings. Part of being a person is having the ability to think. Humans can know, remember, forget, and reason. They can know and believe something true and be deceived into thinking something is true when it is not.
4. Humans are *emotional* beings. Part of being a person is having the capacity to feel. Babies feel before they think or choose.
5. Humans are *volitional* beings. Part of being a person is having a faculty of will. Humans have the capacity to make choices and act.
6. Humans are *moral* beings. Part of the mental function in humans is the conscience. This moral indicator of right and wrong can be programmed by society, but every human is born with moral "oughtness."
7. Humans are *physical* beings. Human beings have a body made from the dust of the ground.
8. Humans are functional beings. Humans were designed to have dominion. This probably includes having an ability, talent, or gift to do something. Thus, people are *purposeful* beings.

To say the same thing another way and, at the same time, shorten the above list, what the Bible says about people can be summarized as follows.

1. Humans are spiritual beings. Initially, humans were created with the capacity to have fellowship with God. Then sin entered. Humans are born separated from and in conflict with God (Col. 1:21). Humans can be, and are, influenced by Satan (Eph. 2:2). Humans can, however, be born again (Jn. 3:5) and, thus, have personal knowledge of and fellowship with God (Jn. 17:3). This spiritual relationship can grow (1 Pet. 2:1-3). People are born again when they trust Jesus Christ, who died for our sins and rose from the dead, for the gift of eternal life.

2. Humans are social beings. Humans have the ability to have a relationship with other human beings, but they are born separated from and in conflict with others. They can be, and are, influenced by those around them. The first and foremost influence is their father and mother (Prov. 22:6). The broader community also has an effect (Titus 1:12) as does isolation (Prov. 18:1).
3. Humans are psychological beings. They can feel emotions, think thoughts, choose actions, and perform functions. Every capacity of the human person has been affected by sin and these various components are in conflict with others. Humans are born separated within and are in conflict with themselves!
4. Humans are physical beings. They are a persona united to a body.

This is a broad biblical framework of the make-up of people within which other factors need to be placed. For example, people are born with needs (Phil. 4:12) and desires (Jas. 4:1-2). People develop an image of themselves (Rom. 6:1-11) and a worldview. People are also creative. If the Scripture teaches anything, it teaches that humans are responsible for themselves. From cover to cover, the Bible continually reminds us that we will be judged, indicating that we are culpable before God.

To sum up, humans were created to be spiritual, social, psychological, purposeful, and physical beings. To say the same thing another way, people were designed to be psychological beings (image of God) united to a body (material part), capable of a relationship with God and others, as well as having the ability to work. It is important to keep in mind that, from a biblical perspective, a human being is a unit. Yet, sin separates individuals from God, others, and even themselves.

The Development of People The Bible has more to say about the *make-up* of people than it does the *development* of people. It gives general concepts without a great deal of detail. Nevertheless, it does mention factors that *influence* and *impact* people in their formation in general and their feelings, thoughts, purposes, speech, and choices in particular.

1. Heredity. The Scripture recognizes that heredity plays a part in a person's formation. If nothing else, it teaches that all are born with a sin nature (Eph. 2:1)! Scientists have demonstrated that genes inherited from our parents shape us physically and, no doubt, impact our persona and physical health.

2. Gender. Is not gender a factor in a person's development? The Bible begins by saying God created us male and female (Gen. 1:27). It addresses men as men and women as women (1 Tim. 2:8-9).
3. Needs. People have physical (Phil. 4:19), psychological (Phil. 4:12), social (Gen. 2:18; Rom. 14:7), and spiritual (Heb. 4:16; 5:12) needs. These needs can have an enormous influence on the formation of people.
4. Family. Perhaps the factor that the Bible mentions most is the family. It teaches that parents (or parental substitutes) can have such an influence and impact on a child that whatever that child is trained to do will follow him or her through life (Prov. 22:6).

    In this case, the Bible does give us a glimpse at what some of the details should look like. Ideally, it says that a child should have parents who are in love with the Lord, absorbed with His Word, and are obedient to it (Deut. 6:4-6). Then, those kinds of parents are to teach their children by example and instruction morning, noon, and night (Deut. 6:7-9). Children follow in their parents' footsteps (2 Kings 15:3, 34).

    What if parents do not love the Lord, do not know God's Word, and are not obedient to it? The child will be impacted negatively. For example, the Bible says that the sins of the fathers will be visited on the children to the fourth generation (Ex. 20:5; see 2 Kings 21:22) because they followed in their parent's footsteps (Ex. 20:5). Family environment can have an impact on behavior. Children are taught to be humble or aggressive, polite or rude. If there is no discipline, a child will be rude, rebellious, and disobedient.

    The Bible says to put away anger, wrath, and malice (Eph. 4:31). Can parents impact their children emotionally so that unless the children (as a child or as adults) deal with their emotions, they will haunt them for life? The Scripture warns parents not to provoke their children to wrath (Eph. 6:4), lest they become discouraged (Col. 3:21).

    The old adage says, "The apple does not fall very far from the tree." Another points out, "No matter how high the tree grows, the leaves always fall back to the roots."
5. Age. Scripture addresses people according to their age. For example, Paul told Titus what to say to older men and women and the younger men and women (Titus 2:1-6; see also 1 Tim. 5:1-2). It also hints at the "age characteristics" of people at various stages of their spiritual life. John refers to

believers as little children, young men, and fathers (1 Jn. 2:12-14).

6. Class. The Bible does not speak of "class" as we do today, but it does speak of characteristics that make up what is called "class." It speaks of rich and poor (Jas. 1:9-10) and slaves and masters (Col. 3:22-4:1), implying different class characteristics.
7. Nationality. Paul recognized that the Cretans had national characteristics and even quoted a secular poet to prove his point (Titus 1:12)! An often-told European joke illustrates the point. It says, "Heaven is where the police are British, the chefs French, the mechanics German, the lovers Italian, and it's all organized by the Swiss. Hell is where the police are German, the chefs British, the mechanics French, the lovers Swiss, and it's all organized by the Italians."

    From a biblical point of view, family, class, and nationality could, under certain conditions, be part of the world system. Those conditions are whether or not God is left out of the decision-making process.
8. Individual Choice. Ultimately, individuals make choices. Tendencies and tastes obtained from heredity and environment *influence* those choices consciously and unconsciously, but choices are made nonetheless. Some overcome their heredity, environment, and stress (2 Kings 3:2). Others succumb to their backgrounds, developing into problems of living, which are often brought about by an acutely stressful situation (2 Kings 3:2). Individuals are also influenced by their personality type (personality types are reflected in the biographies in the Bible), coping styles, defense mechanisms, value system, interests, etc.

Recognizing that these factors influence the formation of the persona is one thing. Explaining exactly how that formation takes place is another. While all these factors influence people, in the case of an individual, one or more factors are usually more important than the others. To complicate matters, in any given situation, a different factor may be the determining factor in explaining what a person does or does not do.

The Bible does not explain people in the modern psychological sense of the term, but there are hints here and there. For example, it says, "We love Him because He first loved us" (1 Jn. 4:19). That explains our spiritual experience, but it is true of life in general. The persona needs to experience the love and affection of parents to learn to love in return. Furthermore, according to the Scripture, having realized God's love, our response is not only love but faith. Again, there is a principle here. As humans, we develop trust in response to love or distrust in response to not being loved.

In Romans, when Paul moves from justification to "spiritual growth," he begins with the believer's position in Christ. It is vital to spiritual development for babes in Christ to understand and have a concept of who they are in Christ (Rom. 6:1-11). Likewise, as a person is loved and develops love and trust or is not loved and develops distrust, self-concept and worldview are developed. People's perceptions of themselves and their world determine to a great degree what they do and do not do. This can include emotional impressions as well as cognitive perceptions.

Theory of Pathology

From a biblical point of view, the cause of all problems is sin. As we have seen, sin has affected the whole creation, alienated people from God, separated people from each other, and fragmented individuals within themselves. Thus, there can be, and often are, spiritual, social, natural (meaning from nature), and psychological dimensions of a problem.

Spiritual Factors The most fundamental human problem is their relationship with God (Rom. 1:18-23). People are born alienated from God. They naturally suppress the truth about God (Rom. 1:18; as verse 19 reveals, the "truth" in verse 18 is the truth about God). People restrain, suppress, and obliterate from memory any truth about God. Being unrighteous, that is, having deviated from God's standard, people cannot bear to face the truth, especially the truth about God. Instead of seeking the truth, they seek to hide it.

Consequently, people apart from God are under the influence of Satan (Eph. 2:2). Satan attempts to get people to doubt the goodness of God (Gen. 3:4) and he peddles teachings contrary to God's Word (1 Tim. 4:1). He works through the godless world system (2 Cor. 4:4). He implants ideas (Mk. 8:31-33; note Christ told Peter that what he said was not of men and He called Peter "Satan"). He even invades people (Mk. 7:29). He deceives (2 Cor. 11:3; 1 Tim. 2:14), tempts (1 Cor. 7:5), and uses numerous devices (2 Cor. 2:11), including demon possession (Mk. 1:32-34).

Social Factors People are born separated from one another and must learn how to relate to each other, a skill that should be learned at home. This natural separation among people often results in conflict between individuals (Jas. 4:1-2).

Sinful people sin against people. The recipient of sinful treatment suffers the consequences. Children can be the innocent victims of the sinful behavior of adults.

Adults can receive unjust, sinful treatment from people (Jas. 5:6). In other words, it is not only possible to sin; it is possible to be sinned against by someone else (Mt. 18:15). It is even possible for one person to cause another to sin (Mt. 5:32; 18:6). We are sinned against and we sin against others.

Psychological Factors An individual born with a sin nature and growing up under the god of this world in a sinful society is likely to learn sinful ways. None are righteous (Rom. 3:10). All sin (Rom. 3:23).

As has been pointed out, sin has affected every part of people. The mind is capable of deception (Jer. 17:9). People can be deceived by Satan (2 Cor. 11:3), by others (1 Jn. 2:26), and by themselves (1 Jn. 1:8). The conscience can be weak and defiled (2 Cor. 8:7) and even seared (1 Tim. 4:2). The emotions can be of the most degraded sort, including malice, envy, hate (Tit. 3:3), revenge, etc. Actions can be depraved (Rom. 1:26-32). People make foolish, sinful choices.

People, especially believers, are in internal conflict with themselves (Rom. 7:15; Gal. 5:16; Jas. 4:1). Rather than face the truth and assume responsibility for themselves, people practice denial (Prov. 28:13; 1 Jn. 1:8) and shift blame (Gen. 3:12-13).

Natural Factors People are born into a sin-cursed world filled with defects, disease, disasters, and, ultimately, death. Although not due to personal sin, these events can profoundly affect people. Concerning a man born blind, Jesus said, "Neither this man nor his parents sinned" (Jn. 9:3), yet that man suffered all his life with blindness that affected him and his family. Physical diseases and natural disasters can also have an enormous impact on people. Accidents can leave people affected physically, mentally, and emotionally for years. The loss of a loved one causes grief, pain, and problems of readjustment.

What, then, is the cause of problems? Sin, but sin includes all the aforementioned elements. Most problems often have several of these elements, if not all of them. Problems are rarely (if ever!) simple. They are complex and include all parts of the person, the environment in which that person grew up and now exists, as well as Satan.

Jones and Butman, psychology professors, speak of the "complexity of causation," saying, "Christians would do well to be reminded that emotional and personal problems are nearly always more complex than they appear to be on the surface (that is, they are multiply determined and multiply maintained)" (Jones and Butman, p. 318). "A whole host of biological, psychosocial, and socio-cultural variables are usually involved, even in what appears to be a 'simple' problem'" (Jones and Butman, p. 268).

The Standard of Evaluation

What caused the unsinkable Titanic to sink? Everyone knows the answer to that question—it hit an iceberg! That is true, but it's not the whole truth. No one thing sank the Titanic. There were many contributing factors to the sinking of the Titanic, including 1) The Titanic hit an iceberg. 2) Warmer-than-usual water in the Gulf Stream caused more icebergs to be formed at the intersection of the Labrador Current and the Gulf Stream. 3) The sun, the moon, and the earth were aligned in such a way that on that day, tides sent icebergs southward. 4) The ship was traveling too fast in an area known to contain icebergs. 5) Iceberg warnings went unheeded. [The senior radio operator received multiple warnings about icebergs in the North Atlantic, but the last and most specific warning was not passed along to the captain, apparently because it didn't carry the prefix "MSG" (Masters' Service Gram) that would have required a personal acknowledgment from the captain.] 6) Binoculars were locked up and the key was held by David Blair, an officer who was bumped from the crew before the ship's departure. 7) The steersman took a wrong turn. After the iceberg was spotted, he was commanded to turn "hard starboard," but as the command was passed down the line, it was misinterpreted to mean "make the ship turn right" rather than "push the tiller right to make the ship head left." 8) Just before the impact, the first officer telegraphed the engine room to reverse the ship's engine, reducing the ship's maneuverability. 9) The rivets were too weak and made with low-grade iron. 10) There were too few lifeboats. The lifeboats could only accommodate about 1200 people for 2200 passengers (condensed from a 2010 NBC report on the Titanic).

Simply put, a problem is like a tree; it has one trunk but many roots.

Should such a conclusion surprise biblically knowledgeable believers? The Scripture teaches that the sources of difficulty are the world, the flesh, and the Devil. Do the three not work together? In many situations, we could say this is a case of the flesh, in cooperation with the world and Satan, influencing us to make a choice.

None of this should be interpreted to mean that people are not responsible for their behavior (including thoughts, emotions, choices, and acts). Undoubtedly, people are *influenced* by their heredity, gender, environment, early experiences, etc., but God holds people *accountable* for their choices. How much freedom each has is a question of "mind-boggling complexity" (Jones and Butman, p. 54).

Problems, then, are complex. Heredity, which may predispose a person to something, environment, early experiences, perceptions, assumptions, past and present relationships, expectations (including a lack of goals), etc., influence a person's *choices* in the present.

To sum up, because of a lack of an intimate relationship with God and other people, individuals have deceived perceptions, a defiled conscience, degraded emotions, and, therefore, make defective decisions.

Nature of Health

According to the New Testament, humans are to be "perfect." Jesus commanded us to be perfect as God the Father is perfect (Mt. 5:48). Paul said the goal of all ministry was to present every person perfect in Christ Jesus before the Judgment Seat of Christ (Col. 1:28; Eph. 4:11-16). The Greek word translated "perfect" means "having attained the end or purpose, complete." When used of people, it means "full grown, mature, adult, complete, fully developed" (A-G, p. 809). So, when the Bible says we are to be perfect, it means mature. Since the English word "perfect" means "complete in all respects, without defect, flawless," it conveys more than the biblical word "perfect" intends. Therefore, for this discussion, the best word is "mature."

To say the same thing another way, in 1 Corinthians, Paul divides all human beings into three classes: natural, babes (carnal), and spiritual (1 Cor. 2:14-3:4). In the context of 1 Corinthians, the spiritual person is the mature person (see 1 Cor. 2:6 and 3:1). Later in the book, Paul told them to be babes in malice and mature in understanding (1 Cor. 14:20). From a biblical point of view, all are to be spiritually mature.

As we have seen, humans were created to be spiritual, social, psychological, purposeful, and physical beings. Therefore, ideally, people are to be spiritually, socially, psychologically, and physically mature ("healthy"). Let's be specific.

Spiritually Spiritually mature people have trusted Jesus Christ for eternal life (Jn. 3:16) and, thus, know Jesus Christ (Jn. 17:3). They love God with all their heart (Mt. 22:37), believe God (Gal. 2:20), obey God (Jn. 14:15), trust God (2 Cor. 5:6), are not conformed to this world (Rom. 12: 2), have put on the armor of God (Eph. 6:27), and have submitted to God and resisted the devil (Jas. 4:17).

Part of maturity is recognizing one's sinfulness. Paul said he was the chief of sinners (1 Tim. 1:15). Mature believers are strong in the Lord (Eph. 6:10), but that does not mean they do God's will in their strength. It means that they recognize their weakness (2 Cor. 12:9-10), depend on the grace of God for His strength (1 Cor. 15:10), and, as a result, they are strong in the power of His might (Eph. 6:10).

Mature believers are also people who walk in the Spirit, not to fulfill the desire of the sinful nature (Gal. 5:16). Furthermore, such individuals are growing in the grace and knowledge of Jesus Christ (2 Pet. 3:18) and being conformed to Him (Rom. 8:29; Phil.3:10). They are Christ-like. Jesus Christ was full of grace and truth (Jn. 1:14).

Anyone conformed to Him will also be full of grace and truth.

Mature believers are also grateful (Col. 3:17), content (Heb. 13:5), patient, and kind (1 Cor. 13:4). Paul describes spiritual maturity in detail: "And he Himself gave some to be apostles, some prophets, some evangelists and some pastors and teachers, for the equipping of the saints for the work of ministry, for the edifying of the body of Christ, till we all come to the unity of the faith and of the knowledge of the Son of God, to a perfect man, to the measure of the stature of the fullness of Christ; that we should no longer be children, tossed to and fro and carried about with every wind of doctrine, by the trickery of men, in the cunning craftiness of deceitful plotting, but speaking the truth in love, may grow up in all things into Him who is the head; Christ; from whom the whole body, joined and knit together by what every joint supplies, according to the effective working by which every part does its share, causes growth of the body for the edifying of itself in love" (Eph. 4:11-16).

To sum up, a mature person has a loving, intimate relationship with God, a loving relationship with others, and is grateful, content, sensible, self-controlled, and patient. (For a more detailed discussion of spiritual maturity and the means of obtaining it, see G. Michael Cocoris, *The Spiritual Life: Clarifying the Confusion*, available at Amazon.)

Socially Socially mature people love people. Jesus said, "You shall love the LORD your God with all your heart, with all your soul, and with all your mind. This is *the* first and great commandment. And *the* second *is* like it: 'You shall love your neighbor as yourself'" (Mt. 22:37-39). The ultimate in social interaction is to love (Lev. 19:18; Mt. 22:37-39; Mk. 12:31; Rom. 13:9; Gal. 5:14; Jas. 2:8). Love fulfills the Law (Rom. 13:10). Mature people know how to lovingly, intimately relate to others. They also know when and how to submit to others.

Psychologically As has been pointed out, the psychological makeup of people consists of mind, emotions, and will.

1. Rationally. A Greek word and its cognates are used in the New Testament to describe this quality and more. These Greek words are so rich in shades of meaning that no precise English equivalent exists. One scholar has stated that a translation is almost

impossible because all attempts are too narrow (*Theological Dictionary of New Testament Words*, vol. III, pp. 1097-99). The basic ingredients of these words are sanity, sound of mind, and good sense. The first meaning of the verb form listed in the Greek Lexicon is "to be in one's right mind" (A-G, p. 802; see Mk. 5:15; Lk. 8:35; 2 Cor. 5:13). The second meaning of the verb form is "be reasonable, sensible, serious, keep one's head" (Rom. 12:3; 1 Pet. 4:7).

In Romans 12:3, this verb is rendered "to think soberly" (NKJV). According to this passage, all should think reasonably and sensibly about themselves.

In Titus, the noun form is used to qualify a man to be an elder. It is translated "sober-minded" (Titus 1:8; 1 Tim. 3:2). Elders, of course, are to be examples (1 Pet. 5:3), so this is what all should be. In Titus, this word or a cognate form of it is used of older men (see "sober" in Titus 2:2 NKJV), young women (see "discreet" in Titus 2:5 NKJV), young men (see "sober-minded" in Titus 2:6 NKJV), and of all (see "soberly" in Titus 2:12 NKJV).

It should be added that these rich Greek words, the verbs, the nouns, and adverbs, also mean "to bring one to his senses" (Titus 2:4), "sound mind" (2 Tim. 1:7), "moderation" (1 Tim. 2:9), and "self-control" (1 Tim. 2:15).

A rationally mature individual will not think on evil continually (Gen. 6:5) but will think on things that are true, noble, just, pure, and lovely, things that are of a good report, virtue, and anything praiseworthy (Phil. 4:8). Such a person will also meditate on the Word of God day and night (Ps. 1:2) and will love God with all his or her mind (Mt. 22:37; Mk. 12:30).

The conscience is part of the mind. The Greek word for conscience comes from two Greek words: "with" and "to know." It has been rendered "a knowing with oneself" (*Young's Concordance*, p. 198). The word "conscience" does not appear in the Old Testament but does occur in the New Testament. Furthermore, there are times when the word "heart" is used as an equivalent for conscience (1 Jn. 3:20).

All are born with innate moral "oughtness." Romans 2:14-15 says that Gentiles who do not have the Mosaic Law do *things in the Law by nature*, which shows that the works of the Law are written in their hearts (note: Paul says the *works* of the Law, not the Law itself). In other words, the fact that people not taught the Mosaic Law naturally honor their parents, pay their bills, and show kindness to the poor indicates that a moral "oughtness" is innate in them. Furthermore, in Romans 2:15, Paul states that the conscience also bears witness to a moral code in the Gentiles. Their thoughts either condemn or condone what they do.

While there is a moral "oughtness" in human beings that the conscience uses as a standard, the specific content of that standard can be and is affected by the environment in which one is reared. Ideally, people have had accurate moral instruction and have either lived a moral life or have experienced forgiveness so that they do not labor under a guilty conscience. Paul speaks of having a good conscience toward God (Acts 23:1; 1 Tim. 1:5), a pure conscience (2 Tim. 1:3), and striving to have a conscience without offense toward God and man (Acts 24:16). It is also possible to have a defiled conscience (1 Cor. 8:7; Titus 1:15) and a seared conscience (1 Tim. 4:2).

2. Emotionally. The Scripture does not directly address the subject of emotions. The word "emotions" does not appear in the Bible at all! The words "feeling" (singular) and "feelings" (plural) occur only rarely (see Prov. 29:11). Nevertheless, the Bible has much to say about emotions. If it does not use the word, how does it convey information about the subject of emotions?

The Bible reveals truth to us through precepts, principles, and personalities. Some truths are given in statement form, while other truths are poured through personalities. There is more biographical material in the Scripture than didactic material. If someone took the stories out of the Bible, that big book would be reduced to a much smaller volume. So, what does the Scripture teach indirectly through examples about emotions?

For one thing, it indicates that humans are capable of experiencing a wide range of emotions. For starters, Adam and Eve were afraid (Gen. 3:10). Cain was angry and sad (Gen. 4:6). Laban speaks of joy (Gen. 31:27). Jonah was angry at God (Jonah 4:1)! Others felt discouraged (Ps. 42:5), abandoned, (Ps. 22:1), overwhelmed (Ps. 142:3), grieved (1 Thess. 4:13), and more. Every emotion known to man is directly or indirectly included in the Scripture.

The Bible speaks of "being past feeling" (Eph. 4:19; note the singular). The Greek word rendered by this phrase means "became callous" (A-G, p. 80). Young's concordance renders it "to put away pain." The NIV renders this verse "Having lost all sensitivity." According to the Scripture, not feeling emotions is not good.

The people in the Bible were not only capable of experiencing a wide range of emotions, but they also expressed those emotions. The psalmist expressed feeling abandoned *by God* (Ps. 13:1) and shouts of continual joy (Ps. 35:27-28). When Jonah was angry *at God* and expressed it *to Him*, God did not tell Jonah that he should not be angry, nor did God tell Jonah not to express it (Jonah 4).

Not feeling emotions is not good, but neither is letting emotions get out of control. Proverbs says, "A fool vents all his feelings, but a wise *man* holds them back" (Prov. 29:11). Is Proverbs teaching that only a fool vents all his feelings? Not exactly. The Hebrew word rendered "feelings" is the word "spirit." The NIV renders it "anger." In the context of what the book of Proverbs says about the fool, translating this Hebrew word as "anger" is not a poor choice (see Prov. 29:9 and 14:16-17). The Hebrew word translated "vent" in the NKJV means "to cause to go forth." In other words, this verse says nothing more than a fool does not control his anger. The Scripture teaches that people should exercise self-control, including controlling emotions like anger (Jas. 1:19; Eph. 4:26).

Furthermore, the Scripture says we are to put off some emotions (Col. 3:5-8) and put on others (Col. 3:12-15).

The conclusion is that the Scripture teaches that a person should be able to feel emotions and express them without emotions getting out of control. A mature person is not "past feeling," especially not past feeling such emotions as compassion. Emotionally mature people are sensitive to their emotions and can feel the emotional pain of others to the point that they weep with them (Rom. 12:15).

3. Volitionally. The Scripture constantly commands people to make choices (Jos. 24:15 and the hundreds of commands in the Bible). It recognizes that people can make the wrong choices (Ex. 20:3-7, 12-17; Rom. 12:1-2; 1 Jn. 2:15) and repeatedly urges people to make right choices (Ex. 20:8-12). Beyond making *right* choices, the Scripture directs people to make *wise* choices (Prov. 23:19). It should be remembered that there are two kinds of wisdom; one is divine and the other is devilish (Jas. 3:15). The volitionally mature person follows divine wisdom (Prov. 3:5-8).

Physically According to the New Testament, believers can use their bodies as either instruments of unrighteousness (Rom. 6:13; see 1 Cor. 6:18; Rom. 1:24) or as instruments of righteousness (Rom. 6:13). The spiritually mature will not neglect their bodies to become "spiritual" (Col. 2:23), but will, by the Holy Spirit, put to death the sinful deeds of the body (Rom. 8:13; see Rom. 12:1) and will use their bodies to glorify God (1 Cor. 6:20), and manifest (2 Cor. 4:10), and magnify (Phil. 1:20) Christ and so, be preserved blameless in the body at the coming of Christ (1 Thess. 5:23). In other words, mature believers will exercise self-control and discipline over their bodies (1 Cor. 9:27).

Even though ideally, people should be healthy, physically and spiritually (3 Jn. 2), the Scripture recognizes that it is possible to be what one should be spiritually healthy without being all one can be physically (2 Cor. 12: 7-10). Apart from special circumstances, physical health, as well as spiritual health, is the goal.

The Scripture does not describe physical health or how to get it in detail. In the New Testament, the emphasis is on using the body for spiritual purposes. It says that the body is for the Lord (1 Cor. 6:13). He bought it and the Holy Spirit dwells in it (1 Cor. 6:19-20). Therefore, believers should not sin against their bodies but glorify God in their bodies (1 Cor. 6:18-20). Granted, the subject of the passage is the sin of immorality, but it begins with the general truth that the body is for the Lord (1 Cor. 6:13). Given the fact that the body is the temple of the Holy Spirit, it should be properly handled.

The Bible does recognize that sleep is important. God is said to give it to His beloved (Ps. 127:2; see also Prov. 3:24; Eccl. 5:12; Jer. 31:26). Exercise is profitable (1 Tim. 4:8). Compared to godliness, its profit is small, but it is profitable nonetheless. As for diet, the Old Testament forbids eating some foods, but the New Testament lifts these prohibitions (Acts 10). Now, nothing is to be refused as if abstaining from food would make one spiritual (1 Tim. 4:1-5). Nevertheless, in a passage that specifically mentions food, Paul says, "All things are lawful for me, but all things are not helpful. All things are lawful for me, but I will not be brought under the power of any" (1 Cor. 6:12; see 6:13). Food addiction, or what is called today "food disorders," are unacceptable, because they enslave. Likewise, eating things that are not helpful (harmful) is also inappropriate.

Unless beyond their control because of a disease, believers should do those things that care for the body, namely, get enough sleep, exercise, and eat what is helpful, not harmful.

Given the unity of people's material and immaterial parts, it is possible that not properly caring for the body could affect people psychologically, personally, socially, and even spiritually. The founder of Dallas Seminary, Lewis Sperry Chafer, is often quoted by alumni as saying, "There are times when the best thing you can do for your spiritual life is to get a good night's sleep."

In his massive book on theology, Erickson wrote in one of his chapters on the doctrine of man, "Man is to be treated as a unity. His spiritual condition cannot be dealt with independently of his physical and psychological condition, and vice versa. Psychosomatic medicine is proper. So also, is psychosomatic ministry (or should we term it pneumo-psychosomatic ministry?). The Christian who desires to be spiritually healthy will give attention to such matters as diet, rest, and exercise. Any attempt to deal with man's spiritual condition apart from his physical condition and mental and emotional state will be less than completely successful, as will any attempt to deal with man's emotions apart from his relationship to God" (Erikson, p. 539).

At any rate, a physically healthy (mature) person gets enough sleep, eats what is helpful, not harmful, and exercises.

To sum up, a mature person has a loving, intimate relationship with God, a loving relationship with others, and is grateful, content, sensible, self-controlled, and patient.

Method of Therapy

There is no one method of ministry or "therapy" in the Bible. Jesus did not deal with any two people the same way. He did not heal all blind people the same way! Paul wrote, "Now we exhort you, brethren, warn those who are unruly, comfort the fainthearted, uphold the weak, be patient with all" (1 Thess. 5:14). Paul is saying use different approaches.

The Relationship God's primary method of ministry is *people*. He uses parents (Prov. 22:6), elders, who, if nothing else, are to serve as models (1 Pet. 5:3), gifted believers (Eph. 4:11-16), and fellow believers (see "exhort one another" in Heb. 10:25). It is in a community of believers that individual believers grow (Col. 2:2).

The Counselor Those who would help others must be mature individuals themselves (see "spiritual" in Gal. 6:1; see also Rom. 15:14). People helpers can pray, model, love (see esp. 2 Tim. 2:24-26), comfort, teach, exhort, correct, rebuke, etc. The counselor must also be patient (1 Thess. 5:14). Problems usually take time to develop and usually take time to solve. Therefore, patience is imperative.

The Counselee If people with problems are to grow, they must assume personal responsibility for their attitudes and actions. The means of spiritual growth are meditation in the Word coupled with faith, prayer, obedience with dependence on the Lord, forgiveness, submission to others, fellowship with other believers, service, and enduring trials. Again, much could be written on each of these characteristics.

To sum up, For counseling to be what it should be, there must be a mature counselor, a counselee with a problem willing to assume responsibility to make correct choices and a relationship between the two. An individual is responsible for becoming mature spiritually, socially, and psychologically.

The Standard of Evaluation

Summary: According to the Bible, human beings are complex, spiritual (sinful), social, psychological (emotive/cognitive/volitional, that is, rational, emotional, volitional), purposeful, and physical beings who function as a unit. Since they are born alienated (from God, from others, and even within themselves) and are immature, they make sinful choices. Because of a relationship with God and mature relationships with others, people can grow to maturity if they decide to stop blame-shifting, assume responsibility for their growth, and depend on the Lord for the grace to do so.

People begin as isolated, immature infants who need to grow to maturity. Mature people are those who are not controlled by people or events of the past but have assumed responsibility for themselves and, therefore, are rightly related to God, others, and themselves in the present and have goals for the future.

Mature people are mentally sensible, emotionally self-controlled, volitionally assertive, and relationally loving. Immature people swing to one of two extremes.

	Extreme	Maturity	Extreme
Mentally	all logical	sensible	not reasonable
Emotionally	no emotion	self-controlled	no control
Volitionally	passive	assertive	aggressive
Relationally	withdrawn	loving	enabler

People often react to the people and events in their lives emotionally, mentally, and/or volitionally in one of two ways.

Mentally	obsessive	or	blocked out
Emotionally	out of touch	or	out of control
Volitionally	passive	or	aggressive

From a biblical point of view, believers should have a more "balanced" response.

Mentally	obsessive	sensible	blocked out
Emotionally	out of touch	in touch	out of control
Volitionally	passive	assertive	aggressive

To say all of this another way, what the Bible says about people and their problems is reflected in the life of Adam and Eve. Adam was created in the image of God, which means that he had a mind, emotions, and a will, which, in turn, gave him the capacity for a relationship with God and other human beings and the ability to fulfill a purpose (tend the Garden of Eden). As a result of their disobedience, Adam and Eve were alienated from God (Gen. 3:9), separated from each other (see the fig leaves in Gen. 3:7), fragmented within themselves (Rom. 7:10-20), filled with fear (Gen. 3:10), practiced irresponsibility and blame-shifting (Gen. 3:12-13), and suffered sorrow and pain, even in the ordinary functions of life, such as childbirth and work (Gen. 3:16-19). From this, we learn that people were designed for relationships and purpose, but because of sin, they experience alienation from God, separation from people, fragmentation within themselves, fear, sorrow, and pain. Instead of assuming responsibility for their disobedience, they are irresponsible; they rationalize, and practice blame-shifting.

From the rest of Scripture, we learn that as a result of the sin of Adam and Eve, creation is decaying (Rom. 8:21), the spirit in people is dead, that is, alienated from God (Eph. 2:1; 4:18), human relationships are dysfunctional (Titus 3:3), the mind is deceived (2 Cor. 4:4; darkened, Eph. 4:18), the emotions are degraded (Eph. 4:19), the will is depraved (Eph. 4:19), the conscience is devoid (Eph. 4:19), the body is diseased (1 Cor. 15:53; Eccl. 12:1-5), and purpose in life is diminished (Eccl. 1:2-3).

For people to be all that they were designed to be, they must be reconciled to God, restored to a functional relationship with other people, reestablished in a purposeful life, and renewed mentally, emotionally, and volitionally.

The biblical explanation of the five areas of therapy, especially the biblical teaching concerning people, should be used to evaluate modern psychotherapies. As an introduction to an examination of modern psychotherapies, a brief history of psychology, in general, is given in the next chapter.

Chapter 3

A BRIEF HISTORY OF PSYCHOLOGY

The English word psychology comes from the Greek words *psyche*, which means "soul, life," and *logos,* which means "the study of, the knowledge of." Although no standard definition of psychology is accepted by all branches of psychology, the basic idea is that psychology is the study of people, their life, their behavior, and/or their mind, and/or their emotions. Psychotherapy is treating people who have a psychological problem. Here is a brief history of the explanations of human behavior and the treatments of abnormal behavior

The Ancients

Demons In his college textbook, *Fundamentals of Abnormal Psychology*, Ronald Comer, a professor at Princeton University, says, "The early writings of the Egyptians, Chinese, and Hebrews, for example, attribute psychological deviance to the influences of evil spirits or demons." He says the common treatment was exorcism (Comer, p. 7).

This explanation is compatible with the Bible. From a biblical point of view, demons are fallen angels (Mt. 25:41). Jesus (Mt. 8:28) and the apostles (Acts 5:16; 8:17; 19:12) dealt with demon possession. It is not as common today as some think, but demons do disturb people (see 1 Tim. 4:1). I know a respected Christian psychologist who has, on at least one occasion, cast a demon out of a patient. This "secular theory" is correct. Demons can disturb people.

Astrology The ancients also used astrology to explain human behavior. Astrology is the theory that the position of the heavenly bodies determines, or at least influences, people's behavior. Therefore, it was believed the study of the heavenly bodies could enable a person to foretell the future. Astrology began in Mesopotamia almost five thousand years ago. From there, it spread to Egypt, Greece, and the East. The Babylonians invented the zodiac (Bayly, pp. 13-14).

This notion is not compatible with the Bible. Isaiah ridiculed the Babylonian astrologers. He wrote, "You are wearied in the multitude of your counsels; Let now the astrologers, the stargazers, *and* the monthly prognosticators stand up and save you from what shall come upon you" (Isa. 47:13). He was correct. The zodiac is inaccurate. The original zodiac was based on the seven planets known to exist at the time. Two planets have since been discovered. So, if the position of the heavenly bodies determines events and people's actions, the original zodiac is inaccurate. This theory of human behavior is simply wrong.

Internal Dysfunction The Greek physician Hippocrates (460-377 BC), who is often called the father of medicine, taught that disease and abnormal behavior were not caused by a conflict with the spirits or the gods but by an internal medical problem. According to Hippocrates, the body contains four fluids called "humors." An imbalance among these four humors, yellow bile, red bile (blood), phlegm, and black bile, produce disease. A person with too much yellow bile is choleric or aggressive and irritable and one with too much red bile is warmhearted but might suffer from rapid shifts in mood. If there were too much phlegm, a person would be phlegmatic, sluggish, and apathetic and one whose body contains excess black bile was melancholic or sad. According to Comer, Hippocrates taught that an excess of yellow bile caused mania, that is, frenzied euphoria and an excess of black bile was the source of melancholia, unshakable sadness (Comer, p. 8).

Hippocrates' focus on the internal causes of abnormal behavior was later shared by Plato (427-347 BC) and Aristotle (384-322 BC; Comer, p. 8). In his massive writings on medicine, Galen (d. 216 AD) included the theory of the humors, that is, that the preponderance of one of the four humors had a marked effect on a person's health and personality.

The idea that four internal fluids cause problems is not scriptural or scientific, but the emphasis on an internal cause is biblical. Jesus taught. "Out of the heart proceed evil thoughts, murders, adulteries, fornications, thefts, false witness, blasphemies" (Mt. 15:19). Humans do not have variously colored humors coursing through their veins, but the idea that problems are internal, not external is correct. In this case, the theory of humors is wrong, but there is validity to parts of it.

Morality "The first sophisticated psychologies in the West were developed by Greek philosopher-therapist like Plato, Aristotle, and Epictetus. They attempted to describe human nature, including the fundamental ills, and its reparation, on the basis of personal experience and rigorous reflection in light of prior thought" (Johnson, p.

11). Roberts and Watson explain that Platonists thought "people are more than just physical matter and their happiness more than just maximizing of pleasure.... Platonists thought that human well-being required that we be personally in touch with something eternal and Plato's moral therapy was thus designed to get the soul to 'recollect' its eternal nature and thus come to love what is eternally good." Aristotle thought that happiness "required excellent functioning as a rational social animal in a properly constituted community, along with contemplation of the eternal in a way reminiscent of Plato's thought." The Epicureans thought "that human beings are nothing but physical stuff" and that "psychic well-being was just a matter of maximizing the pleasantness of this temporary life" (Roberts and Watson, pp. 150-151, see Johnson, p. 154).

In his lectures on "The Great Ideas of Psychology," Dr. Daniel Robinson, a professor at Georgetown University, a fellow at Oxford, and a recognized authority on the history of psychology, says, "Aristotle was "the first truly systematic psychologist," in which he included biological, social, cultural, and political issues (Daniel Robinson, "The Great Ideas of Psychology," *The Great Courses*, 1997). According to Aristotle, nature has built into people the desire to be good, defined as a person of virtue and character. Virtue is the golden mean between two extremes of deficiency on one hand and excess on the other.

Deficiency	Golden Mean	Excess
Indecisiveness	Self-control	Impulsiveness
Cowardice	Courage	Recklessness
Stinginess	Generosity	Extravagance
Humility	Modesty	Pride

The Middle Ages

Demons In his textbook *The Abnormal Personality*, Robert White, Professor of Clinical Psychology at Harvard University, says that during the Middle Ages, "It was generally believed that the insane were possessed by evil spirits" (White, p. 7). Various rituals of exorcism were used. Milder forms of exorcism included prayer, chants, and drinking bitter-tasting concoctions. More severe forms involved starvation, whipping, scalding, or stretching (Comer, p. 10). These rites were harsh, but they did not usually result in death. It was in the fifteenth and sixteenth centuries that this belief " reached its extreme development in the institution of witchcraft" and witches were "hunted, captured, tried in court, sometimes tortured to obtain confessions and, if tried and found guilty, were burned at the stake" (White, pp. 7-8).

Lunacy Eventually, the idea of demon possession gave place to the notion of lunacy (White, p. 8). The word "lunacy" comes from the Latin word for the moon. Originally, lunacy was intermittent insanity, supposedly changing in intensity with the phases of the moon. The word "lunatic" was used popularly as synonymous with insanity and was especially prominent in the discussion of who came under the legal qualifications of insanity. By the 18th century, people with abnormal behavior were considered lunatics (White, p. 8). Lunatics were viewed merely as a public nuisance. The less troublesome wandered about the countryside begging and stealing food. Others were thrown into prison as if their problem was that they were guilty of a crime (see White, p. 8; Comer, pp. 8-9).

As with many theories, this one may have an element of truth. There are "many respected institutions and people" who "actively support the idea that behavior is affected by the phases of the moon." They believe that bizarre behavior increases when the moon is full. "Anecdotal evidence abounds" (Comer, p. 8). So, the full moon causes foolish behavior! Over the years, I have had policemen and medical personnel who work in the ER tell me that when there is a full moon, people "get crazy." Is it possible that the full moon does *influence* some people to some degree? It does not affect all.

Some say that since the moon causes the tides, it is reasonable to expect that it has a similar effect on the body since the body is composed of more than 80 percent water (Comer, p. 8). In a class I was teaching, a lady suggested that since the moon affects the tides and the human body is almost all water, it has some *pull* on humans. Some studies support the theory and others do not. Comer says most clinicians are not convinced but admits, "Some people do exhibit strange behavior during the full moon or report strange sensations or increased sexual desire" (Comer, p. 9).

Maybe, as some are more sensitive to environmental factors than others, some are more susceptible to the pull of a full moon than others. There is something similar called Seasonal Affective Disorder (SAD). It is depression that occurs during the winter months. It usually begins around October when the days begin to get shorter and usually subsides around the end of February or March when the days begin to get longer. The diagnosis is made when there is no other known cause for the depression, such as the loss of a loved one, and this pattern of depression occurs over three years. The cause is the body's need of the light produced by the sun for proper hormonal and chemical balance. When the body does not get this light, some develop SAD. No one knows why some are affected and others are not. The treatment is to get in the sun. If that is not possible, sun lamps are used. Medical professionals disagree on the specifics of how to use artificial light.

The Modern Era

Moral Problem White says that milder forms of maladjustment, including people being unhappy and irritable, unduly boastful and self-centered, unable to get along well with their family and friends, frittered away their time or drinking and dissipation of their behavior, was, until recently, considered a sign of "moral inferiority." He adds, "Their deviations from acceptable behavior were felt to lie within the realm of volition. It was up to them to heed wiser counsels, choose nobler ideals, and mend their ways." On the other hand, he says that more severe forms of mental affliction are cases of insanity, where people are unfit to take care of themselves, are an inconvenience to others, and are an occasional danger to themselves or others (White, pp. 5-6).

The Puritans followed this "moral model," calling it the "cure of souls" (an expression from the Latin, *cura animarum*, which is better rendered today as "care of souls;" actually, today, "cure/care of souls" is called "pastoral care"). The cure of souls sought to help "people who were anxious, depressed, and upset with their everyday life" (Abbott, cited by Powlison, p. 149). For the Puritans, the cure of souls consisted in dealing with sin. As Lambert explains, "The Puritans took counseling seriously.... Richard Baxter wrote *The Christian Directory* [1673], outlining in exhaustive detail the spiritual problems Christians face. John Owen wrote, among other things, *The Mortification of Sin* [1657] as a practical guide for dealing with the flesh. *A Lifting up for the Downcast* [1649] was intended by William Bridge to be an encouragement to Christians struggling with all manner of life's difficulties. Writing in the Puritan tradition in America, Jonathan Edwards wrote *A Treatise Concerning the Religious Affections* [1746] to deal with the pastoral issue of judging true works of the spirit from false ones. One of the last Puritan works was Ichabod Spencer's *A Pastor's Sketches in the 1850s*" (Lambert, p. 25).

Notice the Puritan emphasis on sin. John Owen's *The Mortification of Sin* describes how to battle sin and temptation. In 1648, William Bridge, who has been called "a true physician of souls," preached 13 sermons on Psalm 42:11, which were published in a book entitled *A Lifting up for the Downcast*. According to Bridge, the causes of saints' discouragements are such sins as weak grace, failure in duties, want of assurance, temptation, desertion, and affliction.

Given their view of the Bible and the long history of the cure of souls, some Protestant Christians have concluded that counseling is the exclusive domain of the church and that secular psychotherapies are trying to take over what belongs to the church. For example, Adams wrote, "Because of the teaching of the Scriptures, one is forced to conclude that much of clinical and counseling psychology, as well as most psychotherapy, is religion. Psychiatry has been carried on without license from God and in autonomous rebellion against Him. This was inevitable because the Word of the sovereign God of creation has been ignored. In that Word are "all things pertaining to life and godliness" (Jay Adams. *What about Nouthetic Counseling?*, pp. 16-17).

Interestingly, Jung wrote: "Religions are systems of healing for psychic illness..... That is why patients force the psychotherapist into the role of a priest and expect and demand of him that he shall free them from their distress. That is why we psychotherapists must occupy ourselves with problems which, strictly speaking, belong to the theologian" (Jung, "*Psychotherapists or the Clergy, Modern Man in Search of a Soul*." New York: Harcourt, Brace, 1933, pp. 240-241).

Physical Disease Attitudes toward "insanity" changed over several centuries. Slowly the idea that insanity was a disease was more and more accepted. This is called the "Somatogenic Hypothesis" (White) or the "Somatogenic Perspective" (Comer) because it "looks for the genesis of the trouble in the body or soma," which is the Greek word for "body" (White, p. 15).

Apparently, the German physician Johann Weyer (1515-1588) was the first medical practitioner to specialize in mental illness. He believed that the mind was as susceptible to sickness as the body. He is now considered the founder of the modern study of psychopathology (Comer, p. 10).

In 1547, Henry VIII gave the Bethlehem Hospital to the city of London for the exclusive purpose of confining the mentally ill. Patients, restrained in chains, cried out for all to hear. The hospital became a popular tourist attraction; people paid to look at the howling and gibbering inmates. The hospital's name, pronounced "Bedlam" by the local people, has become synonymous with a chaotic uproar. Tourists also viewed mental patients in the Lunatics' Tower in Vienna (Comer, p. 11).

In the eighteenth century, Benjamin Rush (1745-1813), often called the father of American psychiatry, believed that excessive amounts of blood caused abnormal behavior in the brain. He treated some mental patients by drawing blood, a technique used at the time to treat other illnesses (Comer, p. 11).

It was not until the beginning of the nineteenth century that the view arose that the nature of people's problems was a sickness. Philippe Pinel (1745-1826) was made physician-in-chief at a French hospital in the first year of the French Revolution. He declared, "The mentally sick, far from being guilty people deserving of punishment, are sick people whose miserable state deserves all the consideration that is due to suffering humanity. One should try with the most simple methods to restore their reason" (Pinel, cited by White, p. 8). He felt that people were mentally ill because they were deprived of fresh air and liberty.

Pinel removed their chains. When released and treated with kindness, some, but not all, who had been considered completely unmanageable became calm and reasonable (White, p. 9). Some "improved significantly" in a short period when released from their cells and given fresh air, sunlight, and treated with dignity (Comer, p. 12). Pinel introduced case history and record keeping. In 1801, he completed a treatise on mental disorders in which he said there were four groups: mania, melancholia, dementia, and idiocy (White, pp. 9, 13). Pinel's reforms began to spread slowly. Mental hospitals were opened throughout the nineteenth century, especially in the United States (White, pp. 9-10).

Emil Kraepelin (1856-1926), a German psychiatrist, is considered the founder of modern psychiatry. The idea that mental disorders are physical diseases, "analogous in every respect to ailments that have no mental symptoms," culminated in the work of Kraepelin (White, p. 18). He also pioneered the use of drugs to treat mental illnesses. He measured the effects of various drugs on people with abnormal behavior (Comer, p. 14).

Kraepelin concluded that there were two major mental diseases: manic-depressive psychosis and dementia praecox (now called schizophrenia). He was the first to identify manic depression and schizophrenia. White explains, "In forming the first of these two disease entities, he drew together the excited, elated conditions (mania) and the melancholy, depressed states (depression), showing that in many cases, these moods succeeded each other in the same patient.... The symptom complex was centered around abrupt changes of mood and did not include signs of deterioration, such as defects in gait, speech, and memory. The onset was sudden rather than gradual; the course was periodic rather than steadily progressive; the outcome was spontaneous recovery though with a strong likelihood of future recurrence" (White, p. 19).

According to Kraepelin, all the people who had dementia praecox (schizophrenia) "showed an early onset and they all progressed in the direction of incurable dementia.... Its course was progressive rather than periodic, and its outcome was complete dementia, not including, however, paralysis and early death" (White, p. 19). Two-thirds of the patients in mental hospitals had one of these two "diseases" (White, p. 19).

Furthermore, according to Kraepelin, there were physical causes of these mental diseases. "Kraepelin postulated that manic-depressive psychosis was caused by an irregularity in metabolic function. Because the disorder seemed to run in families, he assumed that the metabolic irregularity was based on some kind of hereditary defect. In the case of dementia praecox, he proposed the hypothesis that the sex glands were at fault, producing an unfavorable chemical state, which affected the nervous system. He justified this guess by pointing out frequent associations between the onset of the disease and changes in sexual function: the changes of puberty, menstrual irregularities, childbirth, and the involution period. He thus applied the type of reasoning that prevailed in general medicine and searched for the causes of disorder where any physician would look for them: in tissue changes, endocrine disturbances, hereditary peculiarities; in short, in some specific derangement of the bodily economy" (White, p. 20).

Kraepelin wrote a textbook entitled *Psychiatrie*, which went through eight editions from 1883 to 1913 (White, p. 18). In the 1887 edition of his book, Kraepelin divided psychoses into two types: the curable, caused by external conditions, and the incurable, caused by constitutional factors in the patient. He established the conceptual framework within which psychiatry was to develop for the rest of the twentieth century. His categories live on in the *Diagnostic and Statistical Manual*, the standard reference present-day psychiatrists and psychologists use. He was also a joint discoverer of Alzheimer's disease, which he named after his collaborator, Dr. Alois Alzheimer.

Biological discoveries spurred the somatogenic theory. For example, in 1897, Richard von Krafft-Ebing (1840-1902), a German neurologist, established a direct link between general paresis and syphilis. General paresis is an irreversible, progressive disease with both physical and mental symptoms, including paralysis and delusions of grandeur. Von Krafft-Ebing inoculated paretic patients with matter from syphilis sores and found that none of them developed symptoms of syphilis. Their immunity could have been caused only by an earlier case of syphilis. Since all paretic patients are immune to syphilis, he theorized that syphilis was the cause of general paresis (Comer, p. 14).

The disease approach to people's problems is to put them in a mental hospital and/or give them drugs. While calling people's problems a "disease" is greatly debated, the use of drugs does help with some problems, at least with some symptoms. Opponents of the "disease theory" point out that the lack of aspirin does not cause a headache but can relieve pain (Ross and Pam, p. 41).

Psychological Disorder During the nineteenth century, the idea developed that a psychological disorder caused problems. This is called the "Psychogenic Hypothesis" (White) or the "Psychogenic Perspective" (Comer) because it says the cause of the problem is in the psychological processes. White explains, "Disordered personal reactions occur because the patient's thoughts, feelings, and strivings are disturbed. His somatic processes, even his brain and central nervous system, may be working in an entirely normal fashion; the content of what he feels and imagines throws his personal reactions into disorder. We can begin to speak of psychopathology at the point where ideas or some other psychological processes are held responsible for disordered behavior" (White, p. 20).

The psychogenic theory won its way into modern medicine through the study of hysteria (White, p. 21). Franz Anton Mesmer (1734-1815) was a German physician whose theories and practices led to modern-day hypnotism. His name produced the word "mesmerize," which means to hold one's attention as though that person were in a trance.

Mesmer received his medical degree from the University of Vienna in 1766. In his doctoral dissertation, he described his theory of "animal gravitation," the notion that human health is affected by the gravitational pull of the various planets. Mesmer concluded that people did not need to rely on planetary gravitational pull; they could manipulate their health using any magnetic force. Today, some advocates of alternative medicine use magnets. These magnets are either passed over the body or worn.

By 1775, Mesmer had revised his animal gravitation theory, renaming it "animal magnetism." He decided that magnets were not necessary. Instead, simply passing hands over the body was enough to create the required magnetic forces. Some were "cured" by Mesmer, but many of his patients were not. With the encouragement of the established medical profession, those not cured began to threaten legal action.

In 1778, Mesmer left Vienna and settled in Paris. He developed techniques to put people in trance-like states he called "crises." He believed that these crises acted as a means of forcing the body fluid back to its proper flow. Side effects included convulsions.

Mesmer became popular in France, but the medical establishment was skeptical. In 1784, Louis XVI appointed a group of scientists to examine Mesmer's methods. The commission included some of the leading scientific minds of the day, including Benjamin Franklin. The commission concluded that Mesmer's methods could not be backed up by scientific evidence. After that pronouncement, his following dropped off, and he left Paris in 1785. He died in obscurity.

Mesmer did not know the concept of psychosomatic illness, but he did recognize the role the mind played in disease and he popularized the use of hypnotism to cure ailments. This was a psychological, not physiological, approach.

His followers showed that hypnotized people were highly responsive to whatever was suggested. For instance, they could be temporarily paralyzed and be made insensitive to touch and pain. They could move about, answer questions, talk, and think clearly, but they had no recollection of what had transpired when they woke up. Some patients complaining of aches and pains had them disappear by a suggestion in the hypnotic state so that the patient woke up magically cured, remembering nothing of the process (White, p. 21).

Two physicians, Hippolyte Marie Bernheim (1840-1919) and Ambroise-Auguste Liebault (1823-1904), "were able to make normal people experience deafness, paralysis, blindness, or numbness using hypnotic suggestion—and they could remove these artificially induced symptoms by the same means. In short, they established that a mental process—hypnotic suggestion—could both cause and cure a physical dysfunction" (Comer, p. 15).

Before Wilhelm Wundt (1832-1920), "psychology" was part of the philosophy department. Wundt, the son of a Lutheran minister, was born in Germany. In 1856, he graduated from the University of Heidelberg as a doctor of medicine. He became a professor. He wrote *Principles of Physiological Psychology* (two volumes, 1873-1874), which set out to establish psychology as a science. It stressed the relationship between physiology and psychology and showed how the methods of natural science could be used in psychology. In 1875, he was made professor of philosophy at the University of Leipzig (notice he was a professor of philosophy). In 1879, he opened the first laboratory exclusively devoted to psychological studies. This event is considered to be the beginning of psychology as an independent field of study. In 1881, he established a journal to publish the results of his research. It was called *Philosophical Studies*. There was another journal named *Psychological Studies*; it was about psychic phenomena, such things as clairvoyance (YouTube lecture by Eric Landrum, Boise State University, posted Feb. 5, 2012). Wundt also founded the first graduate program for psychology.

The setting up of Wundt's psychological laboratory is considered the beginning of psychology. Before Wundt, human behavior was a subject thought about by philosophers and theologians. Wundt is credited with turning the study of behavior into a science. At this point, psychology was just the study of human behavior. It was not developed to help people; it was used to study people scientifically. Wundt was anti-metaphysical; he was interested in physical analysis.

J. M. Charcot (1825-1893) was a neurologist in Paris. He received his medical degree from the University of Paris (1853), where he was appointed a professor of pathological anatomy in 1860. In 1862, he was appointed senior physician at a hospital for the treatment of the mentally ill. It became a center for psychiatric training. Charcot's lectures attracted students from all over Europe. By training and experience, he favored the somatogenic theory.

In 1878, at the same hospital in Paris where Pinel had instituted his reforms, Charcot began investigating hysterical symptoms. The word "hysteria" comes from the Greek word for uterus. In popular parlance, it means "wild, uncontrollable excitement." In a psychological sense, it means emotional excitability, excessive anxiety, sensory disturbances, and the simulation of organic disorders, such as total or partial blindness, total or partial deafness, paralyzes, convulsive attacks ("hysterical fits"), etc. Yet "apart from these symptoms, the patient's mind is perfectly clear" (White, p. 22). Comer defines a hysterical disorder as "mysterious bodily ailments that had no apparent physical basis" (Comer, p. 15). In other words, hysteria is the displacement of emotions to a part of the body. It is psychosomatic. In Charcot's time, it was thought that it was only in women.

Charcot himself had never practiced hypnotism, but some of his assistants showed him that by hypnotism, it was possible to produce and remove bodily symptoms of hysteria. By hypnotic suggestion, a patient's perfectly healthy arm could be paralyzed. Charcot himself could not tell the difference between physical paralysis and hysterical paralysis, except that the hysterical paralysis disappeared at a further suggestion (White, p. 22).

These symptoms were not caused by bodily injury to the nervous system. For example, sometimes, a patient would have a paralyzed hand, which stopped at the wrist (roughly the area covered by a glove), but such paralysis is anatomically impossible. A physical injury involving a nerve would affect the arm and the hand. A paralyzed hand alone would be anatomical nonsense. Furthermore, Charcot had one patient who was in an accident during which he thought a carriage ran over his legs. Both legs were paralyzed for months, but in reality, the carriage had not touched the patient (White, p. 23).

Charcot used hypnosis as part of his diagnosis and therapy. He used hypnosis to distinguish true psycho-neurotics from fakes and to treat hysterics. In the hypnotic state, patients recalled events in their lives that were not remembered when awake. Moreover, under hypnosis, they were susceptible to the suggestions of the therapist. Symptoms were relieved. In 1882, Charcot presented his findings to the French Academy of Sciences, where they were favorably received.

Towards the end of his life, Charcot questioned his own work on hysteria, but he made an impression on a man named Sigmund Freud. Freud stayed with Charcot for four months between 1885 and 1886. Freud was so impressed with Charcot that he named his first son after him.

By this time, it was becoming accepted that behavioral abnormalities could originate in a physiological or psychological disturbance. In other words, a psychological process, the disturbance of the person's thoughts, feelings, and strivings, causes hysteria.

Josef Breuer (1842-1925) was a Viennese physician. Between 1880 and 1882, he treated a difficult case of hysteria. A girl in her early 20s named Anna O. had both legs and her right arm paralyzed, her sight and hearing greatly impaired, her neck muscles uncomfortably contracted, and there was a persistent nervous cough, occasional nausea, and periodic difficulty with speech. There were also frequent alternations of her mental state, a confused and dreamy condition Breuer called "absence."

During her periods of "absence," the girl often mumbled to herself as if her thoughts were busy. Breuer took notes of her words and later, after inducing a hypnotic state, repeatedly gave them back to her. When he did, she revealed the "traumatic event" that occupied her in her dreamy state. Having unburdened herself, she felt relieved and was temporarily much improved after being awakened from the hypnosis.

Then, Breuer discovered that a symptom might be permanently removed under certain circumstances. If, during hypnosis, the patient could remember the situation in which the symptoms began and if the accompanying emotions were freely and fully expressed, the symptom would disappear for good.

For example, the girl once nursed her father through a protracted terminal illness. While sitting near his bed, worried and tearful, he awoke and asked what time it was. Her tears prevented her from seeing the clock. Nevertheless, she exerted her eye muscles so she could reply without revealing her distress. When she recalled this forgotten incident and experienced the emotion she had suppressed, her visual symptoms permanently disappeared. A similar origin and cure were found for all her symptoms, and eventually, she was completely cured.

Breuer concluded that thoughts buried in her unconscious resulted in Anna's symptoms and that when these thoughts became conscious and were spoken, the symptoms disappeared. The release of suppressed emotions cured hysteria symptoms (White, pp. 26-29).

Breuer taught his methods to his young colleague, Sigmund Freud, and they worked together for a while. Claiming that the demands of his busy medical practice prevented him from pursuing the work, Breuer ceased to treat patients such as Anna O, but he and Freud discussed Freud's patients. In 1893, they published an article on their work and, two years later, a book (*Studies in Hysteria*), which marked the beginning of psychoanalytic theory.

At about the same time, their friendship came to an end. Apparently, Breuer was ambivalent concerning the value of their work. Their final break came about over the question of childhood memories of seduction. Freud believed that most of his patients had been seduced as children. Only later did he decide that Breuer was correct in believing these to be memories of childhood fantasies.

At this point in history, the psychological disorder theory was that a psychological process, that is, the disturbance of the person's thoughts, feelings, and strivings, causes hysteria. In other words, in reaction to trauma, people could suppress out of their conscious mind emotions, which could produce hysteria. In short, unconscious emotions could produce physical symptoms.

Trauma → suppressed (unconscious) emotions → hysteria symptoms

Furthermore, when the suppressed emotions became conscious and were spoken, the symptoms disappeared. Simply put, the release of suppressed emotions cured hysteria symptoms.

Emotions affect the body. The Bible says, "A merry heart does good, like medicine, but a broken spirit dries the bones" (Prov. 17:22; see also 14:30 and Ps. 51:8). Stress causes illness, such as ulcers and hives. "One standard medical text estimates that 50 to 80 percent of all diseases have their origins in stress" (Kenneth R. Pelletier, "Mind as Healer, Mind as Slayer." *Psychology Today*, Feb. 1977, p. 35). Placebos solve physical problems. A doctor giving sick people sugar pills and telling them that it will cure them works in some cases. Studies indicate that mildly depressed patients have shown the same improvement with placebos as with regular drugs (Norman Cousins, "The Mysterious Placebo: How the Mind helps Medicine Work." *Saturday Review*, Oct. 1, 1977, p. 12).

My brother, a licensed therapist in Texas (before he retired), tells of a psychiatrist who had a blind patient. She thought there was something physically wrong with her eyes. After an examination, the doctor suspected nothing was wrong with her eyes, but when he put a chair in her way, she bumped into it. He told her that he was going to give her a pill that would cure her blindness at 3 pm the next day. He gave her a sugar pill and at 3 pm the next day, she could see.

If the emotions can affect the body, suppressed (forgotten) emotions can affect the body, and released emotions can relieve systems. It is important to note that at the end of the nineteenth century, the psychological disorder theory said that hysteria arose from suppressed emotions. Release the emotions and the symptoms disappear, that is, give the energy of strangulated feelings normal expression instead of letting them spill over into bodily symptoms. Sigmund Freud began with that theory and went from there.

Summary: Before the nineteenth century, the cause of abnormal behavior was thought to be either external forces (demons or heavenly bodies) or internal factors (the concept of temperament or a moral issue), but beginning in the nineteenth century, the ideas developed that the cause of abnormal behavior was either a physical disease or a psychological disorder.

This brief history is an introduction to the examination of modern psychotherapies because it shows that the idea that people's problems are psychological disorders did not develop until the latter part of the 19th century. It indicates how that idea evolved, and it illustrates that from a biblical perspective, some of these suggestions are simply wrong (astrology), some opinions have a wrong theory and a right conclusion (humors), some views have an element of truth (lunacy), and some explanations are right (demon possession; a psychological disorder can cause psychosomatic problems). At this point in history, the cause of problems was thought to be irresponsibility (the moral model), physical sickness (medical model), or suppressed emotional (mental model).

Chapter 4

PSYCHOANALYSIS

The father of psychoanalysis and the grandfather of the psychodynamic approaches to therapy was the Austrian neurologist Sigmund Freud (1856-1939). Freud's efforts resulted in "the most comprehensive theory of personality and psychotherapy ever developed" (Corey, p. 95). He has enormously influenced the public consciousness and directly impacted nearly all academic disciplines, including history, literature, and philosophy (Jones and Butman, p. 66). Some would add "insights into art, religion, social organization, child development, and education" (Arlow, p. 19).

Background

Freud's system of thought evolved over his lifetime (Jones and Butman, p. 66). Hence, a brief summary of his life helps to understand his theories, especially in the early stages.

Sigmund Freud was born to Jewish parents on May 6, 1856, the oldest of seven children. Freud often heard an anecdote growing up: "At the time of my birth, an old peasant woman had prophesied to my proud mother that with her firstborn child, she brought a great man into the world" (Grubin). He dreamed of being famous. He "never lost his thirst for fame" (Lauzun, p. 14). Freud was determined to pursue "power, prestige, and wealth" (Lauzun, p. 23). He grew up in poverty but was a brilliant student.

When he was ten years old, his father told him about an incident that happened when he was a young man. He encountered a Christian who, knocking off his fur cap, called him "Jew." His father picked up the cap and kept walking. Freud was disappointed with his father's response; he wanted him to be heroic. Consequently, Freud lost respect for his father. At the same time, Freud's mother was domineering and dictatorial (Grubin).

Freud was five foot seven inches tall. He used cocaine for a while to relieve depression and for energy, but he was never addicted. When it was discovered that it could be addictive, he gave it up and never used it again, but he did smoke 20 cigars a day (Grubin; Lauzun, p. 24).

Freud was shy, cold, and not particularly friendly (Lauzun, p. 31). He said that from his school days, "I was always in vehement opposition to my teachers, was always an extremist" (Lauzun, p. 31). Lauzun writes, "Freud suffered all his life from various physical ailments: intestinal troubles, rheumatic pains, sinusitis and, above all, frequent migraines. Flashes of temper and attacks of neurasthenia, which sometimes made him ill-humored, were regular occurrences" (Lauzun, p. 31).

As a young scientist, Freud was fascinated with the brain but was unable to earn enough money pursuing science to marry Martha Bernays, the woman he loved. Freud, therefore, abandons scientific research for a career in medicine. Freud earned his medical degree from the University of Vienna and four years later, at 26, he attained a prestigious position there as a lecturer (Corey, p. 95).

In November 1882, the German physician Josef Breuer told Freud about "Anna O.," a hysteric whom Freud had never met. When Breuer put Anna O. under hypnosis and asked her to relate what was oppressing her mind, she would tell of some highly emotional event in her life. She was relieved of her symptoms if a massive outburst of emotion accompanied it (Arlow, p. 24). This was a new method, a "talking cure" (Grubin).

In 1883, Freud went through five months of psychiatric studies, the only course of psychiatric studies he ever undertook (Lauzun, p. 22).

In 1885, Freud went to Paris, where he met the French neurologist Jean-Martin Charcot, who introduced Freud to the problem of "hysteria," people with physical symptoms who had no organic cause. For example, the paralysis that came and went. Charcot treated hysterics with hypnosis. As a result of his experience with Charcot, Freud used hypnosis to treat hysteria. He also used electro-therapy (Grubin).

In September 1886, at thirty, Freud finally married Martha Bernays. They had six children in just over nine years. Martha was a compliant wife who ran an orderly house. Freud lived an organized, conventional lifestyle.

Breuer and Freud worked together and in 1893, they published an article on their work. In 1895, they published *Studies in Hysteria*. At this point, the theory was that unconscious emotions resulted in the physical symptoms of hysteria.

Later, independent of Breuer, Freud concluded that the traumatic events and the resultant unconscious emotions causing hysteria occurred in childhood and were sexual. At first, he believed that an older person had seduced all of his patients. The break between Breuer and Freud came about over the issue of memories of childhood seduction. Freud believed that most of his patients had been seduced as children.

Breuer did not. Later, Freud changed his mind (Arlow, p. 24; Lauzun, pp. 49-50).

Freud said, "When, later, I maintained ever more firmly that sexuality played a part in the aetiology of the neuroses, he [Breuer] was the first to manifest those reactions of disgust and disproval with which I was to become so familiar, but with which I had not yet learned to recognize the inevitable fate in store for me" (Lauzun, p. 42). Lauzun adds, "Freud never forgave him" (Lauzun, p. 42).

During his lifetime, Freud broke with many others. He passed "from one exclusive friendship to another, and alternating, as the years go by, between attraction and repulsion in relation to the same person" (Lauzun, p. 41). Freud said, "An intimate friend and a hated enemy have always been indispensable to my emotional life; I have always been able to create them anew, and not infrequently, my childish ideal has been so closely approached that friend and enemy have coincided in the same person" (Lauzun, p. 41).

In 1896, Freud presented his ideas to Vienna's Society of Psychiatry and Neurology. He said that the origin of hysteria was a sexual assault on an innocent child. His ideas were rejected as a scientific fairy tale (Grubin).

Later that year, his father died (October 23, 1896) and, as a result, Freud began to analyze himself (Grubin). Freud suffered from migraine headaches, mood swings, depression, and phobias, especially an exaggerated fear of dying. Through self-analysis, he explored his dreams and examined his childhood memories. He had patients who said that their father had sexually abused them and he concluded that his father had sexually abused him (Grubin). He decided that as a child, he had intense hostility toward his father and had sexual feelings for his mother (Corey, p. 95; Grubin) and from that, he determined that all children have incestuous feelings; he universalized his feelings (Grubin). Lauzun says that without Freud's self-discovery, "the birth of psychoanalysis could not have taken place" (Lauzun, p. 47).

As Freud went through self-auto-analysis, he confided in Wilhelm Fliess, an ear, nose, and throat specialist from Berlin. For five years, the two exchanged letters, which have been preserved. Fliess had a theory that the key to understanding all vital activities was two numbers, 28 and 23. The first number was derived from menstruation, the second probably from the interval between the close of one menstrual period and the beginning of the next. According to Fliess, these sexual "periods" determine the stages of our growth, the dates of our illness and the date of our death. The mother's periods determine the sex of the infant and the date of its birth. Lauzun says that "such poetic fancy" not only "captivated Freud" but also "obscured his judgment" (Lauzun,

p. 46). Throughout 1907, when Freud was 51 (51 = 23 + 28), he was haunted by fears of imminent death (see fn. in Lauzun, p. 46).

Freud developed various methods of therapy, such as free association, the interpretation of resistance, repression, seeing sexual strivings, and the interpretation of transference and dreams. With Breuer, hypnotism was the treatment for hysteria. At first, Freud used hypnosis (Lauzun, p. 37), but many of his patients could not be hypnotized. So, Freud tried "forced suggestion, a technique of recollection fostered by the insistent, demanding pressure of the therapist" (Arlow, p. 34). Then, a patient named Fräulein Elisabeth complained that these interruptions and interferences hindered her, breaking the flow of memories. "The method of free association was born of this demand" (Lauzun, p. 41). "Freud reduced the element of suggestion to a minimum by a new technical procedure in which he asked his patients to report freely and without criticism whatever came into their minds" (Arlow, p. 34).

He had his patients lie on a couch while he sat out of sight, a method used in hypnosis (White, p. 30). Bair describes the scene. The patient lay on a "daybed draped with a Persian carpet and covered with velvet cushions in muted earth tones, while he sat behind them silently, out of sight in a forest-green velvet armchair" (Bair, p. 218; I saw Freud's couch at the Skirball Cultural Center in Los Angeles on April 22, 2000). As Freud listened, he faced a bronze head of Buddha and an owl from China (Lauzun, p. 86).

Thus, "free association" became Freud's technique for releasing imprisoned emotions. He even claimed that nothing would occur to the patient that was not somehow related to his neurosis.

Patients resisted. In countless ways, they strongly resented telling all, but the resistance did not go on forever. In time, they began to relate memories and feelings (White, p. 31). Based on resistance, Freud formulated his theory of repression. He reasoned that strong forces prevented the patient from remembering emotionally charged experiences and these forces were responsible for their original banishment (White, p. 32).

He also concluded that repression was a device whereby the person is protected from unbearable pain. In the original situation, a wish had been aroused that conflicted with "ethical, aesthetic, and personal pretensions." The appearance of such a wish in the consciousness created sharp and painful conflict, which was solved by repression. Blocked from the ordinary expression, this wish discharged itself into various symptoms of hysteria. Repression is *not* an observable fact. It is a hypothetical concept. The hypothesis is confirmed by recall (White, p. 32).

What kind of strivings ("ethical, aesthetic, and personal pretensions") are so repugnant that they must be denied recognition, yet so strong they take revenge by precipitating a neurosis? From cases other than hysteria (feeling constant fatigue and exhaustion), he found gross disturbances in the patient's current sexual life. Later, he concludes that in all cases of neuroses, including hysteria and obsessive-compulsives, sexual traumas in childhood produced the symptoms. Sex, in this sense, was more than the sex act. It includes a variety of impulses like thumb sucking, display of the naked body, masturbation, etc. (White, pp. 32-33).

His method, which, from the start, he called psychoanalysis, was to replace the unconscious with the conscious. It was a long process of free association. In applying this method, Freud found that patients began to manifest various feelings toward him. He found that an affectionate relationship developed in every case without his encouragement, even in elderly women. He also discovered that sooner or later, hostility and anger displayed themselves. Freud felt that the counseling context alone could not explain these reactions. Therefore, he concluded that they were transferred from the past. He called this transference (White, pp. 34-36).

Freud noticed that his neurotic patients regularly talked about dreams. He dreamed a great deal and, since 1892, had written them down. He decided that dreams were suppressed wishes, unacceptable infantile wishes (Grubin).

In *The Interpretation of Dreams* (1900), Freud related his self-analysis and the concepts of unconscious conflict and childhood sexuality. In it, he also first described the Oedipus complex, the theory that the unconscious contains the sexual drives pressing for expression, but the conscious functions at a logical, realistic, adaptive level.

Much later, Freud began to recognize that his theory did not explain things he saw in his patients. He observed that aggression was present in depression. Even generally, in many ways, people punish themselves. In 1920, he wrote *Beyond the Pleasure Principle,* in which he said there are two drives: a drive of love (*Eros*) and a drive toward death and self-destruction (*Thanatos*).

These drives are often referred to as "instincts," but it has been argued that the German word Freud used should be translated "drive" or "impulse." Jacob A. Arlow, Clinical Professor of Psychiatry at New York University College of Medicine, agrees that "instincts" is inaccurate; the "correct term" is drives (Arlow, p. 29).

Finally, Freud reformulated his theory of the structure of the mind. In *The Structural*

Theory (1923), he described the three major subdivisions of the psyche: the id, the ego, and the superego. One of the major functions of the ego is to protect the mind from the threat of a breakthrough of unconscious impulses.

In *Inhibitions, Symptoms, and Anxiety* (1926), Freud detailed the problem of anxiety. Unconscious wishes try to emerge into consciousness, creating anxiety and causing the ego to use an array of defenses.

Freud's last book was *Moses and Monotheism* (1939). In April 2000, I heard a lecture on Freud's book at the Skirball Culture Center given by Richard Bernstein, author of *Freud and the Legacy of Moses* (1998). He said that, according to Freud, Moses was not a Hebrew but an Egyptian priest. Monotheism was not invented by the Jews but by the Egyptians. The Jews murdered Moses in the wilderness, but the memory of it was repressed. Freud claimed that he was an atheist, yet he also claimed that he was, in his essential nature, a Jew. The essence of Judaism is a life of truth and justice. In a question and answer session after the lecture, Bernstein said that the issue was not history but psychoanalysis, that is, ambivalence to honor the Father and kill him. He said that each generation has to honor and murder his father.

Freud died on September 23, 1939 (Lauzun, p. 110). For sixteen years, from 1923 to 1939, his flesh was slowly eaten away by cancer of the palate and the right side of the jaw. It would go into remission for a while, "then break out afresh to be again held in check, and so on until it finally finished" (Lauzun, p. 83). During those sixteen years, Freud lived with a prosthesis, "suffering atrociously from the inevitable ulceration and sometimes having to struggle for hours to open his mouth slightly to eat or speak" (Lauzun, p. 83). He kept the prosthesis in place with his thumb. The cause of the cancer was smoking; he smoked from ten to twenty cigars a day. He had thirty-three surgical operations (Lauzun p. 88).

Freud's defenders argue that his personal life is irrelevant to his contribution to psychoanalysis. For example, Arnold Richards, editor of the American Psychoanalytic Association newsletter, dismisses any reference to Freud's private conduct, saying, "It has no scientific, practical consequences. It's not relevant to Freud's theory or practice." *Time Magazine* observes that is "a rather odd contention, given Freud's statement that his development of the analytic method began with his pioneering analysis of himself" (*Time Magazine*, November 29, 1993). Since Freud developed his theories through self-analysis, his personal life issues are relevant.

Beyond what has been mentioned, Freud was an inflexible autocrat, had difficulty maintaining relationships with his peers, and had an affair with his wife's sister. Freud was a rigid authoritarian. His belief in the correctness of his theories was absolute. He was an autocrat who was intolerant of dissent (Stevens, p. 16). He had a need for ultimate authority. He admitted, "I don't deny that I like to be right," calling it a "sad privilege" of old age and accusing "younger" men of not knowing how to cope with their "father complexes" (Bair, p. 218).

At dinner one evening during their trip to America, Carl Jung began discussing what they had seen on their tour that morning when Freud suddenly said, "What is it with you and these corpses? Wouldn't it be better if you admitted that you wish I would drop dead?" He, then, *promptly fainted*! Freud blamed Jung for causing it through an "act of resistance against the father" and a "death wish" against him." Jung, of course, denied the charge, but he was frustrated when Freud was incapable of or unwilling to accept his explanation. Jung was furious that despite all the work he had done for Freud's "cause" (more than all his other "students" put together), Freud could still accuse him of "motives that did not exist at all" (Bair, pp. 161-162; Bair quotes Jung as saying, "He always accused me of personal motives that didn't exist at all," Bair, p. 239). On another occasion, during that trip, while overlooking the Hudson River, when they disagreed, Freud urinated in his trousers! (Bair, p. 163).

Several years later, when Jung said something that challenged Freud's support of the father complex, Freud fainted again. He told Jung that it was an unfortunate incident because it made him lose a portion of his authority. Freud attributed fainting to "fatigue, lack of sleep, and too much smoking." He also said that "an unruly homosexual feeling (was) at the root of the matter" (Bair, p. 216).

Freud had a series of broken relationships with colleagues. He once admitted to Jung that his emotional life "demanded the existence of an intimate friend and a hated enemy, and, not infrequently, he encountered both in the same person." Freud was "a strange amalgam of autocrat and masochist." This pattern was apparent in his childhood relationship with his nephew John and with Wilhelm Fliess, who supported him through the period (1894-99) "when he was conducting his self-analysis and establishing the principles of psychoanalysis!" (Stevens, p. 16).

Perhaps his most famous break was with Jung. The break came over Jung's denial of the primacy of sex in his book *Symbols of Transformation* (1911). According to Jung's biographer, in letters between Freud and Jung from June 8 to the end of November 1912, "there is only bitterness, allegation, recrimination, and retaliation" (Bair, p. 227). In his 1914 history of the psychoanalytic movement, Freud "castigated" Jung. As a result of the break, Jung fell into a protracted "state of disorientation," at times verging on psychosis, which lasted four or five years (Stevens, p. 16).

That was "but one of a number of such painful episodes. A similar fate overtook Freud's relationship with Breuer, Adler, Stekel, Meynert, Silberer, Tausk, and Wilhelm Reich. Reich developed a psychosis, from which he recovered only temporarily, while Silberer and Tausk eventually committed suicide" (Stevens, p. 16). Anyone who dared question or refine his theory was "humiliated, discredited, ostracized, and banished" (Bair, p. 282).

Adler's break with Freud is particularly interesting. Adler proposed an explanation of the neuroses, which left sexuality completely out of account. He claimed that everything should be traced back to the feelings of inferiority inherent in every human being. For Adler, it was not sexuality but the pursuit of power that was the main determinant of human action. Choice of goals and cultural factors also play a part in neuroses. Freud declared, "I feel the Adlerian teachings are incorrect and, therefore, dangerous for the future development of psychoanalysis. They are scientific errors due to false methods; still, they are honorable errors" (Lauzun, p. 66).

Freud had an affair with his sister-in-law. In 1896, following the death of her fiancé, Minna Bernays, Freud's wife's sister, moved into the Freud family apartment at 19 Bergasse. She lived with her sister and brother-in-law for the rest of her life. In 1898, Freud and Minna traveled together alone in Switzerland and northwestern Italy. They did so again in 1900. After the trip in 1900, Freud left Minna at a health spa where she spent weeks recovering from respiratory and other troubles. Minna's subsequent symptoms fit those of a septic abortion. Freudian scholars are divided on the nature of their relationship, but Jung said that Minna confessed to having a sexual relationship with Freud (Bair, p. 164).

Drawn from actual events, dates, and circumstances taken from Freud's letters and biographies but with fictional dialogue, Kathleen Daniels has written *Minna's Story: The Secret Love of Dr. Sigmund Freud.* While living in Vienna just blocks from the Freud house, Daniels retraces the documented travels of Freud and Minna, trying to provide authentic details down to hotel names whenever possible. This much is certain: Minna Bernays lived with the Freud family, and she worked closely with Freud for at least ten of those years, translating, proofreading, and editing manuscripts, as well as accompanying him on travels. Minna has been all but obliterated from Sigmund Freud's family history. In accordance with the wishes of Anna Freud, his daughter, some documents and pictures were to be sealed until well after the year 2000. The truth about Minna and Freud's relationship remains in those documents.

The Theory

As the brief review of the development of his theories indicates, they evolved throughout his career. The final form is as follows.

View of People Freud's view of people includes concepts concerning the makeup of people, function within people, and the development of people.

1. Freud developed a detailed concept of the makeup of people. He had five "core assumptions" (Jones and Butman, p. 67).

The economic assumption: the human contains a certain amount of psychic energy in the form of basic drives. This energy is "economic" in the sense that it is neither gained nor lost. Yet, the energy must be released. It can be dispersed without regard to the constraints of reality or social norms, or it can be released in socially acceptable ways (Jones and Butman, p. 68).

The dynamic assumption: every individual has two drives. The life drive (known as *Eros*) is the sexual drive. It includes the urge to create, develop, or maintain intimacy and to love oneself and/or others. In short, all pleasure. The death drive (known as *Thanatos*) is the aggressive drive. It is the wish to die or hurt oneself or others. Freud saw the goal of much of life as gaining pleasure and avoiding pain (Jones and Butman, pp. 67-68; Corey, pp. 96-97).

The structural assumption: a person consists of three systems: the id, the ego, and the superego. These are not three discrete segments; the person functions as a whole. These are psychological processes (Jones and Butman, p. 68; Corey, pp. 97-98).

The *id* is the biological component. It is the seat of the sexual and aggressive drives. It is the pleasure principle, namely, the relentless drive toward personal gratification. The id is illogical, amoral, and largely unconscious.

The *ego* is the psychological component. It is the "executive" that governs and controls the person. The reality principle rules it. The ego is realistic, logical, and formulates plans for satisfying needs. It is largely conscious.

The *superego* is the social component. It is the judicial branch, a person's moral code, that is, the internalization of the standards of parents and society. It represents the ideal, not the real, and strives for the perfect, not for pleasure.

The topographical assumption: there are three levels of consciousness: 1) Consciousness, that is, experiences of which we are aware. 2) Pre-consciousness, that is, experiences of which we are not aware but we can recall. 3) Unconsciousness, that is, stored experiences, memories, and repressed material is not directly accessible to conscious examination (Jones and Butman, p. 67; Arlow, p. 29). Like an iceberg, the greater part of which lies below the surface of the water, the unconscious lies below the surface of awareness (Corey, p. 98). All behavior is largely unconsciously determined. Unconscious processes are the root of neurotic symptoms.

The genetic assumption: current behavior results from unresolved issues from the formative years of childhood (Jones and Butman, p. 67; Arlow, p. 29).

To sum up, people consist of an id (sexual and aggressive drives), an ego (the executive that governs the person), and a superego (the internalization of the standards of parents and society). The ego has repressed material into the unconscious and that unconscious material, which consists of unresolved issues from the formative years of childhood, affects current behavior.

2. Freud also delineated the functions within the person. Within the person, a *conflict* exists between the id, ego, and superego. The id strives to express its drives (sex, that is, pleasure and aggression). The superego seeks to inhibit the id's impulses by persuading the ego to substitute moralistic goals for realistic ones and strive for perfection.

The conflict within the person results in *anxiety*. There are three kinds of anxiety: reality, moral, and neurotic. Reality anxiety is the fear of danger from the external world. Moral anxiety is the fear of one's own conscience. Neurotic anxiety is the fear that the drive will get out of hand and cause one to do something for which one will be punished (Corey, p. 99).

Ideally, the ego controls anxiety through rational means. When the ego cannot control anxiety by direct and rational methods, it relies on ego defense mechanisms. These defense mechanisms transform the threatening anxiety into some alternate form the person can handle (Jones and Butman, p. 69).

Ego *defense mechanisms* help the individual cope with anxiety and prevent the ego from being overwhelmed. These defenses are normal behavior and can have adaptive value (for example, sublimation) if they do not become a lifestyle to avoid facing reality. Ego defense mechanisms are a form of self-deception. They are either a denial or a distortion of reality (Corey, p. 99). In 1946, Freud's daughter, Anna Freud, wrote *Mechanisms of Ego-Defense* (for a brief explanation of them, see Corey, p. 100). Here is a simple summary; it is not exhaustive.

Denial is the simplest defense. It defends against anxiety by denying a threatening reality. It is "closing one's eyes" to the threat.

Psychoanalysis

Repression is the involuntary removal of something from consciousness. Threatening or painful thoughts and feelings are excluded from awareness. It is the basis of neurotic disorders and, thus, one of the most important Freudian concepts. It is assumed that most of the painful events of the first five years of life are repressed, but these events determine adult behavior.

Rationalization is manufacturing a good reason to explain away a bruised ego, failures and losses, and justifying behavior.

Projection is attributing to others one's unacceptable desires. It is "the other people who are lustful or aggressive, not me."

Sublimation is redirecting sexual or aggressive energy into creative behavior. Sexual energy can be put into art. Aggressive energy can be channeled into athletic activity.

Compensation masks perceived weakness or develops certain positive traits to make up for limitations. People who feel socially incompetent compensate by developing their intellectual capacity.

Identification is part of development. Children do it to learn sex roles, but it can become a defense reaction. For example, people who feel inferior identify with successful causes, organizations, or people hoping to be perceived as worthwhile.

Regression is reverting to a form of behavior one has outgrown. In severe stress, it is coping with anxiety by clinging to immature and inappropriate behavior.

Interjection is "swallowing" the values of others. People in concentration camps deal with overwhelming anxiety by identifying with their aggressors.

Reaction formation expresses the opposite impulse.

Displacement shifts impulses from threatening objects to "safe targets."

Ritual and undoing are performing elaborate rituals to undo acts for which one feels guilty.

3. According to Freud, everyone goes through stages of development. The *oral* stage is from birth to the end of the first year. At first, libidinal energy is focused on the mouth. Sucking produces erotic pleasure, so sucking the mother's breast satisfies the infant's need for food and pleasure. Being deprived of oral gratification during this stage leads to problems in adult life.

Oral incorporative behavior involves the pleasurable stimulation of the mouth. Being deprived of oral gratification leads to an oral fixation. Adults who exhibit excessive oral needs such as excessive eating, chewing, talking, smoking, and drinking have this problem.

Oral-aggressive behavior begins when the child starts teething. Again, being deprived can lead to sarcasm, hostility, aggression, gossip, and making biting comments in adult life.

Not getting enough food or love during this period will lead to later personality problems. The child wants food and love from the mother. Not getting these needs met leads to mistrust, fear of reaching out to others, rejection of affection, fear of loving and trusting, low self-esteem, isolation, withdrawal, and the inability to form or maintain intense relationships (Jones and Butman, p. 69; Arlow, p. 30; Corey, pp. 102-105).

The *anal* stage is from one to three years of age. As infants mature, other areas of the body develop and become the focal point of gratification. Next, psychic gratification centers on the retention and expulsion of feces. (On a tour of China, I heard a tour guide call the restroom "the happy room.") According to Freud, the method of toilet training and the parent's attitude toward the child can have far-reaching effects on personality formation.

The anal-aggressive personality is developed if strict toilet-training methods are used. Children may get angry and express it by expelling their feces at inappropriate times and places. This is the foundation of such adult behavior as cruelty, inappropriate displays of anger, and extreme disorderliness.

The anal-retentive personality forms if the mother focuses too much attention on the child's bowel movements. By giving praise when the child defecates, the child may develop an exaggerated view of the importance of this activity. Such a child feels the need to be productive. A fixation at this stage leads to extreme orderliness, hoarding, compulsivity, stubbornness, and stinginess as adults.

This stage is the child's first experience with discipline. Furthermore, the child continually faces parental demands and experiences frustrations when they handle objects and explore their environment. The child experiences negative feelings such as anger, hostility, destructiveness, hatred, rage, etc. (Jones and Butman, p. 69; Arlow, pp. 30-31; Corey, pp. 105-106).

The *phallic* stage is from age three to six. During the phallic stage, the focus for gratification moves from the mouth and anus to the genitals. Sexual activity becomes more intense. The attention is on the genitals themselves, the boys' penises and the girls' clitorises. The basic conflict centers on the unconscious, incestuous desire for the parent of the opposite sex. There is also the unconscious wish to "do away with" the competition, the parent of the same sex. Since these feelings are threatening, they are repressed.

Boys develop the Oedipus complex. (In the famous Greek Oedipus myth, Oedipus murdered his father and married his mother.) Boys experience sexual desires for their mother exhibited by intense attachment to her, jealousy for her attention, etc. Boys also realize that their father is their competition and they get angry with the father, followed by a fearful realization that they cannot compete with their father. Castration anxiety is the fear that the father will retaliate by cutting off the penis. The proper way to resolve the conflict is for the boy to identify with the father and absorb parts of his personality.

Girls develop the Electra complex. Their love is transferred from the mother to the father. They compete with the mother for the father's attention. Penis envy is the realization they do not have a penis. The proper resolution of the conflict is for girls to realize they cannot replace their mothers and begin an identification process by taking on some of their mothers' characteristics.

During this period, many do not resolve their feelings about their sexuality and/or their sex roles. It is during this period the conscience develops. Rigid parental moral standards can lead to over-control by the superego. If parents teach that all impulses are evil, children feel guilty about these feelings and carry the guilt into adult life. This blocks enjoying intimacy with others. These people cannot think for themselves, are rigid, and have low self-esteem, self-condemnation, and severe conflicts (Jones and Butman, p. 70; Arlow, pp. 31-33; Corey, pp. 106-108).

Freud considered the Oedipus complex to be one of his greatest discoveries. He said, "Every new arrival on this planet is faced with the task of mastering the Oedipus complex; anyone who fails to do so falls victim to neurosis" (Sigmund Freud, *Three Essays on the Theory of Sexuality*, published in 1905 and cited by Bobgan, p. 71).

The name for the Oedipus complex is taken from the Greek play entitled *Oedipus Rex* by Sophocles. In the play, the Oracle of Delphi prophesied that any son born to King Laius of Thebes would murder him. Because of the prophecy, when a son was born to Laius, he took the infant, pierced his feet, and left him on a mountain to die. A shepherd found the child, named him Oedipus, and gave him to the childless King and Queen of Corinth, who raised him as their son.

As a young man, when Oedipus was seeking information from the oracle at Delphi, he was told that he would kill his father and marry his mother. Because he loved the two people he thought were his parents, he decided not to return home, lest he fulfill that prophecy. As he traveled along a narrow mountainous roadway, a chariot going in the opposite direction, met him. Since the two could not pass each other, the rider in the chariot ordered Oedipus aside. Oedipus stepped aside, but when the chariot's wheels smashed into his foot, he reacted by killing the driver and the rider. The rider was Oedipus's biological father. Without knowing it, he had killed his real father.

Oedipus journeyed to Thebes. There, he solved the riddle of the Sphinx and was rewarded with the hand of the recently widowed Queen Jocasta. Not realizing that she was his mother, Oedipus married her. At the end of the story, the truth of the relationship is revealed. Jocasta hangs herself and Oedipus pierces his own eyes with a pin from her garment and goes into banishment blind. The story is a classic tragedy. The main character brings about his own destruction.

As Oedipus did not know what he was doing in killing his father and marrying his mother, so for Freud, people are unaware of the negative feelings about the parent of the same sex and the sexual feelings about their parents at an early age because they have deeply repressed many aspects of those feelings.

The *latency* stage is from ages six to twelve. By age six, the personality of id, ego, and superego are largely formed and the stresses of the oral, anal, and phallic stages of psycho-sexual development are passed. The individual enters a period of relative rest. Increased socialization replaces the inwardness of the phallic period. The child develops new interests in the external world, including academics and athletics (Jones and Butman, pp. 70-71; Arlow, pp. 33-34; Corey, pp. 108-107).

The *genital* stage is from ages twelve to eighteen. Again, sexual impulses become predominant. The individual develops an interest in the opposite sex, often experimenting with some sexual activity. Ideally, libidinal energies are redirected into socially acceptable activities like dating and friendships. Each person should develop the capacity to be interested in others, become free of parental influences, and have intimate relationships.

The genital stage continues throughout adult life. The core characteristics of maturity are *lieben* and *arbeiten*, that is, the freedom to love, work, and derive satisfaction from living and working (Jones and Butman, p. 70; Corey, pp. 109-110).

Theory of Pathology According to Freud, everyone has drives, conflicts, and fixations in their formative years and, therefore, has some pathology. No one passes through the stages of development without difficulty. Of course, the more intense the conflicts and fixations are, the more severe the pathology (Jones and Butman, p. 72).

Psychoanalysis

The explanation of a severe pathology (neurosis) begins with the id, the pleasure principle, and the drive to personal gratification of sex and aggression. Because of neurotic anxiety (the fear that a drive will get out of control and cause punishment), the ego uses defense mechanisms to cope with the anxiety and not be overwhelmed. These defense mechanisms are a denial and a distortion of reality.

Anxiety is at the core of all pathology. It operates at an unconscious level. As this unconscious anxiety attempts to intrude into consciousness, the person begins to panic, and symptoms appear. The particular pathology depends on which stage the conflicts and fixation first developed and the specific ego defenses utilized to "bind" the anxiety (Jones and Butman, pp. 72-73). To say the same thing another way, unconscious, unresolved conflicts between the id (sex and aggression drives) and the ego during the first six years of life overwhelm the ego, creating anxiety and neurotic symptoms (Corey, p. 110). Freud's analysis of people's problems looks like this:

Drives → internal conflict → anxiety → defense mechanisms → neurotic symptoms

In short, the problem is unresolved, unconscious internal childhood conflicts.

For example, in one form of agoraphobia, a woman becomes anxious when she goes out on the street because the street represents the place where it is possible to realize her unconscious wish to be a prostitute. The defense mechanisms of avoidance and projection control the sexual impulse. First, the impulse is projected onto the street and then the street is avoided (Arlow, p. 41).

Nature of Health Healthy individuals are those who have "worked through" their childhood conflicts. They have enough conscious awareness of their drives so that they have self-control over them. Freud reportedly said, "Where id was, let ego be." Healthy people have good ego strength and are becoming mature (Jones and Butman, p. 71). Healthy people have socially acceptable behavior.

Method of Therapy The goal of classic psychoanalysis is "to help the patient achieve a resolution of intra-psychic conflict through understanding conflicts and dealing with them in a more mature manner" (Arlow, p. 37). In short, it is to make the unconscious conscious. The client must gain insight, which is not just an intellectual understanding but a re-living of painful childhood experiences and working through them. This is called abreaction or catharsis. Then, the ego is strengthened so behavior is based more on reality and less on drives. The ultimate aim is total personality reconstruction (Jones and Butman, p. 73). Various methods are used.

1. Explaining Free Association. Free association is the basic technique. The client lies on a couch. The therapist sits behind the couch, out of the client's view. The client is to say whatever comes to mind, regardless of how trivial, silly, irrelevant, illogical, or painful it may be. The expectation is that more and more significant unconscious material will emerge.

Nothing the client says is taken at face value. The therapist looks for hidden meanings, for example, a "slip of the tongue." Everything must be interpreted, including free association, resistance, dreams, and transference. Interpretation consists of the therapist explaining and teaching the client the meanings of behavior manifested through these various means.

2. Interpreting Resistance. Resistance is the client's reluctance to bring unconscious material that has been repressed to the surface. Resistance is an unconscious defense against anxiety. It builds in direct proportion to the significance of the unconscious material emerging. Resistance, of course, must be interpreted. These blocks to free association are clues to the nature of conflicts and fixations. If they can be brought to awareness and dealt with, insight can result.

3. Interpretation of Transference. Clients react to their therapist as they did to some significant person in their past. They "transfer" both positive and negative feelings. The interpretation of transference is a critical technique in psychoanalysis. Through experiencing and working through these new editions of early feelings, the client is able to change long-standing patterns of behavior. In essence, the effects of past early relationships are counteracted by working through similar emotional conflicts with the therapist. Counter-transference is feelings on the analyst's part that have been transferred toward the client.

4. Analysis of Dreams. Unacceptable wishes have been repressed into the unconscious. During dreams, defenses are lowered and repressed feelings surface, perhaps even more deeply than in free association (Jones and Butman, p. 75). For Freud, dreams were "the royal road to the unconscious" (Freud, *The Interpretation of Dreams*, p. 769).

Dreams have two levels of content. The manifest content is the dream as it appears to the dreamer. The latent content comprises symbolic and unconscious motives, wishes, and fears. The repressed material is so unacceptable that it is expressed in symbolic form.

"Dream work" is uncovering the latent meanings (Jones and Butman, pp. 74-76). The manifest content must be analyzed to determine the latent content, which is the symbol of the unconscious wish. The dream, then, is a code to be decoded (Stevens, p. 82).

Freud was convinced that he had solved the riddle of dreams that had intrigued people since antiquity, namely, how to unravel their meaning. He was so convinced that in 1895, when he was on vacation in Belle Vue Castle near Vienna, he thought that one day a marble tablet would record that "in this house, on July 24th, 1895, the secret of dreams was revealed to Dr. Sigmund Freud" (Stevens, p. 82).

Arlow, a professor of psychiatry, gives an example of psychoanalysis. Tom was a faculty member at a prominent university, but he could not complete his doctoral thesis. All he had to do was put the final touches on it and defend it before the committee, but he could not finish those last details. He also had difficulties with women. He could not maintain a long-term relationship with them.

The case study contains childhood and adult experiences of Tom, as well as several of Tom's dreams and reactions to the therapist. For example, when Tom was small, he saw his parents having sex. When he was twelve or thirteen, he had a crush on the girl next door, but he did nothing about it. When he was fourteen, he took a girl to a party, but she spent most of the evening with Tom's best friend.

Arlow concludes, "The experiences between the ages of four and five proved to be the crucial ones. They centered on the boy's hostility and envy of the father due to having slept in the same room with his parents at the Jersey shore."

Arlow explains that when Tom saw his parents having sex, "He felt left out, betrayed, and humiliated. In his mind, his mother became a whore who did dirty things and who preferred his father because he was more powerful and had a bigger penis, while he was so small and insignificant.... He no longer trusted his mother, and this affected his attitude toward all women, especially after his sweetheart had turned her affections to his best friend when he was twelve years old" (actually, it was when Tom was fourteen when that happened).

As for the Ph.D. exam, passing it "was to be permitted to enter the council of elders, to have the rights to be sexual, to have a woman, and to become a father." Also, unconsciously, he felt he could not become a husband or father as long as he was in analysis, which meant to him as long as his father was alive. Accordingly, a successful termination of treatment had the unconscious significance of killing his father.... Unconsciously, he imagined that within the woman's vagina was the adversary who would kill or mutilate him."

Arlow says, "After many months of working through the anxieties of these unconscious fantasies of childhood, the patient began to make progress in his work and he became potent again." Tom got the Ph.D. and he got married (a summary taken from Arlow, pp. 49-56).

Evaluation

Philosophical Assumptions Psychoanalysis is based on several philosophical assumptions.

1. Atheism. Freud's atheism is well known. Psychoanalysis is a closed system of cause and effect with no need for God (Jones and Butman, p. 79). In addition, for Freud, religion is an illusion. The threatening universe creates overwhelming anxiety. Religion is our self-protecting response. This illusion stems from our distorted memories of childhood when, as weak and vulnerable, we felt protected by an omnipotent, omniscient, loving parent, especially a father (Jones and Butman, p. 77; Carter and Narramore, pp. 25-26).

According to the Scripture, concerning the issue of the existence of God, Freud was a fool. It says, "The fool has said in his heart, '*There is* no God.'" By the way, Freudianism can explain away atheism as well as theism. Disbelief in God can be explained as a result of the Oedipal complex. What better way to get back at (murder!) a father figure than to simply not believe in him? (Jones and Butman, p. 78). The issue, of course, is "Is there objective evidence that God exists?"

2. Naturalism. There is nothing supernatural about Freud's idea of the soul. Biological and physical laws determine every aspect of human life. Freud was dogmatic about this. For him, there is no room for transcendent reality (Jones and Butman, p. 79). On the other hand, Freud possibly dabbled in "matters of the occult" (Jones and Butman, p. 77). The Bible is full of the supernatural acts of God, beginning with Genesis 1:1.

3. Determinism. Freudianism teaches that all human behavior is determined by unconscious, unresolved conflicts in early childhood. According to Freud, "We are puppets of the unknown and unseen unconscious, shaped by these forces during our first six years of existence" (Bobgan, p. 77). One Freudian has written that determinism is the "first and foremost" principle of psychoanalytic theory (Arlow, p. 29). This has profound ramifications. One author wrote, "Psychoanalysis has taken the meaning out

of all conventional recipes for bringing up children" (Lauzun, p. 117).

Past events undoubtedly influence people, but the psychoanalytic explanation is "overly deterministic" (Jones and Butman, p. 80). That is putting it mildly. Humans are capable of making choices (Jn. 7:17).

View of People Since Freud's view of people is complex, consisting of the makeup of people, the functions within people, and the development of people, each needs to be addressed individually.

1. The Makeup of People. Freud's view is that people consist of an id (two drives), an ego, and a superego (conscience). Granted, people have desires/drives (Jas. 4:1), an ego ("I" in Rom. 7:14 is the Greek word *ego*), and a conscience (Heb. 9:9), but if that is all that is said, it is a notion of the makeup of personality that is a case of reductionism. People have more than two drives (for example, they desire to worship). People have more than three components and capacities. They have a mind, emotions, a will, a conscience, a sinful nature, and a spirit. A more complete view is that people are spiritual, social, psychological, purposeful, and physical beings (see Chapter 2, "The Standard of Evaluation").

People can forget or be deceived, but the concept of the unconscious is debatable and the theory that unconscious, unresolved conflict between the drives and conscience exists at an early age is unprovable. "Although there is a portion of our minds to which we do not seem to have direct access, it does not follow that Freud's theory of the unconscious is true" (Bobgan, pp. 75-76). Furthermore, to say that unconscious motivation determines behavior bypasses human responsibility. Adults have "problems" and, no doubt, have been influenced by past experiences, but to assume that all current behavior results from unresolved issues from the formative years of childhood ignores other factors and choices.

2. The Functions within People. According to Freud, there is a conflict within people. That much is true, but his explanation of the conflict as the id striving to express its drives (sex and aggression) and the superego (conscience) seeking to inhibit the id by persuading the ego to substitute moralistic goals for realistic ones is not the same as the biblical description of the internal conflict in human beings. People have an internal conflict, but that conflict involves the sinful nature (Rom. 7:15-19), which is more than the sexual and aggressive drives. Believers also have a conflict between the flesh and the Spirit (Gal. 5:17).

Freud claims that conflict within the personality results in anxiety. All humans experience anxiety, but to conclude that anxiety is the result of the conflict between the id and the superego is inaccurate and incomplete. The Bible repeatedly speaks of being anxious (Phil. 4:6). People struggle with fear.

Freud says people practice defense mechanisms to defend the ego from anxiety over the conflict between the id and superego, that is, to cope with the fear of the sex drive getting out of control, people practice "defense mechanisms." The Bible speaks of human beings practicing denial (1 Jn. 1:8, 10), rationalization (Gen. 3:11-12), projection (Rom. 2:1), etc. Defense mechanisms have been called forms of "self-deception" (Corey, p. 100). Humans deceive themselves (Jer. 17:9; Jas. 1:22-24; 1 Jn. 1:8). In the final analysis, however, defense mechanisms are forms of not assuming responsibility and shifting the blame to someone or something else. Fear is undoubtedly involved, but guilt is also present (Gen. 3:8-11).

3. The Development of People. For Freud, people pass through stages, all of which are sexual. Humans develop through discernible stages, but the stages are not sexual/pleasure stages. After Freud, Erikson developed much more realistic stages of development (see Chapter 6, Psychodynamic Psychotherapies).

The concept of childhood sexuality is speculation. The Oedipus complex and penis envy are myths. Freud's notion that all children between the ages of three and six *desire* to kill the parent of the same gender and have sex with the parent of the opposite gender is a figment of his imagination rather than a universal truth about all children. As Erich Fromm taught, "It is not sexual behavior that determines character, but character that determines sexual behavior" (Lauzun, p. 127).

It has been suggested that Freud missed the point of the Oedipus myth. Incest was only incidental. Oedipus did not desire it, nor was he punished for it (Arlow, pp. 130-31). Moreover, Jesus serves as an anti-Oedipus model. He finds life by obediently doing his Father's will rather than trying to destroy the Father (Jones and Butman, p. 85).

Theory of Pathology Freud concluded that unconscious anxiety over sexual and aggressive drives is at the bottom of *all* pathology. That is simply absurd. Like the fictitious Oedipus story in ancient Greek literature, Freud's Oedipus complex is fantasy! Humans are fearful creatures (Ps. 34:4), but the root cause of *all* problems is not sexual in nature. People's most basic problem is their relationship with God (Rom. 1:18-21) and their irresponsibility (Rom. 3:23).

Nature of Health For Freud, psychologically healthy people have enough conscious awareness of their drives that they have self-control over them. They have good ego strength, are growing toward maturity, and have socially acceptable behavior. The psychoanalytic view of health stresses individualism and subjectivism to the point that it can become so all-consuming that it breeds unhealthy narcissism and self-absorption (Jones and Butman, p. 83). It is a self-contained system that, even for healthy people, "relationships with other beings are of value only insofar as they facilitate instinctual gratification" (Storr, cited in Jones and Butman, p. 82).

Healthy individuals are mature, but maturity consists of more than self-awareness (see column on self-knowledge in Jones and Butman, p. 84) and self-control. They have socially acceptable behavior, but ultimately, the standard of behavior is not society. An objective system of ethics is lacking (Jones and Butman, p. 13). Maturity includes other personal virtues (Gal. 5:22-23; 2 Pet. 1:5-7), loving relationships with others, and dependence on the Lord.

Method of Therapy Freud utilized several different methods of therapy, each of which is flawed. With free association, the counselor is "unduly restrictive" (Corey, p. 129; 2 Thess. 5:14). Clients often resist counselors, but client reluctance is not a clue to the conflict between the id and the ego or a clue to fixation. It is often nothing more than embarrassment or unwillingness to assume responsibility. Counselees develop fond feelings and anger toward their counselors, but it is not necessarily that the patient transfers the feelings from one person to another or from the past to the present. Clients angry at their fathers or mothers get angry at *any* father or mother figure. The Steven Principle is "If you don't like the message, stone the messenger" (see Acts 7).

Subjective interpretations of dreams are given as though they are the objective truth (Bobgan, p. 69). There is no doubt that dreams reflect a person's experience or thinking, but they are not a "royal road to the unconscious." As Korchin wrote, they are "hardly a freeway with unlimited visibility, nor do hidden meanings roll forth with simple clarity" (Korchin, cited by Jones and Butman, p. 75). Dream research has proven that Freud's hypothesis concerning dreams is untenable. Since all mammals and human infants devote much of their time both in the womb and post-natally to Rapid Eye Movement sleep, which is when dreams occur, dreams cannot be disguised expressions of repressed wishes (Stevens, pp. 82-83).

Summary: Freud believed that unconscious, unresolved internal conflicts between the id and the superego during the first six years of life overwhelm the ego, creating anxiety and neurotic symptoms. Through free association and the interpretation of resistance, dreams, and transference, the unconscious is made conscious, so the emotions can be transferred to the therapist and be relieved and, thus, released. As a result, the ego is strengthened.

From a biblical perspective, psychoanalysis is a myth because it is atheistic, naturalistic, deterministic, and subjective in the extreme. It has a reductionist view of people, an inaccurate notion of how people function because it ignores human responsibility, and has an explanation of the development of the personality that is bizarre (all stages of development are sexual). It has an absurd view of pathology (all problems are caused by anxiety over sexual and aggressive drives), a concept of psychological health that breeds narcissism and self-absorption, and a method of therapy that is unproven, unrealistic, and unnecessary.

Many have criticized Freud. Jung once asked Freud to observe a patient. Freud's main reaction was to ask Jung how he could tolerate "spending hours and days with this phenomenally ugly female." Jung was "dumbfounded" by Freud's "lack of objectivity." Jung attributed Freud's thoughtless remark to "how little he knew of psychiatry." Years later, Jung said Freud "was really a layman when it came to psychiatry…. He simply only knew *his* theory. And his theory did not suffice. It suffices for a certain area but not for the whole" (Bair, p. 149). In 1909, William James wrote in a letter that Freud "made on me personally the impression of a man obsessed with fixed ideas" (*Time Magazine*, November 29, 1993).

In his book *Seductive Mirage: an Exploration of the Work of Sigmund Freud*, Allen Esterson documents discrepancies, doctored evidence, and apparent lies in Freud's account of his cases. Freud regularly sounds like a detective who solves a crime before interviewing the first witness. Once he made a diagnosis, that case, as far as he was concerned, was closed, although the treatment continued (*Time Magazine*, November 29, 1993).

In their book, *Father Knows Best: The Use and Abuse of Power in Freud's Case of "Dora,"* Robin Tommach Lakoff and James C. Coyne relate the story of Freud's most famous botched analysis. In 1901, when "Dora" was 18, she sought Freud's help. Her father was having an affair with the wife of Herr "K," a family friend. Herr "K" had been paying unwanted sexual attention to Dora since she was 14 and her father was now encouraging her to pursue this, presumably as a way of deflecting attention away from his affair. Freud decided that Dora really desired Herr K sexually, plus her father to boot. He criticized her "hysterical" refusal to allow herself to follow her true inclinations and make everyone, including herself, satisfied and fulfilled. She left Freud's sessions after three months (*Time Magazine*, November 29, 1993).

Psychoanalysis

Many criticisms have been leveled against Freud's theories. Harding wrote that Freud receives criticism "from the academic psychologist for being unscientific, from humanists and theistic psychologists for being too reductionistic, and from the behaviorist for not being reductionistic enough" (Jones and Butman, p. 76). It is a psychosexual system that eliminates psychosocial factors in human development (Jones and Butman, p. 76). Jones and Butman concluded, "Unfortunately, the theory all too often lacks precision and testability and runs the risk of leading to 'nothing, but,' or reductionistic interpretations of behavior (e.g., everything becomes the result of aggressive or sexual drives)" (Jones and Butman, p. 71).

Freud got his theories by analyzing himself. Freud's theories are a projection of his sexuality on all mankind (Bobgan) and they are improbable. It is impossible to verify or refute such a subjective system. For example, in the interpretation of dreams, the same symbol could have entirely different implications for different people. "It is akin to shoveling smoke" (Bobgan, p. 78). In his book *Validation and the Clinical Theory of Psychoanalysis*, Adolf Grumbaum, a professor at the University of Pittsburgh, examines a number of psychoanalytic premises, including the theory of repression, the investigative capacities offered by free association, and the diagnostic significance of dreams. He argues that neither Freud nor his successors have ever proved a cause-and-effect link between a repressed memory and a later neurosis or a retrieved memory and a subsequent cure (*Time Magazine*, November 29, 1993).

It is questionable whether the system works at all. Freud mentions 133 cases in his writings, but he only provided extensive reports on six. Of these six, he only saw two for more than six months and only one, the famous "Wolff Man," for a full course of psychoanalysis. The Wolff Man was "not quite the advertisement for psychoanalysts which Freud had hoped for" (Storr, cited by Jones and Butman, p. 76). "Apparently, while Freud reported his analysis to be a complete success, a follow-up study suggested that the Wolff Man's analysis with Freud was only somewhat helpful, allowing him to live a life of moderate maladjustment" (Jones and Butman, p. 76).

The cover of the November 29, 1993 issue of *Time Magazine* asked the question, "Is Freud Dead?" The cover story by Paul Gray entitled "The Assault on Freud" refers to a number of individuals and authors who have attacked Freud. Concerning whether or not psychoanalysis would be covered in a national health plan, Dr. Frederick K. Goodwin, director of the National Institute of Mental Health, said, "It is clear that classical psychoanalysis, which is four to five times a week for four to five years in duration, will not be covered. It will not be covered because there is no evidence that it works."

Frank Sulloway, a visiting scholar of science history at MIT, says, "Psychoanalysis is built on quicksand. It is like a 10-story hotel sinking into an unsound foundation. The analysts are in this building. You tell them that it is sinking and they say, 'It's OK; we are on the 10th floor'" (*Time Magazine*, November 29, 1993). From a Freudian point of view, any criticism of psychoanalytic principles is resistance and resistance amounts to the actual evidence in favor of the correctness of the theory! (*Time Magazine*, November 29, 1993).

Psychoanalysis is unrealistic. Even if it were accurate and worked, it would only be for a select group of people. Jung once wrote Freud for advice concerning a patient. In his reply, Freud said he was pleased to hear that this patient was a student because people without education make unsuitable subjects (Bair, p. 108). One psychoanalyst wrote, "Not all forms of mental disturbances can or should be treated by psychoanalysis. Paradoxically, the demands of psychoanalysis require the cooperation of a patient with a fairly healthy ego who is well motivated to change and capable of facing himself honestly" (Arlow, p. 57).

Furthermore, the process usually takes multiple sessions every week for three years or more, which is very expensive. Therefore, analysis is not for the average person because of what it takes and how much it costs, even if it were true. It has been called "inappropriate and unrealistic for the vast majority of suffering persons" (Jones and Butman, p. 86). The time and expense alone eliminate most people.

Perhaps Freud should have pursued his original theory. Initially, Freud felt that the origin of hysteria was in sexual traumas suffered in childhood, often at the hands of parents or other caretakers and that these early traumas had lasting damaging effects on the victims. He later abandoned the "seduction theory," deciding that the childhood traumas described to him by his patients, mostly women, were fantasies rather than reality. He then developed theories of childhood sexuality, including the Oedipus complex. In his book, *The Assault on Truth: Freud's Suppression of the Seduction Theory*, Jeffrey Moussaseff Masson insists that Freud was wrong to abandon the seduction theory because the stories Freud heard were real, not the fantasies of hysterical women. He cites evidence that incest and other sexual abuse of children were more common in Freud's time than his contemporaries would acknowledge and that Freud knew this. He quotes Freud's daughter Anna as writing in 1981, "Keeping up the seduction theory would mean to abandon the Oedipus complex and with it the whole importance of fantasy life, or unconscious fantasy. In fact, I think there would have been no psychoanalysis afterward" (Joan Sweeney, "Is Psychoanalysis Flawed by Freud's Own Failing?" *The Los Angeles Times*, Feb. 14, 1984).

    Children are sexually abused, and sexual abuse does cause great psychological problems. What Freud saw was probably the result of actual sexual abuse. He should have pursued the seduction theory instead of concocting the concept of childhood sexual fancies.

    While the notion that unresolved, unconscious internal conflicts create anxiety that results in the use of defense mechanisms and explains *all* adult behavior is absurd, there are traces of truth in psychoanalysis.

1. The two drives discussed by Freud are an oversimplification, but people do have drives (Jas. 4:1).
2. The internal conflict described by Freud is not the total explanation, but people have internal conflicts (Rom. 7:15-19).
3. Neurotic anxiety is not at the bottom of all problems, but people are anxious and anxiety is a major problem for some people (Phil 4:6-7).
4. The use of defense mechanisms is not to defend the ego from anxiety over the conflict between the id and superego, but people do practice denial (Gen. 3:12), projection, and repression. The theory of suppressed emotions in the unconscious predates Freud. He gave this concept a new interpretation. While his explanation is speculation at best, people do suppress emotions, are deceived (Jas.1:22), and are unaware of forces that influence them.
5. The stages of development in Freud's system are not accurate (they are not sexual!), but people do go through discernable developmental stages, even spiritually (1 Jn. 2:12-14).
6. The influence of childhood on adult life is not as Freud theorized, but people are influenced by their childhood experiences (Ex. 20:5; 2 Kings 21:22; Prov. 22:6).
7. Transference is not what Freud proposed, but counselees often have favorable and unfavorable emotional reactions to a counselor (Acts 7).

Chapter 5

ANALYTICAL PSYCHOTHERAPY

Analytical psychotherapy originated with Carl G. Jung (1875-1961). Only a small percentage of clinicians would call themselves "Jungian," but his concepts have been "widely disseminated." Part of the reason for his influence is his considerable legacy of written material, which is often difficult to understand. His work "resists summarization." He has been influential with some because of his insistence on the importance of the "spiritual" aspect of the person and the meaning of life (Jones and Butman, pp. 119-120).

According to Stevens, "In addition to psychology, psychiatry, and medicine, he [Jung] had an encyclopedic knowledge of religion, philosophy, Gnosticism, and alchemy, knew English, French, Latin, and Greek, as well as his native German and was at home in the literature of each" (Stevens, p. vii; Bair, Jung's biographer, says that Jung was fluent in four languages, Bair, p. 244). He was awarded honorary degrees from numerous universities, including Oxford and Harvard (Hall and Nordby, p. 27).

Background

Jung was born in Kesswil, Switzerland on July 26, 1875. Since Jung's family influenced some of his interests, information about them is pertinent.

Jung's grandparents on his mother's side were Samuel and Augusta Preiswerk. Samuel was a theologian who devoted his life to the study of Hebrew, believing it was the language spoken in heaven (Stevens, p. 2). He wrote a highly respected Hebrew grammar (Bair, p. 15). He was also a Zionist, had visions, and held conversations with the dead (Stevens, p. 2). He kept a chair in his study for the ghost of his first wife, with whom he had intimate conversations. As he wrote his sermons, he had one of his four daughters sit behind him, making occasional motions to chase away the ghost, who, he insisted, was trying to scramble his thoughts (Bair, p. 16). Most members of the Preiswerk family were clergymen who shared Samuel's preoccupation with the occult (Stevens, p. 2).

Augusta (a.k.a. Gustele), Jung's grandmother, is credited with bringing the occult strain into the family. She had "fainting fits" followed by trances during which she uttered prophecies. Emilie, Jung's mother, also had nieces, nephews, and cousins who had similar visions and believed in ghosts and visits from spirits and some even talked in tongues. Hence, Emilie grew up thinking visionary experiences were "an ordinary part of everyday family life" (Bair, pp. 15-17).

Augusta was the first to speak of No. 1 and No. 2 personalities, terminology Jung later used. For Augusta, the No. 1 and No. 2 personalities were two monks she called the Good Monk and the Bad Monk. Augusta also described incidents with the monks in past lives, which her husband verified in historical accounts that she could not have read. When Jung began investigating the collective consciousness, he remembered this (Bair, pp. 15-17).

Jung's father, Paul, was a Swiss Reformed pastor (Bair, p. 7) who specialized in Aramaic and wrote his dissertation on a scholar's commentary on the Song of Solomon (Bair, p. 13). Paul Jung was complacent in public, but when he was alone, he was often "engaged in a quiet rage and seething fury" (Bair, p. 13). Young Jung heard his father's anger resonate throughout the house (Bair, p. 20). Early in his ministry, Paul lost his faith, but because he did not have any other source of income, he stayed in the ministry (Stevens, p. 3).

Jung's mother was Emilie. Her contemporaries described her as fat, ugly, authoritarian, haughty, and afflicted with depressive moods. She had a caustic wit and sharp tongue. Her husband, Jung's father, could not bear her barbs and found it easier to leave her alone. He was dazed before her towering anger (Bair, p. 18). Her excuse for not going to church was that pews were uncomfortable, "but in reality, she was too fat to sit on them." She did not ride on trains: "She could barely squeeze through the door" (Bair, p. 316).

Jung's parents were not happily married. The villagers gossiped openly about it (Bair, p. 20). They slept in separate bedrooms and Jung shared a bedroom with his father (Hall and Nordby, p. 17), apparently in the same bed (Stevens, p. 3).

When Jung was three years old, his mother had a breakdown and spent several months in a hospital (Stevens, p. 3). In his autobiography *Memories, Dreams, Reflections*, Jung wrote, "From then on, I always felt mistrust when the word 'love' was spoken. The feeling I associated with 'women' was for a long time that of innate unreliability" (Jung, *Memories, Dreams, Reflections*, p. 23).

Also, when he was "nearly four," he had a dream that he kept secret until he was 65, when he revealed it to his wife. In the dream, he saw a hole in the ground in which there was a golden throne. On the throne was a large, tree trunk-looking object that he decided years later was a phallus and still years after that, a ritual phallus. "Throughout his long life, the dream of the phallus preoccupied him" (Bair, p. 24).

Jung felt that he was made up of two separate personalities, which he referred to as "No. 1" and "No 2." No. 1 was the son of his parents, who went to school and coped with life. No. 2 was remote from society but close to nature, animals, dreams, and God. It had "no definable character at all—born, living, the dead, everything in one, a total division of life" (Jung, *Memories, Dreams, Reflections*, p. 92). Later in his life, he came to believe that there were two personalities present in everyone and he renamed them the "ego" and the "self" (Stevens, pp. 4-5). He believed that his No. 2 personality conferred on him direct access to the mind of God. His dreams contained images he considered must come from a source beyond himself (Stevens, p. 6).

Jung had a vision of the Almighty seated on a golden throne, defecating on the roof of the Basel Cathedral, which had to signify that God did not have much respect for the church. These revelations gave rise to heated discussions between him and his father. When his father became irritated and defensive, he told Jung, "You always want to think. One ought not think but believe." Jung said to himself, "No, one must experience and know" (Stevens, p. 6).

As a boy, Jung was sexually assaulted by a man he once "worshiped." He revealed that to Sigmund Freud in a letter dated October 28, 1907. Nothing is known about the man or the circumstances, but all of his descendants now agree that the most likely suspect was a Catholic priest who became his father's best friend and in whose home his father spent regular vacations away from his family. Jung wrote to Freud that, as a result of that experience, any time any man tried to become a close friend, it was "downright disgusting." Throughout the rest of his life, most of his friendships with men began positively but ended badly in bitterness, rejection, and recrimination (Bair, p. 71).

When Jung was confirmed in the church, he was appalled to discover that he had experienced nothing whatsoever (Stevens, p. 6). He said, "I now found myself cut off by the church and from my father's and everyone else's faith" (Jung, *Memories, Dreams, Reflections*, p. 65). Throughout his adolescence, he experienced the Self as God-like, which took precedence over all other relationships. "He did not feel himself to be among people, but alone with God" (Stevens, p. 6).

In school, Jung loathed gymnastics. When he developed fainting spells, he missed more than six months of school. Physicians were unable to diagnose the problem. Then, one day, he overheard his father telling a friend, "The doctors no longer know what is wrong with him. It would be dreadful if he were incurable. I have lost what little I had, and what will become of the boy if he cannot earn his living?" Later, Jung said it was from this experience that he learned what neurosis was (Hall and Nordby, p. 18).

Jung received most of his education in Basel (Kaufmann, p. 124). During the summer after his junior year in college, "several occult experiences occurred which were to influence Jung's vocational choice. Dreams, fantasies, and para-psychological phenomena always played a great role in Jung's life, especially when he had to make an important decision" (Hall and Nordby, p. 21).

The first para-psychological phenomenon happened as he was studying in his room. When he heard a loud noise, like a pistol shot, he went into the next room where his mother was sitting. He discovered that the large dinner table was "split from the rim to the center through solid wood and not along any joint or seam." Jung was baffled by the splitting of the aged walnut table because it could not have been caused by a change in temperature or humidity (Hall and Nordby, p. 21; see Bair, p. 42).

On another occasion, a large bread knife lying in a breadbasket shattered into several pieces. When Jung had the pieces examined, he was told, "This knife was perfectly sound; there is no fault in the steel. Someone must have deliberately broken it piece by piece." Years later, when Jung's wife was fatally ill, Jung "took the pieces from a safe and had them mounted as a whole knife" (Hall and Nordby, p. 21).

"Shortly after these events, Jung began attending séances and table turnings. His interest in the occult never diminished" (Hall and Nordby, p. 21). Helene Preiswerk, his cousin, conducted these séances. For two years, he collected detailed observations on these séances, which became the basis for his doctoral dissertation, "On the Psychology and Pathology of So-called Occult Phenomena." When Helene was in a trance, her "control" spirit (Ivenes) spoke in high German instead of Helena's Basel dialect. Jung concluded that Ivenes was the adult personality developing in Helena's unconscious (Stevens. p. 9).

On September 28, 1900, Jung passed his final exam to become a medical doctor (Bair, p. 43). On December 10, 1900, Jung became an assistant at the Burghölzli Mental Hospital in Zurich. It was the most famous mental hospital in Europe. The director was Eugene Bleuler, who was "world-famous for his treatment of psychoses and his development of the concept of schizophrenia." Jung remained in Zurich for the rest of his life (Hall and Nordby, p. 22).

In 1902, Jung briefly studied with Pierre Janet (1859-1947) in Paris (Stevens, p. 11). Janet was a student of Charcot. In the 1890s, he published his observations of the mental state of hysterical patients (White, p. 24).

In 1903, Jung married Emma Rauschenbach (1882-1955), the daughter of a rich industrialist. Between 1904 and 1914, they had four daughters and a son (Stevens, p. 16). Jung was wealthy because of his wife's inheritance (Bair, p. 84).

In 1905, at thirty, he became a lecturer in psychiatry at the University of Zurich and senior physician at the Psychiatric Clinic. He also conducted a private practice (Hall and Nordby, pp. 22-23).

Bleuler assigned Jung the task of studying the association test. People were given chosen words and asked to respond with the first word that spontaneously came to mind. Jung discovered that each person responded to certain words either too quickly or slowly, compared to their average response time to the rest of the words. He concluded that those particular words carried special meaning for that person. For Jung, these words led to ideas that were accompanied by an effect. He called the effect a complex. Moreover, these complexes were usually unknown to the subject. Jung then concluded that these complexes were unconscious by repression (Kaufmann, p. 125; see also Stevens, p. 11).

Jung was "familiar" with Freud and Breuer's *Studies in Hysteria* (1895) and read Freud's *The Interpretation of Dreams* (1900; see Hall and Nordby, p. 22), but he did not necessarily get the concept of unconscious from Freud. G. W. Leibnitz had postulated it a hundred years before (Kaufmann, p. 124). Jung felt he had provided "proof" of the unconscious and the process of repression, which were key concepts in Freud's theories.

In 1907, Jung sent Freud "copies of his articles and his first book, *The Psychology of Dementia Praecox* (1907), in which he upheld the Freudian viewpoint, although with some reservations, especially concerning the importance of infantile sexual traumas" (Hall and Nordby, p. 23; see also Bair, p. 209).

Freud invited Jung to visit him in Vienna (Kaufmann, p. 125). In March 1907, they met and when they did, they talked continuously for thirteen hours (Stevens, p. 12). When they met, Jung was an established scholar with an international reputation (Bair, p. 115). After that visit, they corresponded "on a weekly basis" for the next six years (Hall and Nordby, p. 23).

Soon after their first meeting, Jung wrote Freud, "Let me enjoy your friendship not as one between equals, but as that of a father and the son." Later, Freud formally anointed Jung as his "Son and heir" and his "Crown Prince." The problem was that Freud wanted a son "who would be willing to defer unconditionally to his authority and to perpetuate, without modification, the doctrines and principles of his rule" (Stevens, p. 13).

In 1909, they traveled together for seven weeks on a trip that included speaking together at Clark University in the United States (Hall and Nordby, p. 23).

In 1910, when the International Psychoanalytic Association was formed, Freud insisted that Jung become its first president. Jung was also the chief editor of the first psychoanalytic journal, the *Jahrbuch* (Stevens, p. 14).

Sometime during this period of his life, Jung developed the concept of the *collective unconscious*. Emile Schwyzer (1862-1931), later known as "the Solar Phallus Man," began having delusions in 1882. He had been hospitalized for almost two decades in other institutions before he was admitted to the Burgholzli on October 27, 1901. He suffered from severe anxiety coupled with hallucinations. He thought he was God and became agitated by his "obligation to distribute his semen since, otherwise, the world would perish." He insisted that he was "capable of producing weather." When asked how he did this, he said that the sun had a gigantic phallus and if he looked at it with eyes half shut and moved his head from side to side, he could make the phallus move, thus creating wind and, by extension, the weather (Bair, pp. 174-175).

At first, Jung wondered if the content of the delusion was connected to a myth, which Schwyzer might have encountered before or during his various hospitalizations. Jung decided that was unlikely. Schwyzer came from an uneducated, impoverished family. It was doubtful that printed material ever came their way. None of the hospitals where Schwyzer had stayed had patient libraries and, besides, Schwyzer could not have concentrated long enough to comprehend such material (Bair, p. 176).

In 1910, Jung found similar images in literature and art. For example, in one painting, the Holy Spirit, represented as a dove, flies down a tube from heaven and up the robe of the Virgin Mary to impregnate her. Jung became convinced that a "universal human characteristic" was involved and humans possessed a "disposition to produce the same or very similar ideas." Later, he called this the "archetype" of the collective unconscious (Bair, p. 177). Jung concluded that there were primordial imageries and archetypes in the unconscious of all human beings (Kaufmann, p. 125;

see Stevens, p. 40).

There is a controversy over who exactly was the originator of the concept of the collective unconscious. Johann Honegger, Jr. (1885-1911), a man who himself had mental problems and eventually committed suicide, came to Burgholzli as a medical school graduate desiring to specialize in psychiatry and looking for a dissertation topic. He became Jung's research assistant and was assigned to analyze Schwyzer. Honegger was to write down everything Schwyzer did or said, which Honegger did from December 31, 1909 to the end of February 1910. He amassed approximately 240 hand-written pages of Schwyzer's delusional ramblings, to which he added his own observations and interpretations in the margins. These pages were followed by what was probably intended to be Honegger's dissertation. This has come to be called the "Honegger Papers," a total of 350 pages. Later in his life, Jung took credit for the concept of the collective unconscious based on Schwyzer's phallus delusion, but some contend that Jung stole Honegger's research and lied about his role in the Schwyzer case. There is evidence, however, that Jung recognized something universal in Schwyzer's solar phallus vision as early as 1901 (see Bair, pp. 171-190, 641-647, including footnotes).

Eventually, Freud and Jung parted ways. Jung's book *The Psychology of Dementia Praecox* (1907), which was the application of psychoanalytic principles to schizophrenia, contained "serious misgivings about some of Freud's ideas" (Kaufmann, p. 125). Jung's book *Symbols of Transformation* (1911) marked the final break with Freud. In that book, Jung identified libido as general psychic energy rather than sexual energy. Thus, he dethroned sexuality "as the all-encompassing causative element in things psychic" (Kaufmann, p. 126; see Bair, p. 201). Stevens says that Jung found two of Freud's assumptions unacceptable, namely, that the human motivation is exclusively sexual and that the unconscious mind is entirely personal and particular to the individual (Stevens, p. 14; for Jung's view of the Oedipus complex, see Stevens, p. 15). He also says that this book was the first in which he put forth his idea of a collective conscious (Stevens, p. 38).

Jung was sure his book *Symbols of Transformation* would cost him Freud's friendship. For several months, Jung was so tormented by this thought that he could not complete the final chapter, "The Sacrifice" (Hall and Nordby, p. 24).

In June 1992, Martin S. Fiebert (California State University Long Beach) presented a paper entitled "Sex, Lies, and Letters: A Sample of the Significant Deception in the Freud/Jung Relationship" to the San Diego American Psychological Society Convention meeting. In that paper, Martin demonstrated a pattern of mutual deception throughout their entire relationship. For example, Freud deceived Jung about his affair with Minna Bernays and Jung deceived Freud about his affair with Sabina Spielrein. They also deceived each other about their homosexual feelings for each other. Fiebert writes, "It is my contention that when Jung discovered that Freud, his mentor, was having a secret and culturally forbidden affair with Minna Bernays, this stimulated and sanctioned his growing desire for his patient and student Sabina Spielrein" (Fiebert, www.csulb.edu).

In 1913, Jung resigned from his presidency of the Association, his editorship of the Jahrbuch, and his lectureship at the University of Zurich. He also withdrew from the psychoanalytic movement (Stevens, p. 15). In October 1913, Jung broke with Freud once and for all; in February 1914, Freud published a paper entitled "History of the Psychoanalytical Movement." His purpose was to establish his own and his followers' right to the term "psychological analysis." He discussed Jung's and Adler's concepts at length. He considered Adler's more significant but rejected both (Lauzun, p. 69).

After his association with Freud terminated, Jung described himself as being in a state of confusion and inner uncertainty. He said he was "completely devastated" (Bair, p. 244). A "fallow period" followed when he could do no research, reading, or writing. This period began in the autumn of 1913 and lasted until the end of 1917 (Bair, p. 242). During this period, he devoted his time to exploring his own unconscious by analyzing his dreams and visions (Hall and Nordby, p. 24; see Bair, pp. 242-244). Stevens suggests, "It was triggered as much by upheavals in his domestic life as by the loss of his friendship with Freud" (Stevens, p. 16).

In the autumn of 1913, Jung had a "horrifying vision" and disturbing dreams. They were so severe they brought him to the edge of madness. "He played in his garden like a child, heard voices his head, walked about holding conversations with imaginary figures and, during one episode, believed his house to be crowded with the spirits of the dead" (Stevens, p. 18). He wrote that he ran into "the same psychic material which is the stuff of psychosis and is found in the insane" (Jung, *Memories, Dreams, Reflections*, p. 181). He understood all of this to be material bursting forth from his unconscious, which became the basis of his theory (Stevens, p. 22). Jung wrote, "Philosophical criticism has helped me to see that every psychology—my own included—has the character of a subjective confession. Even when I am dealing with empirical data, I am necessarily speaking about myself" (Jung's *Collective Writings*, vol. IV, para. 774).

There has been much discussion of what happened to Jung during these years.

It has often been compared to what happened to Freud. It has also been compared to similar experiences of shamans, religious mystics, artists, writers, and philosophers (Stevens, pp. 22-23).

He returned to studying myth, philosophy, and religion to find parallels to what he had experienced. The result was his book *Psychological Types* (1921; Stevens, p. 24), "which many scholars considered his most important contribution to the literature of psychoanalysis" (Bair, p. 246). Jung did not insist that his was "the only true or possible type-theory" (Bair, p. 287). Freud was among the first to read it and he dismissed it as "the work of a snob and a mystic, no new ideas in it" (Bair, p. 286).

Jung traveled extensively. He went to Tunis and the Sahara Desert to observe the mentality of primitive people. He had learned Swahili before he penetrated to the heart of Africa on a safari, returning by way of Egypt. He traveled to New Mexico to learn about the Pueblo Indians' religious beliefs. He also traveled to India and Ceylon (Hall and Nordby, p. 25).

In 1927, Richard Wilhelm sent him a German translation of a Taoist alchemical treatise called *The Secret of the Golden Flower* (Stevens, p. 26). Jung studied alchemy at great length. The alchemists of the Middle Ages were known for their attempts to convert base metals into gold. Alchemy was "a very complex philosophy that expressed itself through chemical experimentation." The modern science of chemistry grew out of it. Jung was attracted to this subject because he felt that the symbolism in alchemical philosophy and experimentation revealed many, if not all, of man's inherited archetypes (Hall and Nordby, p. 113). Later, Jung published *Psychology and Alchemy* (1944).

Throughout the 1920s and well into the 1930s, Jung spent "a significant amount of time examining 'spiritism' and attending séances'" (Bair, p. 328).

Jung was indirectly responsible for the founding of Alcoholics Anonymous. In 1931, Jung saw Roland H., an American alcoholic, as a patient. Jung failed to keep Roland away from binge drinking. Finally, Jung told him, "It was unrealistic to seek a cure through psychiatry. Jung suggested that he join the Oxford Group, which conducted its meetings through strict, ritualistic procedures, hoping that such structure might lead Roland H. to undergo a conversion experience of a religious or spiritual nature that would give him the strength to stop drinking" (Bair, p. 377).

Roland H. followed Jung's advice and began to devote himself to helping other alcoholics. When he returned to the United States, he told his friend Bill W. of his conversion experience. Shortly after, Bill W. had "a similar religious event that was enhanced by the image of a group of alcoholics who would inspire each other to abandon alcohol." Hence the formation of the Society of Alcoholics Anonymous (Bair, p. 377).

In 1944, Jung broke his foot and shortly after had a heart attack. Following his recovery, he embarked on a productive period of writing. He attributed this prolific writing period to the numerous visions, dreams, and deliriums he experienced during the months of recovery (Hall and Nordby, p. 26).

Jung used self-analysis as "the starting point to formulate what he believed were enduring objective truths" (Bair, p. 5). His custom began with observations about himself, his ideas, intuitions, and dreams, to which he compared what his patients revealed during therapeutic sessions. He attempted to determine what was common and what was uniquely individual. Then, he looked for archetypal antecedents by reading widely (Bair, p. 525). He insisted that he did not propound "theories" but made "discoveries" (Bair, p. 551). Thus, he developed his theories by observing people, his vast knowledge of mythology, religion, alchemy, travels, and self-analysis, which he engaged in all his life (Hall and Nordby, p. 28). Jung said every psychological theory is "a subjective confession" (Bair, p. 514).

Before he died in 1961, Jung wrote *Memories, Dreams, Reflections*, which is his autobiography. It was published in 1963.

Jung has been criticized for being an occultist, a womanizer, and an anti-Semite. Jung did dabble in the occult. He not only attended séances as a college student, but he also did so during his years at the Burgholzli hospital and from time to time until the early 1930s, he attended séances "either as an official participant or a private observer" (Bair, p. 135). It can be argued he did so to study it. For example, concerning his dissertation, his biographer says, "his intention was to make the point that psychiatric powers emerge from the psychological state of mind and have nothing to do with the so-called supernatural" (Bair, p. 63).

Hall and Nordby write, "Jung has often been criticized for the interest he took in such scientifically suspect subjects as alchemy, astrology, divination, telepathy and clairvoyance, yoga, spiritualism, mediums and séances, fortunetelling, flying saucers, religious symbolism, visions, and dreams. In our opinion, these criticisms are not justified. Jung approached these subjects not as a disciple or a 'believer' but as a psychologist. The central question for him was what these subjects revealed about the mind, especially that level of the mind, which Jung called the collective unconscious. Jung learned very early in his career that the unconscious mind shows itself most clearly in the symptoms, verbalizations, hallucinations, and visions of patients such as those at Burghölzli. Later, he was to discover that in more normal people, the unconscious manifested itself most clearly in so-called occult phenomena, religious symbolism, mythology, astrology and dreams" (Hall and Nordby, pp. 25-26).

On the other hand, Jung had some strange experiences, including visions and dreams (see Bair, pp. 242, 244). Throughout the winter of 1924, he experienced a "ghostly presence." He heard music and envisioned a host of young peasant men who seemed to be "encircling his house with much laughter singing and roughhousing" (Bair, p. 330).

In her extensive biography of Jung, Bair said he practiced yoga for over 20 years (Bair, p. 434). In a presentation introducing her book at the C. G. Jung Institute of Los Angeles, she said that he practiced yoga all of his life (I heard her there on 1/9/2004).

Jung was an adulterer. From the beginning, he had a reputation as a ladies' man (Bair, p. 98). Early in his marriage, he probably had an affair with Sabina Spielrein (Stevens, p. 17). In 1904, after several acute attacks of hysteria, Sabina was admitted to the Burgholzli Hospital. Jung supervised her treatment for the following year. She was released and, in 1911, received a medical degree. For seven years, their lives were entwined personally and professionally (Bair, p. 86). Sabina said they had an affair (Bair, p. 181) and everyone believed they were having an affair. Jung, however, insisted that it was friendship gone awry in that he told her his secrets, although he did admit that he had "polygamous components." According to his biographer, "no definite proof has yet been found to prove one right and the other wrong" (Bair, pp. 154-155, but see Bair, p. 181).

Jung gathered around himself a number of female devotees who came to Zurich to analyze and study with him and could seldom bring themselves to leave (Stevens, pp. 17-18). The diaries of several women hint at liaisons and one woman describes in fairly graphic detail several "treatment sessions" in her home that became sexual encounters (Bair, p. 181).

Jung maintained that two kinds of women were important for a man: a wife to create his home and to bear and rear his children and a spiritual companion to share his fantasies and inspire his greatest works. In a letter to Freud, he said that there were "polygamous components" in him, asserting, "The prerequisite for a good marriage, it seems to me, is the license to be unfaithful" (*The Freud/Jung Letters*, 289, January

30, 1910).

In 1910, Antonia Wolff ("Toni"), whom he first met as a patient (Bair, p. 195), became a lifelong intimate and colleague (at the time, Jung was 35 and Wolff was 22, Bair, p. 199; for a description of Wolff, see Bair, p. 221). When Emma, Jung's wife, insisted that he give up the extra-marital affair with Toni, he insisted that Toni was far too important for him to do without her. Emma gave in "as much out of fear for his sanity as a determination to preserve her marriage" (Stevens, pp. 17-18). He treated his mistress, Toni, as a second wife (Bair, p. 266) and insisted upon a discrete triangular relationship that lasted their entire lives (Bair, p. x.). Sometime before or during Emma's (Jung's wife) pregnancy with her fifth and last child, this "unorthodox emotional triangle" began. Jung and Wolff left on vacation two weeks after Emma gave birth, leaving Emma at home (Bair, p. 248). The three often appeared together in public, but in private, the tension between the two women "intensified to such a degree that both found it difficult to keep it under control in public." They became increasingly openly sarcastic to each other (Bair, p. 327).

Besides Wolff, there were other affairs that Jung's wife accepted because "she knew if she left him, he would fall apart" (Bair, p. 321; see also p. 391 and esp. p. 777, fn. 67). There were also serious financial ramifications. Emma, Jung's wife, had inherited a large estate. Her wealth was enormous, but according to Swiss law at the time, her husband was "head of the family" and her fortune was subject to his authority. If she had divorced him, her only recourse to what had been hers would have been "a claim for compensation," which he could have agreed to or not (Bair, p. 566).

In attending a number of lectures at the C. G. Jungian Institute of Los Angeles, I heard several speakers justify Jung's infidelity with such arguments as "the ethical standards of therapist had not yet been developed" (see Bair, p. 260). According to his biographer, Jung described "his adulterous behavior" in a variety of ways. He dismissed responsibility, saying, "Back then, I was in the midst of the anima (that is, a feminine; see below) problem." At other times, he was apologetic, saying, "What could you expect from me?—the Anima bit me on the forehead and would not let go." Most often, "He was filled with anguish over being caught in a situation he felt he could not control and made no attempt to offer either rational or self-serving explanations. He merely kept on doing what he felt he had to do to explain himself to himself" (Bair, pp. 248-49). Nevertheless, it was difficult for him. His turmoil over how to treat both women equally was so overwhelming that "one day while swimming in the lake, he thought the only solution was to stop trying to stay afloat and let himself drown" (Bair, p. 266).

Jung also had a less-than-ideal relationship with his children. His biographer said he "had little interest in children per se." When he ate with the family, he ate silently, except when he conducted a monologue that no one dared interrupt (Bair, p. 250). He had an "exceedingly formal relationship" with his daughters. He never hugged or kissed them. "When they said hello or goodbye, they shook hands—if they touched at all" (Bair, p. 565).

Jung's son, Franz, tells the story of a rare occasion when Jung took his four older children sailing. He bought them candy when they docked at a village on the lake. Franz says, "When we got home, Marianne ran across the lawn to her mother and cried, 'Just look! Franz's father bought me a little cake.' Of course, the mother immediately said, 'Now, look, Marianne, you must remember that Franz's father is *your* father, too'" (Bair, p. 251). By the way, their mother only kissed the children on their birthdays and other ceremonial occasions (Bair, p. 250, also p. 565).

Jung once said, "Personal relationships don't count very much for me" (Bair, p. 541). The psychiatrist Michael Fordham said, "Jung was a narcissistic personality and had a lot of paranoia to deal with. Such people are never satisfied, you know" (Bair, p. 818, fn., 24).

It might be argued that the issue is not Jung's personal life but his theories of psychotherapy, but remember, he said, "Every psychological theory should be criticized in the first instance as a subjective confession" (Jung, *Collected Works*, X, para. 1029).

The charge that he was a Nazi sympathizer and anti-Semitic arose because 1) He wrote articles arguing that there are psychological differences between Jews and Aryans and 2) In 1933, he became president of the German Medical Society of Psychotherapy.

Jung did not dispute what he said about the differences between Jewish and Aryan psychology, but he strenuously denied that he was either a Nazi sympathizer or racist (Stevens, p. 114). He accepted the presidency of the Medical Society of Psychotherapy specifically to protect its Jewish members (Stevens, p. 115).

There is plenty of evidence to support that Jung was not a Nazi sympathizer or anti-Semitic. He gave generous assistance to his Jewish colleagues fleeing Nazi persecution and the Jews who knew him condemned the charges against him (Stevens, p.120). As a side note, he was infatuated with England and all things English. There was "something oddly English about his appearance" (Van de Post, cited by Bair, p. 304). He wore "Harris-tweed jackets, tiny-checkered woolen sports shirts, paisley ties, corduroy trousers, and comfortable cardigan sweaters as well as English brown brogan shoes" (Bair, p. 304).

The Theory

View of People Like Freud, Jung had a comprehensive view of people, including the structure of personality, the dynamics of personality, and the development of personality. Jung's view of people has been called "an exceedingly complex structure" (Hall and Nordby, p. 55).

1. Jung's concept of the personality structure begins with the *psyche*. For Jung, the *psyche* is the total personality. It is composed of several subsystems, each of which is independent and yet interdependent (Kaufmann, p. 127). People are not made up of parts; they are whole individuals (Hall and Nordby, p. 32). The sub-systems of the *psyche* are the *ego, personal unconscious*, and *collective unconscious*. He added that archetypes are in the collective unconsciousness.

The *ego* is the center of consciousness. Jung used "ego" and "consciousness" interchangeably (Stevens, p. 46). Two "attitudes" determine the orientation of the conscious mind, namely, extraversion and introversion, which brings up Jung's theory of personality types.

In 1921, Jung published *Psychological Types*. His biographer says that he wrote with Freud's primacy of sex and Adler's power in mind and expressed his differences with both of them (Bair, p. 286). In a lecture on the "Personality Types in Relationship to Self and Other" at the C. G. Jung Institute of Los Angeles (2/11/03), Michele O'Brien Daniel, a Jungian analyst, said that Jung developed his theory of personality types to understand the breakup between him and Freud. Stevens says, "Jung's motive in devising his typology was derived only in part from his wish to explain why he and Adler had quarreled with Freud; it was also, I believe, a further attempt to compensate for his sense of personal oddity and isolation just as he had to discover what he shared in common with the rest of humanity, so he had also to explain how he was different" (Stevens, p. 77).

To trace the evolution of Jung's theories, Gary V. Hartman read everything Jung wrote up to 1935 and wrote a paper entitled "A Time Line of the History and

Development of Jung's Works and Theories (1902-1935)." In this paper, Hartman explains that Jung's first formal paper on types, "A Contribution to the Study of Psychological Types," was delivered at a conference on psychoanalysis in Munich in October 1913. At that point, his typology was only a pair of opposites: extroversion and introversion. In "The Psychology of the Unconscious Processes," four years later, Jung added thinking and feeling, resulting in a paired structure of extroversion/feeling and introversion/thinking (1917). Only when Jung wrote *Psychological Types* (1921) did he arrive at the two types, four-function paradigm (Hartman, www.cgjungpage.org). Hans Schmid and Toni Wolff suggested that Jung give equal status to "intuition" and "sensation" (Bair, p. 287). Jung sums up this information on types in *Man and Symbols,* which was published two years after his death (Jung, chapter X in volume VI of the *Collected Works*; see Stevens, p. 66).

In the foreword of *Psychological Types,* Jung explains how he developed his concept of personality types. He wrote that the book was "the fruit of nearly twenty years' work in the domain of practical psychology. It grew gradually in my thoughts, taking shape from the countless impressions and experiences of a psychiatrist in the treatment of nervous illnesses, from intercourse with men and women of all social levels, from my personal dealings with friend and foe alike, and finally from a critique of my own psychological peculiarity" (Jung, *Collected Works*, vol. 6, p. xi). In the preface to the seventh edition of *Psychological Types*, he said, "My typology is a result of many years of practical experience, and such experience is, of course, not available to the academic psychologist" (Jung, cited by Stevens, p. 78).

Stevens sums up the content of *Psychological Types.* "He embarked on an extensive investigation of some of the great quarrels of history (e.g., those between St. Augustine and Pelagius, Tertullian and Origen, Luther and Zwingli) and some of the major categorical distinctions made by philosophers and poets in the past (e.g., Nietzsche's contrast between the Apollonian and Dionysian, Spitteler's between Prometheus and Epimetheus, and Goethe's between the principles of diastole and systole). In all instances, he concluded the distinctions represented a fundamental difference between extroverted and introverted attitudes" (Stevens, p. 77; see also Bair pp. 278-283 and see p. 287 for her summary of his book).

At any rate, according to Jung, two "attitudes" determine the orientation of the conscious mind. "The extroverted attitude orients consciousness toward the external, objective world; the introverted attitude orients consciousness toward the inner, subjective world" (Hall and Nordby, p. 33, 97).

Within the broad "attitudes" of extroversion and introversion are four types: 1) the thinking type (logical, objective), 2) the feeling type (subjective experience), 3) the sensation type (stimuli from the senses) and 4) the intuitive type (creative, imaginative and integrative). Jung concluded that there were eight classifications of psychological types (Jones and Butman, p. 124). According to Jung, one's type was as much determined by genetics as environmental factors (Stevens, p. 79). Michele O'Brien Daniel, a Jungian analyst lecturing at the C. G. Jung Institute of Los Angeles (2/11/03), said that Jung believed that extrovert and introvert types were innate and she added that preference toward one attitude could be seen at birth.

Jung writes, "These functional types correspond to the obvious means by which the consciousness obtains its orientation to experience. *Sensation* (i.e., sense perception) tells us that something exists; *thinking* tells us what it is; *feeling* tells you whether it is agreeable or not; and *intuition* tells you whence it comes and where it is going" (Jung, *Man and His Symbols*, p. 61).

Jung believed that thinking and feeling are rational functions and sensation and intuition are irrational functions. For Jung, feeling is not an emotion. Feeling makes value judgments about the inner or outer events to determine whether they are pleasant or unpleasant, beautiful or ugly, desirable or undesirable, good or bad, etc. This process requires evaluation in light of past experience and is, therefore, rational. When feeling is powerful enough to trigger biochemical or neurological changes in the body, it can give rise to emotions. In other words, for Jung, the feeling function is a judgmental process concerned with values. "Non-rational" would be a better term for "irrational" and *evaluating* function would be a more appropriate term for feeling (Stevens, p. 67).

Individuals do not use all four of these mental functions in equal proportions. They usually utilize one function considerably more than the others. The predominant use of one of these functions is what differentiates one person from another. For instance, a thinking type differs significantly from a feeling type (Hall and Nordby, p. 33).

The ego is highly selective, that is, it eliminates most of the experiences people have before those experiences reach consciousness. Feeling types permit more emotional experiences to enter the consciousness. Thinking types admit more thoughts into the consciousness. What is allowed to reach consciousness depends on a number of factors, including the amount of anxiety that the experiences arouse in the ego, the level of individuation reached and the intensity of the experience (Hall and Nordby, pp. 34-35).

The *personal unconscious* includes everything repressed (Kaufmann, p. 127). All experiences disregarded for various reasons, such as depressing thoughts, unresolved problems, personal conflicts, and moral issues, are stored in the personal unconscious. The content of the personal unconscious is like an elaborate filing system or memory bank. The contents of it are ordinarily readily accessible to consciousness when the need arises. On the other hand, unnoticed experiences during the day may appear in dreams that night (Hall and Nordby, pp. 35-36).

Within the personal unconscious, groups of contents might clump together to form a cluster or constellation. Jung called these cluster experiences "complexes" (Hall and Nordby, p. 36), which are defined as emotionally toned ideas and behavioral impulses (Kaufmann, p. 127). In modern parlance, a complex is a "hang-up." Lauzun says that Jung invented the word "complex" (Lauzun, p. 70).

People with a mother complex are extremely sensitive to everything their mother says and feels and her image is always foremost in their mind. They tend to imitate their mother and will try to introduce her or something associated with her in every possible conversation, whether it is pertinent or not. As a child, such a person is a "mother's boy"; as an adult, such an individual is "tied to his mother's apron strings." According to Jung, "a person does not have a complex; the complex has him." A complex may be a tyranny over someone's life or a source of inspiration and drive (Hall and Nordby, p. 37). Jung speaks of the artist's "ruthless passion for creation." "He is fated to sacrifice happiness and everything that makes life worth living for the ordinary human being" (Jung, vol. 15, pp. 101-102).

The *collective unconscious* is not dependent on personal experience. It is a reservoir of latent images, which Jung called "primordial images." People inherit these images from their ancestral past, including all human ancestors and pre-human and animal ancestors (Hall and Nordby, p. 39). This non-personal unconscious is the transpersonal, collective unconscious, "the storehouse of all the latent memories of our human and pre-human ancestry." It contains the "wisdom of the ages" and should be the guide for development (Jones and Butman, p. 121). The unconscious is not just the sum total of everything that a person has repressed; it contains "well-springs of creativity and sources of guidance and meaning" (Kaufmann, p. 119).

The contents of the collective unconscious are called *archetypes*. By "archetypes," Jung means an original model after which other things are patterned. It is a "pattern of behavior," a "mode of functioning," corresponding to the inborn way a bird builds its nest (Stevens, p. 37). In other words, an archetype is a "prototype" (Hall and Nordby,

p. 41).

Jung wrote, "There are as many archetypes as there are typical situations in life" (Jung, *Collected Works*, vol. 9, p. 48). In a lecture on the "Archetypes of the Collective Unconscious" at the C. G. Jung Institute of Los Angeles (1/21/03), a Jungian analyst, Barry Miller, said there is nothing that is not an archetype. He said that "walking" seen in a dream is an archetype.

Archetypes Jung identified include birth, rebirth, death, power, magic, the hero, the child, the trickster, God, the demon, the wise old man, the mother earth, the giant, and many natural objects such as trees, the sun, the moon, wind, rivers, fire, and animals as well as man-made objects such as rings and weapons (Hall and Nordby, pp 41-42).

Archetypes are universal. Everyone inherits the same basic images. They are "psychic structures common to all" (Jung, *Collective Works*, vol. V, para. 224). Everyone inherits a mother archetype. This mother archetype is developed into a more definite image by people's experiences with their mothers (Hall and Nordby, pp 42-43).

Archetypes can form combinations. If a hero archetype combines with a demon archetype, the result would be a "ruthless leader" (Hall and Nordby, p. 42).

Archetypes can form complexes. An archetype can function as a magnet, attracting its relevant experiences to form a complex (Hall and Nordby, p. 43).

Some archetypes are important in shaping personality and behavior. These include the animus and anima, persona, the shadow, and the self (Hall and Nordby, p. 42). These archetypes are "inborn psychic predispositions to perception, emotion, and behavior" (Kaufmann, p. 127).

The masculine and feminine archetypes are two great archetypal principles expressed in the interplay of yin and yang in Taoist philosophy. Jung rejected the *tabula rasa* theory, that is, the idea that people are born as a blank slate and, therefore, gender differences are due entirely to culture. Jung taught that gender differences began with biological or archetypical predispositions (Stevens, p. 51). The masculine archetype is driving, penetrating, aggressive, and disciplined, while the feminine is yielding, containing, nurturing, concrete, and intuitive (Jones and Butman, p. 123).

The animus and anima are archetypes of contra-gender. Every man has an anima, that is, a feminine element. All women have an animus, a masculine element in their unconscious (Stevens, p. 54). These archetypes are often underdeveloped. Men who exhibit only masculine traits have not developed their feminine traits. Women who exhibit excessive femininity have unconscious qualities of stubbornness and willfulness (Hall and Nordby, pp. 47-48). Whole individuals are those who are willing to embrace both of these dimensions (Jones and Butman, p. 123).

The persona is the archetype of adaptation (Kaufmann, p. 128). The word "persona" originally denoted a mask worn by actors, which enabled them to play a role. In Jungian thought, the persona archetype is the faēade people exhibit publicly (Hall and Nordby, p. 44), the mask that is worn in social situations (Jones and Butman, p. 123), our public self (Kaufmann, p. 128). It is "a public-relations expert employed by the ego to ensure that people will think well of us" (Stevens, p. 47). People have more than one mask. Collectively, these masks constitute a person's persona. It enables people to get along with others in an amicable manner, even those they do not like (Hall and Nordby, p. 44).

The shadow is the archetype of our "other side," "all that we would like not to be" (Kaufmann, p. 128). In a lecture on "The Shadow: The Dark Side of the Self" at the C. G. Jung Institute of Los Angeles (3/18/03), Steven Galipeau, a Jungian analyst, lecturer, and author, said that the shadow is the opposite of a person, extrovert versus introvert, feeling versus thinking. Although often seen as our "evil side," if it is controlled and expressed responsibly, it can be a source of creativity (Jones and Butman, p. 124). In fact, "inspirations are always the work of the shadow" (Hall and Nordby, p. 49). Since it is unconscious, it is experienced as a projection on others. For Jung, projection is the main mechanism of the psyche (Kaufmann, p. 128). We see the shadow in others (Galipeau).

The Self is the central archetype. In everyday usage, the "self" is the ego or persona. For Jung, the Self (capital S) transcends the ego (Stevens, p. 45). It is the organizing principle of the personality. It unites the personality, giving it a sense of oneness (Hall and Nordby, p. 51). It is the psychic predisposition to wholeness, centeredness, and meaning in life. The god within us does not affirm or deny the existence of a God outside of us (Kaufmann, p. 129). The process of achieving this goal is called "individuation," finding one's unique way (Kaufmann, p. 130). The Self "seeks fulfillment in the spiritual achievements of art, religion, and the inner life of the soul" (Stevens, p. 45).

Jung never explained how he would have combined archetypes with types and functions (Hartman, www.cgjungpage.org).

Different analogies have been employed to illustrate Jung's view of the makeup of people (the psyche, the total person). It has been compared to a "psychic ocean," consisting of the conscious and the unconscious. The conscious is an island floating on the ocean and the collective unconscious is the ocean floor (MacGregor, p. 363).

Another illustration is a hand submerged in water with just the fingertips protruding above the surface of the water. The fingertips above the water are *conscious* experiences. The submerged shafts of the fingers symbolize the *personal unconscious* and the body of the hand represents the *collective unconscious*, which all share in common (Jones and Butman, p. 121).

2. The dynamics of people concern the distribution of energy within the structure of the people. Two principles are involved. Both are derived from physics (Hall and Nordby, p. 64).

The principle of equivalence states that if the amount of energy consigned to a psychic element decreases, that amount of energy will appear in another psychic element. In other words, energy is not lost from the psyche; it is simply transferred from one position to another. The loss of interest in something always results in gaining interest in something else. When a boy loses interest in model airplanes, he becomes interested in automobiles (Hall and Nordby, pp. 64-65).

The principle of entropy states that the distribution of energy in the psyche will seek equilibrium or balance among all the structures of the psyche. The aim is to achieve a completely balanced system, which is never fully realized (Hall and Nordby, pp. 68-69).

Simply put, the psyche is a self-regulating system that perpetually strives to maintain a balance between opposing propensities and simultaneously seeks its growth and development (Stevens, p. 54). The theory of compensation is that "too little on one side results in too much on the other" (Jung, *Collective Writings*, XVI, para. 330). Stevens says, "The principle of compensation is the key concept of Jungian psychodynamics, that is, it is central to Jung's understanding of how the psyche adapts and develops in the course of the life cycle" (Stevens, p. 55).

3. "Jung's key developmental concept is *individuation*" (Hall and Nordby, p. 82). People are born with a drive to achieve individuation, that is, wholeness. In addition to drives of sex and aggression, etc., there is a drive toward individuation, which is "constantly trying to launch us on a process of fulfilling our truest self, thereby finding our own wholeness and particular meaning in life" (Kaufmann, p. 120). Human beings are born with an elaborate program for life, which is incorporated into the Self and includes the natural life cycle of humanity (Stevens, p. 55).

Analytical Psychotherapy

An individual's personality is destined to individuate like the body is destined to grow. As the body needs proper food and exercise for growth, so the personality needs proper experiences and education for individuation. Also, as the body can become sick due to an inadequate diet or lack of exercise, the personality can become deformed by deficiencies in experience or education. The process by which this is done is by making conscious that which is unconscious (Hall and Nordby, pp. 82-83).

Jung believed in "causality," that is, the cause of a present difficulty might be the past. He also believed in "teleology" or "finalism," namely, that present behavior is determined by the future. To understand present behavior, past events and future goals must be considered. Individuation, integration, and selfhood are finalistic in the sense that they are goals.

Later in his life, Jung proposed a principle he called "synchronicity," that is, events occurring together without one causing the other, for example, dreaming of an event at the exact time the event occurred. He felt mental telepathy, clairvoyance, and other types of paranormal phenomena could not be explained by chance coincidences. They suggest that another kind of order is in the universe in addition to that described by causality (Hall and Nordby, pp. 128-129). Jung was influenced by the ancient Chinese concept of reality in *I Ching* (*Book of Changes*), namely that anything that happens is related to everything else that happens at the same time (Stevens, p. 42). More specifically, the maturity process follows a natural sequence of steps, which Jung describes in his essay "The Stages of Life" (Jung, *Works*, vol. VIII, para. 749-95).

Jung recognized four basic stages of life. The childhood stage begins at birth and lasts until puberty or sexual maturity. The children live enclosed in the psychic atmosphere of their parents. Later, the ego begins to form. The youth and young adulthood stage begin during puberty. The psyche begins to take its own shape. The individual has to make his or her place in the world. Hence, the strengthening of the will is of the utmost importance. The middle age stage starts between the ages of 35 and 40. The main task is to re-center life around a new set of values. The old age stage is the period of extreme old age. This stage held little interest for Jung (Hall and Nordby, pp. 90-94). He did say, "The afternoon of life must have a significance of its own and cannot be merely a pitiful appendage of life's morning" (Jung, *Collected Works*, VIII, para. 787).

As people pass from one stage to the next, new aspects of the Self demand expression. In the first half of life, the primary concerns are biological and social.

In the second half, the concerns are cultural and spiritual. In the first half, the natural aim is to have children, protect them, and acquire money and a social position. Only when that aim has been achieved does the cultural aim become feasible (Stevens, p. 55).

Hall and Nordby explain that many of Jung's patients were "successful in their vocations and enjoyed an enviable societal position. They were often highly creative, intelligent individuals." They felt the need to consult Jung because life had lost its zest and sense of adventure and its meaning. "Things which had formerly been extremely important to them were no longer important. Their lives seemed empty and meaningless. They felt depressed." Jung discovered that the energy that had been invested in attaining a position in society had been realized. So, new values must arise, filling the vacuum (Hall and Nordby, p. 93). Hall and Nordby add that the new values must be beyond the purely materialistic. They must be spiritual and cultural. "It is time for self-realization through contemplation and meditation, rather than activity" (Hall and Nordby, p. 94).

The assessment of Hall and Nordby is accurate. Once Jung left Burgholzli, most of his patients were educated, well off, and in the second half of life. A number were psychologically sophisticated and had already received some form of psychotherapy. A fair proportion had little that was psychiatrically wrong with them (Stevens, p. 103; Bair, p. 300). Jung observed, "Most of my patients are socially well-adapted individuals, often of outstanding ability, to whom normalization means nothing" (Jung, cited by Bair, p. 300) and "About a third of my cases are not suffering from any clearly definable neurosis, but from the senselessness and aimlessness of their lives. I should not object if this were called the general neurosis of our age" (Jung, *Collected Work*, XVI, para. 83).

The transition from one stage to another is a time of a potential crisis. To assist individuals through these crisis periods, primitive societies developed rites of passage, including puberty initiation rites, rites of incorporation into the hunter, warrior, or shamanic role, marriage rites, rites on the birth of children, and the death of relationships. These are of great value because they provide public affirmation that a significant transition has occurred. The symbolism of the ritual activates archetypal components, the collective unconsciousness, and the archetypal potential are then incorporated into the personal psyche (Stevens, p. 56).

Growth consists of the individuation of the various structures and the integration of these structures into a unified whole (selfhood). Heredity, childhood experience, parents, education, religion, society, and age influence this growth process, either positively or negatively (Hall and Nordby, pp. 94-95).

Jung acknowledged that environmental factors enormously influence people's psychological development. Nevertheless, he maintained that these influences act by bringing out the "subjective aptitudes" with which all are born. For Jung, these aptitudes included gender awareness, psychological type, and archetypes (Stevens, pp. 50-51).

Theory of Pathology The analytical psychotherapy theory of pathology is "sketchy." The basic idea is that people ignore the messages they receive from their personal and collective unconscious. As a result, they develop one-sidedly. Pathology is our attempt to compensate for a lack of balance. This compensation is most often expressed in a specific complex that forms in the conscious ego and inhibits the emergence of the true self (Jones and Butman, p. 126).

In other words, an archetype can become deflated (underdeveloped) or inflated (overdeveloped), causing an imbalance (Hall and Nordby, p. 48). "If one part of the personality is neglected, this neglected part will find abnormal ways of expressing itself. The inflation of a system will create a lopsided personality" (Hall and Nordby, p. 83).

For example, when people become too preoccupied and involved with their role (their persona), their ego begins to identify solely with that role, and the other sides of their personality are shoved aside. Such persona-ridden people become alienated from their nature and live in a state of tension because of the conflict between their overdeveloped persona and the underdeveloped parts of their personality. This ego identification with the persona is called inflation (Hall and Nordby, p. 45).

An archetype in the collective unconscious becomes a center, attracting relevant experiences to it to form a complex. Additional experiences strengthen the complex until it penetrates the conscious. For example, the God archetype exists in the collective unconscious. As the person experiences the world, those experiences that are relevant to the God archetype become attached to it to form the complex. The complex becomes stronger and stronger by accumulating new material until it is strong enough to force its way into consciousness.

When the God complex becomes dominant, the behavior is governed by it. A person with a God complex perceives and judges everything in terms of good and evil, preaches hellfire and damnation for the wicked and eternal paradise for the virtuous, accuses people of living in sin, and demands repentance. Such an individual believes himself to be God's prophet or God Himself and is considered a fanatic or psychotic. This example is one complex operating in an extreme capacity. If this person's God complex had functioned as a *portion* of his personality instead of taking over his *total* personality, he might have been of great service to humanity (Hall and Nordby, p. 43). What Freud called the superego, Jung called the moral complex. This inner watchdog is not, as Freud said, "a fear of being castrated by the Father as a reprisal for entertaining incestuous desires." Instead, it is "a fear of being abandoned by the mother for being unacceptable. The dread of being rejected because of some bad aspect of the Self seems to be at the bottom of all guilt, desire for punishment, and longing for atonement and reconciliation. The moral complex forms based on an archetypical imperative to learn and maintain the values of the culture into which we are born. The moral complex imposes severe restraints on the Self" (Stevens, p. 49).

Complexes have been called "personifications of archetypes." They are how the archetypes manifest themselves (Stevens, p. 35).

Paula Smith-Marder lectured on complexes at the C. G. Jung Institute of Los Angeles (2/4/03). She said Breuer and Freud were the first to speak of the key to complexes. Freud dropped all but one, the Oedipus complex. Quoting another author, she defined a complex as a "feeling-toned cluster of images, affects, and thoughts with an archetype at its core."

The archetypes are in the subconscious, so people do not come in direct contact with them. An experience (often a traumatic childhood experience) activates an archetype, causing anxiety, which produces a complex. It is only a complex if anxiety is connected with it, or at least a lot of the emotion.

$$\text{Archetypes} \rightarrow \text{activation} \rightarrow \text{anxiety} \rightarrow \text{complex}$$

Every complex has two opposite poles. For example, an inferiority complex has a superiority complex. A victim will act like a bully (aggression). Smith-Marder mentioned the following complexes: inferiority complex, superiority complex, savior complex (spending too much energy rescuing others), martyr complex, mother complex (nurturing on one end and devouring on the other), father complex (authority, dominancy, wisdom, and guidance), wise old man complex, and the eternal boy complex.

Jung believed "illness is always an intensely individual phenomenon" (Jung, *Collected Works*, p. 98). Nevertheless, as a general rule, illness is an extreme expression of the two basic attitude types. Extreme introversion results in a withdrawal from outer reality, leading to an entirely private world of fantasy. Extreme extroversion leads away from inner integrity to an exaggerated concern with one's influence in the world. In other words, schizophrenics (psychotics) live in the unconscious, while hysterics (neurotics) live in their "persona" (Stevens, p. 98).

The origins of neurosis lie in early childhood, but neurosis is caused by failure to contend with contemporary circumstances. Early trauma may predispose the individual to neurosis, but such trauma is not the cause of the neurosis. Rather, neurosis is essentially an escape from a challenging life event that the individual feels unequipped to meet. Jung taught his students that when they were confronted with a new patient, they should ask themselves, "What task is the person trying to avoid?" (Stevens, p. 100).

Neurosis is a form of adaptation, an "inferior adaptation." It is a creative act (Stevens, p. 99). The closest he came to a definitive definition was that the suffering soul had not found its meaning (Stevens, pp. 99-100).

Nature of Health The nature of health is individuation. Individuation is a biological process "by which every living creature becomes what it was destined to become from the beginning" (Jung, *Collected Works*, XI, para. 144). What people are meant to be is in their subconscious. Healthy people, therefore, follow the urgings of their unconscious.

The ideal Self is actualized by becoming what one was meant to become, which is done by experiencing all of the archetypes in their proper balance (Jones and Butman, p. 126). The goal of complete balance and unity is rarely if ever, reached, except in a Jesus or a Buddha (Hall and Nordby, p. 82). "For healthy development, all facets of the personality must be given an equal opportunity to become individuated" (Hall and Nordby, p. 83).

Kaufmann uses the Naskapi Indians to illustrate individuation through listening to the unconscious. They believe that they carry within themselves an inner companion whom they call "the Great Man, who is immortal and toward whom an attitude of total honesty is required." They communicate with the "Great Man via dreams and inner voices. Life is viewed as a deepening communication with this inner companion" (Kaufmann, p. 120).

Jung's view is more complex than listening to one inner voice. There are several archetypes and they must be in balance.

In a rather small room at the C. G. Jung Institute, I was sitting only a few feet away from Dr. Claire Douglas, an authority on Carl Jung. She was lecturing on the roots of analytical psychology. The room was warm. So, a man sitting next to me on the front row removed his jacket. The speaker asked if the temperature needed to be adjusted. Several responded in the affirmative and someone adjusted the thermostat. With a smile, the speaker said, "Let's not go to the other extreme and get it too cool." Knowing Jung's emphasis on balance, I said softly so that the speaker but not many others could hear me, "We will strive for balance." When she heard that, she looked at me and said, "That is my message tonight" (Lecture at the C. G. Jung Institute of Los Angeles, 1/14/2003). That is Jung's ultimate—balance.

Method of Therapy Jung said, "I have no method at all, when it comes to the individual case" (Blair, p. 382). He also said, "The shoe that fits one person pinches another; there is no universal recipe for living." His biographer writes that he invented, adjusted, or changed his therapeutic technique with each new patient. Furthermore, he formulated his theory while he was writing. Hence, "many seeming discrepancies" exist in his writing (Bair, p. 300). "There is no one standard Jungian therapeutic method" (Hall and Nordby, p. 126). He perceived therapy "as a process of self-knowledge, a reconstruction of the personality, or even as education" (Kaufmann, p. 132). He used many methods, including having people dance, act, sing, play musical instruments, paint, etc.

Consequently, analytical therapy does not pose a specific method of psychotherapy, but the core concept is to help the unconscious become conscious. The therapist affirms whatever direction the unconscious provides, especially through the self-archetype (Jones and Butman, p. 127). Also, a common theme is the need for techniques to be adjusted or modified depending on the psychological type of the client.

Jung divided analysis into four stages, which are not necessarily in regular order and inevitably overlap. The four are: 1) Confession. Clients share their secrets. 2) Elucidation. Symptoms are examined and areas of failed development are located. 3) Education. Clients explore and experience new modes of existing. 4) Transformation. Working with the unconscious brings clients face-to-face with archetypal components, "which are activated, as a natural homeostatic compensation, for one's previously narrow, neurotic, or one-sided development." At this stage, the individuation quest is underway and is associated with coming to selfhood, "a state reaching beyond mere 'normality 'social adaptation' to a full affirmation and acceptance of oneself as a whole entity in one's own right" (Stevens, p. 105).

"The real therapy only begins when the patient sees that it is no longer father and mother who are standing in his way, but himself"(Jung, *Collected Works*, VII, para. 88). People need to understand that their "illness" is not their "fault," but they alone can find a cure (Stevens, p. 106).

Jung's biographer points out that despite his many inconsistencies in therapy, there was one major constant, namely, the first stage in therapy was for his clients to have no doubt about their personality type and function (Bair, p. 376).

Although Jung took the past into account, he was far more interested in what the person was in the process of becoming in the present (Stevens, p. 106). The psychiatrist sees the patient is a victim of the illness. Jung therapists see them as "candidates for individuation" (Stevens, p. 102).

Dreamwork is the core of Jungian therapy. "One of the most fruitful ways to understand a person's unconscious is through dreams." The interpretation of dreams is the "backbone" of analysis (Kaufmann, p. 132). The aim is "to help the unconscious become conscious, and for the therapist to affirm whatever direction and guidance the unconscious provides, especially through the self-archetype" (Jones and Butman, p. 127). According to his estimate, Jung analyzed and interpreted no less than 80,000 dreams during his professional lifetime (Hall and Nordby, p. 122).

Both Freud and Jung believed that dreams are the clearest expression of the unconscious mind (Hall and Nordby, p. 118), but they had different interpretations of dreams. Freud viewed dreams as the emergence of repressed material. They are distorted and need to be unraveled. For Jung, dreams are unconscious messages in symbolic form, not necessarily repressed but rather trying to reveal themselves (Kaufmann, p. 136). For Freud, dream symbols represent a repressed wish. For Jung, a dream symbol was an attempt to individuate the anima, persona, shadow, etc., to unify them into a harmoniously balanced whole. Dreams point to the future as well as the past. Dreams are a form of compensation; they try to compensate for the neglected aspects of the psyche and bring about the balance that is lacking (Hall and Nordby, p. 119).

A simple illustration of how the two could differ in interpreting a symbol in a dream is Rollo May's example of a church steeple, which the Freudian interpreted as a phallic symbol and the Jungian as spirituality (Kaufmann, p. 123). It should be pointed out that Jung did not believe symbols had a fixed meaning. The same symbol could have different meanings to different people and to the same person at different times (Hall and Nordby, p. 122).

Since archetypes are deeply buried in the collective consciousness, unknown and unknowable to the individual, they can only express themselves in symbols. Therefore, only by analyzing and interpreting symbols, dreams, fantasies, visions, and art can one obtain any knowledge of the archetypes in the collective unconsciousness. Consequently, Jung studied symbolism extensively. "Five of his eighteen volumes are devoted exclusively to symbolism in religion and alchemy and the subject is discussed frequently throughout virtually all of his writings" (Hall and Nordby, p. 111).

Because of his knowledge of the alchemy literature, Jung was able to point to parallels between the symbols in the dreams and those found in old alchemical texts. He concluded that the strivings of the medieval alchemists were projected into their chemical experiments and those of the patients in their dreams were precisely the same. The dreamers were trying to individuate themselves in their dreams to achieve unity, just as the alchemists tried to individuate (transform) matter to obtain a perfect substance. Jung concluded that the correspondence between the images in dreams and the tools and practices of alchemy was evidence of the existence of universal archetypes. Moreover, he found the same archetypes expressed in the myths of primitive races as well as in religion and art, both primitive and modern (Hall and Nordby, pp. 114-115).

For example, using dreams, myths, art, and historical references, Jung "demonstrated" that flying saucers symbolize totality. They come from another planet (the unconscious) and contain strange creatures (archetypes). This analysis (Jung's name for his analysis was "amplification") is purely psychological, that is, it does not depend on the reality of the flying saucers. In a similar fashion, others find a symbolic representation of selfhood in eastern religion or primitive Christianity (Hall and Nordby, p. 115).

On January 21, 2003, I heard a lecture at the C. G. Jung Institute of Los Angeles on "Archetypes of the Collective Unconscious" by Barry Miller, a Jungian analyst in private practice. Miller explained that there are a number of ways to tap into the collective unconscious. Mystics, artists, religious fanatics, and even psychotics have done so. Sometimes, the experience is called by another name, such as the 12-step program's concepts of a higher power. For Jungians, dreams are the best way to reach the collective unconscious.

In dreams, everything is an archetype. Miller told of dreams one of his patients had. The patient was walking on the beach, but the waves constantly knocked him down. An older man in the dream told the beach walker about a peninsula on which there was a lighthouse. According to Miller, everything in the dream was a symbol of something. The man was walking. He was not sitting. Walking is symbolic of being in a state of movement. In response to a question from the audience, Miller said that he was happy the man's feet were on the ground and that he only became concerned when the person in the dream was flying. Miller suggested that the beach represented something, the line between the known and the unknown. Later in the lecture, Miller said the water was the womb. One of the mistakes some therapists make is to make someone in the dream the therapist, such as the older man. The reason that is a mistake is that it fosters dependency. In Miller's view, the older man symbolizes what the patient will be in the future, namely, a man of wisdom. Miller thought it was significant that the man saw a lighthouse, not the sun. In contrast to the sun, a lighthouse is a man-made object.

Miller ran out of time before he could explain in detail the outcome of all the therapy, except to say that as a result of therapy, the patient became a more responsible person who was becoming himself. Miller stressed that the ego does not know what to do, but something inside the person knows what to do, meaning the collective unconscious.

Jung believed in treating human beings rather than patients and taught that every appointment was a social occasion and a clinical interview. People should be treated as essentially normal, while accepting, incidentally, that they might have a problem. His patients were struck by the fact that he was completely in the analytic situation, not aloof or out of sight. In his view, only wounded physicians heal. He greeted one patient with a grin, saying, "So you are in the soup, too" (Stevens, p. 101).

Jung thought psychoanalysts did not need to see patients intensively for a long period of time. Instead of three or four times a week, as a rule, he met with patients twice a week. He said, "I break off the treatment every ten weeks or so to throw him (the patient) back into his normal milieu" (Jung, *Collected Works*, XVI, para. 43).

In the book *Current Psychotherapies*, Yaam Kaufmann, a Jungian with a private practice, gives a case study of the analytical psychotherapy approach to therapy. Michael came to therapy because of his homosexuality. He was not feeling guilty because of it, and his family, including his wife and friends, knew about it. His problem was that he had failed to find satisfaction in the homosexual world. He wanted therapy to help him form lasting and meaningful relationships in either the homosexual or heterosexual world. The case study consists of an analysis of nine dreams.

The interpretation of the first dream was that Michael's ego is under the dominance of the mother archetype. Hence, his masculinity is chained. The point of the third dream, in which Michael saw the therapist climbing a mountain, was that the analyst represented the Self on the road to individuation. The result of the fourth dream is that Michael is getting in touch with his repressed masculinity, and now he can expect a new attitude toward his feminine side. At the end of the eighth dream, Michael recognizes that he must assume masculine qualities rather than look for them in others.

Kaufmann concludes the case study by saying that there were scores of other dreams, not all of which were understood. He adds, "Dreams point to possibilities, not actualities. Michael's concrete problems are far from solved" (Kaufmann, pp. 145-49).

Evaluation

Philosophical Assumptions Analytical psychotherapy is built on several philosophical assumptions.

1. Atheism. Jung's father was a Protestant minister in the Calvinistic tradition. He considered himself a member of the Swiss Reformed Church, but Jung never attended services. He and his wife sent their children to church, but when it came time for the children to be confirmed, none were because of their father's coldness and mother's disdain. As adults, the children drifted away from the church, and later in life, they insisted they did so because they sensed that that was what their father wanted (Bair, p. 321). Yet, Jung's son said that late in his life, his father insisted that he believed in the existence of God (Bair, p. 756, fn. 32).

Even so, a concept of a God who is absolute and beyond all human experience would be alien to Jung (Jones and Butman, p. 134). He did not believe the death and the resurrection of Christ were historical facts. The notion of a God who died and rose again to give us eternal life is the "symbolic representations of deep archetypal, and thus purely psychological realities" (Jones and Butman, p. 129). Jung said, "If Christ means anything to me, it is only as a *symbol*.... I do not find the historical Jesus edifying at all, merely interesting because controversial" (Bair, p. 526). Jung rejected the Christian notion of God as containing only "positive characteristics" (Bair, p. 527). He believed that the Christ of Christianity was an incomplete symbol of the Self because he did not have a dark side (Bair, p. 526). In his book *Answer to Job* (1952), he claimed that to insist upon the absolute goodness of Christ in the traditional Christian sense would deny him "the shadow that probably belongs to the Christian image of the Self (Bair, p. 527).

He once described himself as a "Christian-minded agnostic" for whom God was a certainty and a mystery (Bair, p. 127). Jung dealt with religion, but in his view, religion represented archetypes. Self is "our god within ourselves" (Kaufmann p. 129).

On the other hand, his grandmother was a medium and his mother had psychic experiences. His medical thesis was on the occult phenomena and he had repeated mysterious encounters with "spirits" throughout his adult life.

Jung's views about God and Jesus are figments of his imagination rather than conclusions based on the objective evidence for the existence of God and the historicity of Jesus Christ (see the next paragraph).

2. Subjectivism. Reason and rationality are viewed with suspicion (Jones and Butman, p. 135). Jung's ultimate criteria for truth have been described as "vague and undefined" and "decidedly subjectivistic" (Jones and Butman, p. 122). It is "highly subjective" and "experiential" (Jones and Butman, p. 131). The collective unconscious is completely trusted for guidance (Jones and Butman, p. 131). This is subjective epistemology in the extreme. For Jung, external validation is not needed.

3. Individualism. Jung's approach has been called "exaggerated individualism." The focus is almost exclusively on the "isolated, autonomous individual." Self-awareness is needed, but not a focus on the individual to the exclusion of dependence on God and relationships with others (Jones and Butman, p. 132).

4. Optimism. Jungianism is not the deterministic, pessimistic system of Freudianism because Jungianism combines an optimistic teleology with a deterministic view of causality. People are shaped not only by their immediate and inherited pasts but also by their aspirations for the future (Jones and Butman, p. 122).

View of People The different dimensions of Jung's view of people should be evaluated separately.

1. The Makeup of People. People have a conscious self (an ego). They think, feel, and act. There are masculine and feminine types. God created humans, male and female (Gen. 1:27), each with distinct characteristics. Jung's explanation is not

the final word on this subject, but gender differences are obviously present and need to be understood.

Although Jung's explanations of personality types lack precision, the concept is valid. This approach has been "sufficiently researched and validated to be responsibly adapted for clinical application, assuming that it is sensitively and accurately interpreted" (Jones and Butman, p. 132). The Myers-Briggs Type Indicator (MBTI) is loosely based on Jung's concepts (Jones and Butman, p. 125). Myers and Briggs added judging and perceiving (Michele O'Brien Daniel, in a lecture on the "Personality Types in Relationship to Self and Other" at the C. G. Jung Institute of Los Angeles, 2/11/03).

The concept of personality types is reasonable. It is common sense. It is hard to doubt the obvious that some people are extroverts and others are introverts. Careful observation also leads to the conclusion that there are distinctive "temperaments" or "types" of people beyond just extroverts and introverts. Theologians and psychologists recognize that human beings have a mind, emotions, and will. Upon reflection, it seems that while every person has all three capacities, the mind predominates in some, the emotions in others, and the will in others.

Ole Hallesby, a Norwegian theologian (for 40 years, he was a professor at the Independent Theological Seminary in Norway), wrote *Temperament and the Christian Faith*. He defines "temperament" as people's response to their surroundings. He asks, "Is it in the emotions, in the mind, or in the will that one is first and most strongly stirred to action? Or are two of these facilities aroused strongly at the expense of the third? Or do all three share equal reactions?" (Hallesby, p. 10). Using the same names as Hippocrates, Hallesby says that in the choleric, the will is predominant (Hallesby, p. 60); in the sanguine, the feelings are predominant (Hallesby, p. 13); in the melancholic, reflective thought, as well as feeling, are predominate, impressions are analyzed thoroughly (Hallesby, p. 37); and in the phlegmatic, no one aspect is especially active (Hallesby, p. 79).

While the Bible does not directly discuss temperaments, the people in the Bible reflect the different temperament types. Peter was noticeably an impulsive sanguine (Mt. 26:51; Mk. 14:47; Lk. 22:50; Jn. 18:10, 26). Paul was recognizably a goal-oriented choleric (Rom. 15:24, 28). Jonah was visibly an analytical melancholic (Jonah 4:1-3). Abraham was perceptibly a compliant phlegmatic (Gen. 13:11-20). For a detailed description of the four temperaments and their combinations, see John T. Cocoris's *Why We Do What We Do, New Insights Into The Temperament Model of Behavior*, available at Amazon.com.

Analytical Psychotherapy

People also have had experiences of which they are not aware (personal unconsciousness), but the concept of a collective unconscious is a "slippery concept" that is "unmeasurable," which makes it a "disturbing" item, especially since so much depends on it (Jones and Butman, p. 132). If the Freudian concept of the unconscious is debatable, the Jungian idea of the collective unconscious is definitely debatable!

The concept of archetypes within the collective unconscious is another figment of a psychoanalyst's imagination, but history and literature reveal that there are patterns of behavior that are repeated patterns in people. There are universal "roles" (Eph. 5:22-6:9).

There is a shadow side to people. Jung's concept of the shadow is not the same as the biblical view of sin, but people do have a "dark side." In biblical terms, there are none righteous (Rom. 3:10); in theological terms, humans have a sinful nature.

2. The Dynamics of People. Whether or not the psyche is a self-regulating system that perpetually strives to maintain a balance might be debatable, but there is a sense in which people should be balanced. Healthy people are characterized by balance, not necessarily the balance described by Jung, but balance none-the-less (Jn. 1:17). The concept of compensation ("too little on one side results in too much on the other") probably has some validity in some cases, but it is not as central to how people adapt as Jung makes it.

3. The Development of People. There is a drive toward individuation, but the process by which this is done is not making conscious that which is unconscious. Individuals have talents (believers also have spiritual gifts, Rom. 12:6), which should be developed.

People go through stages from birth to death (1 Jn. 2:12-14).
Present behavior is and should be determined by the future. People are shaped by their past and by their aspirations for the future (Phil. 3:12-14). The goal is growth (2 Pet. 3:18) to Christ-like spiritual maturity (Eph. 4:10-16).

Theory of Pathology Humans are rarely what they were intended to be, but that is not because they failed to pay attention to the archetypes in their unconscious or attempt to compensate for the lack of balance. The Jungian view is an extremely narrow view of pathology. To suggest that people's problems are a result of a failure to listen to the unconscious is reductionism in the extreme. Jung's system does not consider the biological and socio-cultural variables. It has been called "dangerously irresponsible" because "problems in living" are "multiply determined" (Jones and Butman, p. 137).

Nature of Health The ideal "self" is not determined by following the urging of the archetypes in the unconscious to experience all of the archetypes in their proper balance, that is, healthy people are not the people who just become what they were meant to be. Many people have realized their potential and have not been healthy individuals. The ideal is to be what *God* intended each individual to be: to be "conformed to the image of His Son" (Rom. 8:29).

More specifically, health is determined by developing every area of personhood, including talents and abilities and by becoming like Jesus Christ (Rom. 12:1-8; Eph. 4:10-16). Healthy individuals do have a balance between the anima and the animus, but not because these are embedded in the unconscious.

Method of Therapy Since people have different personality types, approaches to them should be chosen with their individual type in mind. Making the unconscious conscious through dream interpretation is not the way to help people be all they were meant to be. To think that is dreaming!

Summary: Jung taught that not paying attention to the unconscious and attempting to compensate for the lack of balance causes symptoms. Following the urging of the unconscious, learned primarily through the interpretation of dreams, leads to actualizing the ideal self.

From a biblical perspective, analytical psychotherapy is flawed because it is atheistic, subjective, and individualistic in the extreme, with no place for God or a relationship with people. Its view of people, pathology, and health are reductionistic.

In addition, Jung's work has been criticized for being "inconsistent and contradictory with so many conflicting ideas that a reader can find something within it to support whatever contention he or she wishes to put forth" (Bair, p. 300). In the *New Republic*, Walter Lippmann said that one of Jung's books was "a personal adventure in search of a philosophy far more than a contribution to psychoanalytic understanding a series of grandiose generalizations about human destiny" (Bair, p. 306). Jung's system has been described as "complex, esoteric, and obscure." Defining or testing the core concepts experimentally is extremely difficult (Ryckman, cited by Jones and Butman, p. 120). Jung was an "intellectual pack rat" who picked up ideas from many places and integrated them into his system (Hartman, www.cgjungpage.org).

Nevertheless, with all of his foibles, Jung had some keen insight into the obvious.

1. People are born with gender differences (Gen. 1:27).
2. Jung's concept of personality types (temperaments) lacks precision, but the basic concept is valid. Therapy should consider an individual's personality.
3. The notion that archetypes are in the unconscious is speculation, but there are universal "roles" (Eph. 5:22-6:9).
4. People go through stages from birth to death (1 Jn. 2:12-14).
5. People are shaped by their past and their aspirations for the future. The goal is growth (1 Pet. 2:1-3; 2 Pet. 3:18).
6. Healthy people are characterized by balance, not necessarily the balance described by Jung, but balance nonetheless [implied in the Bible by a Greek word translated "to bring one one to his senses" (Titus 2:4), "sound mind" (2 Tim 1:7), "moderation" (1 Tim. 2:9), and "self-control" (1 Tim. 2:15)].

Chapter 6

PSYCHODYNAMIC PSYCHOTHERAPIES

Psychodynamic psychotherapies are those approaches that have been influenced by Freudianism but have developed significantly beyond psychoanalysis.

Background

Freud In his book *The Ego and the Id* (1923), Freud began to acknowledge again the role of the environment and relationships in the development of the internal workings of the mind. Some say Freud intended this to be a major paradigm shift, but the classical psychoanalytic school contends that Freud was only fine-tuning his system. They continue to insist that the instinctual drive model is "the only viable focal point for understanding human nature" (Jones and Butman, p. 93).

At any rate, after Freud, psychodynamic approaches developed. These approaches moved beyond seeing individuals as deterministically and irrationally driven by instinctual drives and personalities solely molded by internal psychic structures. They continued to see humans as beings profoundly impacted by early relationships and shaped by unconscious processes and psychological conflict, but these neo-Freudians shifted away from Freud's emphasis on the id to an emphasis on the ego and relationships. They are less biological and mechanistic and more cognitive and interpersonal (Jones and Butman, p. 93). They moved from psychosexual to psychosocial.

The psychodynamic approaches are usually divided into three camps.

Ego Psychology Anna Freud, Erik Erikson, Henry Hartmann, and others developed ego psychology. It is called the "American school." The model is an adaptation of Freud's ideas with a heightened emphasis on ego and relationships. It does not deny that some conflicts reflect drives striving for gratification, but it adds that the ego is also striving for adaptability, competency, and mastery. Beyond the tension surrounding sex and aggression, there are also issues of identity, intimacy, and integrity. It also stresses the development of the personality across life's span (Jones and Butman, p. 94).

Psychotherapies, A Simple Explanation and Biblical Evaluation

Erik Erikson was born in Frankfurt, Germany, on June 15, 1902. Anna Freud psychoanalyzed him. He taught at the Harvard Medical School and practiced child psychoanalysis privately. Later, he taught at Yale and at the University of California at Berkeley. During this period, he did his famous studies of modern life among the Lakota and the Yurok (American Indians). In 1950, he wrote *Childhood and Society*, which contains summaries of his studies among the Indians and analyses of Maxim Gorkiy and Adolph Hitler, a discussion of the "American personality," and the basic outline of his version of the Freudian theory. The themes of the influence of culture on personality and the analysis of historical figures were repeated in other works, one of which, *Gandhi's Truth*, won him the Pulitzer Prize. In 1950, he moved back to Massachusetts, where he spent ten years working and teaching at a clinic. Then, he went back to Harvard until he retired in 1970. He died in 1994.

The two books that lay out his theory are *Childhood and Society* and *Identity: Youth and Crisis*. These are more like collections of essays on subjects as varied as Native American tribes, famous people like William James and Adolph Hitler, nationality, race, and gender. His most famous books are two studies in "Psychohistory," *Young Man Luther* on Martin Luther, and *Gandhi's Truth* (from the article on Erikson by C. George Boeree of the Psychology Department at Shippensburg University. www.ship.edu).

Erikson is known for his work on identity and human development. He coined the phrase "identity crisis."

Erikson had a personal identity crisis. His biological father was a Danish man who abandoned his mother before he was born. His mother, a young Jewish woman, raised him alone for three years before she married Theodor Homberger. Until early adulthood, he was Erik Homberger and his parents kept the details of his birth a secret. "So here he was a tall, blond, blue-eyed boy who was also Jewish. At temple school, the kids teased him for being Nordic; at grammar school, they teased him for being Jewish. When he became an American citizen, he officially changed his name to Erik Erikson. No one seems to know where he got the name!" (Boeree).

Erikson is credited with bringing an emphasis on social factors to psychoanalysis. His theory of development is that psychosexual and psychosocial growth take place together. According to Erikson, at each stage of life, we face a "crisis," a turning point, when we can either regress or move forward. To a large extent, life results from choices made at these various stages. Instead of being based on the *id,* as in psychoanalysis, the focus is on the *ego*, which offers ways of dealing with life's tasks (Corey, p. 102).

Erikson's epigenetic principle is that people develop through the predetermined unfolding of their personality in eight stages (Boeree). The following is a summary of the explanation given by Corey of those eight stages (Corey, pp. 102-111; see also Boeree).

1. Infancy (1st year): Trust versus mistrust. If, during the first year of life, significant others provide basic physical and emotional needs (being cared for and caressed), infants develop a sense of trust. If these needs are not met, the result is mistrust of others (Corey, p. 105).

2. Early childhood (1 to 3): Autonomy versus shame and doubt. If, from the ages of one to three, parents allow their children to explore and experiment, to make mistakes, and to test limits, they will develop autonomy. If, however, parents promote dependence, children will not develop self-control but a sense of shame and doubt about their abilities and will, thus, be hampered in their capacity to deal with the world (Corey, p. 106).

3. Preschool age (3 to 6): Initiative versus guilt. If, from ages three to six, parents allow their children the freedom to select meaningful activities, the children tend to develop a positive outlook characterized by the ability to initiate and follow through. If children are not allowed to make some of their own decisions, they tend to develop guilt over taking the initiative. Such individuals withdraw from taking an active stance and permit others to make decisions for them (Corey, p. 108).

4. School age (6 to 12): Industry versus inferiority. During the early school years, individuals need to expand their understanding of the physical and social worlds, continue to develop an appropriate sex role identity, and learn the basic skills required for school success; in short, they need to achieve a sense of industry. Failure to do this results in feelings of inadequacy and inferiority (Corey, p. 109).

5. Adolescence (12 to 18): Identity versus role confusion. During adolescence, individuals need to develop a personal identity and integrate a system of values that will give life direction. Models are especially important. Diverse pressures from parents, peers, and society often make gaining a clear sense of identity difficult. Failure to achieve a sense of identity results in role confusion. When Erikson died at 91, the papers reported that he was the one who coined the phrase "identity crisis" (Corey, p. 110).

6. Young adulthood (18-35): Intimacy versus isolation. Young adults need to develop intimacy with others, which involves sharing and giving to others. One of the key characteristics of psychologically mature people is the ability to form intimate relationships. Failure to achieve intimacy leads to alienation and isolation.

7. Middle age (35 to 60): Generativity versus stagnation. Middle-aged people need to learn how to live creatively with themselves and others. People should be creative through a career, family, leisure time activities, etc. The main quality of productive adults is the ability to love, work, and play well. If adults fail to achieve a sense of productivity, they begin to stagnate and die psychologically.

8. Later life (60 plus): Integrity versus despair. Elderly people need integrity, achieved by those who have few regrets; they have lived a productive life and have coped with failure and success. They are not obsessed with what might have been. Failure to achieve integrity leads to feelings of despair, hopelessness, guilt, resentment, and self-disgust.

Object Relations M. S. Mahler, W. R. D. Fairbairn, Otto Kernberg, and others developed object relations theory. The approach is called the "British school" (Jones and Butman, p. 94). Freud used the term "object" to "refer to that which satisfies a need or to the significant person or thing that is the object or target of one's feelings or drives. Rather than being an individual with a separate identity, others (objects) are perceived by an infant as objects for gratifying needs" (Corey, p. 112).

The main determinant of personality is the internalized images of the primary relational figures in our past ("objects" such as mother and father). These images are the primary psychic structures replacing id, ego, and superego. The interrelations of the objects create our drives, not the id. Thus, the drives are relational rather than sexual and aggressive (Jones and Butman, p. 94).

Early experiences of self shift to an expanding awareness of others. Once self/other patterns are established, they influence later relationships. People search for relationships that match the patterns established by their earlier experiences. People are either overly dependent or overly detached (Corey, p. 112).

According to Mahler, the self develops through four broad stages. The individual begins in a state of psychological fusion with the mother and progresses gradually to separation. Psychological development can be thought of as the evolution of the way in which individuals separate from and differentiate themselves from others. The following is a summary of Mahler's stages of development (Corey, pp. 112-14).

1. Normal Infantile Autism (first 3 or 4 weeks). At this stage, the infant is unable to differentiate itself from its mother. There is no whole self and there are no whole objects. According to Melanie Klein, the infant perceives parts, breasts, face, hands, and mouth rather than a unified self. The infant responds more to physiological tension than to psychological processes. Adults who have a fixation at this stage show the most extreme forms of lack of a sense of self.

2. Symbiosis (3rd to 8th months). Instead of being an interchangeable part, the mother is clearly a partner. The infant seems to expect a high degree of emotional attunement with the mother and has a pronounced dependency on the mother. Psychotic disorders are linked to the failure to pass beyond this stage.

3. Separation/individuation (beginning the 4th or 5th month). This stage, which overlaps the second stage, involves the infant moving through several sub-phases away from the symbiotic forms of relating. The child experiences separation from significant others yet still turns to them for a sense of confirmation and comfort. The child may be torn between states of independence and dependence.

Children who do not differentiate and who do not idealize others while also taking pride in themselves may suffer later from narcissism and problems of self-esteem. Narcissism is characterized by a grandiose and exaggerated sense of self-importance and an exploitive attitude toward others, which is a mask for a frail self-concept. Such individuals have a tendency toward extreme self-absorption, unrealistically exaggerate their accomplishments, seek attention and admiration from others, and are exhibitionists. Kernberg adds that they can be, at times, parasitic.

Borderline conditions are also rooted in this period. People with Borderline Personalities have moved into the separation process but have been thwarted by maternal rejection of their individuation. In other words, the mother is unable to tolerate the beginning of individuation. Borderlines are characterized by instability, irritability, self-destructive acts, impulsive anger, and extreme mood shifts. They typically experience extended periods of disillusionment, punctuated by occasional euphoria.

In their book on borderline personality, entitled *I Hate You–Don't Leave Me,* Jerold J. Kreisman and Hal Straus explain the evolution of the term "borderline." It was first used in 1938 by Adolph Stem to describe patients who did not fit the "neuroses" or the "psychoses" classifications. In 1942, Helen Deutsch described patients who overcame a sense of emptiness by altering their internal and external emotional experiences to fit their current situation. Then, in 1953, Robert Knight revitalized the term "borderline." After that, the term became more popular and Stem's concept of it became more accepted (Kreisman and Straus, pp.171-180).

Various explanations have been given to explain borderline personality. John Gunderson of Harvard defines it based on observable behavior. Otto Kernberg of Cornell proposes a description based on intrapsychic functioning and defense mechanisms.

In *I Hate You–Don't Leave Me,* Kreisman and Straus say that if a person has five of the following eight criteria, Borderline Personality Disorder is confirmed (Kreisman and Straus, pp. 27-41).

1. Unstable and intense interpersonal relationships with marked shifts in attitude
2. Impulsiveness in at least two areas that are potentially self-destructive, such as drug abuse, excessive spending, anorexia nervosa, bulimia, etc.
3. Radical mood shifts
4. Inappropriate, intense anger or lack of control of anger
5. Recurrent suicidal threats or gestures or self-mutilation
6. Persistent identity disturbance manifested in at least two of the following: self-image, sexual orientation, long-term goals or career choice, type of friends desired, and preferred values.
7. Chronic feelings of emptiness or boredom
8. Frantic efforts to avoid real or imaged abandonment

Since Kreisman and Straus published their work, the *Diagnostic and Statistical Manual III* (DSM-III) has been updated to the DSM-IV. To meet the criteria for BPD, one must have five (or more) of the following:

1. Frantic efforts to avoid real or imagined abandonment. Note: Do not include suicidal or self-mutilating behavior covered in criterion five.
2. A pattern of unstable and intense interpersonal relationships with themselves and others characterized by alternating between extremes of idealization and devaluation

3. Identity disturbance: markedly and persistently unstable
4. Impulsivity in at least two areas that are potentially self-damaging (spending, sex, substance abuse, reckless driving, binge eating)
5. Recurrent suicidal behavior, gestures, threats, or self-mutilating behavior
6. Affective instability due to a marked reactivity of mood (intense irritability or anxiety usually lasting a few hours and only rarely more than a few days)
7. Chronic feelings of emptiness
8. Inappropriate, intense anger or difficulty controlling anger (frequent displays of temper, constant anger, recurrent physical fights)
9. Transient, stress-related paranoid ideation or severe dissociative symptoms

My brother, Dr. John T. Cocoris, a retired licensed therapist, wrote *Born with a Creative Temperament* (available at Amazon.com). In it, he describes a group of people who are similar to BPDs. He differs from the traditional approach in the explanation of the cause. Whereas most mental health professionals point to a chemical imbalance or some aspect of the environment, he contends that a better explanation is rooted in the temperament concept. When Sanguine-Melancholies fail to control their natural tendencies and fail to develop coping skills, they become a problem to themselves and others.

4. Move toward Constancy of Self and Object (pronounced by the 36th month). The child can begin to relate to others without being overwhelmed with fears of losing a sense of individuality. By now, others are more fully seen as separate from the self.

Self-Psychology Heing Kohut and his followers established self-psychology. If early relationships are healthy and nurturing, a stable or "true self" will develop that is capable of mature relationships. Deprivation results in a "false self," which is limited in capacity for relationships. The individual cannot value both autonomy and community. A mature identity is open to input from others without a competing fear of being overwhelmed.

The object-relations theory focuses on psychological relations between internalized objects. Self-psychology goes a step further, positing a strong entity of self that is not a separate psychic structure but instead is the sum of all the intra-psychic entities plus an unnamed integrating function (Jones and Butman, pp. 94-95).

Thus, Ego psychology accommodates classic psychoanalysis. It modifies the id-drive model by emphasizing early formative relationships. Object-relations, however, is a more radical, alternative strategy. It completely replaces the drive concept with a strong interpersonal model. Self-psychology is model mixing. It adapts drive-model concepts and mixes them with the relational model (Jones and Butman, p. 95).

Other neo-Freudians include Karen Horney, Erich Fromm, and Harry Stack Sullivan, all of whom agreed that social factors were of great significance in shaping the personality. Heinz Ansbacher suggested that because they moved away from Freud's biological and deterministic point of view toward Adler's social-psychology and non-deterministic perspective, it would be more appropriate to refer to them as neo-Adlerians (Corey, p. 137). Karen Horney (1885-1952) was born in Germany on September 16, 1885. Her father was a ship's captain, a religious man, and an authoritarian. His children called him "the Bible-thrower" because, according to Horney, he threw Bibles! She felt deprived of her father's affection and became especially attached to her mother.

At about nine, she developed a crush on her young teenage brother, who was embarrassed by her attention and pushed her away. This led to her first bout with depression, a problem that plagued her for the rest of her life.

She entered medical school in 1906 and in 1909, married Oscar Horney. They had three daughters. She and her daughters moved out of Oscar's house in 1926 and in 1930, she moved to the U.S., eventually settling in Brooklyn, which, at the time, was the world's intellectual capital. There, she became friends with such intellectuals as Erich Fromm and Harry Stack Sullivan, even having an affair with the former. The website of Sonoma University, a California State University, contains lecture notes by an unnamed professor which say that Karen and Oscar were separated when she was 41 and that she then had affairs with Hans Liberman and Erich Fromm (1931-early 40s) as well as "many affairs with student and clients much younger than she was" (www.sonoma.edu).

Boeree says that Horney's theory of neurosis is perhaps the best theory we have. She saw neurosis as an attempt to make life bearable, a way of "interpersonal control and coping." Everyone strives to do that, but while most seem to be doing alright, neurotics seem to be sinking fast. Two things make a normal need a neurotic need. First, with neurotics, the need is unrealistic, unreasonable, and indiscriminate. All need affection, but everyone does not expect it from everyone they meet, nor do they expect their loved ones to show affection at all times in all circumstances. Secondly, with neurotics, the need is much more intense. If the need is not met, there is great anxiety. For example, affection has to be shown clearly at all times in all circumstances by all people, or there is panic. The neurotic makes that need (or some other need) too central to their existence.

According to Boeree, Horney listed the following neurotic needs.

1. The neurotic need for affection and approval, the indiscriminate need to please others and be liked by them.
2. The neurotic need for a partner, for someone who will take over one's life. This includes the idea that love will solve all of one's problems.
3. The neurotic need to restrict one's life to narrow borders, be undemanding, be satisfied with little, and be inconspicuous.
4. The neurotic need for power, control over others, and a facade of omnipotence.
5. The neurotic need to exploit others and get the better of them. This is manipulation and the belief that people are there to be used. It may also involve a fear of being used or of looking stupid.
6. The neurotic need for social recognition or prestige. All have this need, but neurotics are overwhelmingly concerned with appearances and popularity. They fear being ignored, being thought plain, "uncool," or "out of it."
7. The neurotic need for personal admiration. All need to feel important and valued, but some are more desperate and need to remind everyone of their importance. Their fear is of being thought of as nobodies, unimportant, and meaningless.
8. The neurotic need for personal achievement. Neurotics are obsessed with it. They have to be number one at everything they do. They devalue anything at which they cannot be number one.
9. The neurotic need for self-sufficiency and independence. Neurotics feel that they should not ever need anybody. They tend to refuse help and are often reluctant to commit to a relationship.
10. The neurotic need for perfection and unassailability. Neurotics are driven to be perfect and scared of being flawed. They cannot be caught making a mistake and must always be in control.

Horney said that neurotic needs can be clustered into three broad coping strategies:

1) Compliance, which includes needs one, two, and three. 2) Aggression, including needs four through eight. 3) Withdrawal, including needs nine, ten, and three. She added three here because it is crucial to the illusion of total independence and perfection that you limit the breadth of your life!

Horney used other phrases to refer to these three strategies. She referred to compliance as the moving-toward strategy and the self-effacing solution. Boeree points out that this is the same as Adler's getting or leaning approach or the phlegmatic personality. Horney called aggression moving-against and the expansive solution. Boeree suggests that it is the same as Alder's ruling or dominant type or the choleric personality. Horney described withdrawal as moving-away-from and the resigning solution. Boeree says it is somewhat like Adler's avoiding type, the melancholy personality.

The compliant person believes, "I should be sweet, self-sacrificing, and saintly." The aggressive person says, "I should be powerful, recognized, a winner." The withdrawing person believes, "I should be independent, aloof, and perfect."

The Theory

There is no one theory of psychodynamic psychotherapies as there is with other schools of psychotherapies. At the same time, each camp within this approach shares similar concepts.

View of People Psychoanalysis and psychodynamic theories, in general, claim that each individual has an internal world that is affected by the past and which, in turn, affects one's functioning in the present. The way the past impacts the individual is variously explained. For example, object relations theories say the past affects us through internalized memories and images of relationships and events. People are usually not conscious of these imprints, but they profoundly influence our daily lives (Jones and Butman, p. 97).

When we interact with a person, we are not relating to the real person but to our internal representation or idea of that person. Furthermore, our internalized representation is rarely based on the reality of who the person is. Instead, our perception is colored by past images of events and people. Thus, we relate to people through our internalized representations of past relations. In short, we transfer parts of past images of people onto others. If the past images are strong enough, and we do not sort out the distortions, we may feel and act in unrealistic ways toward others (Jones and Butman, p. 97).

We also have an internal representation of ourselves, which we formed during our earliest interactions with others. If treated with adequate nurturing, we developed a whole and integrated sense of self, which included a realistic awareness of both good and bad qualities. When the needs are not met, an integrated sense of self is not developed. The development of an integrated or mature self occurs in stages through the first few years of life. For the child to adequately complete a stage, parents must meet the needs of the child (Jones and Butman, pp. 97-98).

Theory of Pathology Freud divided psychopathology into two categories: neurosis and psychosis. Neurosis reflects unresolved conflicts from the Oedipal period. Psychosis is the inability of the ego to interact with the reality of the external world. It is basically untreatable through traditional psychoanalysis (Jones and Butman, p. 101). For the psychodynamic psychotherapies, pathology develops because the necessary nurture was not provided and, as a result, an immature personality was formed. Deprived of a nurturing relationship, the individual remained stuck in the early phase of viewing others for their usefulness in meeting needs. The child's internal sense of self also became distorted (Jones and Butman, p. 100).

$$\text{No nurture} \rightarrow \text{immaturity} \rightarrow \text{problems}$$

Initially, Borderlines were viewed as walking a fine line between neurosis and psychosis. Eventually, Borderlines were seen as a separate personality disorder. There is, however, a wide variety of explanations of Borderlines. Stone says the term has six different uses (Jones and Butman, p. 101). All claim that disruptions in early relationships leave the personality in an immature or incomplete state, incapable of forming mature adult relationships. Such an individual has remained "stuck" in pre-Oedipal development (before age four) and thus seeks ways to satisfy unmet needs. By comparison, a neurotic has a reasonably developed personality but is still unable to effectively manage anxiety (Jones and Butman, pp. 101-102).

Nature of Health Healthy people are mature people, that is, people who realize their full potential as a person in personal relationships. More specifically, mature adults see themselves and others realistically, meaning viewing themselves and others as having both good and bad qualities without having to either idealize or reject on the basis of passing moods or pressing needs.

Years ago, in a conversation, Bruce Narramore told me that all psychodynamic theories basically say the same thing. He described their concept like this.

Threat → anxiety → defense → symptoms → impoverishment of personality → conflict → guilt

He went on to explain that the threat/conflict may be either external or internal and that anxiety/guilt was anything that "feels" bad. Defense includes denial of reality (thinking it did not happen), repression (being unaware that it happened), projection, and splitting. The impoverishment of personality includes dependency, inflexibility, intolerance, rigidity, the need for certainty, etc.

In a mature adult, the internal representations (objects) of self and others have developed adequately and come close to external reality. Mature individuals see the world and others accurately and, therefore, have no need for exaggerated psychological defenses. Defenses are initially used against real hazards-pain inflicted by people or events in our childhood. Later, we project the threat of pain onto people or the world when these threats do not exist. Mature individuals trust others and, at the same time, know that at times of potential pain, the self may need to be defended (Jones and Butman, pp. 99-101).

Method of Therapy Because humans are fundamentally relational beings, healing can only come through relationships. Healthy relationships have therapeutic potential. In psychoanalysis, the relationship is not a real relationship at all. The relationship is defined by transference. Any feeling on the part of the analyst is seen as counter-transference. In the psychodynamic model, the therapy is a relationship. The therapy may likely be the first authentic or consistent intimacy the client has experienced (Jones and Butman, pp. 102-103).

In object-relations, theories and techniques are not prescribed. The spontaneity and mutual exploration of the relationship constitute the healing process. In that relationship, the vital internal representations of primary figures that form the core of personality will begin to emerge. The therapist's counter-transference, or responsive and reactive state, is the primary tool. Therapy hinges on it.

The therapist cannot lead the patient to greater maturity than the therapist has attained. Through a relationship with the therapist, a client strives to develop the ability to relate to self and others in healthy ways, unencumbered by painful relationships from the past. This is a chance to meet unmet needs since childhood (Jones andButman, pp. 103-104).

Evaluation

Philosophical Assumptions The psychodynamic approach is built on several philosophical assumptions.

1. Atheism. The subject of God is never addressed as such. The theory assumes the need is for a mature self and relationships. There is no need for God.

2. Humanism. It assumes that all will be well if a person has one really good relationship with another human. Such a person will be able to function autonomously through the direction of the ego once the bad internalized objects are straightened out (Jones and Butman, p. 113).

3. Moderate Determinism. The psychodynamic approach rejects "hard" determinism, which contends that psychological causation and human freedom are incompatible and accepts a "soft" determinism, which redefines freedom to make it compatible with psychological determinism. "In both cases, internal forces exert powerful influences on our thoughts, feelings, and behaviors." Past relationships influence us, but a "limited freedom" approach does not assume that our history "forces" us to behave in a predetermined way. Our past only provides "probabilities" of how we will act. Within boundaries, we have freedom and are, therefore, still accountable for our actions (Jones and Butman, pp. 107-108).

View of People Humans are affected by past unconscious perceptions of themselves and others, but the explanation of how early this happens (though there may be some elements of truth in it) is speculation and the limitation of the experience to the treatment of the parents is an oversimplification.

It is reasonable to assume that infants feel before they think; therefore, early impressions are made on them about themselves and others. It is speculation, however, to suggest that the mother's treatment of a small infant alone causes problems in adult life. It is more likely that the conditions of *all* of early childhood combined produced (or contributed to) the difficulties one has in adulthood.

Theory of Pathology Parents profoundly impact children (Deut. 6:7; 1 Kings 15:3; Prov. 22:6), but the psychodynamic view places a disproportionate responsibility for the adequacy of the child's personality on the shoulders of the parents. Parents have a responsibility to nurture children (Eph. 6:4) and children have a responsibility to respond (Eph. 6:1-3), but in the psychodynamic approach, "the child is not able to have much volitional control over the development or preparation of his or her personality until late adolescence at the earliest" (Jones and Butman, p. 102).

Nature of Health Healthy individuals are mature. The Scripture uses the analogy of maturity to describe spiritual health. When people trust Christ, they are "born again" (Jn. 3:3) and are said to be babes (1 Cor. 3:1; Heb. 5:13; 1 Pet. 2:1). The object of the spiritual life is to grow (2 Pet. 3:18) to maturity (Eph. 4:13-16). The problem is that some get stuck in childhood (1 Cor. 3:2-3).

Healthy, mature adults have a realistic view of themselves and others through the explanation of how these developed or did not develop is too limited to early infant experience. Healthy, mature individuals do indeed trust others, but not blindly.

Maturity consists of more than realistic relationships. It includes the development of personal virtues, loving relationships, and dependence on the Lord. Moreover, as Jones and Butman point out, "Since contemporary Psychodynamic psychology is agnostic regarding the existence of reality or truth outside of this temporal world, it cannot allow for choices or values which call for the sacrifice of the needs of self" (Jones and Butman, p. 112).

Method of Therapy A healthy relationship can be therapeutic, but the psychodynamic assumption that all will be well if the client has one really good relationship is overly optimistic. Therapists can be helpful, but in this approach, "there is little faith in the client's capacity to grapple directly and rationally with the true determinants of his or her problem" (Jones and Butman, p. 104). A good relationship with a counselor is part of the therapeutic process but by no means the only one. Other methods are also effective and, in some cases, more so than a relationship.

Summary: The psychodynamic psychotherapies say the lack of necessary nurture in early childhood resulted in the formation of an immature personality, one in which the internal sense of self and others was distorted. Through a healthy relationship with a therapist, the immature person grows to a place where he or she can see themselves and others realistically.

From a biblical perspective, the psychodynamic theory is an improvement over its processors, but it still falls short because, like its psychoanalytic roots, it is atheistic and humanistic with no need for God. It also places too much responsibility on the parents for the formation of the personality and the presence of problems in one's adult life without focusing on personal responsibility enough.

At the same time, the psychodynamic theory has correct emphases.

Psychodynamic Psychotherapies

1. Although too much responsibility is placed on parents, it is true that parents, others, and early experiences have a profound impact on adult life (Prov. 22:6).
2. Although all the details of the stages of development might not be exactly correct, the concept is accurate and helpful (1 Jn. 2:12-14).
3. Although perhaps not developed as much as needs to be done, the psychodynamic approach substantially understands our rational capacities as humans (Col. 3:10).
4. Psychological health is best described as maturity. Spiritual maturity is the biblical goal (Col. 1:28).

Chapter 7

ADLERIAN THERAPY

Adlerian therapy is named after Alfred Adler (1870-1937). Adler has been "very influential in counseling, but he has received little attention. His ideas are widely used professionally, but seldom are they attributed to him" (Jones and Butman, p. 226). It has been suggested that neo-Freudians, such as Karen Horney, Erich Fromm, and Harry Stack Sullivan, would more appropriately be called "neo-Adlerian," because "they moved away from Freud's biological and deterministic point of view and toward Adler's social-psychological and nondeterministic view of human life" (see Corey, p. 137).

The social orientation of individual psychology eventually led to an interest in group methods and Adler's introduction of family therapy (1922). In the mid-1920s, Dreikurs initiated group therapy in private practice, a natural evolution from the Adlerian axiom that people's problems are always social problems. Dreikurs is credited with the first use of group psychotherapy in private practice.

Adler is also said to have influenced the thought of ego psychologies, rational-emotive therapy, family therapy, and many other systems. It has been noted that "most observations and ideas of Alfred Adler have subtly and quietly modern psychological thinking to such a degree that the proper question is not whether one is Adlerian, but how much of an Adlerian one is" (Mosak, p. 108).

His system is one of the most adaptable for Christian counselors (Jones and Butman, p. 226).

A two-minute film of Adler, recorded on June 17, 1929, can be seen on the website of the Alfred Adler Institutes of San Francisco and Northwestern Washington (home.att.net/~adlerian/video4.htm).

Background

Alfred Adler was born near Vienna on February 7, 1870 (Mosak, p. 74). He was a sickly child. At the age of four, he almost died of pneumonia. It was about that time he decided to become a doctor. In childhood, he struggled to overcome physical difficulties, weaknesses, and feelings of inferiority. He was also a poor student. One of his teachers advised his father that he would be fit to be a shoemaker but not much else (Corey, p. 137).

Nevertheless, with determination, Adler eventually rose to the top of his class and went to the University of Vienna, where he studied medicine. Note: he shaped his life rather than being determined by his fate. After graduation in 1895, he entered private practice as an ophthalmologist, then shifted to general medicine and eventually specialized in neurology and psychiatry with a keen interest in incurable childhood diseases. In 1898, he wrote a book on the health of tailors (Mosak, p. 74; Corey, p. 136).

Adler wrote two defenses of Freud's theories, which, in 1902, gained him an invitation by Freud to join Freud's Wednesday evening discussion circle. Adler was, at least for a while, a colleague and collaborator with Freud. Adler's *Study of Organ Inferiority* won Freud's unqualified endorsement (Mosak, p. 74).

In 1908, however, when Adler introduced the aggression instinct, he met with Freud's disapproval. Their differences grew. "Adler criticized Freud's sexual stance; Freud condemned Adler's ego psychology. They disagreed on 1) the unity of neuroses, 2) penis envy (sexual) versus the masculine protest (social), 3) the defensive role of the ego in neuroses, and 4) the role of the unconscious." After a series of meetings designed to discuss these issues, but characterized by fencing and heckling, Adler resigned as the Vienna Psychoanalytic Society president in 1911 (Mosak, pp. 74-75).

Freud took the position that Adler was a heretic. He asserted that it was impossible to support Adlerian concepts and remain in good standing as a psychoanalyst. In 1912, Adler founded the Society for Individual Psychology (Corey, p. 137). Years later, Adler discarded the aggression instinct theory and, in 1923, Freud incorporated it into psychoanalysis. Adler said, "I enriched psychoanalysis by the aggressive drive. I gladly make them a present of it!" (Mosak, p. 74).

As an adult, Adler was converted from Judaism to liberal Protestantism. Politically, he was a socialist (Jones and Butman, p. 228).

After serving in World War I as a medical officer, he created numerous child guidance clinics in Vienna's public schools and began training other professionals such as teachers and physicians. The clinics he founded grew in number and popularity. He was a tireless speaker and author traveling in America and

Europe (Corey, p. 137).

The Theory

View of People Adler's view of people is less extensive than Freud's. Adler's view can be summarized under the two topics of the makeup of people and the development of people.

1. Adler's makeup of people does not dissect a person into parts like Freud's id, ego, and superego. Adler insisted on a holistic approach. A person is to be regarded as "indivisible" from the Latin word *individium*, meaning "indivisible" or "holistic." Hence, Adler's system is known as "individual psychology" (Jones and Butman, p. 229).

According to Adler, "To live is to feel inferior." All children by virtue of their size and lesser capabilities, feel inferior. Out of these feelings of inferiority, the drive to feel significant emerges (Jones and Butman, p. 229). All crave a sense of mastery and meaning, superiority, and significance. By superiority, Adler does not mean being superior to others but attaining a greater degree of one's potential perfection. People cope with feelings of helplessness by striving for competence, mastery, and perfection. The unique way we develop a style of striving for competence is what constitutes individuality (Corey, p. 139).

Hence, Adler was in opposition to Freud on many personality issues. Case in point, Adler believed consciousness, not the unconscious, is the center of personality. Humans are motivated primarily by social urges rather than sexual urges. Behavior is purposeful and goal-directed. Unlike Freud, Adler stressed choice, responsibility, meaning in life, and striving for success and purpose (Corey, p. 138).

Thus, the cornerstone of Adler's view of people is that people are decision-making, social beings with a unified purpose.

2. According to Adler, a number of factors influence the development of people. One factor is *birth order*. A child begins to cope with feelings of inferiority in the context of the family. Of supreme importance is the child's position in the family constellation. Birth order is one of the prime determinants of personality (Jones and Butman, p. 229). To be more specific, birth order is not as important as an individual's interpretation of his or her place in the family (Corey, p. 141).

Adler identified five psychological positions: only, oldest, second of only two, middle, and youngest. He and others have described the influence of birth order as follows.

- The only child (and the oldest until another comes along) receives a great deal of attention and is, hence, somewhat spoiled. The "only" child does not learn to share or cooperate with other children but learns to deal with adults well. The "only" want to have the center stage all the time.
- The oldest tends to be dependable and hard-working and strives to keep ahead.
- The second typically behaves as if he or she were in a race and is generally under full steam at all times. The second born is often the opposite of the firstborn.
- The middle child feels squeezed out, becomes convinced of the unfairness of life, and feels cheated. This child can assume a "poor me" attitude and become a problem child.
- The youngest is always the baby and tends to be the most pampered one. Youngest children tend to go their own way, developing in ways no others in the family thought about (Corey, pp. 141-142).

A second factor in the development of people is *subjective perception*. Each individual develops a subjective frame of reference, a phenomenological orientation. This "subjective reality" includes the individual's perceptions, beliefs, and conclusions. Behavior is understood from this "cognitive perspective" (Corey, p. 138). Along with birth order, personal perception is a prime determinant of personality (Jones and Butman, p. 229).

The concept that a person's subjective worldview as a basic factor in explaining behavior is incorporated in existential therapy, person-centered therapy, Gestalt therapy, cognitive-behavioral therapies, and reality therapy (Corey, p. 138).

A third factor is *purposeful behavior*. All human behavior has a purpose. Adler rejected Freud's biological and instinctual determinism and replaced those ideas with teleological (purposeful, goal-oriented) ones (Corey, p. 139).

Adler was influenced by Hans Vaihinger's view that people live by fictions, that is, views of how the world should be. For example, "If I were important, I would be accepted." Adler called the imagined central goal that guides a person's behavior "fictional finalism" (Corey, p. 139).

When people experience inferiority, they are immediately pulled by strivings for compensation and superiority. Superior does not mean being superior to others but attaining a greater degree of one's potential. We seek to change a weakness into a strength.

A fourth factor is *lifestyle*. Family interactions impart an understanding of life and the child's place in it. The developing person, what an individual becomes in adult life, is largely influenced by the first six years of life, forms a "lifestyle," a psychological map, and an individual's basic orientation to life. It is not the critical childhood experiences; it is a person's interpretation of those events. This map of self and world guides action as one strives to overcome feelings of inferiority. Through their "lifestyle," people move toward their life's goals (Corey, p. 140). Jones and Butman say, "Mosak (1984) has understood the lifestyle to be composed of four elements: the *self-concept,* or view of the self "as is;" the *self-ideal* or self as one ought to be; the *picture of the world,* one's model or "myth" about why things work as they do outside of oneself; and one's *ethical convictions.* This map determines who we each are, as it determines the choices we make" (Jones and Butman, p. 229).

It is not exactly another "factor" in developing the personality, but a critical issue in understanding people is the concept of *life tasks*. Life presents challenges in the form of life tasks. Adler originally proposed three: living in a society with others, work or occupation, and sex and marriage (Jones and Butman, pp. 229-230). Others added two more. Thus, everyone must master five life tasks: 1) self-acceptance (getting along with ourselves), 2) friendship (relating to others), 3) love and family relations (achieving intimacy), 4) work (making a contribution), 5) religion (developing our spiritual dimension, including values, meaning, life goals, and our relationship to the universe or cosmos) (see Corey, p. 141; Mosak, p. 68).

Corey adds, "Furthermore, it is essential that we define our sex roles and learn to relate to others. Because we are not self-sufficient, we need to learn to become interdependent. Work is basic to survival; therefore, it is important that we createmeaning in work and accept our part in this social enterprise. Our feelings about ourselves and our level of self-acceptance are determinants of how effectively we are able to form interpersonal relationships" (Corey, p. 141).

Theory of Pathology "Generally, symptoms begin when an individual is not prepared to meet a life task and begins to feel the shock of his anticipated failure" (website of the Alfred Adler Institutes of San Francisco and Northwestern Washington, home.att.net/~adlerian).

The heart of the abnormality is discouragement. "When people lose courage in facing life's demands and achieving significance, they may move from having inferior feelings to having an inferiority complex, a concept which originated with Adler" (Jones and Butman, p. 231).

In a discouraged state where people are unconsciously convinced of inferiority, they use face-saving maneuvers to divert their attention from their troubling feelings (Jones and Butman, p. 231). The result of discouragement is self-deception (Jones and Butman, p. 239).

Neurotic symptoms protect people from having to struggle with discouragement. For example, "How can I do well at work when I am as depressed as I am?" (Jones and Butman, p. 231).

Inferior feeling → "lifestyle" → loss of courage → inferiority complex

Nature of Health It is normal to have problems. Life consists of ongoing problems. No problem is ever solved perfectly. The healthy person is likely to have grown up in a family where the parents modeled how to choose attainable goals and effective, flexible ways of solving problems. They are likely to have a functional or productive lifestyle. When persons are functioning well, they will naturally embrace the highest value, namely, social interest, which is a concern for the welfare of others (Jones and Butman, p. 230).

So, to live well is to have the "courage to be imperfect." Healthy persons have the courage to do their best to accomplish life's tasks, take risks, and be content to do "good enough" rather than perfectly, and, thus, face life squarely without evasion or excuse. Being imperfect is part of living. Healthy people are the ones who cope with courage and grow in their concern for others (Jones and Butman, p. 230).

Social interest is one of Adler's most distinctive and significant concepts. He equated it with a sense of identification and empathy with others. He said it is "to see with the eyes of another, to hear what the ears of another, to deal with the heart of another." It also involves finding a place in society, acquiring a sense of belonging, and contributing. The degree to which people are concerned about the welfare of others and successfully share with them is the measure of mental health. As social interest develops, feelings of inferiority and alienation diminish (Corey, p. 140).

Corey puts it this way: "Because we are part of society, we cannot be understood in isolation from the social context. Humans seek a place in the family and society. There is a basic need to feel secure, accepted, and worthwhile. People must discover their unique ways of contributing and sharing activities and responsibilities. Many of the problems we experience are related to the fear of not being accepted by the group we value. If our sense of belonging is not fulfilled, anxiety is the result. Only when we have the sense of belonging are we able to act of courage in facing and dealing with our problems" (Corey, pp. 140-141).

Method of Therapy For Adler, therapy is a process of encouraging and changing one's lifestyle. The process contains four phases. These are not linear and do not progress in rigid steps (Corey, p. 146).

1. Relationship. The first phase is establishing and maintaining a "good" (that is, cooperative) relationship with the client (Jones and Butman, p. 231). It is a friendly relationship between equals (Mosak, p. 84). It is based on deep caring, involvement, and friendship. Therapeutic progress is possible only when the goals of counseling are clearly defined and when there is an alignment of goals between the therapist and the client (Corey, p-. 146).

2. Analysis. The second phase is the analysis and assessment of the lifestyle. Interview techniques are used to understand how clients see themselves, their world, and their goals (Jones and Butman, p. 231). The client's family constellation is explored to ascertain prevailing conditions when the child was forming lifestyle connections (Corey, p. 148). The client's "early recollections" are interpreted ("I remember" is a recollection. "We used to" is a report.). People selectively recollect incidents from their past that are consistent with their lifestyle (Mosak, p. 86).

The summary of early recollections, that is, the story of one's life, permits the determination of the patient's "basic mistakes," which include 1) overgeneralization: "life is dangerous," 2) impossible goals of security: "I have to please everyone," 3) misconceptions of life and life's demands: "Life is so hard. Life never gives me any breaks," 4) minimization of one's worth: "I'm stupid," 5) faulty values: "Be first even if you have to climb over others" (Mosak, p. 87; see also Corey, pp. 152-153).

Other forms of analysis are also used. Dreams are rehearsals of possible future courses of action. They are purposeful and unique to the individual. Thus, there is no fixed symbolism. One cannot understand dreams without understanding the dreamer (Mosak, pp. 88-89).

3. Insight. The third phase is interpretation, resulting in insight (Jones and Butman, p. 231). Adlerians are supportive and confrontive. They challenge clients to develop insights into mistaken goals and self-defeating behaviors. Yet they assume that no one knows the truth about another's world. Therefore, they offer suggestions in the form of questions or qualified statements (Corey, pp. 153-154). They also assume a difference between an intellectual and an emotional insight. An intellectual insight is the patient's desire to play the game of therapy rather than the game of life. Real insight is understanding translated into constructive action (Mosak, p. 89).

4. Reorientation. The fourth phase is reorientation (Jones and Butman, p. 231). This action-oriented phase involves re-education or putting insights into practice. Clients make decisions and modify their goals. They are encouraged to act "as if" they were the people they want to be. Clients must be willing to set tasks to do something specific about their problems. A number of techniques are employed (Corey, p. 154).

Harold H. Mosak, an Adlerian in private practice, writes about a case using Adler's therapy method. He tells of a 53-year-old man suffering from depression, obsessive-compulsive behavior, phobic behavior, especially agoraphobia, who was divorced from the social world, had somatic symptoms, and invalidism. The man was also on medication, which he received from a previous therapist.

According to Mosak, the patient was pampered as a child and was using "illness" to tyrannize the world and to gain exemption from life's tasks. He demanded special attention from his therapists, who decided to wean him from medication, to give him no special attention, and not be manipulated by him.

Mosak gives a brief summary of many of the counseling sessions. In one, the therapist tells the patients of the logical consequences of his actions. In another, the therapist encourages the patient. A summary of the family constellation is taken. The therapist tells the man that he is a little boy who wants to be big but doesn't think he can make it. He is a pampered tyrant. In another session, the therapist encourages the man to decide by himself. In still another, the therapist tells the man that his salvation will come from within and that he can choose to live life destructively (and self-destructively) or constructively.

As the therapy continues, the patient's discussion of symptoms is superseded by a discussion of realistic concerns. Resistance wanes. When he ended treatment, he understood his tyranny and was able to accept it. He had the opportunity to ask himself how he preferred to live his life—usefully or uselessly. After resolving the issue of his tyranny, the therapy moved on to his other "basic mistakes," one at a time. The frequency of interviews was decreased and termination was by mutual agreement (a summary taken from Mosak, pp. 101-106).

Evaluation

Philosophical Assumptions As with other psychotherapies, Adlerianism also has its philosophical assumptions.

1. Atheism. Adler was a liberal Protestant, but in the final analysis, Adlerianism is atheistic. Adler regarded the idea of God as "a concretization of the idea of perfection, greatness, and superiority." God is seen as a projection of our psyche, which is the same as Freud's view. Nevertheless, Adler saw no serious conflict between his psychology and Christianity (Jones and Butman, p. 232).

Today, Adlerians usually say that "religion is health-promoting insofar as it alleviates an individual's own self-bounded concern with his demise and encourages him to contribute to the usefulness of the ongoing social order" (Brink cited by Jones and Butman, p. 232). In other words, the therapist and pastors are after the same goal.

2. Humanism. The highest intrinsic value is social interest. For Adler, social interest is the pinnacle value because humans are the "center of the world" and, in a sense, are to be worshiped. This is not the purely humanistic psychology that boils down to self-gratification, but it is humanistic nonetheless (Jones and Butman, p. 235).

3. Relativism. Ultimately, Adlerianism is relativistic. Everyone has a guiding goal ("fictional finalism" is an imagined central goal that guides a person's behavior) and the relative merits of each one's goal is to be judged by how that goal aids his or her pursuit of social interest (Jones and Butman, p. 234).

4. Optimism. Adler rejected hard determinism in favor of limited libertarianism. With an appreciation for the formative impact of the family and a person's "lifestyle," choice and responsibility are emphasized. An individual can transform his or her life by changing how he or she thinks about it. This is a balance between determinism and the radical freedom of humanistic psychologies (Jones and Butman, p. 234).

View of People Humans should be viewed holistically (Eph. 4:17a), but to view them as a unit without conceding the possibility of atomistic analysis (Eph. 4:17b-19) is superficial. Perhaps many feel "inferior," especially before God (Ps. 8:1-4) and they have mastery and a significant drive (Gen. 2:15), but to conclude that they only have just one of these or both of these is reductionistic. People have a drive to worship, a sex drive, etc.

Humans develop in the context of their family (Prov. 22:6) based on their subjective experience. The Scripture occasionally mentions birth order but does not delineate birth order characteristics. Some generalizations about birth order characteristics seem appropriate. Mosak cautions, "If these general characteristics possess any validity, at best, they exist as statistical probabilities and not as defining traits. Considering the family constellation in terms of birth order or ordinal position creates the problem of characterizing, let us say, the fifth child in the family. Although the fifth child is often encountered in the therapy situation, he or she never receives any attention in the literature. Birth order, per se, also ignores the gender position of the child. The children in two-sibling families in which the possible configurations are boy-boy, girl-girl, boy-girl, and girl-boy do not possess similar characteristics based upon ordinal position alone" (Shulman & Mosak, 1977).

"The Adlerian prefers to study the family constellation regarding the *psychological* position. A simple example illustrates this point of view. Take two siblings separated in age by ten years. In birth order research, these would be treated as first and second child. From the Adlerian point of view, the psychological position of each would most *likely* be that of an only child with perhaps the older child functioning as an additional parent figure for the younger" (Mosak, p. 77).

Humans have a subjective perception (Prov. 14:12). They have a self-concept (Rom. 12:3), a self-ideal (Rom. 6:1-6), and a worldview (Rom. 12:2).

Whether or not *all* human behavior is purposeful, at least to a great degree, it should be (Phil. 3:13-14).

Humans have tasks as well, including relating to themselves (Eph. 4:17-32), others (Eph. 5:1-21), family (Eph. 5:22-6:4), work (Eph. 6:5-9), and God (Eph. 2:1-22; 3:14-21).

Humans are ultimately to be understood in a social context. Psychological theories tend to be individualistic or collectivistic (for example, family therapy). In the former, the community disappears; in the latter, the individual disappears. Adler has a balance of the individual rooted in relationships (Jones and Butman, p. 237).

Theory of Pathology Humans get discouraged (Heb. 10:25, where the Greek word translated "exhort" also means "encourage"), but to say that discouragement is the source of pathology is "too bland and benign a concept by itself" (Jones and

Butman, p. 239). To say that discouragement rather than sickness is the problem does restore a modicum of responsibility to a person, but this view assumes that a person possesses all the resources they really need; they are discouraged and, hence, are not utilizing their resources. It suggests that people do not really become enslaved to real problems (Jones and Butman, p. 239).

Humans do have a propensity for self-deception (Jer. 17:9; Jas. 1:22-24; 1 Jn. 1:8), but it is not an attempt to preserve self-esteem. We do not deceive ourselves because we fear inferiority and shy away from a forthright confrontation of our limitations. In some cases, that may be the explanation, but self-deception usually has more sinister motives. People deceive themselves, justify themselves, and rationalize themselves. "Persons in the Adlerian view are merely discouraged persons needing encouragement; in the Christian view, we are this but are pre-eminently fallen beings deserving judgment" (Jones and Butman, p. 239).

Nature of Health Healthy individuals have the courage to accomplish life's tasks, take risks, strive for perfection, and yet accept imperfection, but courage alone is not the key to normalcy. Other virtues are involved (Gal. 5:22-23; 2 Pet. 1:5-7). Healthy individuals are concerned for the welfare of others (Eph. 4:15).

Method of Therapy A counselor should be a deeply caring, involved individual with clearly defined goals that the counselor understands and to which the counselee is committed (1 Thess. 5:14-15).

An analysis and assessment of the family constellation and the child's lifestyle connections render insight (Prob. 22:6).

Counselors should use cognitive/verbal intervention and insist on action. If cognitive change does not produce practical results in terms of behavioral change, that is, if it is not spontaneous, it should be deliberately programmed (Gal. 6:1-4)

Summary: Adler believed that in the context of the family, having formed a "lifestyle" (non-conscious, cognitive concepts about self and the world) based on subjective experience, people get discouraged. When they lose the courage to face life's demands and achieve significance directly, they move from having feelings of inferiority to having an inferiority complex. Through a relationship with a therapist who analyzes and assesses "lifestyle," interpretation results in insight and reorientation.

From a biblical perspective, Adlerianism moves in the right direction, but it still lacks a comprehensive view because it sees no necessity for God and is humanistic and relativistic. It is not, however, anti-God. It says religion is health-promoting in that it encourages social interest. Its view of people is superficial. Its explanation of pathology, health. and its estimate of motivation are reductionistic. The term "lifestyle" needs to be changed because today it means something different than it did for Adler.

Nevertheless, as Jones and Butman state, "We are most powerfully struck by the compatibility of Adlerian thought with Christianity when we examined its model of psychotherapy" (Jones and Butman, p. 241). One reason for their conclusion is that Mosak describes "the Christian virtues of faith, hope, and love" as necessary ingredients of a good therapy relationship (see Mosak's explanation, pp. 83-84 and Jones and Butman, p. 214). It has been said that a psychiatrist took Adler to task after a lecture with the criticism, "You are only talking common sense." Adler replied, "I wish more psychiatrists did." Adler had a number of common-sense concepts that help understand people.

1. People are decision-makers and social beings with a purpose (Gen. 3:6; 1:26; 2:15).
2. They are all unique individuals who are responsible, rational, socially interconnected, and capable of change (Gen. 2:16, 19-20, 21-24).
3. Birth order, as understood as an individual's interpretation of his or her role (position) in the family, is compatible with the Bible but not taught in the Bible.
4. Humans have a self-concept and worldview (Rom. 12:2-3).
5. Humans do have life tasks (demands), including relating to themselves (Eph. 4:17-32), others (Eph. 5:1-21), family (Eph. 5:22-6:4), work (Eph. 6:5-9) and God (Eph. 2:1-22; 3:14-21).
6. Individuals are an integral part of a social system (the Bible repeatedly speaks of people being members of a family, a nation, and believers being members of the church).
7. Health includes social interest (Mt. 22:39).

Chapter 8

BEHAVIOR THERAPY

Behavior therapy is popular in academic clinical psychology because researchers have successfully generated empirical studies (Jones and Butman, pp. 145-146).

Behavior therapy today consists of a wide variety of procedures with different theoretical rationales. Some branches rely heavily on cognitive theories.

Background

The roots of Behaviorism go back to the early 1900s. Around the turn of the century in Russia, Ivan Pavlov established the foundations of classical conditioning (Wilson, p. 246). He "taught" a dog to drool at the sound of a bell (a conditioned response involving substituting one stimulus for another). In the United States, E. L. Thorndike demonstrated the influence of consequences (rewards and punishments) on behavior (Wilson, p. 246). In the 1920s, John B. Watson first clarified philosophical behaviorism. He directly challenged the idea that the mind or consciousness was the proper subject matter of psychology because it could not be examined empirically (Jones and Butman, p. 147). He claimed that all behavior could be understood as a result of learning (Wilson, p. 246).

The formal beginnings of behavior therapy began in the 1950s as a radical departure from the then-dominant psychoanalytic practice. In America, B. F. Skinner published Science and Human Behavior (1953). Criticizing psychodynamic concepts, he reformulated psychotherapy in behavioral terms (operant conditioning). In 1958, in South Africa, Joseph Wolpe presented the results of his application of learning principles to adult neurotic disorders. He pioneered the technique called "systematic desensitization." In 1959, Hans J. Eysenck of the Institute of Psychiatry of London University published a paper defining behavior therapy as the application of modern learning theory to treating behavioral and emotional disorders. In his view, behavior therapy is an applied science with features that canbe testable and falsifiable (Wilson, p. 247).

The Theory

View of People There is nothing special about humans. Needs, drives, motives, and conflicts are disregarded. Their concepts are "vague pseudo-explanations of behavior" (Wilson, p. 250). Some behaviorists have even said, "personality' is not a real thing" (Jones and Butman, p. 148). The focus is on principles of behavior that apply to all behaving organisms, both animals and humans (Jones and Butman, p. 148).

A person is a bundle of behavior patterns, reflexes, perceptions, and impressions. The "self" is nothing more than a cluster of a person's empirical characteristics. Persons are understood by looking at the "atoms" of their behavior patterns and how these atoms are arranged and related. These atoms are not "held together by or emanating by a comprehensive core, which might be called a 'self'" (Jones and Butman, p. 148). Behaviorists assert that classical conditioning and operant learning processes explain all behavior. These topics may sound simple, but they, in fact, are immensely complex. Summaries, such as the one given here, tend to be an oversimplification and, thus, can be misleading (Jones and Butman, p. 149).

Classical conditioning is the process by which a stimulus brings out an involuntary response that it did not previously elicit. All humans respond to stimuli, such as salivating at the smell of food. These responses are unconditional and unlearned; they are reflexive.

Pavlov demonstrated that these reactions can be associated with new stimuli that had previously not elicited these responses. Pavlov's dog learned to salivate at the sound of a bell because the bell was repeatedly associated with food. The food without the bell was an unconditioned stimulus, eliciting an unconditional response. After conditioning with the bell, it became a conditioned stimulus, which could elicit a conditioned response of salivation even when no food was present (Jones and Butman, pp. 151-152).

Operant learning is the process by which behavior is modified over time by the consequences that follow. Skinner showed that the behavior of a rat in a box could be modified by the consequences arranged to follow the behavior. Responses (lever pressing) followed by food or drink or the removal of an unpleasant voice or shock are likely to increase the frequency of the behavior (reinforcement). Negative responses, like the removal of food or drink or a spray of ice water or shock, are likely to decrease the frequency of the behavior (punishment). Changes in behavior are based on reinforcement patterns (Jones and Butman, p. 149).

Operant learning can lead to new and very complex behavior. For example, "shaping" can teach a new behavior. Shaping involves reinforcing closer and closer approximations of a goal response. A chicken can be taught to peck a key on a piano by reinforcing the behavior of being closer and closer to the piano, then reinforcing the behavior of touching the piano nearer and nearer to the keyboard until a peck on the keys can be reinforced. "Chaining" can create new complex patterns of behavior. Chaining consists of more and more "links" (specific behaviors) occurring together until an entire "chain" of behavior occurs before the final reinforcement. The chicken now raises a curtain, moves a stool and then plays the piano (Jones and Butman, p. 149).

As has been pointed out, behaviorists of both the classical conditioning and operant learning schools exclude any reference to mediational concepts such as thinking, attitudes, and values. Since the 1970s, however, the behavioral movement has conceded a legitimate place to thinking. Behavior therapy is "no longer grounded exclusively in learning theory, nor is it a narrowly defined set of techniques" (Corey, p. 292).

Motivation is very simple and very complex. It is simple because it sees only one motivation behind behavior: the drive for survival. It is complex because almost anything can become a reinforcer through its association with a limited number of primary reinforcers. Because of prior conditioning, what may motivate one may not be for another. Thus, no one core motivation explains human behavior. Instead, human motivation is individual. Each person's motivation may be different from those of his or her neighbors (Jones and Butman, pp. 159-160).

Theory of Pathology Human problems occur 1) when people learn inappropriate responses, 2) when people fail to learn appropriate responses because of previous learning environments, and 3) when people respond to the wrong environmental factors. The cause may be a combination of all three (Jones and Butman, pp. 149-150). Pathology develops because of the response to the environment. The learned conditioned response interferes with the capacity to deal adaptively with the challenges of life. Moreover, the problem is a particular behavior, like an anxiety disorder, depression, cigarette smoking, overeating, etc.

For Wolpe, a central feature of most adult pathology is anxiety. He understood anxiety in terms of its physical, observable manifestations, and, thus, the response most antithetical to anxiety was muscular relaxation (Jones and Butman, p. 152).

Environment → conditioned response → problem (anxiety; depression; etc.)

Freud tells the story of Little Hans, a boy who developed a phobia for horses. Little Hans was terrified when he saw an accident in which a fast-moving horse drawing a loaded cart was knocked down and apparently killed. According to Freud, the horse pulling the loaded cart was a symbol of pregnancy. What Little Hans saw (the external stimuli) had little effect on the phobia; the fear of horses per se was less significant than the underlying conflict. The cause of the phobia was attributed to castration anxiety and Oedipal conflict. As Freud put it, "The anxiety originally had no reference to horses but was transposed onto them secondarily."

Wolpe and Rachman concluded that seeing the horse killed created a classically conditioned phobic reaction. They pointed out that Little Hans had a discriminating fear. He only feared a single horse pulling a loaded cart, not two horses, a larger rather than a small horse, a rapidly moving horse-drawn cart more than slowly moving ones, and so on. Since Little Hans believed that he saw a single, large, rapidly moving horse killed and that he was only fearful when he saw that kind of situation, a simple conditioning response was a plausible explanation for Little Hans' fear (Wilson, p. 252).

Nature of Health In a sense, in Behaviorism, health is simply the modification of a particular behavior, such as an anxiety disorder, depression, cigarette smoking, or overeating. Indirectly, Behaviorism suggests that optimal human well-being is the development of competencies (Jones and Butman, p. 164).

Method of Therapy Based on the theory that behavior is caused by its environment, behavior therapy begins with assessing the "controlling" conditions influencing the problematic behavior. It is not the person that is assessed; it is the behaviors. This is called conducting a "functional analysis" of the problem behavior.

The therapist then proceeds to foster a collaborative relationship with the client by showing as much of the conceptualization with the client as is feasible, modifying the conceptualization as needed, and enlisting the client as a collaborator in the therapy process. If informed consent is not possible (psychotics, antisocial adolescents, etc.), permission is obtained from the legal custodian. Modification procedures are implemented. Continuing assessment is done throughout and after the intervention period to verify that change is occurring as expected (Jones and Butman, pp. 153-154).

Perhaps this is an oversimplification, but Behaviorism could be summed up like this. There are different types of responses: 1) involuntary (a dog salivates at food), 2)Perhaps this is an oversimplification, but Behaviorism could be summed up like this. There are different types of responses: 1) involuntary (a dog salivates at food), 2) conditioned (a dog salivates at a bell), and 3) learned (a chicken plays the piano). In response to stimuli, people develop problems. So, the solution is to retrain the response with different stimuli.

G. Terence Wilson, a professor of psychology at Rutgers University, presents the following as an example of behavior therapy. Mr. B was from a successful, middle-class family. He was 35 and married with two sons aged eight and five. He was a persistent exhibitionist whose pattern over the past 20 years had been to expose his genitals to unsuspecting adult women as often as five or six times a week.

Mr. B had had fifteen years of intermittent psychoanalytic treatment, several hospitalizations at psychiatric institutions, and a six-year prison sentence. He was under a grand jury indictment for exposing himself to an adult woman in the presence of a group of young children. Given his repeated behavior, he would likely receive a life sentence.

He was hospitalized and treated daily for six weeks, a total of about 50 hours of direct contact with a therapist. After developing a trusting personal relationship with Mr. B, the therapist conducted a series of interviews to ascertain the specific environmental circumstances and psychological factors maintaining Mr. B's deviant behavior. The wife was also interviewed. Mr. B's exhibitionist behavior was not directly caused by an unhappy marriage or lack of sexual satisfaction from his wife.

Based on this behavioral assessment, a detailed picture of the sequence of internal/external stimuli and responses that preceded his acts of exposure was developed. Mr. B hoped that his victim would express some form of approval, either by smiling or by making some sexual comment.

The therapist explained that success could only be achieved with his active cooperation. Mr. B. was told that he would learn new behavioral self-control strategies. Treatment would be multifaceted, meaning that several different techniques would be employed. It was explained that the time to break this behavioral chain, to implement the self-control strategies he would acquire as a result of treatment, was at the beginning when the urge was weakest. To do this, he would have to learn to be aware of his thoughts, feelings, and behavior and to recognize the early danger signals.

Mr. B. was trained to reduce tension through relaxation. "Instead of exposing himself, he learned to relax, an activity incompatible with exposing behavior." Assertion training was used to help Mr. B cope constructively with feelings of anger and express them appropriately rather than seek relief through deviant behavior. Aversion conditioning was used. During repeated presentations of a videotape of his exposure scene, on an unpredictable schedule, a loud police siren was blared over his earphones.

The therapist strongly recommended that the court give Mr. B a suspended sentence, which it did. A five-year follow-up showed that Mr. B had refrained from any exhibitionism, experienced very few such desires, and felt confident in his newly found ability to control any urges that might arise (a summary of Wilson, pp. 273-76).

Although presented as a case of behavior therapy, there are numerous references to issues beyond behavior, such as thoughts, feelings, and causes. A purer example of behavior therapy is the desensitization approach to agoraphobia, the fear of being in public places. The fearful person is taken more and more into public by small degrees.

Jones and Butman list several successful applications of behavior modification. Conceding that the cause of autism is obscure, the application of operant procedures has provided the most effective treatment for it. In one application, autistic children were given intensive training for hours every day. Nearly half of the autistic children in the program were indistinguishable from normal children by late elementary school age, and most of the others were improved (Jones and Butman, p. 150).

In the classroom, positive reinforcement has been shown to be effective in increasing positive social behavior and academic performance and has even been used to teach children greater self-control (Jones and Butman, pp. 150-151).

Behavior modification has also been effective in assertiveness training. With the assumption that individuals with interpersonal difficulties lack relationship skills, the treatment simply teaches them social skills (Jones and Butman, p. 151).

"It can be argued that behavior therapy is the treatment of choice for phobias" (Wilson, p. 265). Wolpe pioneered the technique called "systematic desensitization." He viewed the phenomenon of anxiety largely in terms of its physical, observable manifestations and, thus, reasoned that the response most antithetical to anxiety was muscular relaxation. So, he first taught anxious people to relax and while maintaining that relaxed state, he had them slowly and gradually imagine closer and closer approaches to the anxiety-provoking stimulus. After that, he guided them to closer real-life approaches to the feared stimulus (Jones and Butman, pp. 152-153).

Evaluation

Philosophical Assumptions Like all psychotherapies, Behaviorism has philosophical assumptions. They are as follows.

1. Atheism. Behaviorism is based on logical positivism and inductive empiricism. Logical positivism claims that all meaningful assertions must be either analytic (something is true by definition, like 2 + 2 = 4) or empirically verifiable or falsifiable. According to this view, statements like "God exists" are not merely false; they are meaningless because they are neither analytic nor verifiable by empirical means. Empirical sense data is the highest court of meaning and determines truth (Jones and Butman, pp. 146-147). Skinner explains all religion away by saying it was just reinforcement (Collins, p. 97).

2. Naturalism. Naturalism assumes that the universe is composed exclusively of matter and energy. If the material universe is all there is, humans are only material beings and are entirely explicable via natural laws. Because mental phenomena are not accessible to empirical study, behaviorism eschews all "mentalism." John B. Watson, the first to give clear articulation to philosophical behaviorism, directly challenged the notion that the mind or consciousness (the psyche) was the proper subject matter of psychology because it could not be empirically examined (Jones and Butman, p. 147). If a study is limited to external behavior, it will automatically result in external explanations.

3. Determinism. All behaviors are the inevitable results of relevant conditions. Skinner said, "A person is not an originating agent; he is a locus, a point at which many genetic and environmental conditions come together in a joint effort." Wolpe says, "We always do what we must do." Ultimately, human choice is an illusion. Our actions are the inevitable results of causal forces (Jones and Butman, p. 148). In short, events outside the person, operating through the laws of learning, totally determine behavior. "Christian belief requires a rejection of determination" (Jones and Butman, p. 156).

Speaking about the development of an addiction, Marlatt said, "The fact is that an individual who acquires a maladaptive habit pattern based on past conditioning and the effects of reinforcement is no more 'responsible' for his behavior than one of

Pavlov's dogs would be held responsible salivating at the sound of a ringing bell" (Marlatt, cited by Jones and Butman, p. 200).

View of People Behaviorism has been criticized for "losing sight of the importance of the person—and lacking a theory of personality" (Wilson, p. 250). No wonder. There is no self! To deny self, to disregard thinking and feelings, and to reduce a person to "atoms" of behavior, making people only passive agents subject to environmental determinants, is to eliminate personhood. Such "atomism" is unacceptable to a biblical Christian (Jones and Butman, p. 159). In only recognizing the bodily existence, behaviorists miss the "soul" within humans and the interplay of body and soul-spirit (1 Thess. 5:23; see Jones and Butman, p. 155). "Christians cannot accept a position that belief and thought are not effectual causes of behavior" (Jones and Butman, p. 156).

Man is reduced to something less than human. Watson said, "Man is an animal different from other animals only in the types of behavior he displays." Man is more than a dog, rat, or chicken. The theory itself makes humans so mechanical they are treated like machines. Hence, it's determinism.

Humans can be influenced and even conditioned by their environment (Rom. 12:2a), but to conclude that they are only a response pattern that needs to be modified is reductionism in the extreme. In Christ, it is possible to experience a transformed life by an inward renewal (Rom. 12:2b; 2 Cor. 3:18).

Humans can be changed by external consequences such as reinforcement and punishment, but ideally, they should be motivated internally, not externally (Jn. 14:15). Granted, believers should be motivated by rewards (Mt. 6:19-20), but the behaviorist concept of reinforcement is not the same as the biblical concept of rewards. Behaviorists use "reinforcement" in a technical sense that implies things about personality that are contrary to the Scripture. The biblical concept of rewards implies moral worthiness, not just manipulation by consequences (Jones and Butman, p. 164). Humans are motivated by survival, but to say that is the one and only drive (even though it can be appealed to in a wide variety of ways) is again reductionistic.

Theory of Pathology No doubt, humans learn incompetent responses, but there is more to pathology than maladaptive behaviors. According to Jesus, "For out of the heart proceed evil thoughts, murders, adulteries, fornications, thefts, false witness, blasphemies" (Mt. 15:19). As Glasser has pointed out, stimulus-response psychology "ignores, or tries to ignore, the fact that we are internally motivated" (Glasser, *Stations of the Mind*, p. 30). Classic Behaviorism gives no place to the mind, emotions, will, or choice and, hence, to responsibility. Since there is no "person" to hold responsible, a concept of general human responsibility is impossible (Jones and Butman, p. 158).

Nature of Health, As a therapy, behavior modification has a much less well-developed notion of human health than the classic psychoanalytic or person-centered models. Healthy people certainly have some level of competence, but Behaviorism lacks a clear distinction between competent and incompetent and adaptive and maladaptive behavior patterns (Jones and Butman, p. 167). In the final analysis, behavior modification lacks a built-in explicit model of healthy humanness. Healthy individuals are competent, but they are much, much more.

Method of Therapy Behaviorism ignores people's feelings and history. While some argue that feelings must be changed before behavior can change, behaviorists answer that empirical evidence has not born out that criticism. Behavioral practitioners contend that when a person changes his or her behavior, the feelings are likely also to change. Likewise, when criticized for ignoring historical causes and not providing insight, behaviorists respond that behavior is changed directly. While behaviorists acknowledge that deviant responses have historical origins, they contend that history is seldom important in the maintenance of current problems and that there is a lack of clear evidence that insight is critical to the outcome (Corey, pp. 315-316).

Nevertheless, while focusing solely on learning a new coping skill has enabled individuals to break maladaptive habits, focusing *solely* on behavior can be superficial in that feelings, rationality, relationality, and historical factors are ignored.

Behavior Modification has been successful in helping some phobias, but according to Wilson, "therapeutic failures (figures that range from roughly 10 percent to 40 percent with agoraphobics) remain a problem" (Wilson, p. 266).

People do not just need behavior modification; they need spiritual regeneration and sanctification.

Summary: Behaviorism says that people learn conditioned responses, motivated by survival and the drive to adapt to a challenging environment. Learning new coping skills breaks maladaptive habits, enabling the person to be competent at meeting life's challenges.

From a biblical perspective, Behaviorism is woefully lacking because it is atheistic, naturalistic, and deterministic. Its view of people, pathology, and health is reductionistic in the extreme.

This is a case where the theory is wrong, but the technique works in some applications, such as autism, classroom discipline, assertive training, and especially phobias. There are a few insights that are helpful in Behaviorism.

In his book *Stations of the Mind*, William Glasser gives the "common sense" rebuttal to what he calls "stimulus-response psychology." He imagines an observer being sent from Mars to Earth to investigate how people on Earth function. The alien studies humans by observing how they handle the telephone. Being invisible, she can observe a man working in a busy office without his knowing it. When the telephone rings, he answers it. Again and again, he responds to its ring. She observes a hundred people worldwide "react" to the ring of a telephone, and all except one do the same thing. When she returns to Mars, she reports that people on Earth respond to the stimulus of bells, buzzes, or lights on their phones very specifically by picking them up and talking. When questioned, she defends her belief that stimulus-response is how humans function by appealing to the writings of a prominent psychologist, B. F. Skinner (Glasser, *Stations of the Mind*, p. 31). Glasser says that all Pavlov and Skinner proved is that "when something gets our attention, we will consistently do something about it *if* what gets our attention is in some way important to us. If stimulus-response is correct, the one who did not answer the phone should have" (Glasser, *Stations of the Mind*, p. 33, italics his). "Any theory that explains how the brain works must explain how it works all the time, not just almost all the time" (Glasser, *Stations of the Mind*, p. 34).

1. *Doing*, as opposed to merely *talking* about problems and gathering insights, should be part of many types of therapy. Sometimes, just dealing with behavior works (the Bible is full of behavioral commands).
2. Specific, systematic and successful techniques have been developed to help children, adolescents, and people with phobias which are compatible with the Bible.

Chapter 9

RATIONAL-EMOTIVE THERAPY

Albert Ellis (1913-2007) is the father of rational-emotive therapy (RET) and the grandfather of cognitive-behavioral therapy. He once said that he wanted to be remembered as "the main pioneering cognitive and cognitive-behavioral theorist and therapist" (Corey, p. 325). In a 1982 poll of 800 clinical psychologists, Ellis was voted the second most influential psychotherapist in history. Carl Rogers, the father of humanistic psychology, was number one and Sigmund Freud, the founder of psychoanalysis, was number three (from Albert Ellis's obituary in the *Los Angeles Times*, July 25, 2007). Robert O'Connell, the executive director of the Albert Ellis Institute (founded in 1959 by Ellis), said that Ellis was the progenitor of the self-help philosophy that propelled figures such as Wayne Dyer and "Dr. Phil" McGraw to celebrity (*Los Angeles Times*, July 25, 2007).

Background

Albert Ellis was born in Pittsburgh and moved to New York at four. Except for a year in New Jersey, he lived in New York City all of his life. He was hospitalized nine times as a child, but by vigorously taking care of his health and stubbornly refusing to make himself miserable about it, he lived an unusually energetic life (Corey, p. 325).

At age 12, Ellis decided to be an author. He majored in business administration at the City College of New York, hoping to make enough money in business to write. The Depression influenced him to give up getting rich as a businessman, but he wrote. His writing about sex, love, and marriage convinced him he could counsel people and that he enjoyed doing it (Corey, p. 325).

Eight years after graduating from college, he entered the clinical psychology program at the Teacher's College of Columbia University. He obtained a master's degree in 1943 and a doctorate in 1947. He was analyzed and supervised by the training analyst of the Karen Horney School. From 1947 to 1953, he practiced classical analysis and analytically oriented psychotherapy.

Ellis concluded that psychoanalysis was relatively superficial and unscientific (Corey, p. 325).

He experimented with several other systems and then, early in 1955, he combined humanistic philosophy and behavioral therapy to form rational-emotive therapy. Ellis developed his approach around how he dealt with his problems, especially during his youth. For example, during his adolescence, he was extremely shy around girls. At age 19, he forced himself to talk to 100 girls in one month. He did not get any dates, but he did desensitize himself to his fear of rejection by women (Corey, pp. 325-326).

Ellis traces the origins of RET to the ancient Greek Stoic philosopher Epictetus (15-130 AD), who said, "People are disturbed not by things, but by the view which they take of them." Ellis gives credit to Adler as a modern forerunner of RET. Adler said, "I am convinced that a person's behavior springs from his ideas" (Ellis, p. 202). Adler's motto was, "Everything depends on opinion" (Ellis, p. 202). Ellis also wrote, "RET agrees with almost all of Adlerian theory, but has a much more hardheaded and behavioral practice. It also minimizes most of the Adlerian emphasis on early childhood memories, lifestyle, and the importance of birth order" (Ellis, p. 211; see also p. 200). Adler taught that our emotional reactions and lifestyle are associated with our basic beliefs and are, therefore, cognitively created (Corey, p. 327). This is one of the basic tenets of RET.

Ellis explains that during the late 1940s and early 1950s, after practicing classical psychoanalysis and psychoanalytic oriented psychotherapy, he "discovered that no matter how much insight his clients gained or how well they seem to understand the events of their childhood, they rarely lost their symptoms and they still retained strong tendencies to create new ones." He realized that this was because they were not merely indoctrinated with irrational ideas of their own worthlessness when they were young, but they actively *reindoctrinated* themselves with the original irrationalities they picked up and even invented (Ellis, p. 203).

Ellis was one of the most prolific writers in counseling. He wrote 78 books (*Los Angeles Times*, July 25, 2007) and 600 articles (Corey, p. 326). His books and articles have been criticized for being "repetitive and self-promoting" (Jones and Butman, p. 174).

Rational-Emotive Therapy

The Theory

View of People RET does not have a comprehensive theory of people. Ellis views the self as merely a collection of empirical characteristics; therefore, he is much like the traditional behaviorist. There isn't a *self* that is at the core of a person. The core assertion of RET is that a person's thoughts are central to understanding that person. At the same time, RET recognizes that people are feeling and doing creatures (Jones and Butman, p. 176).

The basic concepts of the RET's views of people are 1) "People are born with a potential to be rational as well as irrational," 2) "People's tendency to irrational thinking, self-damaging habitations, wishful thinking, and intolerance is frequently exacerbated by their culture and their family group," and 3) "Humans tend to perceive, think, emote, and behave simultaneously" (Ellis, pp. 197-198).

As for the development of people, RET recognizes but does not explore the fact that the family and the culture impact the individual. For RET, the issue in the development of the people and emotional disturbance is beliefs. Ellis writes, "The basic tenet of RET is that emotional upset, as distinguished from the feeling of sorrow, regret, annoyance, and frustration, is caused by irrational beliefs" (Ellis, p. 207). In his writings, Ellis explains the preceding using an ABC format.

People come to a therapist because of a consequence (C), that is, an emotional or behavioral consequence that is disturbing them ("I'm depressed"). People attribute their emotional or behavioral consequences to an activating experience or event (A) as if there were some necessary causal relationship between A and C ("I lost my job, that's why I'm depressed"). (A) can be an external event, an internal thought, or the person's behavior. People are not disturbed by events but by their beliefs (B) about those events (Jones and Butman, p. 176).

Theory of Pathology The heart of Ellis' explanation of pathology is irrational beliefs. These irrational beliefs come from absolutizing and demanding that the universe should, ought, and must be different (Jones and Butman, p. 188), which he has called "musterbating." Irrational beliefs result in undesirable emotional consequences. On the other hand, rational beliefs result in appropriate emotional consequences (Jones and Butman, p. 177).

Ellis has developed a list of major irrational beliefs, but the list has changed over time. Early in the development of RET, Ellis listed eleven common irrational beliefs (Ellis, *Reason and Emotion in Psychotherapy*, 1962, cited in Jones and Butman, p. 178).

1. The idea that it is a dire necessity for an adult human being to be loved or approved by virtually every significant person in his community.
2. The idea that one should be thoroughly competent, adequate, and achieving in all possible respects if one is to consider oneself worthwhile.
3. The idea that certain people are bad, wicked, or villainous and that they should be severely blamed and punished for their villainy.
4. The idea that it is awful and catastrophic when things are not the way one would very much like them to be.
5. The idea that human unhappiness is externally caused and that people have little or no ability to control their sorrows and disturbances.
6. The idea that if something is or may be dangerous or fearsome, one should be terribly concerned about it and should keep dwelling on the possibility of its occurring.
7. The idea that it is easier to avoid than to face certain life difficulties and self-responsibilities.
8. The idea that one should be dependent on others and needs someone stronger than oneself on whom to rely.
9. The idea that one's history is an all-important determiner of one's present behavior and that because something once strongly affected one's life, it should have a similar effect.
10. The idea that one should become quite upset over other people's problems and disturbances.
11. The idea that there is invariably a right, precise, and perfect solution to human problems and that it is catastrophic if this perfect solution is not found.

Later (1985), Ellis summarized these into three main irrational beliefs (Jones and Butman, p 177), namely:

Rational-Emotive Therapy

1. I must do well and win approval, or else I rate as a rotten person.
2. Others must treat me considerately and kindly in precisely the way I want them to treat me; if they don't, society and the universe should severely blame, damn, and punish them for their inconsiderateness.
3. under which I live must be arranged so that I get practically all I want comfortably, quickly, and easily, and get virtually nothing that I don't want. The irrational quality comes from demanding that the universe should, ought to, and must be different.

These irrational beliefs are at the root of problems.

Irrational beliefs → emotional consequences

Nature of Health In Ellis' words, the goals of RET are to "help people think more rationally, feel more appropriately, and act more functionally to achieve their goals of living longer and more happily." The healthy person, then, has developed an effective rational philosophy. Such a person will feel appropriately and act functionally (Jones and Butman, p. 181).

More specifically, Ellis believes that people should strive to acquire and internalize the following values, many of which can be thought of as rational attitudes: self-interest, social interest, self-direction, high frustration tolerance, flexibility, acceptance of uncertainty, commitment to creature pursuits, scientific thinking, self-acceptance, risk-taking, long-range hedonism, non-utopianism, and responsibility for our emotional disturbances (Jones and Butman, p 173).

Ellis' view of a healthy person has been described as one who is "emotionally flexible and adaptable, relatively content regardless of what happens." Ellis has linked RET to ancient Stoic philosophy. Experiencing cultural decline, repeated invasion, and military defeats, the Stoics developed a philosophy that sought to control the inner world of the mind and be unaffected by the outer world, which was out of control. Ellis' view is Stoic in nature. In his view, nothing is of ultimate value and, therefore, there is nothing to be upset about; only one's happiness is highly valued (Jones and Butman, pp. 185-186).

Method of Therapy On the one hand, Ellis writes, "In RET, the attempt to help clients minimize their dictatorial, dogmatic, absolutistic core philosophy is attempted in three main therapeutic ways: cognitive, emotive, and behavioristic" (Ellis, p. 213).

On the other hand, he explains, "The many roads taken in RET are aimed at one major goal: minimizing the client's central self-defeating outlook and acquiring a more realistic, tolerant philosophy of life" (Ellis, p. 214). He adds, "Rational-emotive practitioners often employ a fairly rapid-fire, active-directive-persuasive-philosophic methodology. In most instances, they quickly pin the client down to a few basic irrational ideas" (Ellis, p. 215). He calls this the cognitive-persuasive aspect of RET its "most distinguishing characteristic" (Ellis, p. 214).

In other words, after ABC comes D, that is, disputing. Disputing is applying the scientific method to help clients challenge their irrational beliefs. The three components of disputing are detecting, debating, and discriminating. Eventually, the client arrives at E, an effective philosophy. A new and effective rational philosophy replaces inappropriate thoughts with appropriate ones. Finally, the client comes to F with a new set of feelings (Corey, p. 332).

Corey summarizes the RET therapeutic process in four steps: 1) Show the clients that they have incorporated many irrational "shoulds," "oughts," and "musts." The therapist serves as a scientist who challenges the self-defeating ideas of the client. 2) Demonstrate that the clients keep their emotional disturbances active by thinking illogically and repeating self-defeating meanings and philosophies. 3) Help them modify their thinking and abandon their irrational ideas. 4) Challenge clients to develop a rational philosophy of life so that in the future, they can avoid other irrational beliefs (Corey, p. 333).

Ellis says, "Rational-emotive therapists do not believe a warm relationship between counselee and counselor is a necessary or sufficient condition for effective personality change. They believe it is desirable for therapists to accept clients fully but criticize and point out the deficiencies of their behavior" (Ellis, p. 198).

RET also uses a number of techniques, including homework, imagery, role-playing, shame-attacking exercises, etc. (Corey, p. 340).

Ellis gave a case study using RET. Sara R. was a 25-year-old computer programmer. Although fairly attractive, she was always ashamed of her body, did little dating, and occupied herself with her work. Since her college days, she had been overeating and overdrinking. Three years of fairly classic psychoanalysis disillusioned her with therapy, but the president of her company told her he would no longer put up with her constant drinking and insisted that she see Ellis.

The RET therapy lasted for six sessions, followed by 24 weeks of RET group therapy and one week of rational encounter. She was repeatedly shown cognitively that her central problem was that she devoutly believed she had to be almost perfect and that she must not be criticized in any major way by significant others. Ellis writes, "She was persistently taught, instead, to refrain from rating herself, but only to measure her performances; to see that she could never be, except by arbitrary definition, a worm even if she never rid herself of her overeating, her compulsive drinking, and her other foolish symptoms; to see that it was highly desirable but not necessary that she relate intimately to a man and to win approval of her peers and her bosses at work; and first to accept herself with her hostility and then to give up her childish demands on others that led her to be so hostile to them."

Ellis goes on to say she was finally "induced" to replace her "shoulds" with "it would be better" both in her vocabulary as well as in her internalized beliefs. Ellis adds, "Sara was fully accepted by the therapist as a person, even though he strongly assailed many of her ideas and sometimes humorously reduced them to absurdity." She was also "assertively confronted" by some of the group members. In the marathon weekend of rational encounters, some "used vigorous, down-to-earth language with her, which she initially disliked but later began to use to some extent herself." There was also steady support of phone calls and visits when she was going through a difficult time with drinking. Then, they went after her defenses with RET analyses and revealed her foolish ideas. She was given homework assignments and shown how to stay on a long-term diet. Role-playing was also used. Ellis concludes by pointing out that cognitive, emotive, and behavioristic approaches were used.

As a result, Sara stopped drinking completely and lost 25 pounds. She became considerably less condemnatory of herself and others and began making some close friends. She had satisfactory sex relations with three different males and began to go steadily with one of them. She only rarely made herself guilty or depressed, accepted herself with her failings, and began to focus much more on enjoying than on rating herself.

Sara had individual and group sessions for six months and occasional follow-up sessions for the next year. She married her steady boyfriend about a year after she had originally begun treatment. Two and half years after the close of therapy, things were going well in their marriage, her job, and their social life (Ellis, pp. 216-220).

Evaluation

Philosophical Assumptions Rational Emotive therapy is based on philosophical assumptions that Ellis feels are rational.

1. Atheism. Technically, atheism is not an essential part of RET, but Ellis is an unabashed atheist and his atheism dramatically shapes some of the positions. Ellis says, "In the final analysis, then, religion is neurosis.... If there were a God, it would be necessary to uninvent him" (Ellis, cited by Carter and Narramore, p. 25).

Jones and Butman contend, however, that Ellis does allow for the possibility that individuals with some religious faith can be emotionally healthy as long as they do not go overboard (Jones and Butman, p. 174). They also say that Ellis claims that devout belief tends to foster human dependency and increase emotional disturbance. Hence, too much religion is necessarily bad. For Ellis and RET, ultimately, God is irrelevant and unnecessary. For example, according to Ellis, God is not needed to explain the creation of things, nor is He needed to create an ethical code (Jones and Butman, p. 175).

2. Humanism. Ellis believes that the reasoning individual is the source of wisdom, not Almighty God. He admonishes, "People had better define their own freedom. Cultivate a good measure of individuality, live in dialogue with others and learn to accept their own human limitations and the fact that they will eventually die." Jones and Butman conclude, "Clearly, in RET, people are the only real measure of people; God is irrelevant to the human outlook" (Jones and Butman, p. 175).

3. Hedonism. Ellis assumes that all humans are basically hedonistic, that is, they are happiness-seeking beings. Hedonism usually implies short-term pleasure seeking. Ellis, however, would allow for delayed gratification of an immediate desire to maximize a greater amount of happiness in the long term. Hence, he prefers the term "long-range hedonism" (Jones and Butman, pp. 174-175).

4. Optimism. In the psychological sense, optimism is the opposite of determinism. Optimism is the concept that humans can choose and change. According to RET, to change, people must simply change their beliefs. Ellis said, "RET holds that virtually all serious-emotional problems directly stem from magical, empirically unvalidatable thinking and that if disturbance-creating ideas are vigorously disputed by logico-empirical thinking, they can be eliminated or minimized and will ultimately cease to reoccur" (Ellis, p. 199). Now, that is optimism! While that might work in some cases, it certainly does not work in all. The fact that RET teaches that people can change is

good, but it takes more than changing one's thinking.

View of People Humans are thinking, feeling, and behaving creatures and rationality is prominent among human capacities. Unlike other approaches to psychotherapy that de-emphasize rationality or explains it in such a way as to leave it an empty shell (psychoanalysis, behaviorism, etc.), RET assumes that people can think and reason and that these processes are important to understanding human behavior.

Beliefs should and do affect behavior, but to conclude that beliefs defined as rational (or irrational) thoughts are the *sole factor* in determining behavior is an oversimplification. Many Christians have embraced RET (Jones and Butman claim that Crabb's early books on counseling were a form of RET, p. 179), perhaps because it sounds biblical. Does not the Scripture say, "For as he thinks in his heart, so is he" (Prov. 23:7; see also Rom. 8:5; 12:2; Eph. 4:23; Phil. 4:8; 1 Cor. 2:16, etc.)?

Proverbs 23:7 is not making a universal statement about all humans at all times to the effect that a people's mental thoughts determine who they are. The context is talking about a miser (a stingy) man (Prov. 23:6). As the rest of verse 7 explains, the man, in this case, says one thing ("eat and drink") but thinks something else in his heart ("his heart is not with you"). The point of the passage is, do not eat a miser's food because, when he hypocritically feigns generosity (eat and drink while in his heart he is thinking something entirely different), you will be repulsed (you will vomit, Prov. 23:8). Such a man is not what he *says*, but what he *thinks*. That, of course, is true anytime anyone says one thing and thinks another. That is vastly different, however, than teaching that this verse is saying that a man's thoughts determine his behavior. The Greek word translated "mind" in Romans 8:4 and other passages means more than "thoughts" or "beliefs." It includes the thinking, the will, and even the emotions. One commentator says it includes one's outlook, assumptions, values, desires, and purposes (Cranfield, p. 386).

While cognition might often shape and determine emotional experience, the reverse is also the case; emotions can come before and shape cognition (Jones and Butman, p. 184).

Theory of Pathology Irrational beliefs can cause or, at least, contribute to pathology, but irrational belief alone is not the cause of problems. People make choices. Furthermore, one should not reject all "shoulds" and "oughts" (the Ten Commandments). At the same time, accepting absolutes must be balanced with accepting that we miss the mark.

Some of the original eleven RET irrational beliefs are accurate. It is irrational to believe: 1) It is a dire necessity for an adult human being to be loved or approved by virtually every significant person in his community. 2) One should be thoroughly competent and adequate and achieve in all possible respects if one is to consider oneself worthwhile. 3) It is awful and catastrophic when things are not how one would like them to be. 5) Human unhappiness is externally caused and people cannot control their sorrows and disturbances, etc. (see also the last 3).

Some of the RET irrational beliefs are not correct (they are irrational!). For example, one of his original eleven is that dependency on another is irrational. It is rational to assume that humans need something or someone beyond themselves. Is the rationale behind this irrational belief the secular assertion of human autonomy? Depending on others and interdependence is not pathological; it is psychologically healthy (Jones and Butman, p. 189).

Nature of Health Healthy individuals think rationally, feel appropriately, and act functionally. Healthy individuals are emotionally flexible and adaptable but are not stoic; they do not believe that nothing is of ultimate value, that there is nothing to be upset about, or that only their happiness is of high value (Jones and Butman, p. 186). RET can be used to change particular irrational beliefs, but the grander goal is "committing" the person to a rational life philosophy, that is, adapting RET as a religion, a way of life, for the sake of future prevention (Jones and Butman, p. 179). As a substitute religion, RET is a false religion.

Method of Therapy Ellis speaks of having "three main therapeutic ways: cognitive, emotive, and behavioristic" (Ellis, p. 213), but as he himself admits, the one major goal is to minimize "the client's central self-defeating outlook and acquiring a more realistic, tolerant philosophy of life" (Ellis, p. 214). The therapy is virtually totally cognitive.

The core of therapy is "D," that is, the disputation of irrational beliefs. Many methods are used to dispute irrational beliefs. Ellis personally uses a great deal of Socratic questioning and challenging of clients to produce scientific evidence for their irrational beliefs or to examine the practical, emotional impact of those beliefs. The client is enabled to engage in self-disputation of their own irrational beliefs. Also, RET practitioners commonly use many of the active change strategies of the behavior and cognitive-behavior therapists, as well as some techniques designed to be emotionally evocative, such as imagery exercises and role-playing (Jones and Butman, p. 179).

Ellis' idea that a warm relationship between counselee and counselor is not a necessary condition for personality change may be true in some cases, but it is certainly not the biblical way to minister to people. Like the Holy Spirit (Jn. 14:16-17), Christians are called alongside to help in a tenderhearted, compassionate way (1 Pet. 3:8).

Therapy should, in some cases and at an appropriate time, dispute irrational beliefs, but to challenge beliefs along with a few other techniques is a narrow approach. Jones and Butman say it is "one of the narrower approaches" (Jones and Butman, p. 193).

Summary: RET says irrational beliefs produce emotional upsets. By using an active-direct-persuasive philosophic approach, individuals with irrational beliefs can be persuaded of rational beliefs, which will make "amazing" curative and preventive changes in their disturbance-creating tendencies.

From a biblical perspective, RET misses the mark because it is atheistic, humanistic, and hedonistic. Its view of people and pathology is reductionistic, and its therapy is too narrow. I once had the opportunity to hear Ellis lecture in person to a class of college students. He was extremely rough and rude with people, and his language was filled with profanity. Some of his ideas may have merit, but if he is an example of the product of RET, it is a far cry from the meek and gentle Jesus.

There are a few valuable ideas in RET.

1. Ellis gave rationality a prominent place in psychology, unlike most of his predecessors. "After a person has experienced a cathartic or highly intensive emotional experience related to earlier traumas, some attempt at conceptualization and giving meaning to the experience is essential if it is to have any lasting effect" (Corey, p. 356). The Bible puts a premium on being rational (Rom. 12:2).
2. While it is true that other people and events in our past have contributed to the shaping of our current philosophy of life and our current lifestyle, we are responsible for maintaining certain self-destructive ideas and attitudes that influence our daily lives. What could be more biblical?
3. Unlike most therapies that precede his, Ellis' theory is dogmatically optimistic and not deterministic, which is certainly compatible with the Scripture, especially when God's grace is taken into consideration.

Chapter 10

COGNITIVE THERAPY

Cognitive-behavioral therapy is a "highly influential descendent of behavior therapy and RET" (Jones and Butman, p. 196). Cognitive-behavioral therapy differs from traditional Behaviorism in that it teaches that internal (mental) events cause some human behavior and that this internal behavior operates on different principles than the laws of learning (operant learning and classical conditioning) used to explain animal behavior. Cognitive-behavioral therapy differs from RET in being more integrated into the overall discipline of psychology, more scientific, well-researched, and less dogmatic (Jones and Butman, pp. 197-198).

Unlike most schools of psychology, cognitive therapy does not have one founding theorist. There are many variations of this model. Its lack of cohesiveness makes it hard to summarize and digest (Jones and Butman, pp. 196-197).

Background

While there are many variations of cognitive therapy, three groups are representative (Jones and Butman, p. 196).

In the early 1960s, Aaron T. Beck developed the approach known as "cognitive therapy" as a result of his research on depression. Beck, who was trained in psychoanalysis, attempted to validate Freud's theory of depression as having at its core "anger turned on the self." Rather than finding retroflexed anger in their thoughts and dreams, Beck observed a negative bias in their cognitive process. From these observations, Beck developed his theory of emotional disorder and a cognitive model of depression (Beck and Weishaar, p. 290). Beck did his work independently of Ellis but reached similar conclusions (Corey, p. 344).

In the 1970s, Donald Meichenbaum, whose work evolved out of traditional behaviorism (Jones and Butman, p. 197), developed cognitive behavior modification

(CBM). He concluded that a person's cognitions are explicit behaviors that can be modified in their own right. His approach focuses on the clients' self-verbalizations. For change to occur, clients need to interpret the scripted nature of their behavior so they can evaluate it (Corey, p. 351). He wrote *Cognitive Behavior Modification* (1977).

Walter Mischel (1973) and Albert Bandura (1986) wrote about the social-cognitive approach to human personality, which has been the most aggressive attempt to understand human personality from a behavioral and cognitive perspective. They have not developed a corresponding school of therapy (Jones and Butman, p. 197).

The Theory

Beck's Cognitive Therapy Cognitive therapy is based on the premise that how one thinks largely determines how one feels and behaves (Beck and Weishaar, p. 285). To say the same thing another way, an individual's emotional and behavioral responses to a situation are largely determined by how that individual perceives, interprets, and assigns meaning to that event (Beck and Weishaar, p. 293).

People with emotional difficulties tend to commit "characteristic logical errors" that tilt objective reality toward self-depreciation (Corey, p. 345). These "distorted cognitions" are not the symptom of the problem; they are the cause of the problem (Jones and Butman, pp. 204-205). Beck has identified common cognitive distortions in processing information that leads to faulty assumptions and misconceptions (see Beck and Weishaar, pp. 295-296 and Corey, pp. 345-346).

1. Arbitrary Inference is reaching a conclusion without supporting evidence or even in the face of contradictory evidence (Beck and Weishaar, p. 295). This distortion includes "catastrophizing," thinking of the absolute worst scenario for a situation (Cory, p. 345).

2. Selective Abstraction is forming conclusions based on an isolated detail taken out of context while ignoring other information (Beck and Weishaar, p. 295). This misses the overall significance (Cory, p. 345).

3. Overgeneralization is holding an extreme belief based on a single incident and applying it inappropriately to dissimilar events (Cory, p. 345).

4. Magnification and minimization is seeing something as far more significant or less significant than it is (Beck and Weishaar, pp. 295-296). It consists of overestimating the significance of negative events (Cory, p. 346).

5. Personalization is relating external events to oneself without evidence for making such a connection (Beck and Weishaar, p. 296).

6. Dichotomous (or polarized) thinking is interpreting experiences in all-or-nothing terms or categorizing experiences in either/or extremes (Cory, p. 346). It categorizes experience as either a complete success or a total failure (Beck and Weishaar, p. 296).

Both RET and cognitive therapies teach the primary importance of cognition in psychological dysfunction. Nevertheless, there are a number of differences between the two approaches. RET says the cognitive problem is irrational beliefs and assumes that all problems have a similar set of irrational beliefs, while cognitive therapy claims that the cognitive problem is distorted thinking and that each disorder has its own typical cognitive content (Beck and Weishaar, p. 288). Beck stresses inaccurate conclusions. He maintains that certain ideas are not irrational but too absolute, broad, and extreme. "RET views the problem as philosophical; cognitive therapy views it as functional" (Beck and Weishaar, p. 288).

Therapy proceeds in three stages: 1) The presentation of the therapeutic rationale. 2) The development of dysfunctional thoughts. 3) Alteration of the dysfunctional thoughts and the substitution of more functional thinking (Jones and Butman, p. 205). RET views the therapist as a teacher and does not think a warm relationship with a client is essential. Beck believes successful counseling rests on genuine warmth, accurate empathy, nonjudgmental acceptance, and the ability to establish trust and rapport. RET is highly directive; Beck emphasizes a more Socratic dialogue. He places more stress on helping the clients discover their misconceptions for themselves (Corey, pp. 346-347). Beck uses persistent but gentle logic and persuasion to change the clients' thinking (Jones and Butman, p. 205).

Beck is considered one of the leading authorities on depression. According to Beck, a "cognitive triad" consisting of a negative view of the self, the world, and the future is the pattern that triggers depression (Corey, p. 349).

The Beck Depression Inventory (BDI) is a standardized device to assess the depth of depression. It contains twenty-one symptoms and attitudes: 1) sadness, 2) pessimism, 3) sense of failure, 4) dissatisfaction, 5) guilt, 6) sense of punishment, 7) self-dislike, 8) self-accusations, 9) suicidal ideation, 10) crying spells, 11) irritability,

12) social withdrawal, 13) indecision, 14) distorted body image, 15) work inhibition, 16) sleep disturbance, 17) tendency to become fatigued, 18) loss of appetite, 19) weight loss, 20) somatic preoccupations, and 21) loss of libido (Corey, pp. 349-350).

Self-criticism is a central characteristic of most depressed people. Another characteristic is an exaggeration of external demands, problems, and pressures. Painful emotions are a typical experience. People feel overwhelmed. Some behavioral symptoms are inactivity (too tired to do anything), withdrawal, and avoidance. Some harbor suicidal wishes.

Therapeutic procedures include Socratic questioning ("How do you know that it is pointless to try?"), exposing negative thinking, helping clients make a list of their responsibilities, setting priorities, and developing a realistic action plan. Graded tasks are to be completed. Easy tasks are completed first, so they will begin to be active, meet with some success, and become slightly more optimistic (Corey, pp. 350-351).

Studies have documented cognitive therapy's success in dealing with depression. Thirty of thirty-four studies have supported the hypotheses of bias in information processing. Studies from seven independent centers have compared the efficacy of cognitive therapy to antidepressant medication, a treatment of established efficacy. Comparisons of cognitive therapy alone to drugs alone have found cognitive therapy to be superior or equal to antidepressant medication. "Follow-up studies, observing patients from three months to two years after treatment, indicate that cognitive theory has greater long-term effects" (Beck and Weishaar, p. 291).

Merchenbaum's Cognitive Behavior Modification (CBM) "Cognitive structure" is the organizing aspect of thinking, which monitors and directs the choice of thoughts. It is this cognitive structure that needs restructuring. This is done through self-instructional therapy (self-statements). Merchenbaum proposes that "behavior change occurs through a sequence of mediating processes involving the interaction of inner speech, cognitive structures and behaviors and their resultant outcome" (Corey, p 351). He uses a three-phase process of change in which these three aspects are interwoven. Focusing on only one of these will probably prove insufficient (Corey, p. 352).

Phase 1: Self-observation. When clients begin therapy, their internal dialogue is characterized by negative self-statements and imagery. They must be willing and able to listen to themselves. This process involves increased sensitivity to their thoughts, feelings, actions, physiological reactions, and ways of reacting to others.

Phase 2: Starting a new internal dialogue. If clients hope to change, what they say to themselves must instate a new behavioral chain, one that is incompatible with their maladaptive behaviors. Their new internal dialogue serves as a guide to new behavior. In turn, this process impacts the client's cognitive structures.

Phase 3: Learning new skills. Clients are taught more effective coping skills, which are practiced in real-life situations. At the same time, clients continue to focus on telling themselves new sentences and observing and assessing the outcomes. As they behave differently in situations, they typically get different reactions from others. The stability of what they learn is greatly influenced by what they say to themselves about their newly acquired behavior and its consequences.

Merchenbaum has also developed procedures for teaching coping skills and stress management. His five-step treatment procedure for teaching *coping skills* is: 1) using imagery and role-playing to expose clients to anxiety-producing situations, 2) having clients evaluate their anxiety levels, 3) teaching clients to become aware of their anxiety-provoking cognitions in stressful situations, 4) helping client reevaluated their self-statements, and 5) having clients note their level of anxiety following their reevaluation (Corey, pp. 352-353).

"Research studies have demonstrated the success of coping skills programs when applied to problems such as speech anxiety, test anxiety, phobias, anger, social incompetence, addictions, alcoholism, sexual dysfunctions, and social withdrawal in children" (Corey, p. 353).

Stress-inoculation training (SIT) is a coping skills program for *stress management*. It inoculates people psychologically and behaviorally as immunization does biologically. Beginning with relatively mild stress stimuli, individuals gradually develop a tolerance for stronger stimuli. It is based on the assumption that people can cope with stress by modifying their beliefs and self-statements in stressful situations. It consists of giving information, Socratic discussion, cognitive restructuring, problem-solving, relaxation training, behavioral rehearsals, self-motivating, self-instruction, self-reinforcement, and modifying environmental situations. There are three stages in stress-inoculation training (Corey, pp. 353-55).

Phase 1: The conceptual phase. Clients often begin treatment feeling they are the victims of external circumstances, thoughts, feelings, and behaviors over which they have no control. They are provided with a conceptual framework designed to help them understand how they respond to stressful situations. They must become aware of their role in creating their stress. They become aware of it by "systematically observing the statements they make internally as well as monitoring the manipulative behavior that flows from this dialogue" (Corey, p. 353).

Phase 2: The skill acquisition and rehearsal phases. Clients are given a variety of behavioral and cognitive coping techniques to apply to stressful situations. Direct actions include "gathering information about their fears, learning specifically what situations bring about stress, arranging for ways to lessen the stress by doing something different and learning methods of physical and psychological relaxation." Cognitive coping consists of being taught that adaptive and maladaptive behaviors are linked to inner dialogue. In this phase, they acquire and rehearse a new set of self-statements. Training also consists of reevaluating priorities, time management, instruction, and developing support systems. Relaxation techniques may include relaxing muscle groups, breath control techniques, meditation, yoga, walking, jogging, gardening, knitting, or other physical activities. Relaxation is as much a state of mind as it is a physical state (Corey, p. 354).

Phase 3: The application and follow-through phase. Clients must practice self-statements and apply their new skills in real-life situations. They practice behavioral assignments, which become increasingly demanding (Corey, p. 354).

This approach to stress management has been applied to anger management, anxiety management, assertive training, improving creative thinking, treating depression, and dealing with health problems (Corey, p. 355).

Mischel's Five Person Variables In the cognitive-behavioral camp, only Mischel has proposed anything approaching a grand personality theory. He suggests "idiographic analysis," where each person is analyzed individually without reducing individual differences to measurements of universal traits such as extroversion, etc. Each person is unique and must be understood as such. Five categories develop differently in each person. These are not psychoanalysis traits or psychological structures such as the id, ego, and superego (Jones and Butman, pp. 200-201).

1. Cognitive encoding strategies. Everyone sorts the raw data of their sensations of the world in different ways. The encoding strategy transforms the perception of someone's mouth movement into either an accepting smile or a judgmental gesture. "Persons with sophisticated, broad, adaptable ways of sorting or encoding their experiences will be more adjusted and adaptable than persons with simplistic, rigid, and narrow encoding strategies" (Jones and Butman, p. 201).

2. Cognitive and behavior construction competencies. In response to the data taken in through the senses and their encoded perceptions, people "figure out" their world by constructing a cognitive model of it, and then they construct actions to respond to it. Once they have given a label to their experience, they combine bits of experience in a way that seems to make sense. These models may vary from highly accurate and productive to highly inaccurate and destructive. Based on their model and utilizing their available skills, the people act (Jones and Butman, p. 201).

3. Subjective stimulus values. People differ in what they value and, hence, what motivates them (Jones and Butman, p. 201).

4. Operant and classical conditioning. Though he moved beyond traditional behaviorism, Mischel believes that basic learning processes still influence human behavior. For him, these do not operate mechanistically (Skinner) but at a cognitive level (Jones and Butman, p. 202).

5. Self-regulatory systems and plans. Through memory, expectancy, and language, people take their environment inside of themselves and, thus, the thoughts they engage in become powerful determinants of their actions as the external environment (Jones and Butman, p. 202).

Mischel's view of people has not resulted in a formal therapeutic approach per se, but his model provides the best framework for understanding all cognitive-behavioral therapy (Jones and Butman, p. 202).

Bandura's Social Cognitive Therapy Bandura is a prolific researcher who has contributed many important concepts to cognitive-behavioral therapy. He focused on modeling—the capacity of humans to learn not just by direct experience but by watching the behavior or hearing the thoughts of others. He developed the concepts of self-regulation (see #5, Mischel) and reciprocal determinism (see the evaluation of the philosophical assumptions).

He also developed the concept of self-efficacy, that is, the concept that it is not just the root consequences of an action that determines its occurrence or even the expectation of a future consequence, but it is also our evaluation of our competency or effectiveness in behaving that determines action. The point is that people do not attempt things just because there are rewards, but they also consider our expectancy that we can be effective at the behavior it takes to obtain the reward. The therapist cannot simply create a reward but must also create a sense of personal effectiveness to get the fearful person to act courageously. This concept has become central in cognitive-behavioral practice today (Jones and Butman, p. 203).

Cognitive therapists will say that there is no single cause of pathology. "Psychological distress is ultimately caused by many innate, biological, developmental, and environmental factors interacting with one another." Yet, on the other hand, they say, "System errors in reasoning, called cognitive distortions, are evident during psychological distress (Beck and Weishaar, p. 295). In the final analysis, cognitive therapy teaches that cognitions and beliefs are the causes of pathology (Jones and Butman, p. 213). "In Beck's mind, the distorted thinking is not the symptom of the problem; it is the cause of the problem" (Jones and Butman, p. 205).

Distorted thinking → emotional disturbance

In a chapter written by Beck and Weishaar, the following case study, which has been edited, is given here.

The patient was a 21-year-old male college student who complained of insomnia, halting speech, stuttering, feelings of nervousness, dizziness, and worrying. His sleep difficulties were particularly acute before exams or athletic competitions.

The patient was raised in a family that valued competition. His father taught, "Never let anyone get the best of you." As a consequence of viewing others as adversaries, he developed few friends, for he could not self-disclose, fearing that others would discover he was not all he would like to be.

After gathering initial data regarding diagnosis, context, and history, the therapist attempted to define how the patient's cognitions contributed to his distress. He asked, "What situations are most upsetting to you?" "What thoughts go through your mind, let's say when you do not do so well at swimming?" and "Do you *see* any connections here among these thoughts?"

At this point, the therapist began to hypothesize about the patient's organizing beliefs: that others determine his worth, that he is unattractive because there is something inherently wrong with him, or that he is a loser. The therapist looked for evidence to support the centrality of these beliefs and remained open to other possibilities.

The therapist assisted the patient in generating a list of goals to work on in therapy, including 1) decreasing perfectionism, 2) decreasing anxiety symptoms, 3) decreasing sleep difficulties, 4) increasing closeness in friendships, and 5) developing his own values apart from those of his parents.

The first problem addressed was anxiety. To reduce ruminations about his performance, the therapist asked him to name the advantages of dwelling on thoughts of the exam. The patient came up with his own rationale for decreasing his ruminations. He was then ready to consider giving up his maladaptive behavior and risk trying something new. The therapist taught the patient progressive relaxation, and the patient began to use physical exercise as a way to relieve anxiety.

The patient was also instructed on how cognitions affect behavior and mood. The therapist picked up on the patient's statement that worries can be distracting. The patient was instructed to record automatic thoughts, recognize cognitive distortions, and respond to them. For homework, he was asked to record his automatic thoughts if he had trouble falling asleep before an exam. By observing his automatic thoughts across various situations—academic, athletic, and social—the patient identified dichotomous thinking ("I'm either a winner or a loser") as a frequent cognitive distortion. Perceiving the consequences of his behavior as either totally good or completely bad resulted in major shifts in mood. It also gave him a false sense of himself, for others should be attracted to him if he was good. The fact that not everyone was attracted to him was interpreted as evidence that he was bad and a loser. Two techniques that helped with his dichotomous thinking were reframing the problem and building a continuum between his dichotomous categories.

The therapist reframed the problem from a situation in which something was inherently wrong with the patient to one characterized by a problem with social skills. Moreover, the theme "I am a loser" appeared so powerful to the patient that he labeled it his "main belief." This assumption was traced historically to the constant criticism from his parents for mistakes and perceived shortcomings. By reviewing his history, he was able to see that his lies prevented people from getting closer, reinforcing his belief that they did not want to be close. In addition, he believed that his parents made him whatever success he was and that no achievement was his alone. This had made him angry and lacking in self-confidence.

As therapy progressed, the patient's homework increasingly focused on social interaction. He practiced initiating conversations and asking questions to learn more about other people. He also practiced "biting his tongue" instead of telling small lies about himself. He monitored people's reactions to him and saw that they were varied but generally positive. By listening to others, he found that he admired people who could openly admit shortcomings and joke about their mistakes. This experience helped him understand that it was useless to categorize people, including himself, as winners and losers.

In later sessions, the patient described his belief that his behavior reflected on his parents and vice versa. Recognizing how he was different from his parents freed him from their absolute standards and allowed him to be less self-conscious when interacting with others.

Subsequently, the patient was able to pursue interests and hobbies that had nothing to do with achievement. He was able to set moderate and realistic goals for schoolwork, and he began to date (Beck and Weishaar, pp. 312-315).

Evaluation

Philosophical Assumptions The philosophical presuppositions of this group of approaches are not as conspicuous as behaviorism, but cognitive therapy is built on the foundation of behaviorism and, therefore, the basic presuppositions are consistent with that perception (Jones and Butman, p. 198).

1. Atheism. In the final analysis, both behaviorism and cognitive behavioral therapy are atheistic.

2. Naturalism. Like its predecessor, behaviorism, cognitive therapy is naturalistic and, thus, materialistic, denying the existence of the spiritual.

3. Moderate determinism. Bandura developed the notion of reciprocal determinism and other cognitive-behaviorists usually enthusiastically endorsed it (Jones and Butman, p. 200). According to Bandura, our environment determines us, but, to a limited degree, we are also the determiners of our environment. For example, we may be affected by what we watch on TV, but we choose what we watch. We can determine how other people treat us by how we treat them (Jones and Butman, p. 200).

In other words, freedom is the exercise of self-influence, but the exercise of self-influence is itself causally determined. We have freedom whenever the self exercises its influence even though the self-system operates by determining rules and, therefore, *could not have done otherwise* (Jones and Butman, p. 208).

Something other than the decision of the person causes behavior. People may be honest, but ultimately, the development of honesty is caused by factors over which they have "no control." They learned honesty by the laws of learning. "Moral choice becomes just another behavior that is acquired the way all behaviors are acquired" (Jones and Butman, p. 208).

This is soft determinism (see the discussion on psycho-dynamic psychotherapy), which redefines freedom in such a way as to make it compatible with determinism, thus creating the illusion of freedom. Although there is talk about freedom, humans are not free in the sense of having any choices over which we exercise ultimate control as responsible agents. Bandura states that there is no "psychic agent that controls behavior" (Jones and Butman, p. 208).

The soft determinism of cognitive-behavioral therapy is a more balanced position than other theories. Jones and Butman go so far as to say that even though Bandura's view is faulty, it comes the closest to a Christian view of freedom. They say it avoids the "suffocating determinism" of classic psychoanalysis and behavior modification. It also avoids the radical suggestion about freedom embraced by humanistic psychotherapies (Jones and Butman, p. 209).

Is this a view of limited freedom that Christians can accept? Not exactly. In neither behaviorism nor cognitive therapy do people have true limited freedom. Both models are "dangerous" in that people are mechanisms *always doing what they must do*. In behaviorism, people are non-cognitive machines. In cognitive therapy, they are thinking machines. Only a theistic view of persons that asserts that we are created for moral accountability is an adequate grounding for a full conception of limited freedom (Jones and Butman, p. 209).

Yet, at a therapeutic level, cognitive-behavioral therapy practitioners try to enlist the client as a "collaborator" in the change process. This concept carries a high view of the client's power of freedom and choice. In practice, cognitive-behavioral therapy acknowledges a person's capacity for change through "self-control" and related processes (Jones and Butman, p. 209).

View of People Because cognitive therapy focuses on micro-theories of specific pathologies, there are no grand postulates about personality (Jones and Butman, p. 211).

In explaining the cognitive theory of personality, Beck and Weishaar say, "An individual's emotional, behavioral responses to a situation are largely determined by how that individual perceives, interprets, and assigns meaning to that event" (Beck and Weishaar, p. 293). They add that the personality is shaped by cognitive structures "that consist of the fundamental beliefs and assumptions, which develop early in life from personal experiences and identification with significant others. People form concepts about themselves, others, and how the world operates. These concepts are reinforced by further learning experiences and, in turn, influence the formation of other beliefs, values, and attitudes" (Beck and Weishaar, p. 293).

This view of people is atomistic. It virtually focuses solely on the cognitive. People are a loose collection of cognitive beliefs and habits. This is not a holistic view; it is reductionism. People are "thinking machines" (Jones and Butman, p. 209).

The strength of cognitive therapy is its high view of rationality and its emphasis on behavior. It stresses the cognitive and behavioral aspects of personality. Knowledge (2 Pet. 1:6) and belief (Rom. 6:11) are involved in behavioral change. The Scripture often addresses behavior directly in the form of commands. Some Christians have even suggested, "The process of change which takes place in sanctification is the same as the process of change which occurs with cognitive therapy" (Pecheur, cited by Jones and Butman, p. 212). Passages on renewing the mind (Rom. 8:5; 12:2; Eph. 4:23) are quoted to support such a position.

One of the weaknesses of cognitive therapy is the overemphasis on rationality. Knowledge without love puffs up rather than builds up (1 Cor. 8:1). Belief alone does not determine behavior. More than "belief" is involved in renewing the mind and behavioral change.

The Greek word translated "set their minds" in Romans 8:5 (see also Col. 3:2) means "think, form or hold an opinion, judge, set one's mind on, be intent on, be minded or disposed" (Arndt and Gingrich). It includes the thinking, the will, and even the emotions (Godet; Hodge). Cranfield says it also includes one's outlook, assumptions, values, desires, and purposes (Cranfield, p. 286). Murray says it is to have something as the absorbing object of thought, interest, affection, and purpose, including "not simply the activities of reason, but also those of feeling and will" (Murray, p. 285).

The Greek word rendered "mind" in Romans 12:2 and Ephesians 4:23 means "the understanding, the mind" as a faculty of thinking, the part of man which initiates his thought and plans, "attitude, way of thinking" and the result of thinking as in "thought, opinion" (Arndt and Gingrich). It means "mind, thought, purpose" (Abbott-Smith).

Thus, the biblical concept of renewing the mind is more than having information in the brain, thinking differently about something, or even changing beliefs. It involves emotions, will, values, attitudes, opinions, intentions, and purpose. Along with the "belief" are an attitude, emotion, intention, and purpose. A renewal of all that is within a person is involved in behavioral change.

In cognitive therapy, emotions are cognitively caused and hence incidental. The attitude is, "Get your thoughts and actions straight, and your emotions will fall in line." Emotions are often treated as an add-on, a nuisance that can be controlled, modified, or explained. This is a demeaning view of emotions. Granted, cognition can produce emotion in some cases, but not all emotions are caused by cognition. Furthermore, emotions are a human capacity that enriches life (see Jones and Butman, p. 212).

Cognitive therapy gives some attention to the interpersonal environment but does so impersonally. Other people are seen as "stimuli" in an environment. They are resources of reinforcement, punishment, or modeling. "The more human and 'warm' concepts such as love, wisdom, and compassion are missing" (see Jones and Butman, p. 215). Thus, cognitive therapy underestimates the critical part relationships play in growth.

Cognitive therapy undermines the indispensable need for the direct experience of God's grace. Pecheur concedes that the major difference between Christian sanctification and cognitive therapy is God's active participation in the process of sanctification (see Jones and Butman, p. 212).

Theory of Pathology While it is true that people with problems usually have distorted thinking (Jer. 17:9), to say that distorted thinking is the basic cause of problems is reductionism. Ultimately, problems are not just cognitive; they are volitional and relational.

Nature of Health This school of thought focuses on specific pathologies and does not have a well-defined view of health other than solving the immediate issue, such as depression or a phobia. There is no grand postulate about the ideal. Nevertheless, cognitive-behavioral therapists often emphasize competence. A healthy person is a competent person. Competent is defined as "effective" at accomplishing a specific task or getting what one wants (Jones and Butman, p. 215).

Healthy individuals are competent, at least to some degree, but that needs to be delineated in more areas than the one or two areas where a person may have a "problem." Healthy individuals are more, much more than just competent. Cognitive-behavioral therapy has been characterized as "amoral," meaning the tendency is to go along with the individual's definition of abnormality (Jones and Butman, p. 219). Amorality is problematic. Jones and Butman cite an example of a therapist who taught an adulterous woman to tolerate sex with her husband, whom she did not love. To tolerate sex with an unloved husband might have "solved" the "problem" she thought she had, but that "solution" would not be tolerated by many wives, not to mention the husband's view of her intolerable adultery (Jones and Butman, p. 220).

Method of Therapy "Cognitive therapy aims to correct faulty information processing and to help patients modify assumptions that maintain maladaptive behaviors and emotions" (Beck and Weishaar, p. 299). Therapy aims to eradicate pathological reactions, which come from beliefs and cognitions (Jones and Butman, p. 213).

Cognitive and behavioral methods are used to challenge dysfunctional beliefs and promote more realistic adaptive thinking. The cognitive therapist does not tell the client that the beliefs are irrational (RET) or wrong or that the therapist's beliefs should be adopted. "Instead, the therapist asks questions to elicit the meaning, function, usefulness, and consequences of the patient's beliefs. The patient ultimately decides whether to reject, modify, or maintain all personal beliefs, being well aware of their emotional and behavioral consequences (Beck and Weishaar, p. 299).

It has been suggested that there are three major types of cognitive-behavioral therapy interventions: 1) cognitive restructuring, where the focus is on the direct form of modification of maladaptive thought patterns, 2) coping skills training, where clients are assisted in developing cognitive and behavioral skills for dealing with challenging situations, 3) problem-solving training, where clients expand their general capacity for understanding and facing challenging problems (Jones and Butman, p. 207).

Distorted thining and maladaptive thinking be addressed, but focusing on these, believing that the emotions will follow, is to ignore the emotional element in therapy. In some situations, emotional issues need to be addressed directly.

Summary: Cognitive therapy teaches that there is no single cause of pathology, but cognitive distortions are evident during psychological distress. (Distorted thinking causes an emotional disturbance.) By asking questions to elicit the meaning, function, usefulness, and consequences of a client's beliefs, he or she can ultimately decide whether to reject, modify, or maintain those beliefs, being aware of their emotional and behavioral consequences.

From a biblical perspective, cognitive therapy is inadequate because it is atheistic and naturalistic. Its view of people, pathology, and help are oversimplifications of the complexity of human problems.

Nevertheless, several of the cognitive therapy thoughts are accurate and workable.

1. People, especially those who are "disturbed," have distorted thinking. (Actually, all have "blind spots.") Cognitive therapy's description of distorted thinking is broader and more flexible than the irrational thinking of RET.
2. Beliefs are a critical part of problems (Rom. 12:2).
3. Self-talk is appropriate (Ps. 42:5).
4. It is appropriate to address behavior directly. The Bible does!

Chapter 11

REALITY THERAPY

Reality therapy was developed by William Glasser (1925-2013). According to Glasser, he developed reality therapy based on practical experience, common sense, some basic ideas from the cognitive neurosciences, and perceptual psychology, along with some indirect influence from existential thought through his mentor, G. L. Harrington. He acknowledges broad similarities to Adlerian Psychology and rational-emotive therapy, but he says these systems did not have any formative impact on his thinking. Others, however, have suggested that Adler's model is a direct ancestor to reality therapy (Jones and Butman, p. 243). In his obituary, the *Los Angeles Times* said, "Glasser's interest in psychology stems from an eagerness to deal with his own intensely shy nature" (*Los Angeles Times*, 8/28/2013, p. A5).

Reality therapy has not had much impact on the professional psychotherapeutic community at large. It has, however, been very popular among teachers, youth guidance counselors, substance-abuse treatment counselors, and rehabilitation counselors. It has been suggested that it is not more widely practiced because Glasser maintained such tight control over all "certified" reality therapy training (Jones and Butman, p. 243).

Background

Glasser became a chemical engineer at 19 and a physician at 28. In 1953, he finished medical school at Case Western Reserve University. He took his psychiatric training at the Veterans Administration Center in West Los Angeles, did his final year at UCLA (1957), and was board-certified in 1961 (Corey, p. 370).

During his training, Glasser was taught to follow the Freudian model, but it did not seem to him that it worked. He felt that rather than the therapist being aloof and detached, a close and warm involvement backed by personal interest and some self-revelation by the therapist seemed necessary for a good outcome.

Also, rather than being victims of their own impulses or victims of those around them, clients seemed to choose what they did with their lives. He was reluctant to express his dissatisfaction with psychoanalytic therapy until he met a sympathetic faculty supervisor named G. L. Harrington, to whom he gives full credit for many contributions to the ideas he formed (Corey, p. 370).

In 1956, Glasser became a counseling psychiatrist at the Ventura School for Girls, a California State facility for delinquent adolescents. This experience further convinced him of the futility of classical psychoanalytic concepts and techniques. He began to develop and experiment with different therapeutic approaches (Corey, p. 370).

In 1961, Glasser published his first book, *Mental Health or Mental Illness*, which laid the foundation for reality therapy. His book *Reality Therapy* (1965) contains his fundamental beliefs that all are responsible for what they choose to do and that in a warm, accepting, non-punitive therapeutic environment, people are willing to learn choices that are more effective or ways that are more responsible (Corey, p. 370). Other books followed, including *Control Theory* (1985), *The Quality School* (1990), and *Choice Theory: A New Psychology of Personal Freedom* (1998). The name "Control Theory" was changed to "Choice Theory."

The Theory

View of People Glasser does not have a formal theory of personality (Jones and Butman, p. 244). He does not reduce a person to interacting parts. He views people holistically. Humans are teleological and phenomenological beings who work to meet their needs as they perceive them. People are responsible for their choices (Jones and Butman, p. 245). Glasser works within a framework he calls "control theory" (later called "choice theory") of how the brain functions. Choice theory is the concept that all organisms and people act to control their environment to achieve survival and meet other needs. The assumption is that we create an inner world that satisfies our needs. What Glasser says about the makeup of personality can be summarized as follows.

1. Needs. In his book *Reality Therapy*, Glasser said that all humans have two basic psychological needs: "the need to love and be loved and the need to feel that we are worthwhile to ourselves and others" (Glasser, *Reality Therapy*, p. 9). The first is established in relationships and the second through achievement. "Although the two needs are separate, a person who loves and is loved will usually feel that he is a

worthwhile person, and one who is worthwhile is usually someone who is loved and who can give love in return" (Glasser, *Reality Therapy*, p. 10). People "vary remarkably in their ability to fulfill" these needs (Glasser, *Reality Therapy*, p. 9).

In *Control Theory* (1985), Glasser expanded the list of needs to four: 1) belonging (to love and be loved), 2) power (to define and establish one's sense of personal worth, power, and purpose, which is strikingly parallel to Adler), 3) freedom, and 4) fun (Corey, p. 372; Jones and Butman, p. 244).

In *Choice Theory* (1998), Glasser wrote that humans have five basic needs: survival and the four psychological needs of love and belonging, power, freedom, and fun (Glasser, *Choice Theory*, pp. 25-43). In other words, he added the need for survival.

1. Personality. The way we usually relate to others, best called our personalities, is, in part, written into our genes. What gives us our different personalities is that our five basic, or genetic, needs differ in strength. Some of us have a high need for love and belonging. Others have a high need for power and freedom. "The strength of each need is fixed at birth and does not change" (Glasser, *Choice Theory*, p. 91).

2. Quality World. The quality world consists of mental pictures, which fall into three categories: 1) The people we most want to be with, 2) the things we most want to own or experience, and 3) the ideas and systems of belief that govern much of our behavior. People want to feel as good as possible. Therefore, they choose to put particular pictures in their personal world of the people, things, and beliefs that make them feel much better than they do with other people, things, and beliefs (Glasser, *Choice Theory*, p. 45).

Glasser puts it like this: "If I want a lot of power, I may put politics into my quality world. If survival is all I want, I may make Ebenezer Scrooge my role model. If freedom dominates the pictures in my quality world, I may buy a small sailboat and blissfully sail the sea alone. If I want a lot more sex, I may ignore my mate and look for a sexier partner who matches the one I picture in my quality world." "As we attempt to satisfy our needs, we are continually creating and recreating our quality worlds" (Glasser, *Choice Theory*, p. 48).

Happiness is feeling good in a relationship. Happy people have at least one person in their quality world (Glasser, *Choice Theory*, p. 49).

3. Total Behavior. Behavior consists of four inseparable components: activity (walking, talking, eating), thinking, feeling, and physiology (the heart pumping blood, the lungs breathing, and neurochemistry associated with the functioning of our

brain). All four components work simultaneously. Thus, the concept of "total behavior." Behavior always consists of four components: acting, thinking, feeling, and physiology associated with all our actions, thoughts, and feelings (Glasser, *Choice Theory,* p. 72). Total behavior is labeled by its most obvious component. A person walking down the street is described as walking. Yet that person is also thinking and feeling and has a beating heart (Glasser, *Choice Theory,* p. 76).

People do not have direct control over the way they feel in the way that they have direct control over the way they act and think, but because all four components of behavior are inseparable, they have a lot of indirect control, not only over how they feel but even over a great deal of their physiology (Glasser, *Choice Theory,* p. 73). "All our feelings, both pleasurable and painful, are indirectly chosen. But an indirect choice is still a choice" (Glasser, *Choice Theory,* p. 72).

In his workshops, Glasser explained his concept of "total behavior" by comparing how we function to how a car functions. Just as the four wheels guide a car, so do the four components of our total behavior determine our direction in life. It is impossible to choose a total behavior and not choose all its components. Glasser emphasized the "two front wheels" (doing and thinking), which steer us, just as the front wheels of a car steer its direction. It is difficult to directly change how we feel separately from what we are doing or thinking. We have, however, an almost complete ability to change what we are doing and thinking despite how we might be feeling. Therefore, the key to changing a total behavior lies in choosing to change what we do and think, thus changing our emotional and physiological reactions.

4. Responsibility. The definition of "responsibility" is "the ability to fulfill one's needs and to do so in a way that does not deprive others of the ability to fulfill their needs" (Glasser, *Reality Therapy,* p. 13).

5. Creativity. When we want good relationships and are not able to get them, we create totally self-destructive behaviors. Depressing is the most common, but there are also anxieting, headaching, back aching, etc. (Glasser, *Choice Theory,* pp. 136-137).

The Development of People Choice theory challenges the deterministic philosophy of human nature. Although external forces influence our decisions, our behavior is not caused by these environmental factors. People are not "naturally endowed with the ability to fulfill" these needs; this ability is learned (Glasser, *Reality Therapy,* p. 14). Glasser writes, "Children ordinarily learn by means of a loving relationship with responsible parents, an involvement which implies parental teaching and parental example. Also, responsibility is taught by responsible relatives, teachers, ministers, and friends with whom they become involved. The responsible parent creates the necessary involvement with his child and teaches him responsibility through the proper combination of love and discipline" (Glasser, *Reality Therapy*, p. 16).

In most cases, the first person people put into their quality world is their mother. By the time infants are six months old, they are well aware that feeling good is highly related to their quality world picture of their mother. As infants learn to help themselves, they begin to put strong pictures of themselves in their own quality world. They are now planting the first seeds of personal freedom. Around the age of two, babies begin to be driven by a new discomfort; they want power. The ultimate goal of power is to get rid of every discomfort. No one, of course, achieves it, though some babies come pretty close, at least, for a while. Babies say to themselves, "Why not find out how much I can get others to do for me?"

Between the ages of two and four, toddlers discover there is a limit and begin modifying the pictures of their parents doing everything for them. "Preschoolers begin to learn that wanting things that depend on others who don't want, or can't give them, what they want is just too painful; it isn't worth it. As children begin school, they learn that external control is a two-way street and most of the traffic is coming the other way. When the sex hormones start to flow freely, the power struggle between parent and child escalates." Glasser's advice is, "Pay close attention to what they do but little attention to what they say" (see Glasser, *Choice Theory*, pp. 56-61).

Human behavior is purposeful and originates from within rather than from external forces. We are completely motivated internally and all of our behaviors are attempts to get what we want and, in doing so, form effective control of our lives (Corey, pp. 372-73).

To be more specific, Glasser suggests that our brain systems compare their pictures of our needs with their pictures of available behavioral responses and, thus, choose ways of dealing with perceived reality. In other words, we choose the world we want (that is, goals) and then choose the behavior that is our attempt to move the real world closer to the in-the-head quality world we want. Actions, thoughts, and even emotions are actively chosen ways of responding to the perceived world and, therefore, we are responsible for all aspects of our personal reality. Even destructive emotions are chosen behaviors. Thus, Glasser never says someone is depressed, which is a passive description, but they are depressing (as in "depressing themselves as a way of control").

Theory of Pathology Psychopathology is ineffective behaviors, that is, poor attempts to meet needs. Depression, schizophrenia, and all other problems are unsuccessful or marginally successful attempts to control one's environment to meet needs.

People have problems because they are unable to fulfill their essential needs. "The severity of the symptom reflects the degree to which the individual is unable to fulfill his needs" (Glasser, *Reality Therapy*, p. 5).

Also, all people who have problems "deny reality." "Denial of some or all of reality is common to all patients" (Glasser, *Reality Therapy*, p. 6). A neurotic is afraid of reality and a psychotic denies reality (Glasser, *Reality Therapy*, p. 49).

All problems are caused by choosing to meet one's needs in an unrealistic way. The ever-present problem is irresponsibility (Glasser, *RT*, p. 49).

According to Glasser, happiness and pleasure are the two forms of feeling good. Happiness is feeling good in a relationship. Happy people have at least one person in their quality world. Unhappy people keep trying to satisfy a picture of themselves and someone being close. A lot of people, however, have not found somebody they trust and enjoy being with; they have been rejected and abused. As a result, they give up on happiness. To feel good, they began to replace people pictures with non-people pleasure pictures—pictures of violence, drugs, and unloving sex. As they do so, they separate themselves further from people and happiness (Glasser, *Choice Theory*, p. 49). In other words, people replace happiness with pleasure (Glasser, *Choice Theory*, p. 50).

Depression is something people choose to do. They choose the misery that they feel. Glasser changes the adjective *depressed* to the verb *to depress* (Glasser, *Choice Theory*, p. 63). There are three logical reasons why people choose to depress: angering, asking for help without begging, and avoidance (Glasser, *Choice Theory*, pp. 79-88). These reasons explain the whole gamut of what is commonly called mental illness. Even sickness may be explained by the same three reasons. "The *psycho* of *psychosomatic* means that the way we are thinking may have a lot to do with what is going on in the *soma*, our bodies" (Glasser, *Choice Theory*, p. 79).

Needs → quality world (my happy world) → choice → ineffective behaviors

Nature of Health Psychological health is scantily defined as the result of responsibly and effectively meeting one's needs. When we meet our needs in a responsible way, we develop an identity characterized by success and self-esteem and the behaviors we use to meet them feel good. If people act responsibly and in accord with reality, they can meet all of their basic needs to some degree (Jones and Butman, p. 245).

Over the years, Glasser's concepts have been refined. To sum up, according to the website of the William Glasser Institute (www.wglasser.com, accessed March 2003), reality therapy says that since unsatisfactory or non-existent connections with people we need are the source of almost all human problems, the goal of reality therapy is to help people reconnect. This reconnection almost always starts with the counselor/teacher first connecting with the individual and then using this connection as a model for how the disconnected person can begin to connect with the people he or she needs. To create the relationship vital to reality therapy, the counselor, teacher, or manager will:

- Focus on the present and avoid discussing the past because present unsatisfying relationships cause all human problems.
- Avoid discussing symptoms and complaints as much as possible since these are how counselees deal with unsatisfying relationships.
- Understand the concept of total behavior, which means focusing on what counselees can do, directly act and think. Spend less time on what they cannot do directly: change their feelings and physiology. Feelings and physiology can be changed, but only if there is a change in acting and thinking.
- Avoid criticizing, blaming, and/or complaining, and help counselees to do the same. By doing this, they learn to avoid these extremely harmful *external control* behaviors that destroy relationships.
- Remain non-judgmental and non-coercive, but encourage people to judge all they are doing by the Choice Theory axiom: *Is what I am doing getting me closer to the people I need?* If the choice of behaviors is not getting people closer, the counselor works to help them find new behaviors that lead to a better connection.
- Teach counselees that, legitimate or not, excuses stand directly in the way of making needed connections.
- Focus on specifics. Find out who counselees are disconnected from as soon as possible and work to help them choose reconnecting behaviors. If they are completely disconnected, focus on helping them find a new connection.
- Help them make specific, workable plans to reconnect with the people they

need and follow through on what was planned by helping them evaluate their progress. Based on their experience, counselors may suggest plans but should not give the message that there is only one plan. A plan is always open to revision or rejection by the counselee.
- Be patient and supportive, but keep focusing on the source of the problem: disconnectedness. Counselees who have been disconnected for a long time will find it difficult to reconnect. They are often so involved in the symptoms they are choosing that they have lost sight of the need to reconnect. Help them understand by teaching choice theory and encouraging them to read the book *Choice Theory: A New Psychology of Personal Freedom*. Whatever their complaint, reconnecting is the best possible solution to their problem.

Method of Therapy In his book *Reality Therapy*, Glasser teaches that for people to learn how to meet their needs in a realistic way, they "must be involved with other people." "Therefore, essential to the fulfillment of our needs is a person, preferably a group of people, with whom we are emotionally involved *from the time we are born to the time we die*" (Glasser, *Reality Therapy*, p. 8, italics his). The person (or people) with whom we are involved "must be in touch with reality" (Glasser, *Reality Therapy*, p. 7). Therapy is guiding irresponsible people toward more responsibility (Glasser, *Reality Therapy*, p. 20).

Glasser says that reality therapy is made up of three separate but intimately interwoven procedures. First, is involvement. "The therapist must become so involved with the patient that the patient begins to face reality and see how his behavior is unrealistic" (Glasser, *Reality Therapy*, p. 21). Second, the therapist must reject the unrealistic behavior while still accepting the patient and maintaining his involvement with him. Third, depending upon the patient, in varying degrees, "the therapist must teach the patient better ways to fulfill his needs within the confines of reality" (Glasser, *Reality Therapy*, p. 21).

Glasser says, "All we can do that has any chance of succeeding is to build relationships with them and get into their quality worlds" (Glasser, *Choice Theory*, p. 50).

In an article in the 3rd edition of *Current Psychotherapies*, Glasser listed the eight major steps in conducting reality therapy.

1. Make friends and ask clients what they want.

2. Ask, "What are you doing now?"
3. The therapist helps the client realize that what he or she is currently doing is ineffectual. ("Is what clients choose to do getting them what they want?")
4. Make a plan to do better.
5. Get a commitment to follow the plan worked out in step number 4. (Those with failure identities are particularly reluctant to commit to change.)
6. No excuses. (Excuses are always part of the ineffectual patterns of the past. Reality therapists are interested in the future.)
7. No punishment. (Punishment usually involves another person controlling the client's life. The only possible punishments available to a therapist are temporary and naturally and logically tied to an infraction.)
8. Never give up. (To give up is to be controlled by the client's ineffectual behavior; see Jones and Butman, pp. 246-47.)

Though the principles are applied progressively, they should not be thought of as discrete and rigid categories. It is more than following procedures in a step-by-step or cookbook fashion. The process takes skill and creativity (Corey, p. 378).

In *Choice Theory*, Glasser illustrates a counseling session, using Francisca from James Waller's *The Bridge of Madison County* as the counselee (Glasser, *Choice Theory*, pp. 118-133). Francisca is a woman from Italy who marries an Iowa farmer. While her husband and children are away, she has a four-day affair with a stranger named Robert. After Robert leaves, she is seriously depressed, which is why she comes to see a counselor. The counselor asks her to tell him her story, assuring her that he will not judge her. The counselor observes that she has an internal conflict between loyalty and love. The counselor stays strictly with her present problem, not talking about her unhappy life with her husband or the life she could have had with Robert. In talking with her, the counselor tries to figure out ways she can see some hope, showing her she has some satisfying choices even in this painful situation. He tries to find something she wants now, something she has control over and something that depends on her and that no one else can take away from her. In his opinion, this is the way to live through a conflict, that is, not focusing on the conflict, but focusing on something possible that isn't part of a conflict that will give her hope. According to the counselor, teaching counselees that life is not fair is also critical.

In the summer of 2003, my wife, Patricia, and I took the "Basic Intensive Week" of training from Carlene Glasser, William Glasser's wife, in their home in West Los

Angeles. On the last day of the class, we had the opportunity to spend time with Glasser. One of the things he did with the class was role-playing with several different counseling situations. My wife and I were guinea pigs for marriage counseling. Both of us adopted the role of a couple we had counseled. As counselees, we tried to explain our opinions of our marriage problems to Glasser, the counselor. Instead of delving into the problems we thought we had, Glasser insisted that each of us tell him one thing we could do to improve our marriage in the next week. In other words, he emphasized our responsibility.

Evaluation

Philosophical Assumptions Here are some of the philosophical assumptions of reality therapy.

1. Atheistic. Perhaps it would be more accurate to say, "There is no concept of transcendent reality built into reality therapy" (Jones and Butman, p. 249). It is not that reality therapy is actively atheistic. It does not address the issue. The result is that reality therapy does not take ultimate reality into consideration and, therefore, in that sense, reality therapy is not entirely dealing with reality!

2. Relativistic. Adler's concept of lifestyle and Glasser's idea of internal pictures are inherently relativistic because, according to both, all we can ever know are these internally constructed fictions (Jones and Butman, pp. 248-49).

3. Optimistic. Human beings are not passively determined responders but actors pursuing desired ends. Glasser rejects determinism (Jones and Butman, p. 245). People can change.

View of People Humans have a need for love, purpose, freedom, and fun. Belonging and purpose, or worth, are central needs.

Humans have capacities for doing, thinking, feeling, and physical activity, but they also have spiritual capacities.

Humans are responsible but more responsible than even reality therapy acknowledges. According to reality therapy, we are to do what is loving and what satisfies our needs as long as we do not interfere with the needs of others. This is a human-centered system of morality that is an inadequate guide. It is a law without a lawgiver, a law where right is judged primarily in terms of how actions impact human needs and not in the relations of those actions to God's will. Moreover, obedience to human law and even divine law is not sufficient for the fulfillment of our intended humanness. Glasser's system is all law and no grace (Jones and Butman, p. 249).

Theory of Pathology In a sense, all problems are in the present, but insight into the extent of the influence of the past helps deal with problems in the present.

Ineffective behaviors and irresponsibility are factors in many problems, but not all problems are the result of irresponsibility. Just emphasizing responsible behavior in the present is sometimes a dead-end street (Jones and Butman, p. 250).

Nature of Health Reality therapy does not define the normative traits of the healthy person (Jones and Butman, p. 245). The assumption is that if a person acts responsibly and in accord with reality, they will be able to meet all of their basic needs, at least to some degree. This enables them to achieve survival and thereby experience a modicum of a sense of belonging, self-worth, fun, and freedom.

Healthy individuals act responsibly, but health is more than acting responsibly.

A healthy individual is not only independent but also dependent and interdependent.

Method of Therapy While the cognitive dimensions of reality therapy are similar to those of Adler, they are underdeveloped as compared to Adler (Jones and Butman, p. 248).

Dealing with the cognitive and behavioral aspects is a balance, but it is also superficial in that it does not view individuals as having a necessary conflict built into their very being (Jones and Butman, p. 240).

Summary: Based on personal perception, people's attempts to meet their needs produce ineffective behaviors. Individuals must act responsibly and effectively according to reality to meet their needs in ways that do not interfere with others fulfilling them. Responsible people are autonomous because they know what they want from life and make plans to meet their needs and goals. In short, responsibility means that people have learned to take effective control of their lives (see Corey, p. 375).

From a biblical perspective, reality therapy is insufficient because it is atheistic and relativistic.

There are correct concepts in it.

1. Humans are indeed creatures with needs who are trying to get those needs met (Jas. 4:1; Phil. 4:11-12).
2. Humans have personal perceptions that affect their behavior (Rom. 12:2).

3. Humans are responsible for their choices and should control themselves (see "self-control" in Gal. 5:23).
4. To help people become more responsible, someone must become involved with them (1 Thess. 5:14).

Chapter 12

MULTIMODAL THERAPY

Multimodal therapy was formulated by Arnold A. Lazarus (1932-2013). Arnold Lazarus was the first person to introduce the terms "behavior therapy" and "behavior therapist" into the professional literature (see Lazarus, A. A. "New Methods in Psychotherapy: a Case Study." *South African Medical Journal*, 1958, 32, pp. 660-664).

Background

Lazarus was born and educated in Johannesburg, South Africa. At an early age, he felt that racism and discrimination were totally unacceptable. He received a master's degree in experimental psychology (1957), a Ph.D. in clinical psychology (1960), and entered private practice in Johannesburg.

In 1963, Lazarus was invited by Albert Bandura to teach at Stanford University. After one year, he returned to private practice in Johannesburg because he was "extremely homesick." In 1966, he returned to California to head the Behavior Therapy Institute. In 1967, he was appointed a full professor at Temple University Medical School in Philadelphia, where he worked with Dr. Joseph Wolpe, his mentor. They parted company when Lazarus criticized Wolpe for being too rigid and narrow. In 1970, Lazarus went to Yale University as Director of Clinical Training and in 1972, he became a Distinguished Professor at Rutgers University. After that, he taught in the Graduate School of Applied and Professional Psychology and conducted a private practice in Princeton, New Jersey. He wrote eighteen books and hundreds of articles.

While still getting his education, Lazarus became a "neo-behaviorist" (Lazarus, p. 511). In 1965, he wrote a paper on the need to treat alcoholism from a multi-dimensional perspective. Later, he published *Broad-spectrum Behavior Therapy and the Treatment of Agoraphobia* (1966). In other words, early in his career, he demonstrated a penchant for broad-based or comprehensive psychotherapeutic procedures (see his article in Corsini and Wedding, pp. 512-513 for an excellent explanation of his evolution).

His first presentation of multimodal therapy as a distinctive orientation was in 1973. His first book on multimodal procedures, which had eleven contributors, was published in 1976.

The Theory

View of People According to Lazarus, "We are products of the interplay among our genetic endowment, our physical environment, and our social learning history" (Lazarus, p. 514). The closest Lazarus comes to a theory of personality is to postulate the premise that human beings are complex creatures that can be divided into seven areas of functioning. This concept is the "essence" of the multimodal approach (Corey, p. 309).

As Lazarus explains, "In the final analysis, we are biochemical-neurophysiological entities. Human life and conduct are products of ongoing behaviors, affective processes, sensations, images, cognitions, interpersonal relationships, and biological functions" (Lazarus, p. 504). The first letter of each of these "modalities" spells BASIC IB," but in Lazarus' view, the final "B" refers to "drugs/biology" because one of the most common biological interventions is the use of psychotropic medication. Therefore, he changed BASIC IB to BASIC ID or the preferred Basic I.D. (I.D. as in "identity"). "D" stands not only for drugs, medication, or pharmacological intervention but also includes nutrition, hygiene, exercise, and all basic physiological and pathological inputs (Lazarus, p. 504). The seven major areas of functioning are (Jones and Butman, pp. 309-10):

1. Behavior. This modality refers primarily to overt behaviors, including acts, habits, and reactions that are observable and measurable.
2. Affect. This refers to emotions, moods, and strong feelings.
3. Sensation. This area refers to the five senses.
4. Imagery. This pertains to how we picture ourselves and includes memories and dreams.
5. Cognition. This function refers to insights, philosophies, ideas, and judgments that constitute one's fundamental values, attitudes, and beliefs.
6. Interpersonal relationships. This, of course, refers to interactions with other people.

7. Drug/biology. This includes more than drugs. It takes into consideration one's nutritional habits and exercise patterns.

To sum up, an individual's complex personality can be divided into seven areas of functioning: behavior (B), affective responses (A), sensations (S), images (I), Cognition (C), interpersonal relationships (I), drugs, biological functions, nutrition, and exercise (D). Hence, BASIC ID. These modalities are interactive, yet they can be considered discrete functions.

Lazarus says, "The BASIC ID is presumed to comprise human temperament and personality, and it is assumed that everything from anger, disappointment, disgust, greed, fear, grief, awe, contempt, and boredom to love, hope, faith, ecstasy, optimism, and joy can be accounted for by examining components and interactions within a person's BASIC ID" (Lazarus, p. 504).

At the same time, Lazarus states it is "essential to recognize and include factors that fall outside the BASIC ID, such as socio-cultural, political, and other macro-environmental events. While external realities are not part of temperament and personality, 'psychopathology and society are inextricably bound together'" (Lazarus, p. 504). For example, he discusses association, modeling, and vicarious processes. He says, "People are capable of overriding the best-laid plans of contiguity, reinforcement, an example by their idiosyncratic perceptions. People do not respond to some real environment, but rather to their perceived environment" (Lazarus, p. 517).

The Development of People According to Lazarus, people are products of the interplay of their genetic environment, physical environment, and social learning history (Lazarus, p. 514).

Theory of Pathology Lazarus says that pathology has no single cause. Genetics can have a role. Learning is a major factor. As Lazarus explains, "The main learning factors are our conditioned associations (respondent and operant responses) and the models with whom we identified and whom we imitated deliberately or inadvertently. During these inputs, we may have acquired conflicting information, faulty cognitions, and a variety of inhibitions and needless defenses. Emotional problems and disorders also arise from inadequate or insufficient (as opposed to faulty) learning. Here, the problems do not arise from conflicts, traumatic events, impositions from significant others, or false ideas. Rather, gaps in people's repertories—they were never given the necessary information and essential coping processes—render them ill-equipped to deal with social demands" (Lazarus, p. 517).

Insufficient learning → emotional problems and disorders

The Nature of Health Multimodal therapy does not propose an idealized model for humans. At best, it seems to be saying that the healthy person is the untroubled, functioning individual. To a great degree, what that means is left up to the client. Like its father behaviorism, multimodal therapy lacks a definitive description of psychological health.

Method of Therapy According to multimodal therapy, it differs from other systems where the presenting problems are clustered into "ill-defined" constructs and one or two procedures are directed at them. In multimodal therapy, the emphasis is on the uniqueness of each individual. Hence, there is no typical treatment format. A basic premise is that patients are usually troubled by a multitude of specific problems and that these problems should be dealt with by a multitude of specific treatments (Lazarus, p. 503). For example, in discussing existential psychotherapy, May and Yalom say that Lazarus uses some existential presuppositions (May and Yalom, p. 375).

Multimodal therapists practice "technical eclecticism." They borrow techniques from other therapy systems. Most of the techniques listed by Lazarus are standard behavioral procedures, but these techniques are never used in a shotgun manner. Multimodal therapists ask, "What works, for whom, and under what conditions?" (Corey, p. 308).

So, multimodal therapy insists that a multitude of treatments should deal with problems. The basic assumption of therapy is that the durability of results is a function of the amount of effort the client and therapist expend across the seven dimensions of personality (BASIC ID). Multimodal therapists constantly adjust their procedures to achieve the client's goals effectively.

Two specific procedures seem to enhance treatment effects, namely bridging and tracking. Bridging is the procedure in which the therapist deliberately tunes into the client's preferred modality before branching off into other dimensions that seem likely to be more productive. Tracking is the firing order of the different elements in BASIC ID (Lazarus, pp. 505-507).

Here is a case study written by Lazarus himself (Lazarus, pp. 534-538). A 33-year-old woman came to a counselor with the fear of becoming pregnant and with several somatic symptoms, including headaches, chest pains, and gastrointestinal distress. A medical exam indicated no organic pathology. When her husband became very successful in his work over the previous three years, he strongly desired children. That is when she realized that pregnancy and childbirth terrified her.

She had gone to a psychologist, who explored her relationship with her mother, father, brother, and general home atmosphere. She found all of that interesting but not necessarily effective. She then went to a behavior therapist who attempted unsuccessfully to desensitize her to the fear of pregnancy. Then, she decided to try multimodal therapy.

The multimodal therapist had her fill out a life history questionnaire, which revealed aspects of her behavior (excessive smoking), affects (anger, resentment, fear), sensation (physical pains), imagery (failing), cognition (perfectionist), interpersonal, (passive-aggressive tactics), and drugs data (for menstrual dysfunction). The profile was discussed in the second session. It became immediately clear to the counselor that the modality (BASIC ID) firing order almost invariably followed that SICA sequence (sensation-imagery-cognition-affect). Based on her firing order, the following treatments were given: 1) biofeedback. 2) associated imagery. She was asked to relax, close her eyes, and picture her grandmother's heart attack. Then, she was to focus on other images that emerged. She was told to imagine going forward in the time remaining free from organic disease until she reached her late seventies. 3) positive statement implementation. Then, she carried out the deserted island fantasy, which indicated that she felt let down by her husband. At that point, therapy focused on assertive training.

After eight sessions, she showed gains across the BASIC I.D. For example, she stopped smoking, expressed her feelings more openly, was more relaxed, etc. At the start of the ninth session, she requested that they go for a walk instead of talking in the office, which the therapist agreed to do since he had no fixed rules. The client revealed she had been having an affair for the past year and a half. She was to practice imagery, exercises, and other homework assignments between sessions. For a month, she was making progress. Then, she began having palpitations, chest pains, and tension headaches. She admitted to having stopped using the relaxation cassettes, the time projection images, the cognitive self-statements, and other techniques. She agreed to go back on the techniques and there were no further setbacks. The sessions were discontinued by mutual consent after eight months. The client casually mentioned that she had terminated the affair. About four weeks after therapy had ended, the client called to say she felt that she was pregnant and felt "very pleased" about it.

(Was the affair not her problem?)

Evaluation

Philosophical Assumptions Multimodal therapy, too, has philosophical assumptions.

1. Atheistic. It is based on and is a branch of behaviorism. Lazarus says, "Multimodal therapy rests primarily on the theoretical base of social learning theory" (Lazarus, p. 504) and Corey uses Arnold Lazarus as the lead figure of behavior therapy. Granted, Lazarus goes beyond strict behaviorism, but not in this area.

2. Naturalistic. Both behaviorism proper and multimodal therapy are built on naturalism, which has no room for anything supernatural in theory or technique.

3. Moderately deterministic. Multimodal therapy is more moderately deterministic than behaviorism. Although, on the one hand, Lazarus says that we are products of the interplay between our genetic endowment, our physical environment, and our social learning theory, at the same time, he acknowledges that we "deliberately" imitate models. He also says, "People are capable of 'overriding' the best-laid plans of contiguity, reinforcements, an example by their idiosyncratic perceptions" (Lazarus, p. 517).

View of People Multimodal therapy has taken more facets of the human personality into systematic consideration than most approaches, yet it still omits any spiritual function. Multimodal therapy considers behavior, mind (C and I), emotions, body (S and D), and relationships but omits choice.

Theory of Pathology While acknowledging that pathology has multiple causes, Lazarus says, "Most problems are presumed to arise from deficient or faulty social learning processes" (Lazarus, p. 519). Multimodal therapy concentrates on learning, but there is more to pathology than inadequate learning.

The Nature of Health Healthy individuals are "untroubled" and function to some degree, but those concepts need to be clearly defined. Healthy individuals are much, much more than untroubled, functioning people.

Method of Therapy Solving specific problems, even with a systematic and eclectic approach, can be superficial. Corey says it deemsphasizes feelings' role in the therapeutic process (Corey, p. 315). Finding what works, for whom and under what circumstances is indeed commendable and can resolve specific difficulties, but therapy should do more than enable individuals to perform specific functions.

Summary: While people are troubled by a multitude of specific problems, most problems arise from deficient or faulty social learning processes. These problems should be dealt with through a multitude of specific treatments, ensuring that the seven dimensions of personality are addressed.

From a biblical perspective, multimodal therapy is deficient because it is atheistic and naturalistic. Lazarus has made some modifications to behavior modification, but not enough modification.

Nevertheless, some tenets are beneficial.

1. Systematically dealing with seven dimensions of personality is a more comprehensive approach to therapy than most systems. The Scripture is more comprehensive than all psychotherapies because it views people as spiritual, social, psychological, purposeful, and physical creatures.
2. Finding what works, for whom and under what circumstances is desirable (1 Thess. 5:14).

Chapter 13

EXISTENTIAL THERAPY

Existential therapy is not a separate school of therapy or a neatly defined model with specific techniques. It is more of an intellectual approach to therapeutic practice, or philosophy therapists follow (Corey, p. 174). According to a survey some years ago, only 4% of the psychotherapists in America endorsed existentialism as their primary orientation, but this approach has greatly impacted many others (Jones and Butman p. 278).

It has been defined as an approach to therapy that "focuses on concerns that are rooted in an individual's existence" (Yalom, cited Jones and Butman, p. 278). Rollo May is considered one of the main proponents of humanistic approaches to psychotherapy (Corey, p. 173); he is the psychologist most responsible for translating European existentialism into the mainstream of American psychotherapeutic theory and practice (Corey, p. 177).

Background

The existential approach arose spontaneously among a number of psychologists and psychiatrists in Europe in the 1950s. It developed as a reaction to psychoanalysis and behaviorism (Jones and Butman, p. 174). Psychoanalysis says that unconscious forces, irrational drives, and past events restrict freedom. Behaviorism states that socio-cultural conditioning restricts freedom. Existential therapy accepts the premise that external circumstances limit our choices but rejects the notion that our acts are determined. It is based on the assumption that we are free and, therefore, responsible for our choices and actions. We are always more than the victim of circumstances. We are the author or architect of our lives. Furthermore, existentialism is based on the growth model and conceptualizes health rather than sickness (Corey, p. 174).

The thinking of existential counselors has been influenced by several philosophers and writers extending back to the early 19th century. One must be aware of some of the forerunners to understand some of the philosophical underpinnings.

Soren Kierkegaard (1813-1855), the Danish philosopher, was concerned with "angst" (a Danish and German word whose meaning lies between the English words "dread" and "anxiety"). Many, especially in adolescence, are awakened into real life by a terrible uneasiness. Life is one contingency after another, with no guarantee beyond the certainty of death. This is necessary to becoming human. Becoming human is a project (Corey, p. 175).

Friedrich Nietzsche (1844-1900), a German philosopher, set out to prove that the ancient definition of humans as rational was entirely misleading. We are far more creatures of will than impersonal intelligence, but society makes us impotent by surrounding us with moral, political, and religious injections. If we release ourselves by giving free rein to our will to power, we will top our potential for creativity and originality. This is the way of the leader, the "Superman" (Corey, p. 175). Nietzsche said, "He who has a *why* to live can bear with almost any *how*" (Nietzsche, italics his, cited by Frankl, p. 12).

Martin Heidegger (1889-1976) developed phenomenology, a method of studying experience. It reminds us that we exist "in the world." The way we fill our everyday life with superficial conversation and routine shows that we assume we are going to live forever and can afford to waste day after day. We can inauthentically construct our lives around the expectations of others, or we can live authentically (Corey, p. 174).

Jean-Paul Sartre (1905-1980), the French philosopher and novelist, was convinced by his part in the French Resistance in World War II that humans are even freer than earlier existentialists had believed. The existence of a space—nothingness—between the whole of our past and the now frees us to choose what we will, but this freedom is hard to face up to, so we like to invent excuses, that is, my past conditioning. No matter what I have been, I can choose as I will and become something different (Corey, p. 176).

Early figures of the existential practice of psychiatry in Europe include Ludwig Binswanger, Medard Boss, and Viktor Frankel. They did not develop a cohesive ideological school, but they believed in common that therapists must enter the client's subjective world without presuppositions that would get in the way of this experiential understanding (Corey, pp. 176-177).

Viktor Frankl (1905-1997) is a key figure because his life illustrates his theory and his because of popularity. He was born and educated in Vienna. He received his

MD in 1930 and his Ph.D. in 1949, both from the University of Vienna. He held honorary doctorates from more than 120 universities worldwide (Corey, p. 172). He was a student of Freud and he began his career with a psychoanalytic orientation but reacted against most of Freud's deterministic notions (Corey, p. 177). Before World War II, he developed an existential approach to clinical practice. From 1942 to 1945, Frankl was a prisoner in Auschwitz and Dachau, where his parents, brother, wife, and children died (Corey, p. 172). His experience confirmed his views. His book, *Man's Search for Meaning* (1959), has been a best-seller around the world (Corey, p. 172).

Rollo May (1909-1994) grew up in an unhappy home, which had something to do with his interest in psychology. He struggled with his existential concerns and the failure of two marriages (Corey, p. 173). He studied in Vienna with Alfred Adler. In 1938, he received a Master of Divinity from Union Theological Seminary and in 1949, he received his first Ph.D. in clinical psychology from Columbia University (Corey, p. 173). His book, *Man's Search for Himself* (1953), which dealt with the meaning of existential loneliness and the anxiety that characterizes the contemporary person, distinguished him as the key American existentialist and psychoanalytic writer. He believed that psychotherapy should be aimed at helping people discern the meaning of their lives and should be concerned with the problems of being rather than with the problem of solving (Corey, p. 173). He also believed, like Adler, that our individualism should be balanced by social interest. There is too much concern about self and not enough concern about society.

Irvin D. Yalom (1931-) graduated from George Washington University in 1952 (BA) and from Boston University School of Medicine in 1956 (MD). After his internship, residency, and Army service, he began his academic career at Stanford University (1963), eventually becoming Professor of Psychiatry (1973). He retired in 1994. He authored a number of books, including *The Theory and Practice of Group Psychotherapy (1970), Existential Psychotherapy (1980), Love's Executioner (1989), The Gift of Therapy (2005), etc.* His writing on existential psychology centers on what he refers to as the four "givens" of the human condition: isolation, meaninglessness, mortality, and freedom. His book, *Existential Psychotherapy*, is considered the American textbook of the movement.

Yalom's eleven factors that influence change and healing in group therapy are: "1) The instillation of hope creates a feeling of optimism. 2) Universality helps group members realize they are not alone in their impulses, problems, and other issues. 3) Imparting information helps educate and empower people with knowledge about their specific psychological situation. 4) Altruism allows clients to gain a sense of value and significance by helping other group members. 5) Corrective recapitulation provides for the resolution of family and childhood events within the safety of the group family. 6) Socializing techniques promote social development, tolerance, empathy, and other interpersonal skills. 7) Through imitative behavior, group members learn to adopt other group members' coping strategies and perspectives. 8) Interpersonal learning teaches clients how to develop supportive interpersonal relationships. 9) Group cohesiveness gives members a sense of acceptance, belonging, value, and security. 10) Catharsis releases suppressed emotions and promotes healing by disclosing information to group members. 11) Existential factors incorporate learning to exist as part of something larger than oneself. This factor brings a client into the awareness that life will continue with pain, death, sadness, regret, and joy. By living existentially, clients learn to accept these conditions without escaping them. Instead, they learn how to live with and through them" (www.goodtherapy.org/famous-psychologists/irvin-yalom.html, accessed July 5, 2018).

Yalom says, "Our deepest wants can never be fulfilled: our wants for youth, for a halt to aging, for the return of vanished ones, for eternal love, protection, significance, for immortality itself. It is when these unattainable wants come to dominate our lives that we turn for help to family, friends, to religion—sometimes to psychotherapists." He goes on to say that the people he writes about in this book came to him "suffering the common problems of everyday life: loneliness, self-contempt, impotence, migraine headaches, sexual compulsivity, obesity, hypertension, grief, a consuming love obsession, mood swings, depression." Yet therapy "uncovered deep roots of these everyday problems—roots stretching down to the bedrock of existence." They were struggling with "existence pain" (Yalom, *Love's Executioner, hereafter LE*, p. 4).

Yalom says the primal stuff of psychotherapy is always "existence pain." His "primary clinical assumption" on which he bases his techniques "is that basic anxiety emerges from a person's endeavors, conscious and unconscious, to cope with the harsh facts of life, the 'givens' of existence" (Yalom, *LE,* pp. 4-5). The four "givens" that are "particularly relevant to psychotherapy" are: "the inevitability of death for each of us and for those we love; the freedom to make our lives as we will; our ultimate loneliness; and, finally, the absence of any obvious meaning or sense to life" (Yalom,

LE, p. 5).

As for death, "at one's core, there is an ever-present conflict between the wish to continue to exist and the awareness of inevitable death. To adapt to the reality of death, we are endlessly ingenious in devising ways to deny or escape it. When we are young, we deny death with the help of parental reassurance and secular and religious myths.... As we grow older, we learn to put death out of mind; we distract ourselves; we transform it into something positive (.... peace at last); we deny it with staining myths; we strive for immortality through imperishable works by projecting our seed into the future through our children, or by embracing a religious system that offers spiritual perpetuation" (Yalom, *LE,* pp. 5-6). Death anxiety surfaces "only rarely, sometimes only once or twice in a lifetime. Occasionally it happens during waking life, sometimes after a personal brush with death, or when a loved one has died, but more commonly, death anxiety surfaces in nightmares" (Yalom, *LE,* p. 6). [It has been suggested that people suppress the fear of death in one of three ways: 1) the biological mode, living through one's prodigy; 2) the theological mode, believing in an afterlife/reincarnation; 3) the creative mode: living through one's work (source unknown)].

"Freedom means that one is responsible for one's own choices, actions, one's own life situation.... Every therapist knows that the critical first step in therapy is the patient's assumption of responsibility for his or her life's predicament. As long as one believes that one's problems are caused by some force or agency outside oneself, there is no leverage in therapy. If, after all, the problem lies out there, then why should one change oneself? It is the outside world (friends, job, spouse) that must be changed—or exchanged" (Yalom, *LE,* pp. 8-9).... The assumption of responsibility is not synonymous with change. "Freedom not only requires us to bear responsibility for our life's choices but also posits that a change that requires an act of the will. Though *will* is not a concept therapists seldom use explicitly, we nonetheless devote much effort to influencing a patient's will" (Yalom, p. 9, italics his own). "When years of interpretation have failed to generate change, we may begin to make direct appeals to the will" (Yalom, *LE,* p. 10). Effort is needed.... "When direct exhortation fails, the therapist is reduced, as these stories bear witness, to employing any known means by which one person can influence another. Thus, I may advise, argue, badger, cajole, goad, implore, or simply endure, hoping that the patient's neurotic worldview will crumble away from sheer fatigue. It is through willing, the mainspring of action, that our freedom is enacted" (Yalom, *LE,* p. 10).

"Existential isolation" is "the unbridgeable gap between self and others, a gap that exists even in the presence of deeply gratifying interpersonal relationships" (Yalom, *LE,* p. 11). Interpersonal isolation is loneliness.

"In therapy, as in life, meaningfulness is a byproduct of engagement and commitment, and that is where therapists must direct their efforts—not that engagement provides the rational answer to questions of meaning, but it causes those questions not to matter." The existential dilemma is that a being "searches for meaning and certainty in a universe that has neither" (Yalom, *LE,* p. 13).

Since it is so popular and a good illustration of the existential approach, Viktor Frankl's book, *Man's Search for Meaning*, is briefly summarized here. In the Preface, Gordon W. Allport, a former professor of psychology at Harvard University, explains that Frankl asked his patients who suffered from multiple torments, "Why do you not commit suicide?" They spoke of love for their children, a talent that needed to be used, and even lingering memories worth preserving. Their answers provided guidelines for Frankl's psychotherapy (Frankl, p. 9).

Man's Search for Meaning is divided into three parts. The first part is entitled "Experiences in a Concentration Camp." It describes three phases of an inmate's mental reaction. The first phase is the period following admission. First, there is shock (Frankl, p. 26). Nearly everyone lives under the delusion that he will be reprieved, that everything will be well. One by one, these illusions were destroyed. Then, most are overcome by a grim sense of humor (Frankl, p. 34) and curiosity (Frankl, p. 35). Cold curiosity detaches the mind from its surroundings. Curiosity evolved into surprise (Frankl, p. 35).

The second phase is when the prisoner is well entrenched in the camp routine. It is a phase of relative apathy in which there is a kind of emotional death (Frankl, p. 39). First, there is a boundless longing for home and family followed by disgust with all the ugliness. Then, feelings are blunted and the prisoner watches unmoved (Frankl, pp. 39-40). Apathy is a necessary mechanism of self-defense (Frankl, p. 47).

Yet, despite living in a concentration camp, spiritual life can deepen (Frankl, p. 55). "A man who has nothing left in this world still may know bliss, be it only for a brief moment, in the contemplation of his beloved" (Frankl, p. 57). "Humor was another of the soul's weapons in the fight for self-preservation. More than anything else in the human make-up, Humor can afford an ability to rise above any situation, even if only for a few seconds" (Frankl, p. 63).

Frankl's point is that apathy can be overcome. "Everything can be taken from a man but one thing: the last of human freedoms—to choose one's attitude in any given set of circumstances, to choose one's own way" (Frankl, p. 86). "The sort of person the prisoner became is a result of an inner decision and not the result of the camp influences alone. Fundamentally, therefore, any man can, under such circumstances, decide what shall become of him—mentally and spiritually. This inner freedom cannot be lost. It is this spiritual freedom—which cannot be taken away—that makes life meaningful and purposeful" (Frankl, p. 86).

"What was really needed was a fundamental change in our attitude toward life. We had to learn ourselves and, furthermore, we had to teach the despairing men that *it did not really matter what we expected from life, but rather what life expected from us*" (Frankl, p. 98, italics his).

The third phase of an inmate's mental reaction to camp life is the period following his release and liberation. At first, they could not grasp the fact that they were now free. They had lost the ability to feel pleased and had to relearn it slowly. The body began to eat ravenously (Frankl, p. 110). "Many days passed, until not only the tongue was loosed, but something within oneself as well; and feelings suddenly broke through the strange fetters which every restrained it.... Step for step, I progressed until I again became a human being" (Frankl, p. 111).

People suddenly released from mental pressure can suffer damage to their moral and spiritual health. Being free, they could use their freedom licentiously and ruthlessly. For some, the only thing that had changed was that "they were now the oppressors instead of the oppressed" (Frankl, pp. 112-113). Two other fundamental experiences threatened to damage the character of liberated prisoners, namely bitterness and disillusionment when they returned to their former lives (Frankl, p. 113).

Part two of the book, entitled "Logotherapy in a nutshell," explains Frankl's therapeutic theory. He explains that *logos* is a Greek word that denotes "meaning." In other words, Logotherapy focuses on the meaning of human existence and man's search for meaning (Frankl, p. 121).

When asked about how his approach differed from psychoanalysis, Frankl said, "During psychoanalysis, the patient must lie down on a couch and tell you things which sometimes are very disagreeable to tell. In Logotherapy, the patient may remain sitting erect, but he must hear things which are sometimes very disagreeable to hear"

(Frankl, p. 120). Psychoanalysis is retrospective and introspective, whereas Logotherapy focuses on the meaning to be fulfilled by the patient in the future (Frankl, p. 120).

The following material is taken from *Man's Search for Meaning*, but the order has been rearranged.

The existential vacuum is the feeling of total and ultimate meaninglessness. It is inner emptiness. Modern man experiences this existential vacuum because "no instinct tells him what he has to do and no tradition tells him what he ought to do. Sometimes, he doesn't even know what he wishes to do. Instead, he either wishes to do what other people do (conformism), or he does what other people wish for him to do (totalitarianism)" (Frankl, p. 128).

The existential vacuum manifests itself mainly in a state of boredom. An existential vacuum underlies depression, aggression, addiction, and aging (Frankl, p. 129). Sometimes, the existential vacuum masks itself by a will to power, including the most primitive form of the will to power, the will to money, or the will to pleasure, which is why existential frustration often eventuates in sexual compensation (Frankl, p. 129). According to Logotherapy, the primary motivational force in human beings is the striving to find meaning in one's life, in contrast to Freudian psychoanalysis, which says it is the pleasure principle and Adlerian psychology, which speaks of striving for superiority (Frankl, p. 121).

Man's will to find meaning can be frustrated. Existential frustration can result in neurosis. Logotherapy calls this type of neurosis "noogenic neurosis" from the Greek word *noos*, meaning "mind" (Frankl, p. 123). Noogenic neurosis does not emerge from conflicts between drives and instincts but from existential problems.

A diplomat was discontented with his career and found it difficult to comply with American foreign policy. His analyst told him that he should try to reconcile himself with his father because the United States government and his superiors were "nothing but" father images. In other words, his dissatisfaction with his job was due to his hatred that he unconsciously harbored toward his father. The analysis lasted for five years, and the result was that he was "unable to see the forest of reality for the trees of symbols and images." After a few interviews with Frankl, it was clear that his will to meaning was frustrated by his vocation and he longed to be engaged in some other kind of work (Frankl, p. 124).

"Logotherapy regards its assignment as that of assisting the patient to find meaning in his life" (Frankl, p. 125). "In the Nazi concentration camps, one could have witnessed that those who knew that there was a task waiting for them to fulfill were the most apt to survive" (Frankl, p. 126). Man does not need "homeostasis," a tensionless state, but rather the striving and struggling for a worthwhile goal, a freely chosen task, which Frankl calls noo-dynamics, that is, the existential dynamic in a polar field of tension where one pole is represented by meaning that is to be fulfilled and the other pole by the man who has to fulfill it (Frankl, p. 127).

"The meaning of life differs from man to man, from day to day, and from hour to hour. What matters, therefore, is not the meaning of life in general but rather the specific meaning of a person's life at a given moment. To put the question in general terms would be comparable to the question posed to a chess champion: 'Tell me, Master, what is the best move in the world?' There is no such thing as the best or even a good move apart from a particular situation in a game and the particular personality of one's opponent. The same holds true for human existence. One should not search for an abstract meaning of life. Everyone has a specific vocation or mission to carry out the concrete assignment, which demands fulfillment" (Frankl, pp. 130-131).

Man's main concern is to seek meaning in life. Logotherapy tries to make the patient fully aware of his responsibilities but leaves it to him to decide what or to whom he understands himself to be responsible. In other words, it is up to the patient to determine whether he interprets his life task as responsible to society or his conscience. A painter conveys a picture of the world as he sees it; an ophthalmologist enables people to see it as it is. Thus, the Logotherapist's role consists of widening and broadening the patient's visual field so the whole spectrum of potential meaning becomes visible to him (Frankl, pp. 132-133).

The meaning of life is discovered in the world, not in the person. It is something or someone other than oneself. "The more one forgets himself—by giving himself to a cause to serve or another person to love—the more human he is and the more he actualizes himself" (Frankl, p. 133).

There are three ways to discover meaning in life: 1) by creating a work or doing a deed, 2) by experiencing something or someone, and 3) by the attitude we take toward unavoidable suffering (Frankl, p. 133). Suffering is not necessary to find meaning, but the meaning is possible despite suffering, provided suffering is unavoidable. To suffer unnecessarily is masochistic, not heroic (Frankl, p. 136).

Man has within himself the potential to behave like swine or like saints: which one is actualized depends on decisions, not conditions (Frankl, p. 157). "The Statue of

Liberty on the East Coast should be supplanted by a Statue of Responsibility on the West Coast" (Frankl, p. 156).

The book concludes with a postscript, a speech Frankl gave at the Third World Congress on Logotherapy in 1983. It is entitled "The Case of a Tragic Optimism." The following are excerpts from that speech. "Happiness cannot be pursued; it must ensue. One must have a reason to be happy. Once the reason is found, however, one becomes happy automatically. As we see, a human being is not one in pursuit of happiness but rather in search of a reason to become happy, last but not least, through actualizing the potential meaning inherent and dominant in a given situation" (Frankl, p. 162). "If you want anyone to laugh, you have to provide him with a reason, e.g., you have to tell him a joke. In no way is it possible to invoke the real laughter by urging him, or having him urge himself, to laugh" (Frankl, p. 163).

Frankl tells the story of Jerry Long, a quadriplegic who was paralyzed from the neck down as a result of a diving accident when he was 17 years old. Jerry wrote, "I broke my neck; it didn't break me. I am currently enrolled in my first psychology course in college. I believe that my handicap will only enhance my ability to help others. I know that without the suffering, the growth that I've achieved would have been impossible" (Frankl, p. 172).

"Crime, in the final analysis, remains inexplicable as much as it cannot be fully traced back to biological, psychological, and/or sociological factors. Totally explaining one's crime would be tantamount to explaining away his or her guilt and to seeing him or her not as a free, responsible human being but a machine to be repaired" (Frankl, p. 173).

The Theory

The View of People Like other humanistic approaches, the existential view of people is holistic. The distinctive emphasis of the existential model is the unique experiences of an individual being "in the world." People are radically free and responsible. They are in a continually ongoing process of "becoming," trying to discover and make sense of their existence. They struggle to find meaning. The fundamental questions are "Who am I? Who have I been? Who can I become? Where am I going?" (Jones and Butman, pp. 284-285).

Although it is difficult to describe a particular personality theory as definitively and distinctly "existential," most theoreticians discuss three levels of existence: the *Umwelt*, the *Mitwelt,* and the *Eigenwelt.* The *Umwelt*, meaning "world around," is the biological world. It refers to the physical dimension of existence. It includes biological needs, drives, instincts, the world of natural law and natural cycles, sleep and awareness, being born and dying, desire and relief, finiteness, and biological determinism. It is the world we would exist in if we had no self-awareness. The *Mitwelt*, "with world," is the world of fellow human beings. It is the relational aspect of existence, one's community. The *Eigenwelt*, the "own world," is the personal existential world of meaning. Humans are capable of self-awareness. They can reflect and make choices, thereby increasing their possibilities for freedom (May and Yalom, pp. 366-367; Jones and Butman, p. 286).

Humans can be self-aware, have the freedom to make choices, and are responsible for their lives. Freedom and responsibility are linked together.

Humans are in a constant state of transition, emerging, evolving, and becoming. The significance of our existence is never fixed once and for all; instead, we continually recreate ourselves through our projects (Corey, p. 178). Being a person implies discovering and making sense of our existence (Jones and Butman, pp. 284-285).

The Development of People Humans are alone, isolated, alienated, and have no meaning. Granted, existentially, we are both alone and related, but ultimately, we are alone. The sense of isolation comes when we recognize that we cannot depend on anyone else for our confirmation, that is, we alone must give a sense of meaning to our life. We alone must decide how we will live (Corey, p. 181). Finding meaning is a lifelong struggle. We must, however, accept responsibility for directing our lives. Periods of emptiness, guilt, isolation, loneliness, and meaninglessness are inevitable throughout this quest (Jones and Butman, p. 286).

With awareness of our responsibility for choices and of the consequences of these choices comes anxiety. For existential therapists, anxiety is more basic than fear. Anxiety arises from our personal need to survive, to preserve our being, and to assert our being. May defines it as "the threat to our existence or to values we identify with our existence." Normal anxiety is 1) proportionate to the situation, 2) not repressed, and 3) used creatively. Neurotic anxiety is 1) not appropriate, 2) repressed, and 3) destructive, that is, it tends to paralyze the individual rather than stimulate creativity (May and Yalom, p. 365).

Guilt, resulting from our failure to make authentic choices, is an ally, not a foe, because it reminds us of our refusal to be ourselves in truth (Jones and Butman, p. 286). Normal guilt sensitizes us to the ethical aspects of our behavior, whereas neurotic transgressions (May and Yalom, p. 365). "When we attempt to deny or distort the anxiety or guilt we experience, our *self* becomes strange to our *spirit*, and consequently, we become unknown to ourselves and others" (Jones and Butman, p. 286, italics theirs). guilt feelings often arise from fantasized

To fulfill our destiny, we must be ourselves in truth, relentlessly. To be whole, we must be deeply rooted in our being, not the being of others who are important to us. Although basically alone, we have the opportunity with a clearer sense of identity to relate to others at deeper and more meaningful levels. Healthy relationships are built on the basis of clearly established identities, not by trying to be or become something other than who we are.

In other words, as we develop a clear sense of identity, we have an increasing ability to make conscious and deliberate choices about whether or not we will be ourselves in truth or alternatively protect ourselves from real or imagined threats by becoming more inauthentic.

Theory of Pathology Pathology is caused by refusing to live authentically and responsibly in all levels of existence (that is, the *umwelt*, the "world around," the *mitwelt*, the "with world," and *eigenwelt*, the "own world"). More specifically, at the core of pathology is our response to the issues of death, freedom, isolation, and meaninglessness. We adopt defenses and strategies that are inauthentic and self-deceptive in that they evade freedom and responsibility. In other words, we lie to ourselves and/or others. We lose touch with our own vital center, our capacity to be ourselves, and thereby commit ourselves to an inadequate philosophy of life that leads to symptoms (Jones and Butman, p. 287).

Observing that Frankl did not repudiate Freud, Allport says Freud taught that the root cause of neuroses was conflicting and unconscious motives. Frankl traced some forms of neurosis to the failure of sufferers to find meaning and a sense of responsibility in their existence (Frankl, p. 10). May and Yalom explain that the existential approach retains the basic structure of Freud but with "radically different content" (May and Yalom, p. 360). According to them, the Freudian formula is:

$$\text{Drives} \rightarrow \text{anxiety} \rightarrow \text{defense mechanism}$$

In the existential approach, the Freudian formula is replaced by:

$$\text{Awareness of ultimate concern} \rightarrow \text{anxiety} \rightarrow \text{defense mechanism}$$

In other words, Freud's sequence begins with a drive, whereas the existential framework starts with awareness. The existential approach views people as primarily fearful and suffering rather than driven. Both psychoanalysis and the existential approach place anxiety at the center of the dynamic structure of human beings. Anxiety fuels pathology. Conscious and unconscious psychic operations that is, defense mechanisms, are generated to deal with anxiety. Such strategies provide safety, but they restrict growth (May and Yalom, p. 360).

Nature of Health Healthy individuals are authentic; as they develop a clear sense of identity, they have an increasing ability to make conscious and deliberate choices to be a self in truth. Such individuals have a definite commitment to becoming, which includes seeing themselves as increasingly capable of identifying and removing blocks that thwart their maturing process and having a well-formulated philosophy of life that will guide their current and future actions. Healthy relationships with others are built on the basis of clearly established identities, not by trying to be or becoming something other than who we are (Jones and Butman, pp. 286-287).

Methods of Therapy Unlike most other therapies, the Existential approach does not have a well-defined set of techniques (Corey, p. 189). It is more of an approach or attitude about how best to help others grow than a set of theories and techniques (Jones and Butman, p. 288). It is not a comprehensive psychotherapeutic system but a frame of reference (May and Yalom, p. 382).

Few specific techniques flow from existential therapy. The basic goal is to enable clients to realize that they are free to make choices about the direction of their lives and to help them make commitments that will assist them in becoming more authentic. This is not done through mechanistic techniques but rather through a highly personal encounter between therapist and client. The essential task of the therapist is to understand the world of the client, to clarify that subjective world, and to challenge or confront the client with the need for choice and the need to assume full responsibility for his or her actions, insights, and relationships (Jones and Butman, p. 288).

Corey claims that there are three phases in existential therapy. In the initial phase, the therapist assists clients in identifying and clarifying their assumptions about the world. Clients examine their assumptions, beliefs, and values to determine their validity. During the next phase, clients are encouraged to examine the source and authority of their value system more fully. The final phase focuses on helping clients put what they have learned about themselves into action (Corey, p. 190).

The existential therapy approach is similar to, yet radically different from, Psychodynamic therapies. Like Psychodynamic therapists, the existential therapist assumes that the patient experiences anxiety, which issues from some existential conflict that is at least partially unconscious. The therapist assists the client in embarking on a course of self-investigation in which the goals are to understand the unconscious conflict, to identify the maladaptive defense mechanisms, to discover their destructive influence, to diminish secondary anxiety by correcting these heretofore restrictive modes of dealing with self and others and to develop other ways of coping with primary anxiety. Yet, because the existential view emphasizes the depth of experience at any given moment, the existential therapist does not spend much time helping the client recover from the past. Rather, the therapist strives to understand the patient's current life situation and enveloping unconscious fears (May and Yalom, p. 383).

Conceding that there are similarities between Jungian and existential therapy, May and Yalom criticize Jungians for too quickly avoiding the immediate existential crisis and leaping into theory. They tell of the patient who was afraid to leave the house alone. A Jungian therapist analyzed the patient for six years. The Jungian therapist interpreted several dreams as indicating that God was speaking to the patient. The patient was flattered but still did not leave her house alone. The patient was able to get over her neurosis with the aid of an existential therapist, who insisted that she could overcome her problem only if she actively wanted to, which is a way of insisting that she, not God, needed to take responsibility for her problem (May and Yalom, p. 371).

Rollo May, the psychologist most responsible for translating European existentialism into the mainstream of American psychotherapeutic theory and practice, and Irvin Yalom have described an example of existential therapy. They tell of a 50-year-old scientist they call David. After being married for 27 years, David decided to separate from his wife. He came to counseling because of the degree of anxiety he was experiencing in anticipation of telling his wife.

David's youngest child had just graduated from college. The children had always been the main element binding him and his wife together. Now that they were all gone, he saw no reason to continue in the marriage. He had been dissatisfied with his marriage for many years and, on three previous occasions, separated from his wife, but after only a few days, he became anxious and returned.

The reason for his dissatisfaction was primarily boredom. He met his wife when he was 17, when he had been insecure, especially in his relationship with women. They both came from blue-collar families. He was exceptionally gifted intellectually and won a scholarship to an Ivy League school, obtained two graduate degrees, and embarked upon an outstanding career. His wife was not intellectually gifted and did not go to college, but she did work to support David in graduate school.

For most of their married life, his wife immersed herself in caring for the children while David pursued his professional career. His relationship with his wife was empty and he had always felt bored with her company. He found it constraining to be alone with her and embarrassing to share her with friends. In the meantime, he met another woman who was intelligent, attractive, and 15 years younger than himself.

During David's long and complex therapy, several existential themes, such as responsibility, emerged. What moral responsibility did he have to his wife? Since David had a high moral sense and would torment himself with this question for the rest of his life, it had to be explored in therapy. The most effective way of dealing with this was to leave no stone unturned in his effort to improve and, thus, save the marriage. Also, what about his responsibility for the failure of the marriage? Was he displacing onto the marriage dissatisfaction that belonged elsewhere in his life? A dream pointed the way toward some important dynamics.

One of the major themes of his dream had to do with death and aging (his friend had cancer). In the dream, David attempted to find his friend using a giant auger (a tool for digging a hole). "The symbol of the auger seemed clearly phallic and initiated a profitable exploration of sexuality." A concrete slab elicited associations of morgues, tombs, and tombstones. The dream made it clear that, at an unconscious level, David had considerable concern about being over 50.

The therapist helped David plunge into a thorough exploration of his feelings about his aging and his mortality. The therapist's view was that only by fully dealing with these issues would he be more able to ascertain the true extent of the marital difficulties. As a result, David attempted to deal more honestly with his wife than before, and soon, he and his wife made arrangements to see a marital therapist for several months. David and his wife decided that there was nothing salvageable in the marriage and they separated.

After the separation, David was anxious. The therapist did not try to help David eliminate his anxiety; instead, he attempted to help David constructively use his anxiety.

David's inclination was to rush into an immediate second marriage. The therapist urged him to look at the fear of isolation that each previous separation had sent him back to his wife. It was important to be certain that fear did not propel him into an immediate second marriage. David found it difficult to heed this advice because he felt so much in love with the new woman. (Being in love raises many problems; the pull of romantic love is so great that it engulfs even the most well-directed therapeutic endeavors.) David found his new partner to be the ideal woman. When he was with her, he experienced a state of continual bliss.

When she became somewhat frightened by the power of his embrace, he was willing to look at his extreme fear of being alone and his reflex desire to merge with a woman. Gradually, he became desensitized to being alone. He observed his feelings, kept a journal of them, and worked hard on them in therapy. He noted that Sundays were times of extreme anxiety. Part of that anxiety was that he had to take care of himself on Sunday. He could no longer rely on his wife. These observations led him to face his need to be cared for and shielded. The fears of isolation and freedom buffeted him for several months, but gradually, he learned how to be alone in the world and what it meant to be responsible for his own being. In short, he learned how to be his own mother and father—always a major therapeutic objective of psychotherapy (May and Yalom, pp. 396-399).

Evaluation

Philosophical Assumptions Being a philosophy, existentialism has philosophical assumptions.

1. May or may not be atheistic. Kierkegaard, "the father of existentialism," said, "The self in being itself and is willing to be itself rests transparently in God." In other words, for him, to be a true self is to be self-grounded in Self, that is, the Creator-God (Jones and Butman, p. 281), but not all existentialists are religious. To some extent, nonreligious existentialists usually judge that any answer to authenticity that relies on God and His Word is inauthentic or at least incomplete because it relies on something outside the self (Jones and Butman, p. 290).

2. Can be, and usually is, subjective. The tendency is to assume that the subjective psychological perspective is the most basic perspective. The problem is the extreme emphasis on the subjectivity of our inner experience. The reality "out there" is usually

only understood through the reality "in here." The radical openness to experience can all too easily degenerate into an almost excessive emotionalism (Jones and Butman, p. 293). There is no objective way of measuring the relative worth of the client's experience (Jones and Butman, p. 298).

3. Optimistic. It is, first and foremost, a growth model stressing wellness rather than illness and radical personal freedom rather than psychic or biological determinism. Indeed, the existential approach was developed as a reaction to psychoanalysis and behaviorism (Jones and Butman, p. 283). The psychoanalytic position is that unconscious forces, irrational drives, and past events restrict freedom. The behavior position is that social-cultural conditioning restricts freedom. Existential therapy rejects the notion that our acts are determined. It accepts the premise that external circumstances limit our choices, but it is based on the assumption that we are free and responsible for our choices and actions. We are the authors or architects of our lives; therefore, we are always more than victims of our circumstances (Corey, p. 174).

View of People Humans are responsible, but they are not just responsible for themselves, but they are ultimately responsible to God.

Humans are in a constant state of struggle, but the conflict involves more than finding meaning (Rom. 7:22-23; Gal. 5:17).

Humans need a purpose that gives meaning to their lives. Having a purpose is an important factor in making it through some of the tough times in life. Joe Biden, the former vice president of the United States, lost his son to a brain tumor (2015). Afterward, he wrote a book entitled *Promise Me, Dad: a Year of Hope, Hardship, and Purpose.* It was intended to help people who have lost loved ones understand, "You can find significant hope and purpose" after that loss. From a biblical perspective, that purpose needs to include God's purpose for a person.

Method of Therapy One of the major goals of therapy should be to enable the client to realize that they need to make choices.

A highly personal encounter between a therapist and client can be highly productive, but that alone is not the key to counseling all types of problems.

At least, religious existentialism brings God into the counseling context.
Without more clearly defined models, existentialism leads to a kind of anything-goes anarchy. This was a concern raised by even Rollo May himself in his early writings. There is no "objective" way to measure the relative worth of the client's experience (Jones and Butman, p. 298).

Existential therapy risks overstating the case of conscious and contemporary experience. There is a historical bias that risks ignoring the fact that who we are at any moment reflects where we have come from in the past (Jones and Butman, p. 299).

Nature of Health Healthy individuals are authentic. They are aware of who they are, are removing blocks to their maturity, are making responsible decisions, and are being a self in truth.

Healthy individuals are constantly "becoming" in the sense that they are growing, meaning they are becoming more and more mature, but this process is not just becoming more and more a self in truth; it is becoming more and more Christ-like.

Theory of Pathology Humans have a choice and are responsible, but not all individuals have unlimited internal resources to draw on for making choices. In the broad spectrum of humanity, there are different degrees of capacities of choice and responsibility. Existential therapy works well with high-functioning individuals struggling with the quest for meaning and significance.

An extreme emphasis on choice and responsibility introduces hope into the change process but runs the risk of attributing behavior solely to choice rather than other causal factors. Such an approach tends to ignore or minimize the importance of the creative aspects of our existence, particularly any biological or socio-cultural factors that can play an important role in the cause and maintenance of pathology (Jones and Butman, p. 294).

A view of guilt that is only existentially considered as a manifestation of inauthenticity and not as the result of moral violation is incomplete (Jones and Butman, p. 294).

Summary: In response to the issues of death, freedom, isolation, and meaninglessness, we adopt defenses and strategies that are inauthentic and self-deceptive in that they evade freedom and responsibility. Thus, in a highly personal encounter with a therapist who understands and clarifies the client's subjective world and challenges the client to assume full responsibility for his or her actions and relationships, the client makes choices and, thus, becomes more authentic.

From a biblical perspective, existential therapy is limited because it may be atheistic and can be subjective. Even though existential therapy is unique in that it counts Kierkegaard, a Christian thinker, as one of its founders, it can be and usually is too subjective. Secular existential therapy usually judges answers that rely on God and His Word to be inauthentic or at least incomplete because they rely on something outside the self. Its view of people and pathology is too narrow.

Nevertheless, some of the precepts of existential psychotherapy are compatible and coincide with Christian concepts.

1. Existential therapy distinguishes itself among schools of psychology by grappling with death, aloneness, choice, meaning, growth, responsibility, guilt, etc. No approach mirrors the concern of the faith as well as existential therapy (Jones and Butman, p. 289). What could be more biblical?
2. People need a purpose. They were designed to accomplish a purpose (Gen. 1:15).

Chapter 14

PERSON-CENTERED THERAPY

The essentials of person-centered therapy were formulated by Carl R. Rogers (Raskin and Rogers, p. 155). They evolved predominantly from his experience (Raskin and Rogers, p. 158). Rogers is also recognized for developing the humanistic movement in psychotherapy (Cory, p. 204; Raskin and Rogers say that Abraham Maslow was the founder of humanistic psychology, p. 158).

Background

Carl Ransom Rogers (1902-1987) was born in Oak Park, Illinois. His parents believed in hard work, responsibility, and religious Fundamentalism, frowning on card playing, dancing, and drinking (Raskin and Rogers, pp. 181-182). In 1961, he said close and warm relationships characterized his family atmosphere. Yet, play was discouraged and the virtues of the Protestant ethic were extolled (Corey, p. 204). In an interview, after both parents were dead, when asked what he would want his parents to know about his contributions, he replied he could not imagine talking to his mother about anything of significance because he was sure she would have some negative judgment. His boyhood was somewhat lonely (Corey, p. 204).

Rogers entered the University of Wisconsin as an agriculture major. He switched his major to history, which he thought would better prepare him for the ministry (Raskin and Rogers, p. 182). In 1922, he was chosen to be one of ten American youth delegates to the World Student Christian Federations Conference in Peking (Beijing), China. This experience led him to recognize the wide divergence in people's religious beliefs. He considered this as the time when he achieved his psychological independence. Later, he wrote, "In major ways, I, for the first time, emancipated myself from the religious thinking of my parents and realized that I could not go along with them" (Corey, p. 204).

After graduating from the University of Wisconsin in 1924, Rogers entered the Union Theological Seminary. Two years later, in part because of taking several psychology courses, he entered the Teachers College of Columbia University. After Teachers College, Rogers spent 12 years at a child guidance center in Rochester, New York (1928-1939). There, he began writing. From 1939 to 1963, he held academic appointments at Ohio State University, the University of Chicago, and the University of Wisconsin. In 1964, he joined the Western Behavioral Sciences Institute staff in La Jolla, California. In 1968, he and others established The Center for the Studies of the Person in La Jolla (Corey, 204).

Rogers's presentation at the University of Minnesota on December 11, 1940, entitled "Some Newer Concepts in Psychotherapy," is the single event most often identified with the birth of his approach (Raskin and Rogers, p. 182). In the early '40s, he developed what was known as "nondirective counseling" as a reaction to the directive and psychoanalytic approaches. He later developed a systematic theory of people and applied this self-theory to counseling. He renamed his approach "client-centered therapy" to reflect his focus (1951). Later, his theory became known as the "person-centered approach" (Corey, pp. 205-206).

The Theory

The View of People The person-centered view of people is holistic (Jones and Butman, p. 261). The core assertion is that there is only one motivational force for all humanity: the tendency toward self-actualization. Actualization is not selfishness but the realization of one's potential, which includes the capacity to love. Profound narcissism would be a mark of failure to actualize one's potential (Jones and Butman, p. 257).

The direction of the movement toward self-actualization comes from the "organismic valuing process," an inherent capacity to choose what will enhance us and reject what does not. The organismic valuing process tells each individual what will provide fulfillment. It is presumed to be an infallible and instinctive guide for choice (Jones and Butman, p. 258). The concepts underlying humanistic philosophy are illustrated by an acorn, which, when provided with the appropriate conditions, will automatically grow, pushing naturally to its actualization as an oak tree (Corey, p. 206).

The Development of People Even though children are given a drive toward actualization and an inerrant organismic valuing process to guide them, they still need their parents' acceptance and positive regard. If their parents provide unconditional positive regard, children grow up always exquisitely aware of their natural urges and awareness (self-experience). As the consciousness of self emerges, children begin to define themselves (that is, develop a self-concept) in accord with their experience of themselves and not in terms of how others see them or expect them to be. Furthermore, they have no aspirations to be other than what they are and their ideal self, that is, the perception of what they should be, then perfectly matches the self-concept, which in turn perfectly matches the self-experience. As children mature, their self-concept increasingly shapes and directs the organismic valuing process. Thus, a self-concept unpolluted by distortions caused by other people's judgments of us allows the organismic valuing process to continue to operate as an infallible guide (Jones and Butman, p. 258).

Theory of Pathology Unfortunately, few so develop. Most are subjected to conditions of worth and are loved conditionally, that is, we are expected to act in accord with the expectation of others, usually parents, rather than by our instincts to receive acceptance. The child is confronted with the need to deny certain aspects of his experience and act according to the rules and judgments of authority figures. Thus, the child develops an ideal self-concept formed in part by what the child genuinely experiences of himself and in part by what the child feels he must be. The distorted self-concept quickly warps the organismic valuing process, resulting in impaired perceptions of himself and his world and the choices he can make. For Rogers, Christian discipline would be a prime example of disrespect for the child's self-directedness (Jones and Butman, p. 259).

In person-centered therapy, pathology is seen primarily in terms of incongruence between different dimensions of the self. Psychopathology results when we become more externally oriented than internally oriented trying to manufacture feelings or behavior that others demand before we can be acceptable. The primary problem is the incongruence between what we really are and what we are trying to be. In short, psychopathology is a split or incongruence between self and experience (Jones and Butman, pp. 259-260).

Distorted self-concept (incongruence) → impaired perception of self, choices, etc.

The Nature of Health Healthy individuals have congruence between what they want to become, what they perceive themselves to be, and what they actually experience or are. Fully functioning, healthy individuals live comfortably in the flowing process of this experience. Such people have an intact and functioning organismic valuing process and completely trust it. They are fully aware, honest, personally satisfied, and spontaneous. Health reflects trust of self, openness, and experiencing existential living in the present. This will lead to a new kind of freedom whereby they choose to direct their lives from within rather than by the dictates of the external world. The chief Rogerian virtues are to be fully alive to the moment, completely self-accepting, and strongly committed to an ongoing process of personal growth (Jones and Butman, pp. 258-259).

According to Abraham Maslow, the characteristics of actualization are: the capacity to tolerate and even welcome uncertainty, acceptance of self and others, spontaneity, creativity, a need for privacy and solitude, autonomy, the capacity for deep and intense interpersonal relationships, a genuine caring for others, a sense of humor, an inner-directedness, and an open and fresh attitude toward life (Corey, p. 208).

Method of Therapy Person-centered therapy does not consist of techniques. As Otto Ran once wrote, "My technique consists of essentially in having no technique" (Raskin and Rogers, p. 161). Rogers's approach never involves advice-giving, interpretations, teaching, or other interactions. These, it is argued, are based on a fundamental disrespect of others; they foster dependency and thwart the development of any meaningful sense of autonomy (Jones and Butman, p. 261). A formal assessment of the presenting concerns or underlying dynamics in the form of psychological testing or psychiatric diagnosis are seen as inappropriate and unnecessary. Such a diagnosis may, more often than not, interfere with effective therapy (Corey, p. 212).

In person-centered therapy, the therapeutic relationship is of the utmost importance. Active listening, clarification, and reflection of feelings, personal presence, and "co-participation" are the only necessary "tools" coupled with a profound respect for process and inner directness (Jones and Butman, p. 261).

The basic concepts of the therapist are congruence between his own thoughts and behavior (genuineness), unconditional positive regard for the client, and empathy. The basic concepts of the client include self-concept, locus-of-evaluation, and experiencing. The client's self-concept is wanting (lacking self-esteem) or in conflict. Their locus of evaluation is external, that is, the standards and values of other people. When empathy is at its best, the therapist and the client participate in a process like a couple dancing, the client leading, and the therapist following. The object is for the client to begin experiencing a shift from the rigid mold of experiencing self and the world to one characterized by openness and flexibility. "When clients receive congruence, unconditional positive regard, and empathy, their self-concepts become more positive and realistic, they become more self-expressive and self-directed, they become more open and free in their experience, their behavior is rated as more mature, and they deal better with stress" (Raskin and Rogers, pp. 156-57).

"The basic theory of person-centered therapy is that if the therapist successfully conveys genuineness, unconditional positive regard, and empathy, then the client will respond with constructive changes in personality organization" (Raskin and Rogers, p. 170). "Significant positive personality change does not occur except in a relationship" (Rogers, cited by Raskin and Rogers, p. 212). As I once heard a lecturer say, "The therapist is the therapy."

To be more specific, according to Rogers, the following six conditions are necessary and sufficient for change to occur (Corey, p. 212):

1. Two persons are in psychological contact.
2. The first, whom we shall term the client, is experiencing incongruence.
3. The second person, whom we shall term the therapist, is congruent or integrated in the relationship.
4. The therapist experiences unconditional positive regard or real caring for the client.
5. The therapist experiences an empathic understanding of the client's internal frame of reference and endeavors to communicate this experience to the client.
6. The communication to the client of the therapist's empathic understanding and unconditional positive regard is, to a minimal degree, achieved (Rogers, *Counseling and Values*, pp. 39-41, cited by Corey, p. 212).

No other conditions are necessary. If these six conditions exist over some period, constructive change will occur. These conditions do not vary according to client type, are sufficient for all approaches to therapy, and apply to all personal relationships, not just to psychotherapy. Rogers wrote, "If I can provide a certain type of relationship, the other person will discover within himself the capacity to use that relationship for growth and change, and personal development will occur." As clients experience the therapist listening in an accepting way, they gradually learn how to listen acceptingly to themselves. As they find the therapist caring for and valuing them (even the aspects that have been hidden and regarded as negative), they begin to see worth and value in themselves. As they experience the realness of the therapist, they drop many of their pretenses and are real with both themselves and the therapist (Corey, p. 212).

In psychoanalysis, the analyst interprets connections between the past and the present. In person-centered therapy, the therapist facilitates the client's discoveries of the meaning of his or her current inner experience. In psychoanalysis, the therapist takes the role of the teacher in interpreting insights to the patient and encouraging the development of a transference relationship. The person-centered therapist is as honest and transparent as possible and attempts to establish a relationship in which he or she is authentically caring and listening. In behavior therapy, behavioral change comes about by external control. The emphasis is on specific changes. In person-centered therapy, the therapist believes behavior change involves from within the individual (Raskin and Rogers, p. 159; for the differences between person-centered therapy and RET, see p. 160).

In an article co-authored by Nathaniel J. Ruskin (Professor of Psychiatry and Behavioral Sciences and Philosophy at Northwestern University Medical School, who worked with Carl Rogers for 47 years) and Carl Rogers, the following example of person-centered therapy was given. It has been abbreviated (Raskin and Rogers, pp. 184-187).

For a film series in 1964, Rogers filmed a half-hour interview with a female client and wrote an article about it. Before the filming, Rogers and the client had never met. The client's name was Gloria, a 30-year-old divorcee. Her problem was that she had not been honest with her nine-year-old daughter about having sexual relationships with men since her divorce. She felt great conflict over having lied to her daughter and she wanted to know if telling her daughter about her sexual relationships would affect her adversely.

At the beginning, Gloria tells Rogers, "I almost want an answer from you. I want you to tell me if it would affect her wrong if I told her the truth or what." On two other occasions, she asks again for a direct answer to her question. She wants an "authority" to tell her what to do. Rogers assured her he understood her dilemma and would guide her to her own resources for answering. Each time she asked the question and heard the response, Gloria explored her feelings more deeply.

To her first request, Rogers replies, "I sure wish I could give you the answer as to what you should tell her." "I was afraid you were going to say that," she says. Rogers replies, "Because what you really want *is* an answer."

Gloria explores her relationship with her daughter and concludes that she feels real uncertainty about whether or not her daughter would accept her "devilish" or "shady" side. Gloria is not certain she accepts that part of herself. Again, she asks

Rogers for an answer: "You're just going to sit there and let me stew in it and I want more." Rogers replies, "No, I don't want to let you just stew in your feelings, but on the other hand, I also feel this is the kind of very private thing that I couldn't possibly answer for you, but I sure as anything will try to help you work toward your own answer. I don't know whether that makes any sense to you, but I mean it." Gloria says he really does mean it and begins exploring her feelings. This time, she focuses more on the conflict between her actions and her inner standards.

Shortly, she says, "I want you very much to give me a direct answer." Rogers replies: "I guess, I am sure this will sound evasive to you, but it seems to me that perhaps the person you are not being fully honest with is you because I was very much struck by the fact that you were saying, 'If I feel all right about what I have done, whether it's going to bed with a man or what if I really feel all right about it, then I do not have any concern about what I would tell Pam or my relationship with her.'" Gloria answers: "Then all right, I want to work on accepting me; I want to work on feeling all right about it. That makes sense. Then it will come naturally and I won't have to worry about my daughter."

From this point in the interview, Gloria focuses on her inner conflict. She tells Rogers what she "wishes he would tell her" and says she cannot quite take the risk of being the way she wants to be with her children "unless an authority tells me that." Rogers says, "I guess one thing that I feel very keenly is that it's an awfully risky thing to live. You'd be taking a chance on your relationship with her and taking a chance on letting her know who you are, really." Gloria says, "I do feel like you have been saying to me—you are not giving me advice, but I do feel like you are saying, "You know what pattern you want to follow, Gloria, and go ahead and follow it," I sort of feel a backing up from you." Rogers tells her, "I do believe in backing up people in what they want to do."

Gloria then experiences her inner valuing processes and the conflicts she sometimes feels. She explains that when she follows a feeling, whether it is a bad thing or a good thing, she feels right about herself. Rogers responded that in those moments, she must feel "all in one piece." That brings tears to Gloria's eyes.

In the midst of her weeping, she says, "You know what else I was just thinking? I ... a dumb thing ... that all of a sudden while I was talking to you, I thought, 'Gee, how nice I can talk to you and I want you to approve of me and I respect you, but I miss that my father couldn't talk to me like you are.' I mean, I'd like to say, 'Gee, I'd like you for my father.' I don't even know why that came to me."

The article says that Gloria is now quite close to her inner experiences, allowing her tears to flow. She then explores her relationship with her father, maintaining the same closeness to her inner feelings. She has moved significantly from seeking a solution outside herself to looking inward at a painful hurt.

The article ends with this statement, "Here Rogers presents himself as he really is, offering Gloria the experience of genuine caring from another, an experience she missed in her relationship with her real father. Shortly after this exchange, the interview ends."

Evaluation

Philosophical Assumptions Person-centered therapy, like some other therapies, does not articulate its philosophical assumptions, but it has them.

1. Person-centered therapy is atheistic. It never addresses the issue of God. That is the point; it leaves Him completely out of the process.

2. Person-centered therapy is humanistic. It assumes we are the ultimate force and sole masters of our own destiny. All authority is within. Humanity is the center (Jones and Butman, p. 262). Like Psychodynamic theory, it assumes that all will be well if a person has one good therapeutic relationship with another human. The assumption is that the client will freely choose to translate the changes experienced in the intimate context of therapy to outside relationships with others.

3. Person-centered therapy is subjective. Each person contains within him or herself all (the drive to self-actualization and the organismic valuing process) that is needed. The self assumes a position of supreme importance. The strongly experiential, individualistic, and relativistic "core assertions" of person-centered therapy unquestionably lead to inflated notions of the self (Jones and Butman, p. 262).

4. Person-centered therapy is optimistic. People are seen as having the potential to act and make decisions despite their situations, histories, and limitations. People are responsible (Jones and Butman, p. 263).

View of People Humans are certainly given a drive toward self-actualization, but the self is not all there is and should not be the center of what is. To proclaim oneself to be in control of one's own existence is the ultimate act of rebellion. As has been pointed out, to worship one's self in self-realization is simply idolatry. C. S. Lewis once remarked that a good functional definition of hell would be the kind of place where all acted as if they were the masters of their own lives (Jones and Butman, p.

262).

Humans have a drive to self-actualization, but to argue that this is the only drive, and to be a totally good one at that, is to err, which leads to attributing all human distress to forces external to oneself. Furthermore, if we ever experience conflict, it cannot be due to a true struggle within ourselves but rather to a pseudo-struggle between our true selve (all good) and part of our false self, which originates externally from how others treated us (Jones and Butman, pp. 265-266).

To reduce human growth to the process of pursuing self-actualization by following the direction of one's instinctual organismic valuing processes renders the intricate and complex task of moral decision-making to the merely instinctual. It has been argued that this amounts to listening to our biology. Real freedom requires that we choose responsibly between real options. In the Rogerian scheme, there is only one real option: following our biologically rooted instincts (Jones and Butman, p. 264).

Theory of Pathology Incongruence may be part of pathology, but to say that it is the one and only cause of problems is partial at best, and in the words of Jones and Butman, "This approach seems to have less to add to our overall understanding of human psychopathology than any other mainline approach" (Jones and Butman, p. 268).

Like all humanistic views, this approach is fundamentally flawed in its inability to confront the fundamental depravity of individuals and the reality of evil seriously (Jones and Butman, p. 268).

The Nature of Health Healthy individuals are congruent, but there is more to psychological health than congruence.

Healthy individuals are aware of their feelings, but in person-centered therapy, awareness is an end in itself; awareness is health, which is a deficient view of health.

Healthy individuals experience self-actualization, but health is much more than self-actualization. As Jones and Butman have said, "The person-centered therapy ideal of health is the person without a past (we are always to live in the "now"), a person without any need to submit to authority (we are our own ultimate truth), a person without real dependence on anyone else (we contain all our resources within ourselves), and a person with no firm commitment to truth (all meanings are held tentatively and revised according to changing experiences)" (Jones and Butman, pp. 267-268).

Method of Therapy The therapist is critical in therapy, but to conclude that the therapist is the only crucial element is to ignore other vital elements of effective therapy.

The therapist needs to practice empathy, congruence, and unconditional positive regard, but to do that and that alone can degenerate into a bland, safe, and ineffectual way of relating to people. Should not a counselor be a teacher at some point? (Jones and Butman, p. 273). Is not the person-centered therapist "teaching" by "modeling" congruence?

The unconditional positive regard of person-centered therapy has often been regarded as *agape* love, but in person-centered therapy, there is no discipline, no firmness. Agape love warmly embraces the person, is gracious and unconditionally accepting, but does not cease to be firm and hold the person accountable (Jones and Butman, p. 270).

Person-centered therapy focuses too much on inner subjective experience to the point of completely ignoring the past (Jones and Butman, p. 271).

Summary: As a result of being confronted with the need to deny certain aspects of their experience and acting according to rules and judgments of authority figures, people develop an ideal self—dictated by others, which does not fit who they really are. In other words, there is a split, or incongruence, between the self-concept and experience. The distorted self-concept quickly warps the organismic valuing process, resulting in an impaired perception of one's self, one's world, and the choices one can make. Positive self-regard and, thus, congruence between self-concept and experience can be encouraged by relating to an individual with congruence, empathy, and unconditional positive regard. This will enable the individual to trust the organismic valuing system more fully and move toward greater self-actualization.

From a biblical perspective, person-centered therapy is distorted because it is atheistic (assuming that the self has the position of supreme importance), subjective (assuming that all that is needed is within), and reductionistic (assuming that there is only one drive, namely the drive for self-actualization). It has a reductionistic view of people, pathology, and health. Person-centered therapy contends that the only problem is incongruence and that the sole solution is a relationship with a congruent counselor. At the same time, person-centered therapy contains several useful elements.

1. Empathy, the therapist's capacity to experience and accept the client's inner world, helps facilitate the therapeutic process (Rom. 12:15).
2. Unconditional positive regard can be therapeutic, provided it is not carried to

an extreme. The Bible teaches that we are to be loving, even toward our enemies (Mt. 5:44), and be patient to all, especially when trying to help them (2 Thess. 5 I:14).

Chapter 15

GESTALT THERAPY

Gestalt therapy has been called "perhaps the most phenomenological and pragmatic" of the humanistic approaches (Jones and Butman, p. 303). It is an existential approach based on the premise that individuals must accept personal responsibility if they are to achieve maturity (Corey, p. 231). It is a phenomenological-existential therapy that focuses more on the process (what is *happening*) than the content (what is being *discussed*). "The emphasis is on what is being done, thought, and felt at the moment rather than on what was, might be, could be, or should be" (Yontef and Simin, p. 323). Few therapists would describe themselves as Gestalt purists, but many of the techniques of this approach have been adopted (Jones and Butman, p. 304).

Background

The originator and developer of Gestalt Therapy was Frederick S. Perls (1893-1970), who was born in Berlin into a lower-middle-class Jewish family. Perls received a MD with a specialization in psychiatry. During World War I, he served as a medic in the German Army. After the war, he worked with Kurt Goldstein for brain-damaged soldiers at the Goldstein Institute in Frankfurt. There, he saw the importance of viewing humans as a whole rather than as a sum of discretely functioning parts (Corey, p. 231).

Later, Perls moved to Vienna, where he began psychoanalytic training. Wilhelm Reich analyzed him. He was also supervised by several other key figures in the psychoanalytic movement, including Karen Horney (Corey, p. 231).

In 1946, Perls immigrated to the United States. Around that time, he broke away from Freud's theory. In 1946, his book *Ego, Hunger, and Aggression* (written in 1941-42) was first published in South Africa with the subtitle "A Revision of Freud's Theory and Method." The term "Gestalt therapy" was first used as the title of a book written in 1951 by Perls, Ralph Hefferline, and Paul Goodman. In 1952, Perls established the New York Institute for Gestalt Therapy. Later, he settled in Big

Sur, California (Corey, p. 231). In 1966, the subtitle of Perls' book *Ego, Hunger, and Aggression* was changed to *The Beginning of Gestalt Therapy* (Yontef and Simkin, p. 330).

Gestalt psychology provided the organizing principle for Perls's Gestalt therapy. Gestalt psychologists believe that organisms instinctively perceive whole patterns, not bits and pieces. Whole patterns have characteristics that cannot be gleaned by analyzing parts. Because people naturally perceive whole patterns as they occur, actual awareness can be trusted more than interpretation or dogma (Yontef and Simin, p. 329).

The Theory

The View of People A clearly articulated theory of people is lacking in Gestalt therapy (Jones and Butman, p. 315). Rather than an overall theory of personality, the constructs are phenomenological rather than conceptual (Yontef and Simin, p. 335). The German word "gestalt" means "an organized whole that is perceived as more than the sum of its parts. In Gestalt therapy, it refers to the whole pattern. Gestalt therapy is holistic. It is a hybrid that draws freely on psychodynamic and phenomenological formulations, stressing the unity of mind, body, and feelings (Jones and Butman, p. 305). Corey says Freud's view of people was basically mechanistic, whereas Perls stressed a holistic approach to personality (Corey, p. 232).

Humans are biological organisms with strong needs such as breathing, hunger, thirst, sex, shelter, and survival. They are fully responsible for meeting their needs constructively, creatively, and healthily. Self-actualization is a biologically based drive for fulfillment, as opposed to the Rogerian perspective of "optimization of personal potential" (Jones and Butman, p. 305).

Furthermore, people can deal effectively with their problems provided they make full use of awareness of what is happening in and around them. They are responsible (response-able, that is, able to respond), meaning they are the primary agents in determining their behavior (Yontef and Simin, p. 334).

The Development of People A detailed, developed concept of the development of people is missing in Gestalt therapy. Basically, instead of self-regulation, where learning and choosing happen holistically "with a natural integration of mind and body, thought and feeling, spontaneity and deliberateness," it is "shouldistic," meaning it is based on the "arbitrary imposition of what some controller thinks should or should not be" (Yontef and Simin, p. 333).

Thus, instead of using our energies to meet our biological needs in more adaptive ways, we spend our energy on social roles and symptoms. As a result, the full range of our emotional and sensory-perceptual processes become constricted and we develop increasingly distorted views of ourselves and our environment (Jones and Butman, p. 308). Unfortunately, most would rather avoid experiencing painful emotions than face them and do what is necessary to change. Thus, they are "stuck," blocking their possibility of growth (see Corey, p. 240).

Theory of Pathology In Gestalt therapy, pathology consists of 1) unexpressed emotion, that is, unfinished business, making people fragmented; 2) being deceived, that is, unaware; and 3) being irresponsible in dealing with one's self. Pathology is primarily a personal choice to remain overly dependent, inauthentic, and irresponsible (Jones and Butman, pp. 317-318).

Unexpressed emotions like pain, anxiety, abandonment, grief, guilt, resentment, rage, hatred, etc. are "unfinished" business. In other words, feelings not fully experienced in awareness linger in the background and interfere with the present in one's contact with oneself and others. These "incomplete" feelings can cause compulsive behavior, wariness, self-defeating behavior, etc. (Corey, p. 234). Perls says resentment is the most frequent and worst kind of unfinished business. Unexpressed resentment frequently converts to guilt (Corey, p. 235).

Consequently, the personality becomes "fragmented." We become increasingly preoccupied with our social roles and expressing our other dependence. These roles are "games" and become rigid patterns and self-destructive. They are only part of who we are, but we mistakenly believe they are all of our identity. All problems are "con games" at some level used to run away from awareness (Jones and Butman, p. 308).

In Gestalt therapy, pathology is the failure to take the risk of being a truly alive and responsible person. We surround our core being with layers of deception. Defense mechanisms are used to distort reality so that we lose any real sense of who we are or who we could become. The initial layer of deception is the *phony* layer (acting out what we think others want us to be). The next layer is the *phobic* layer. We fear and avoid awareness because we deny, distort, or disown parts of ourselves. The next layer is *impasse*. Convinced that we cannot find the means to support ourselves, we develop effective strategies of coercing others into "loving" us and "taking care" of us.

We play "stupid," "crazy," "enraged," or "religious" in an attempt to get others to take responsibility for us. Underneath the *impasse* layer is the *implosive-explosive* layers. We vacillate between the experience of deadness to the parts of ourselves we have disowned and the potentially positive explosive energy we have invested in maintaining a false "homeostasis." To encounter our real selves, we must penetrate all these layers (Jones and Butman, pp. 308-309). Because people have developed various ways of avoiding problems, they reach impasses in their personal growth (Corey, p. 233).

Instead of being in the present moment, people invest their energies in bemoaning their past mistakes, ruminating about how life could and should have been different, or engaging in resolutions for the future (Corey, p. 233).

Irresponsibility for not dealing with unexpressed emotions and deception causes problems.

Unexpressed emotions → deception → irresponsibility

Yontef explains that in behavior modification, the therapist's manipulation of their environment changes people's behavior. In psychoanalysis, behavior is caused by unconscious motivation, which is manifested in transference. In Gestalt therapy, people learn to use their internal and external senses so they can be self-responsible and self-supportive (Yontef and Simkin, p. 326).

Nature of Health Perls contends that for people to grow, they must lose their minds and come to their senses, meaning they need to stop thinking too much in self-defeating ways and become fully aware of what they are experiencing, especially emotionally, in any given moment (Jones and Butman, p. 307). Healthy individuals are mature because they have an integrated personality, integrity, and are responsible, growing people. They are truthful with themselves and are not buried under layers of deceit. They are also in touch with their feelings and are living in the moment. They are self-sufficient. Indeed, self-sufficiency is a preeminent virtue in Gestalt therapy (Jones and Butman, p. 306).

The "Gestalt prayer" is: "I do my thing and you do your thing. I am not in this world to live up to your expectations and you are not in this world to live up to mine. You are you and I am I and if by chance we find each other, it's beautiful. If not, it can't be helped." This could be interpreted as a license for self-gratification or irresponsible hedonism. However, in Gestalt therapy it reflects the extreme emphasis placed on "personal autonomy as well as the need for individuals to more fully experience the present moment through increased awareness of what they are thinking, feeling, and doing when they are interacting with others" (Jones and Butman, p. 305).

Method of Therapy Gestalt therapy contends that a person with unexpressed emotions ("unfinished business") and deceptions can be brought to awareness and responsibility for their behavior through an existential encounter. Contact with a person, confrontational contact, and being brought to awareness are therapy tools (see Yontef and Simkin, p. 333). The therapist is to facilitate the client's process of self-discovery and learning, but not teach.

The immediate aim is the attaining of awareness. Increased awareness by itself is viewed as curative. The ultimate goals are 1) personal integration of the fragmented experience of self, 2) greater integrity and responsibility, 3) growth into self-support (Jones and Butman, p. 311).

This encounter with another person is not to gain insight. For Perls, insight is not just a waste of time; it can reinforce the client's defenses against awareness (Jones and Butman, p. 310). "Why?" questions only lead to rationalization and self-deception. Perls felt that much of our thinking is a way to avoid feeling.

Instead, this highly experiential therapy emphasizes *doing* rather than *saying*. The object is to get at the "what" and "how" of behavior in the here and now. Growth is not through affirmation (Rogers) as much as confrontation and encounter. Gestalt therapy is said to be "certainly the most directive and confrontive" approach to therapy (Jones and Butman, p. 310).

According to Perls, verbal communication is usually a lie. The therapists who are content-oriented miss the essence of the person. Real communication is beyond words. So, people's nonverbal clues provide the therapist with information that best reveals feelings of which people are unaware. Thus, the therapist must pay attention to the incongruities between verbalizations and body language (Corey, p. 241).

The "rules" of Gestalt therapy include the following. Clients must communicate entirely in the present tense, using only "I" language rather than "it" or "you" language. Asking questions is strongly discouraged. Clients are not permitted to talk about other people, only to them ("no gossiping"). Clients are to focus on the affective and bodily sensations of their immediate experience. Clients must talk to the therapist or other group members as "equals." These rules are designed to intensify the direct experience and to integrate conflicting feelings within the individual (Jones and Butman, p. 311).

According to Perls, unfolding the personality is like peeling an onion. To achieve maturity, one must strip off five layers of neurosis (Corey, pp. 235-236).

1. The *phony* layer is reacting to others in inauthentic ways. We play games and get lost in roles by trying to live up to a face we or others have created.

2. The *phobic* layer is the fear that if we recognize who we really are and present that person to others, they will reject us.

3. The *impasse* is the point where we are stuck. We feel we cannot survive without external support. At this level, people feel deadness and that they are nothing.

4. The *implosive* level is fully experiencing our deadness.

5. At the *explosive* level, we let go of our phoniness and pretense, release tremendous energy, and become alive and authentic.

For change and growth to occur, there must be contact. Contact is made by seeing, hearing, smelling, touching, and moving. It is interacting with nature and other people without losing one's sense of individuality. When contact is made, change is inevitable, but clients resist contact.

Therefore, the Gestalt therapist focuses on resistance to change, which are defenses we develop to prevent ourselves from experiencing the present fully and realistically. These defense mechanisms prevent people from being authentic. Gestalt therapists challenge five major channels of resistance (Corey, pp. 237-238).

1. Introjection is uncritically accepting the beliefs and standards of others without assimilating them ourselves.

2. Projection is disowning aspects of ourselves by assigning them to others. By projecting onto other qualities we refuse to acknowledge in ourselves, we avoid taking responsibility for our feelings and we also prevent our growth.

3. Retroflection consists of turning back on ourselves what we would like to do to someone else or doing to ourselves what we would like someone else to do to us.

4. Deflection is a distraction through the overuse of humor, abstract generalists, and questions rather than statements, making it difficult to maintain a sustained sense of contact.

5. Confluence blurs awareness of the differentiation between the self and the environment.

Other techniques are used, including dream analysis. Freud calls dreams "the royal road to the unconscious;" Perls says they are the "royal road to integration" (Corey, p. 253).

In 1969, eleven people participated in making a Gestalt therapy training film with James S. Simkin, a Gestalt therapist. A brief summary of the film appears as an example of Gestalt therapy in the chapter on Gestalt therapy by Gary M. Yontef and James S.

Simkin in the book *Current Psychotherapies* by Corsini and Wedding.

A thirty-nine-year-old lady named Peg was angry because her husband committed suicide, leaving her to raise their children. She begins by relating a recurring dream. In the following interchange, Jim, the therapist, asks a series of questions. When the subject of ridicule comes up, Jim has Peg talk about it and after she does, he asks, "So, who is laughing at you?" Since no one in the room is, she says that it is her fantasy. Jim gets her to admit that she creates her fantasy.

She then says that she is incompetent. When Jim discovers that she does not know if she could make someone a good wife again, he has her tell that to all the men in the group. When that is done, she says that what she is experiencing right now is "Satisfaction. Pleasure. I feel good. I feel done."

The article concludes her part of the session, saying, "Although Peg's 'ticket of admission' was a dream, what came to the foreground was her anxiety and fantasies of being ridiculed. The dream served as a vehicle for starting and, as is frequently the case, the work led to a most unpredictable outcome" (Yontef and Simin, pp. 352-355).

Another illustration is the now-famous demonstration by Perls and Shostrum. At the beginning of the interview, Gloria says that she is nervous and afraid of talking with Perls, to which Perls immediately replies, "You said you are afraid, but you are smiling." Then, with a series of direct confrontations, he talks about the incompatibility of fear and smiling. Throughout the interview, he never asked if she would like to discuss it. In other words, he exemplifies how Gestalt therapy pushes for awareness (and "frustrates the neurosis") with the confidence that the aware client will solve her own problem in her own time (Jones and Butman, p. 310).

Evaluation

Philosophical Assumptions The proponents of Gestalt therapy tend not to detail philosophical assumptions. Nevertheless, Gestalt therapy has philosophical assumptions.

1. Atheistic. From their system, it is evident that Gestalt therapy has no need for God.
2. Humanistic. The ultimate goal of Gestalt therapy is meeting one's current organismic needs. Furthermore, each individual is fully capable of and responsible for

accomplishing this. The pre-imminent virtue in Gestalt therapy is self-sufficiency. "Self-sufficiency is ultimately an illusion since we were created to be in relationship with God and others" (Jones and Butman, p. 315).

3. Subjective. As with other humanistic approaches, Gestalt therapy assumes that there is an innate tendency within each human being to become more self-aware and, thereby, move toward greater wholeness. The capacity to regulate ourselves is solely from within ourselves. Awareness is the exclusive authority apart from subjective experience. External criteria are not to be trusted.

4. Optimistic. People are responsible for meeting their own needs and for their behavior. Full responsibility is a key element of Gestalt therapy. Therefore, people have the ability to meet their own needs.

View of People Humans are biological beings with physiological needs, but to assert that humans are *only* biological beings without a relational need for God and others is too narrow a view of mankind. "Gestalt therapy arranges needs into a quasi-moral system by prizing experiencing above all else" (Jones and Butman, p. 313). Humans have needs, but not having our needs met is not the be-all and end-all of life. Under some circumstances, it might be better not to have a need met. Maturity sometimes involves learning to live with some unmet needs (Phil. 4:11-13).

Humans are clearly emotional creatures who are sometimes not fully aware of their feelings; they play "mind games," but the fear of rationalization and intellectualizing should not be used to downplay the cognitive process. The Scripture emphasizes the renewal of the mind and other aspects of being a human (Rom. 12:2; Jones and Butman, p. 319).

"By concentrating day and night on your feelings, potentials, needs, wants, and desires, and by learning to assert them more freely, you do not become a freer, more spontaneous, more creative self; you become a narrower, more self-centered, more isolated one. You do not grow; you shrink" (Yankelovich, cited by Jones and Butman, p. 314).

Theory of Pathology While personal responsibility is a factor in pathology, it is possible to put too much emphasis on it to the exclusion of physical and social elements. Problems are nearly always complex. They are "multiply determined and multiply maintained." To reduce the cause to a single factor is often "naively simplistic" (Jones and Butman, p. 318).

Nature of Health Healthy individuals are integrated, responsible, and growing people, but maturity includes more than those elements. Maturity includes loving others.

Gestalt Therapy

Healthy individuals are at least to a degree self-sufficient, but they are also, to a degree, dependent on God and others.

Healthy individuals live in the present without losing a proper appreciation for the past and a legitimate concern for the future.

"Without any clear sense of obligation or responsibility to anyone except oneself, Gestalt therapy risks epitomizing the philosophy of irresponsible hedonism" (Jones and Butman, p. 314). "We are told repeatedly to embrace justice and mercy, walk humbly and show compassion, not because of what they 'do' for us, but because they are an appropriate response to God's grace" (Jones and Butman, p. 316).

Method of Therapy Confronting and directly encountering "unfinished business" can bring a person to awareness.

Dealing with deception can also bring one to awareness and face-to-face with personal responsibility.

Gestalt therapy needs a cognitive theory to balance its overemphasis on emotions (Jones and Butman, p. 319).

The de-emphasis on the cognitive factor has been the chief criticism of this approach from psychotherapists.

While facilitating the client's own process of self-discovery and learning is valid, so is teaching.

Summary: People are fragmented and unaware Because they do not fully express their emotions. Through existential contact with another person, such individuals can be brought to awareness and responsibility.

From a biblical perspective, Gestalt therapy is defective because it is atheistic, allowing no place for divine intervention, humanistic in that the ultimate goal is meeting man's needs, and subjective in that the capacity to regulate one's behavior is solely within the individual. Its view of pathology and health is reductionistic.

Yet, some things in Gestalt therapy, especially in its understanding of pathology, are worth noting.

1. People, even believers, are deceived (Jer. 17:9).
2. Becoming aware of self-deception is a desirable goal (Jas. 1:22).
3. People are responsible. If the Bible teaches anything, it teaches that people are responsible for themselves and to a holy God.

Chapter 16

TRANSACTIONAL ANALYSIS

Transactional analysis (TA) analyzes the transactions between people. It differs from most other approaches in using a contract (Corey, p. 264). In the 1970s and early 1980s, it was uncritically and enthusiastically adopted by many pastors and churches (Jones and Butman, p. 324).

Background

The originator of TA was Eric Berne (1910-1970). In 1935, he received a MD from McGill University in Montreal. Shortly after that, he completed his psychiatric residency at Yale University. While serving in the U.S. Army (1943-1946), he began experimenting with group therapy. After the war, he moved to Carmel, California, where he resumed his psychological studies with Erick Erikson (Corey, p. 264).

Berne was formally trained in classical psychoanalysis and initially accepted the concept of the Oedipus complex. He departed from that school of thought in the mid-1950s in favor of employing more rapidly effective techniques. His book *Games People Play* (1964) was an international bestseller. In 1970, at age 60, he died from heart failure (Corey, p. 264).

Several factors influenced Berne's thinking. Paul Federn (1952), Berne's analyst, was the first one in the psychiatric field to express the idea that the complete states of the ego are permanently retained and can be reactivated. Later, electrical stimulation and drugs proved this concept (Dusay and Dusay, p. 412). Welder Penfield, who did research at McGill Medical School (1951), where Berne went to medical school, concluded that the memories of people with epilepsy are retained and can be replayed. With electrical stimulation of parts of the brain, epileptics re-experienced the emotions of a past experience and were even aware of the same interpretation they had at the time of the first experience (Dusay and Dusay, p. 412; Harris, pp. 25-28). Chandler and Hartman (1960) saw the reactivation of archaic states using LSD-25. They described two simultaneous states: one related to current reality and the other reliving (not merely recalling) scenes dating back to the first year of life (Dusay and Dusay, p. 412).

Beyond these influences, TA evolved through three phases. The first began with Berne's discovery and description of ego states. In 1955, while working with a group that included a lady named Belle, Berne discovered three distinct ego states (parent, adult, child). An ego system is a coherent system of thinking, feeling, and behaving (Dusay and Dusay, p. 415; think of a lawyer who felt like a little boy).

The second phase (1962-1966) was the *transaction*: one person's ego state responding to another's ego state. The two levels of communication (like the meaningful message on radio with static) are the predictable stereotypes and the destructive actions (games), which are motivated by hidden desires that lead to payoffs (bad feelings). The first is on an overt social level and the second is on the covert psychological level. People base their entire social relationships on finding suitable partners to play their "games" (Dusay and Dusay, pp. 415-416).

The third phase (1960-1970) was script theory. A "script" is "a life plan based on a decision made in childhood, reinforced by parents, justified by subsequent events, and culminating in a chosen alternative" (Berne, *What Do You Say After You Say, "Hello,"* p. 162). Scripts explain why people repeatedly play the same games (Dusay and Dusay, p. 416; see also Corey, p. 265).

Classical transactional analysis was developed by Berne (*Games People Play*, 1964). Thomas A. Harris, a psychiatrist who was a long-time friend and associate of Berne, wrote *I'm Okay—You're Okay* in 1967. Since the late 1960s, TA practitioners have modified Berne's basic concepts. Hence, today, there are several different TA models. One of the major ones was an expansion of Berne's ideas by Robert and Mary Goulding, leaders of the Redecisional School of TA (Corey, p. 265).

The Theory

The View of People According to TA, people have needs and ego states.

Needs. TA assures that humans have needs (Jones and Butman, pp. 327-328) called hungers. Stimulus-hunger is a need for physical and emotional stimulation (Bernie, pp. 13-14). Recognition-hunger is the need for recognition. A "stroke" is "any act implying recognition of another person's presence" (Berne, p. 15). It is any interpersonal event, physical (touching), verbal, or nonverbal, that "recognizes" the existence of another person (Jones and Butman, p. 327). "Hence, a stroke may be used as the fundamental unit of social action. An exchange of strokes constitutes a transaction" (Berne, p. 15).

Positive strokes, essential for healthy psychological development, are affection or appreciation. These strokes are given by touching, holding, and cuddling during infancy and early childhood. Later, between ages two and four, stroking tends to become less physical and more verbal (physical strokes are important throughout life). Positive strokes say, "I like you." Unconditional strokes say, "I am willing to accept you as you are and we can negotiate our differences." Conditional strokes say, "I like you if." These strokes are received for doing something. Negative strokes say, "I don't like you" (Corey, p. 269).

The third need is structure-hunger, which is the need to structure one's life. People "program" their time materially (dealing with external reality, such as building something, work), socially (manners, such as proper greeting, eating, dating, mourning, etc.), and individually (married life, family life, involvement in an organization) (Berne, pp. 16-18). People structure time rituals, pastimes, games, intimacy, and activity (Berne, pp. 18-19).

Later, Berne listed six hungers: 1) stimulus hunger (either intellectual or emotional), 2) recognition hunger (recognition and acknowledgment by others), 3) contact hunger (physical contact with other people), 4) sexual hunger (the need to procreate, romance, passion for something), 5) time structure hunger (filling our lives with things to do), 6) incident hunger (looking for things we find interesting and which add spice to our lives). (http://changingminds.org/explanations/needs/berne_hungers.htm, accessed 8/30/16).

Ego States. According to TA, personality structure comprises three conscious or pre-conscious ego states. Each ego state is an organized psychological system of feelings, thoughts, and behaviors that are distinct and mutually exclusive. The three are the parent (P), the adult (A), and the child (C) (Jones and Butman, p. 325). At any given moment, in a social situation, a person can exhibit any of three ego states and shift from one ego state to another in varying degrees (Berne, p. 24).

The Parent ego state is the re-experience of what we imagined and how our parents or parental substitutes felt, thought and acted toward others. This state contains "shoulds" and "oughts" (Corey, p. 266). It expresses a value system, morals, and beliefs. The Adult ego state processes the data received from the external world and the information from the other two ego states. This part of people is not emotional, passionate, or judgmental. It is realistic, objective, and logical (Corey, p. 266). The Child ego state consists of the feelings, impulses, and thoughts within and spontaneous acts. The child with us never grows up, regardless of how old we are. The Parent is self-righteous. The Child is dominated by feelings, while the Adult is a reasoning, logical, grown-up (Harris, p. 39).

To complicate matters, the Parent and Child ego states can be subdivided. The Nurturing Parent is a composite of the loving, supportive, and accepting messages people receive and the Critical Parent is the composite of the rejecting, controlling, and judgmental messages. The Adapted Child denies or ignores its own instincts and desperately tries to please parents by conforming to their demands. The Natural Child is the spontaneous, joyous, uninhibited responder to the world. Some add a third child, the Little Professor, who delights in learning (Jones and Butman, p. 326).

Berne adds that in this system, the word "childish" is never used; rather, "child-like" is used to describe the Child ego state. Likewise, there is no such thing as an "immature person." "There are only people in whom the "Child takes over inappropriately or unproductively," but all such people have a complete, well-structured Adult who only needs to be uncovered or activated. Conversely, so-called "mature people" are people who are able "to keep the Adult in control most of the time." The "Parent" is exhibited in "direct" and "indirect" forms. In the direct form, the person responds as his own father (or mother) actually responded ("Do as I do"). In the indirect form, the person responds the way his or her parents wanted him or her to respond ("Don't do as I do, do as I say"). The adaptive Child is the one who manifests the behavior under parental influence. The natural Child is a spontaneous expression (Berne, pp. 25-26).

The Parent, Adult, and Child all have a legitimate place in a full and productive life (Berne, p. 28). "In the Child resides intuition, creativity, and spontaneous drive and enjoyment. The Adult is necessary for survival. It processes data and computes the probabilities essential for dealing effectively with the outside world.... The Parent has two main functions. First, it enables the individual to act effectively as the parent of actual children.... Secondly, it makes many responses automatic, which conserves a great deal of time and energy.... This frees the Adult from the necessity of making innumerable trivial decisions so that it can devote itself to more important issues, leaving routine matters to the Parent" (Berne, p. 27).

While there are seeming similarities between Freud's psychic structure and TA ego states, there are major differences. For Freud, only the ego was deemed conscious. In TA, all three structures are part of the ego, and all are conscious or potentially conscious. Perhaps, more importantly, Freud thought psychological experience results from the interaction of all three structures of the personality: the id, the ego, and the superego. In contrast, in TA, personality is largely the function of one ego state at a time. These ego states are essentially mutually exclusive (Jones and Butman, pp. 325-326).

The Development of People The development of people involves scripts, transactions, and games.

Berne thought children are "scripted" early in life, usually by parents. Strokes received from parents and others are either supportive or attacking. From this experience early in life, the child decides that he or she is either basically OK as a person or is not OK. This existential decision is reinforced by verbal and non-verbal messages received from others. The child also decides that others are either OK or not OK. These decisions about oneself and others become one's basic belief system. The script, then, is one's life's themes, direction, or course (Dusay and Dusay, p. 408).

In his book *I'm Okay—You're Okay* (1967), Harris explains that very early in life, every child concludes, "I'm not OK" and as for his or her parents, "You are OK" (Harris, p. 60). "By the end of the second year of life, or sometime during the third year, the child has decided on one of the first three positions:" 1) I'm not OK-you're OK 2) I'm not OK-you're not OK 3) I'm OK-you're not OK 4) I'm OK-you're OK (Harris, p. 66). "Once finalized, the child stays in his chosen position, and it governs everything he does. It stays with them the rest of his life unless he later consciously changes it to the fourth position" (Harris, p. 67).

I'm not OK—You're OK "is the universal position of early childhood, being the infant's logical conclusion from the situation of birth and infancy.... Acknowledging the not-OK Child in each of us is the only sympathetic, thus curative, way games can be analyzed.... Adler's break with Freud was over this point: sex is not at the basis of man's struggle in life, but rather feelings of inferiority, or not OK, were apparently universal. He claimed that the child, by virtue of his small size and helplessness, inevitably considered himself inferior to the adult figure in his environment. Harry Stack Sullivan was greatly influenced by Adler, and I was greatly influenced by Sullivan, with whom I studied the first five years preceding his death. Sullivan, whose central contribution to psychoanalysis thought was the concept of 'interpersonal relationships,' or transactions, claimed that the child built his self-estimate totally on the appraisal of others, what he has called 'reflected appraisals'" (Harris, p. 44)

Goulding and Goulding (1978, 1979) contend that children make decisions responding to real or imagined injunctions and thereby "script" themselves. For them, common injunctions and some possible decisions that could be made in response include (see Corey, pp. 268-269):

1. Don't. Do not do normal things for fear of disaster. A person who accepts this injunction will have problems with decisions.
2. Don't be. Do not exist. It is often delivered non-verbally. The result is, "I'll get you to love me," "I'll pretend I don't exist in this family," or "If things get too bad, I'll kill myself."
3. Don't be close. Do not get physically close. Related messages include "Don't trust" and "Don't lose." Resultant decisions are, "I won't get close and, therefore, I won't get hurt, or people won't leave me or I'll never trust again.
4. Don't be important. The child feels personally discounted when he or she speaks and, consequently, decides never to be or feel important.
5. Don't be a child. The oldest child has to take care of other children and, therefore, finds it extremely difficult to allow himself or herself to have fun or be a child.
6. Don't grow. That is, do not grow up or leave me. The result is, "I'll stay little and helpless."
7. Don't succeed. Too much criticism comes across as "You can't make it." The result is, "I'm a loser."
8. Don't be you. That is, you should have been a boy or girl. The result is "I can't please them."
9. Don't be sane and don't be well. That is, physically ill children feel this. "I'll be ill and then I'll get noticed."
10. Don't belong. The family feels it does not belong in the community or with any group. The result is, "I don't feel at home anywhere."

Other TA practitioners define scripts temporarily as: "always," "never," "almost," or as life theme clichés such as Getting Even, Being Helpful, Carrying My Cross, Looking for the Pot of Gold, or even in terms of childhood mythology such as Cinderella waiting for the invitation to the ball, or Peter Pan refusing to grow up (see Jones and Butman, p. 330).

Transactional Analyis

A transaction is an interaction between people. It is a stimulus and a related response between two ego states. Thus, when two people are relating, six ego states are present. Moreover, this transaction can take place on one of two levels, either on a social (overt) level or on a psychological (covert) level (Dusay and Dusay, p. 407). Healthy individuals can operate out of each of the ego states but will spend most of the time in the Adult, Natural Child, and Nurturing parent—in that order.

The only satisfying answer to stimulus-hunger, recognition-hunger, and structure-hunger is intimacy. At one extreme is "withdrawal," which is predictable and doesn't require risk but is not very rewarding. At the other extreme is intimacy, which is spontaneous, unpredictable, risky, and very rewarding. "Prolonged intimacy is rare, and even then, it is primarily a private matter; significant social intercourse most commonly takes the form of games, and that is the subject principally concerns us here" (Berne, pp. 19-20).

Between these two extremes of withdrawal and intimacy are procedures, rituals, pastimes, and games. Procedures are Adult transactions directed toward manipulating reality, such as piloting an airplane or removing an appendix (see Berne, pp. 35-36). Rituals are parentally patterned transactions, such as greeting one another with "Hi." An informal ritual is the way people greet one another, and a formal ritual is a Roman Catholic mass (see Berne, pp. 36-40). Pastimes are transactions that structure an interval of time. They include such things as chit-chat and small talk, "General Motors" (comparing cars), "Who Won" (sports), "Grocery," "Kitchen," and "Wardrobe." "Pastimes form the basis for the selection of acquaintances and may lead to friendship" (see Berne, pp. 41-44). Games are transactions (at both social and psychological levels) designed to prevent intimacy, resulting in bad feelings for at least one player and advance scripts. The unpleasant feelings that follow the game are called "rackets" (Corey, p. 270). Pastimes and games are substitutes for intimacy (Berne, p. 18).

Rituals are totally predictable interactions with real people; pastimes are impersonal interactions such as talking about the weather or sports; activities are cooperating with people in a spontaneous but safe way (Jones and Butman, p. 328) and games are differentiated from procedures, rituals, and pastimes by two chief characteristics: 1) their ulterior motive (to prevent intimacy) and 2) the payoff (negative feelings).

"Procedures may be successful, rituals effective, and pastimes profitable.... Every game, on the other hand, is basically dishonest.... In the 'insurance game," for example, no matter what the agent appears to be doing in conversation, if he is a hard player, he is really looking for or working on a prospect. What he is after, if he is worth his salt, is to 'make a killing' (Berne, pp. 48-49). There are "unconscious games played by innocent people engaged in duplex transactions of which they are not fully aware and form the most important aspects of social life all over the world" (Berne, p. 49).

Rather than allowing unpredictable intimacy, people play games, that is, they engage in ulterior and cross transactions to make a predictable outcome occur. In other words, they play the game that will predetermine the outcome of the transaction. They do this because they want others to confirm their "I'm not O.K" assumption. Remember, strokes are essential. Positive strokes feel better than negative strokes, but negative strokes are better than no strokes at all. So, if positive strokes are not available, negative strokes are sought. Thus, games are exchanged for strokes. At least the games advance the script (Jones and Butman, p. 329).

Parents often "play games" to control their children and children respond with their own games. For example, children invent games to avoid doing chores. Adults use games such as poor me; martyr, yes, but if it weren't for you, look what you made me do!, harried, uproar, and wooden leg.

In his book *Games People Play*, Berne discusses 36 games and says, "new games are continually being discovered" (Berne, p. 69).

Life games include *Alcoholic* (see how bad I've been and see if you can stop me, Berne, pp. 79-80), *Now I've got you, you son of a bitch* (justification, such as a jealous husband, Berne, pp. 84-86), and *See what you made me do* (vindication and avoidance of responsibility, Berne, pp. 87-90). Marital Games consist of *Courtroom* ("I'm right; reassurance, projection of guilt, Berne, pp. 93-94) and *Frigid Woman* (husband's advances are repulsed, Berne, pp. 99-100). The Party Game is *Why Don't You—Yes, But* (see if you can present a solution I can't find fault with, Berne, p. 116). Sexual Games comprise *Perversion* (fetishism, sadism, masochism, which are symptomatic of a confused Child, and homosexuality (Berne, pp. 124-125; this was written in 1964), *Rapo* (mild flirtation to claiming a criminal assault, Berne, p. 126), and *The Stocking Game* (a woman raises her leg, provocatively exposing herself, and remarks, "Oh my, I have a run in my stockings" to arouse the men sexually, Berne, p. 129). Underworld Games encompass *Cops and Robbers* (see if you can catch me, Berne, pp. 132-137) and *How Do You Get Out of Here?* (an inmate who wants to be free plays the game of "Good Behavior" so he can be released, Berne, p. 137).

Consulting Room Games involve *I'm only trying to help you* (to show that people are ungrateful and disappointing and no one ever does what I tell them., Berne, pp. 143-147), *Indulgence* (looking for a job without the slightest intention of taking one, Berne, pp. 147-151), *Pleasant* (did not take advice, but said the advice-giver was wonderful, Berne, pp. 151-154), *Psychiatrist* ("I am a healer, supported by a diploma," Berne, pp. 154-157), *Stupid* (makes people call them stupid or responds as though they were stupid, Berne, pp. 157-159), and *Wooden Leg* ("What do you expect of a man with a wooden leg?", Berne, pp. 159-162).

Good Games contribute both to the well-being of the other players and to the unfolding of the one who is 'it' (Berne, p. 163), such as *Busman's Holiday* (does something beneficial but with an ulterior motive, Berne, pp. 163-164), *Cavalier* (without ulterior motive takes every opportunity to remark upon someone else's good qualities, Berne, pp. 164-165), and *Happy to Help* (helping with an ulterior motive, such as doing penance for past wickedness, or seeking prestige, Berne, pp. 166-167).

Karpman's Drama Triangle (1968) consists of a persecutor, a rescuer, and a victim. The victim plays the "kick me" game in which the victim may persecute another until that individual "kicks" the victim. The persecutor kicks and the rescuer attempts to save the poor helpless, kicked victim from the ruthless persecutor. It is not uncommon for the victim to then persecute the rescuer. Game switching is usually sudden, abrupt, and dramatic (Corey, p. 270).

Theory of Pathology According to TA, pathology occurs when people confuse their ego states, constantly slipping back and forth between them without completing transactions with others (Jones and Butman, p. 326). Problems also occur when people do not experience their ego-states distinctly; one state contaminates another or when one or two ego-states dominate the personality and exclude the other (Jones and Butman, p. 327). People play games with others rather than experience intimacy.

$$\text{Needs} \rightarrow \text{confused ego states} \rightarrow \text{games}$$

Berne delineates first, second, and third-degree states of games. First-degree games are socially acceptable. Someone may yell, but no one gets physically hurt. Second-degree games result in physical contact like a slap on the face or a punch in the nose. Third-degree games are deadly serious, resulting in a messy divorce, a trip to a courtroom, or a morgue (Dusay and Dusay, p. 423).

Nature of Health Healthy individuals are unscripted, that is, they have abandoned the programming of their parents (or their own early decisions) and have decided to be spontaneous and intimate.

Healthy individuals can function out of each of the three ego states but will spend most of their time in the Adult, Natural Child, and Nurturing Parent. The influence of the Adapted Child and Critical Parent will be minimized (Jones and Butman, p. 326).

Method of Therapy The primary goal of TA therapy is to enable clients to make new decisions about their present behavior. The objective is to replace a lifestyle characterized by a self-defeating life script and manipulative game-playing with awareness, spontaneity, and intimacy. Berne ends his book with a brief word about what happens after games. He says, "For certain fortunate people, there is something which transcends all classifications of behavior, and that is awareness; something which rises above the programming of the past, and that is spontaneity, and something more rewarding than games, and that is intimacy" (Berne, p. 184).

The process begins with a contract between the client and the therapist (Jones and Butman, p. 331). The contract contains specific goals and the criteria to determine whether goals are reached. When the terms of the contract are completed, the therapeutic relationship is terminated unless a new contract is established.

TA is usually done in group therapy; individual counseling is used as an adjunct. It is highly educational. More than any other therapy, TA teaches the theory itself. First, the client is helped to understand the ego states, be enabled to experience blocked states and make choices about what to experience at what time. Then, transactions are analyzed, followed by a confrontation concerning games and rackets. The script is examined and the client is challenged to make a deliberate decision about a new life position. Finally, clients are encouraged to at least change their life script or, even better, to give up scripts entirely and live spontaneously and intimately (Jones and Butman, p. 331).

The co-authors of the article on TA in Corsini and Wedding, John M. Dusay and Katherine Mulholland Dusay, give the following example of TA.

Judd complained about fatigue, headaches, and anxiety. Physicians diagnosed him as a hypochondriac. He nostalgically reminisced about his family's medicine cabinet and remembered his mother taking his temperature, giving him pills, and stroking him for being a weak, sickly child. His wife's attitude toward Judd was similar to his mother's. Both mother and wife were high in Nurturing Parent and Adapted Child.

At Judd's first TA group session, the other members drew his egogram and he established a treatment contract: to experience a full month without having a noticeable headache.

In a subsequent session, Judd was habitually complaining of feeling "sick" and another group member, Wayne, who had a critical personality (high CP), told him, "Stand up for yourself." Judd appeared especially frightened and the therapist, noticing this, asked him if he wanted to work on his feelings. Judd nodded affirmatively.

Knowing that this feeling was a repetitive racket, the therapist did not comfort Judd; rather, the negative feelings were enhanced by instructing Judd to exaggerate his tight jaw and tense, wrinkled brow. When Judd was in obvious pain, the therapist asked him to close his eyes to enable him to leave the here-and-now of the group setting and begin to trace his racket feeling back to a childhood prototype episode of his script decision. Judd "went back" to when he was five and wanted his Mommy to go to nursery school with him, but she would not. He pleaded with his Mommy, "I'm not big enough. I'm scared.... I'm sick!" He was instructed to place his fantasized "Mommy" in the empty chair and tell her what he was feeling. The role-playing served to enhance his emotional state.

After that experience, Judd said he felt great as if he were healthy for the first time in his life. He was no longer dominated by the little boy in his head. Others in the group were happy for him and freely gave him hugs and congratulations. With tears in his eyes, Judd spontaneously said, "There is one more thing I'm going to say to that little boy in me." He then went to another chair and said in a nurturing voice, "You're really an OK person." Judd decided he would be OK, not scared, and thought that getting into good physical shape would be helpful in reinforcing outside of the group what he had re-decided in therapy.

When the re-decision process is not successful, it is due to resistance. The intra-psychic resistance occurs, in Judd's case, when he slips from his Adult or Nurturing Parent into his Adapted Child. In this instance, he would switch back and forth from chair to chair, commiserating with his Adapted Child. When this occurs, the therapist quickly introduces a third observer chair to combat the slippage. The chair is placed perpendicular to the ongoing dialogue chair and Judd is asked to switch and describe what he is observing. Usually, this successfully allows Judd to confront his own resistance. If not, he is probably not ready for re-decision and needs to have more group experience to strengthen his Adult and/or other curative ego-state forces. Then, he will re-approach the problem with increased strength.

In addition to his own internal resistance, Judd challenged the subtle resistances from outside himself: socially at home, institutionally at work, and even culturally in the rest of his environment. He increased his awareness of day-to-day hindrances and gathered support from those who had no vested interest in his being sick, namely, the group members.

Judd's egogram, constructed again after more than a year of rigorous attention to change via diagnosis of weak areas, surfacing inner conflicts, confronting resistance, re-deciding, practicing, exercising both psychologically and physically, and overcoming resistance, showed his Critical Parent gained power as he was able to say no to harmful outside influences and stop being a social patsy. His Adult gained particularly in his ability to see himself more accurately. Also, he laughed more as his Free Child grew. The most dramatic change was the decrease in his Adapted Child as he lived his life with personal strength and freedom (Dusay and Dusay, pp. 444-447).

Evaluation

Philosophical Assumptions Transactional analysis has philosophical assumptions.

1. Atheistic. While claiming to be a complete system, it excludes any reference to spiritual reality inside or outside the individual. Jones and Butman conclude that this is either a denial of the spiritual or an attempt to radically interpret it (Jones and Butman, p. 334).

2. Humanistic. The goal is for the individual to rid himself or herself of restricting scripts and live spontaneously and intimately. For TA, the fully functioning person is acting spontaneously out of the natural child state as moderated by the adult and ego state. Self-actualization is the highest good and evil is excused as nothing more than people (including parents) acting out of their scripts (Jones and Butman, pp. 334-335).

3. Optimistic. It acknowledges the human tendency to be shaped by their past and yet it insists that people can make decisions that will change the direction of their lives. In a sense, this is a view of limited freedom. In another sense, as with all humanistic approaches, TA is too optimistic in that it attests that humans have a boundless capacity to change. In TA, freedom is the capacity to act autonomously, whereas Scripture speaks of freedom to serve God (Jones and Butman, p. 334).

View of People According to TA, the structure of people consists of three distinct, mutually exclusive ego systems, Parent, Adult, and Child.

1. While personhood has different facets, people are not intrinsically divided into three separate parts. In fact, in psychodynamic thought, disassociation within the personality is an unhealthy state, not a normal characteristic; even apart from that concept, ego segregation is unacceptable. People are a unity of capacities, integrated individuals (Jones and Butman, pp. 335-336).

2. People need to have contact with others (affection or appreciation), but humans also have other needs.

3. People should not feel that they are not OK psychologically, but it *is* self-deception to believe that through self-discovery, people can arrive at the self-acceptance of their OKness. People are not OK before God apart from Jesus Christ (Jones and Butman, pp. 338-339).

Theory of Pathology For TA, pathology is being scripted by others in early life (or scripting yourself) with the result that people play games with others rather than experience intimacy.

1. The early childhood messages we receive and accept about ourselves and others affect us in adult life, but the problem is more than our scripts.

2. People play games that prevent intimacy, but a lack of intimacy is not the one and only problem people face in adult life.

Nature of Health Healthy individuals are unscripted, that is, they have abandoned the programming of their parents (or their own early decisions) and have decided to be spontaneous and intimate. Healthy individuals can function out of each one of the three ego states but will spend most of their time in their Adult, Natural Child, and Nurturing Parent (Jones and Butman, p. 340).

1. Healthy individuals are not living according to another human prescription, but health is much more than spontaneously being oneself.

2. Healthy individuals can have intimate relationships with others, but health is much more than intimacy. Furthermore, intimacy with another human is not the ultimate experience in life.

Method of Therapy TA therapy begins with a contract and proceeds through an educational process whereby clients are taught ego states, transactional analysis, and scripts. Clients are also challenged to make re-decisions about their life positions. While therapy is designed to gain both emotional and intellectual insight, the focus is clearly on didactic, rational, and cognitive issues.

1. Beginning with a contract lets the client know up front what is expected. It also provides a definite goal to reach and gives the standard by which success is measured.

2. Teaching the client the theory can be helpful, especially for some clients.
3. Understanding and re-deciding are helpful and necessary techniques in therapy, but those approaches alone will not help all people or address all problems. Corey says the danger is that TA can be primarily an intellectual experience (Corey, p. 283).

Summary: As a result of being scripted (or scripting themselves) in early childhood, adults play games to manipulate people to give them strokes, but the strokes result in bad feelings. TA denies that people can be immature. Transactions and scripts must be analyzed and re-decisions made that will allow spontaneity and intimacy.

From a biblical perspective, TA is not the complete system it claims to be because it is atheistic and humanistic. It claims to be a complete system but excludes any reference to spiritual reality. TA assumes that the only problem is early childhood and adult game scripts.

Be all that as it may, there are elements of TA that can be used profitably.
1. The emphasis on a contract can help some clients assume more personal responsibility for the outcome of therapy (Corey p. 281). This is compatible with the Scripture, which contains covenants.
2. More than any other therapy, clients are taught the theory itself. The Scripture supports adding knowledge to faith, which includes knowledge of interpersonal relationships (2 Pet. 1:5).
3. TA is one of the only systems that addresses interpersonal (as opposed to intrapsychic) reality (Jones and Butman, p. 332). The Bible is full of instructions and illustrations concerning interpersonal relationships.

Chapter 17

FAMILY THERAPY

Family therapy is a generic name given to a diverse group of therapies. These various approaches recognize that a troubled *family* needs treatment rather than just a troubled individual in a family (Jones and Butman, p. 349). A core assertion is that people require relatedness in a family of origin and beyond. It encourages social virtues as well as personal ethical responsibilities. The focus is on "we" (the family) rather than "me" (the individual). The family is the most basic and important social system (Jones and Butman, p. 350).

Background

The precursors of family therapy include Sigmund Freud, Alfred Adler, and Henry Stock Sullivan. Freud saw a connection between a boy's phobic symptoms and his relationship with his father. Adler's concept of sibling position became one of the ideas in the family therapy associated with Murray Bowen. Sullivan suggested that the relationship between a child and the mother was a critical factor in schizophrenia. The actual beginnings of family therapy started in the 1950s (Foley, pp. 459-460).

In 1956, Gregory Bateson, Don Jackson, Jay Holey, and John Weakland published a paper on communication entitled "Toward a Theory of Schizophrenia." They found that double binding occurred regularly in schizophrenic families, that is, when a person was put in a situation where whatever advice was made was unacceptable. If double binding occurred repeatedly, it produced bewilderment and withdrawal (Foley, pp. 460-461).

In 1956, in England, R. D. Laing noted that teenage girls who had been hospitalized for schizophrenia displayed a process of confusion he called mystification. The girls had experienced a form of manipulation where someone sought to induce them to change themselves for the security of the manipulator (Foley, p. 462).

In 1957, at Yale, Theodore Lidy, Alice Cornelison, Stephen Fleck, and Dorothy

Terry observed a pattern in some marriages in which there was an over-attachment to the parental home of one spouse. This "marital schism," as they called it, was particularly evident in a marriage where there was a schizophrenic member. Instead of an alliance between a husband and wife, in this role as parents, there was a violation of boundaries between husband and wife brought about by an alliance between one spouse and that spouse's parents (Foley, p. 461).

In 1958, Lyman Wynne, Irving Rychoff, Juliana Day, and Stanley Hirsch described a false kind of closeness in schizophrenic families they called "pseudo-mutuality," that is, an absorption in fitting together at the expense of differentiation of identities of individuals. Individuals lost their boundaries and became disoriented. The consequence is over-dependency on the family. Nathan Ackerman's book *Psychodynamics of Family Life* (1958) was the first major book that investigated the relationship between an individual and his or her family. He did not work exclusively with schizophrenic families (Foley, p. 461).

In 1962, Ackerman and Don Jackson founded *Family Process*, a journal dedicated to family research (Foley, p. 462).

According to Foley, four schools of family therapy can be identified according to their treatment process: Object relations, family system, structural family therapy, and strategic intervention. The first two spent time clarifying past relationships, while the last two contend that if the present system can be changed, the past need not be an issue (Foley, pp. 462-465).

The Theory

The View of People None of the various groups that fall under the generic name "family therapy" have a theory of people as such. For this approach, a theory of people is more implicit than explicit. They speak more about the functional and dysfunctional family system than about the concept of an individual. The focus is on the family, not on individuals. Thus, it is impossible to summarize a consistent theory of people (Jones and Butman, p. 352).

Nevertheless, some observations about family therapy's view of persons can be made. People are viewed holistically and in relationship to their environment. People are the product of social interaction, which means they are the result of their family of origin. Since family therapy sees people in the family context, it is helpful to understand their view of the family (Foley, pp. 465-466).

A family is a social unit in which people, by mutual choice, attempt to meet their needs for intimacy, power, and meaning. Intimacy is in a heterosexual relationship, power in work, and meaning in having children. When these goals of closeness, self-expression, and meaning cannot be attained, symptomatic behavior like the husband having an affair, the wife becoming depressed, and the children becoming school-phobic occurs. Families must change because they go through stages (husband and wife form a functional "we" in addition to their own personalities, opening the family system for the first child, subsequent children, school, adolescence, and children's marriage. There are also three subsystems in a family: 1) the marital system, 2) the sibling subsystem, and 3) the homeostasis subsystem, namely how the first two subsystems interact (Foley, p. 466).

The Development of People While the various schools within family therapy have different concepts and techniques, all agree that the psychological development of an individual results from the family system. According to this approach, all things being equal, the major force in the development of any person is the family. The family of origin influences how a person looks, thinks, feels, and acts (Foley, pp. 465-466).

A functional family will have conflict, but they will make compromises and the needs of the various family members will be met. "The important difference between a functional family system and a dysfunctional one is not the presence or absence of conflict, but rather the attainment of need satisfaction" (Foley, p. 466). "A functioning family will make compromises; a dysfunctional one will not" (Foley, p. 467).

Theory of Pathology In family therapy, pathology is a dysfunctional family system. Any particular problem an individual might have is a symptom of dysfunction in the family. A family is dysfunctional because of the inability of the family members to meet their needs for closeness, self-expression, and meaning (Foley, p. 466).

The dysfunctional way families face the stresses related to the changes and crises of life includes communication deviance, enmeshment or disengagement, scapegoating, family violence, substance abuse, etc. Communication deviance occurs when verbal content and/or nonverbal behavior are strikingly dissonant. There are other pathological communication patterns, including double-bind, where two messages are logically inconsistent, mystification where what is really going on is befuddled, confused, or masked, symmetrical relationships where a rigidly authoritarian father emphasizes rules, power relationships rather than relating to his children in a personal way, and complementary relationships where personal pathologies feed on each other as in a victim being married to a rescuer. Enmeshment blurs family boundaries (family members are over-concerned and/or over-involved in each other's lives, blurring the distinction between "I-ness" and "We-ness") (see Jones and Butman, p. 354).

Needs →dysfunctional family →symmetrical relationships

Nature of Health Family therapies' concept of the nature of health is viewed from the context of the family system rather than from a more individual perspective. In family therapy, the issue is the well-being of the family.

The family therapy movement has described the qualities of a strong family, which include 1) Responding positively to challenges and crises rather than denying or distorting reality. 2) They have a clearly articulated worldview, often expressed in religious terms. 3) They communicate well, meaning they actively listen, affirm, and support, express their thoughts and feelings, and manage their differences. 4) They spend time together in planned and spontaneous varieties of tasks. 5) They make and honor promises to one another and take tasks and responsibilities seriously. As a result, there is a sense of belonging and respect for individual differences. 6) They know how to express their love and appreciation for one another (Jones and Butman, p. 353).

Method of Therapy As has been pointed out, a number of different approaches go by the name of family therapy. A majority of these consist of individuals who have come out of traditions or individual therapies and have incorporated these theories and practices into their practice. A theoretical basis for family techniques has not been firmly established, nor is there a standard treatment. While techniques differ, family therapists agree that treatment goals are improved communication, individuation, increased empathy, improved role agreement, more flexible leadership styles, reduced conflict, and individual symptomatic improvement (see Foley, pp. 471-472).

At least seven major models of family therapy have been identified. 1) The structural family therapy model uses a very direct and sometimes manipulative approach to reorganize or strengthen the relational structure of the family. 2) The strategic family therapy model attempts to resolve the presenting problem rather than attempting to alter family structures. 3) The family systems model utilizes a direct but non-confrontational approach focusing on the individual's role in the extended family to establish independent identities. 4) The communication model claims that symptoms are nonverbal messages. 5) The behavioral social exchange model stresses establishing concrete and observable goals. 6) The psychodynamic/object-relations model stresses the unresolved conflicts and losses in the family of origin. This approach acknowledges that individuals do have intra-psychic problems, but it also claims that, in addition, family members contaminate each other with their pathologies. Therefore, only intervention in the family can produce effective change. 7) The experiential model emphasizes increased awareness, greater authenticity, and a more fulfilling interaction style (Jones and Butman, pp. 356-358).

Vincent D. Foley gives the following example of family therapy, much of which is quoted from him. Mr. Jones had a problem with drinking. As a result of seeing a minister, Jones quit drinking and joined AA. Shortly after that, his wife became depressed and following that, his son was arrested for stealing. The minister referred the man to a therapist who dealt with "family problems."

Mr. Jones, his wife, and his son attended the initial session. Mr. Jones explained that he had begun drinking 19 years ago, shortly after the birth of his son. When his boss urged him to get help, he went to his minister, who had urged him to join AA and become active in the church. Then, his wife complained of feeling "down." Her family doctor gave her medication. She became worse and was sent to a psychiatrist, who suggested that at age 45, she was beginning to experience a change of life and a loss of feeling sexually attractive to her husband. She began seeing the psychiatrist weekly for private sessions.

During this period, their son, considered a "model child," became more overtly hostile in his comments, careless about his appearance, and indifferent in his schoolwork. Finally, he was arrested for stealing an automobile but was told he would not be charged with the crime if he got "help." The father sent him to a psychiatrist, who referred him to a psychologist whose field of expertise was adolescent problems. The psychologist agreed to see the boy privately weekly.

The father said he did not see any change in his wife or son and was becoming more upset. The wife said she was not being helped but would continue in treatment; the son said his sessions were a waste of time and he wanted to quit. The father said he was tempted to return to drinking.

In retelling the story, the father mentioned his fear of "falling off the wagon," and the son, quiet until then, commented, "At least then we'd know what to do with you." When the therapist asked the son to elaborate on the comment, he said that since sobriety, his father had become a "pompous ass." The mother smiled at this comment as she looked at the son approvingly.

The therapist asked the wife to "tell me something about yourself." She began by mentioning the difference between life before and life after her husband stopped drinking. It was clear that she had more roles while her husband was drinking and also more gratification. When the father was drinking, the son acted in the role of surrogate husband and had a closeness with the mother, which was inappropriate—a violation of the generational boundary.

The therapist began his first intervention by asking the son, John, to change places with him so the son could sit next to his father. The therapist then sat between the father and mother so the boundary between them might be visibly established. Moving his position, he commented to the mother, "As a good mother, Mrs. Jones, I'm sure you'd like to see your husband and son get along better." "Of course," she responded, although her face indicated otherwise. The therapist asked the father and son to talk about interests they had in common.

The case is typical of many in that a number of different analyses can be given. For example, the father can be considered an orally dependent man, as evidenced by his drinking. He could be seen alone in treatment. The drinking of the father and the depression of the mother can be viewed from a communication point of view as signs of their inability to express themselves in words. If this is the problem formulation, the therapist can work on their communication. Or the therapist can see the behavior of all three as related to each other and, more importantly, as contributing to the dysfunction in the here and now. From this viewpoint, one would want to work with all three members of the system. This last viewpoint is known as field thinking and represents family therapy concepts in that each person is viewed in the context of the system.

Two observations may be made about the minister's role in Mr. Jones' sobriety. First, he failed to take into account the positive role of alcohol in the family system. Simply put, drinking served a homeostatic function in the family. Mr. Jones was taken care of, Mrs. Jones had a meaning and purpose, and John received special attention from his mother. When Mr. Jones stopped drinking, everyone's position changed. Second, the initiative for change came less from Mr. Jones than his boss, who promised him a substantial raise. The minister reinforced the passivity by actively moving Mr. Jones toward AA and church involvement. Mr. Jones went from a dependency on his wife to a dependency on the minister and AA.

The problem, in this case, is understanding how each of the family members is entangled in the system and observing the ongoing patterns of interaction that keep the system dysfunctional. The family therapist's role is to see this interaction and make interventions to restructure the system.

One could analyze the family in terms of dysfunctional triangles. By her over-closeness to the son, the wife prevented her husband from getting close. The husband, in turn, triangled in a "bottle." After getting rid of the bottle, he got into a triangle at work and the church. The son's growing up and wanting more distance from the mother, combined with the husband's distancing, produced depression in the wife because she was still isolated from her husband even when he was sober. She got depressed as a way of gaining recognition. This produced some signs of caring by the husband and guilt-induced caring by the son. However, the constant demands of his mother made the son angry and he expressed this in his sullenness and eventually by stealing. The symptomatic response of all the family members can be regarded as tactics for survival and control of the system as well as the properties of each person within it.

The therapist chose to intervene between father and son because he thought the best way to change the system would be to get an alliance between them. At the same time, he puts the mother in a bind by saying she should support such an alliance. He probably would have met massive resistance if he had attacked the over-closeness by suggesting that the mother-son coalition was unhealthy. Rather than attacking, he felt a more effective strategy would be to create more closeness between father and son. This alliance, it is true, would produce more isolation for the mother, but instead of falling into further depression, she could now bring this to the therapist, who in turn could reintroduce it into the system.

At the initial session, the father and son agreed to go fishing, which they both enjoyed. It also gave them a time and place for talking. Predictably, such activity caused the wife to become upset. After several fishing weekends, the wife called the therapist to say that she was pleased about how things were going between her husband and son but that she now felt isolated. The therapist commented that he chose this alliance, knowing it might cause her problems, but did so because he knew she had great strength. He agreed, however, that it might be best to bring this problem up in the next session and further suggested that they leave John out of that session.

Jones and his wife came alone to the next session. Instead of dealing symptomatically with her isolation, Mrs. Jones was able to verbalize it. Mr. Jones, at first, was angry at his wife when she told him of her isolation. She responded to his anger by crying and saying, "It's no use." The therapist commended Mr. Jones for his anger, interpreting it as a way of showing concern, but pointed out that it was ineffective because it turned off his wife. The therapist asked Mr. Jones if he wanted to take responsibility for moving toward his wife. The therapist continued probing the husband, trying to determine how much commitment he wanted to make to the relationship and how much energy he wanted to invest. The delicate and tedious task of rebuilding the marital relationship was underway.

It was decided that the husband and wife would be seen twice a month, Mr. Jones and his son once a month, and the three together once a month. In this way, the marital subsystem, the father-son subsystem, and the family system itself would receive attention. The husband's tentative moves toward his wife diminished her feelings of isolation and, at the same time, made her less demanding of her son's attention. This removal of pressure made John feel better toward his mother, which showed in his willingness to drive her to the store and give other assistance. His father's attempts at moving closer made him feel more confident in the father and his ability to take care of the mother's needs. John could move outside appropriately toward peers without either anger or guilt. Mr. Jones began to spend more time with his wife because she was more responsive.

The resolution of the Jones family meant restructuring the system so each member would have options other than the stereotyped ones they had shown. This was accomplished over 24 sessions without getting involved in why and when and staying with those of what and how.

After 24 sessions, the family was seen twice a month for three months and then once a month for six months, at which time, by mutual consent, therapy was discontinued. In all, 36 sessions were held over a period of one and one-half years. After that time (1972), no further help was requested, and no symptomatic expressions of depression, drinking, or antisocial behavior were reported (Foley, pp. 488-492).

Evaluation

Philosophical Assumptions Family therapy has philosophical assumptions.

1. Atheistic. Like virtually all of the other psychotherapies, God is never mentioned in family therapy. The ultimate goal of family therapy is to improve family communication and, possibly, remove symptomatic behavior.

2. Collectivistic. It is not just humanistic in the sense that being all a human can be is the goal, but it is collectivistic in that it views people as largely or exclusively as a product of social interaction. Individual identification is subservient to a core identity

as part of a collective system. Instead of focusing on the family rather than the individual, both the individual and the family should be considered (Jones and Butman, pp. 361-363).

3. Deterministic. To a great degree, family therapy assumes that individuals have limited resources to directly and responsibly control their lives. The individuals do not directly confront their issues; the family must change for the individuals in it to change (Jones and Butman, pp. 363-364).

View of People Family therapy does not have a theory of people, only a definition of a functioning family within which persons reside (Jones and Butman, p. 366). Family therapy's emphasis on the *family* is needed and refreshing, but it needs a theory of people. Family therapy's explanation of a *functioning family* is insightful and interchangeable with Christian concerns, but the approach requires an emphasis on the individuals within the family as individuals and a view of individuals as part of a family system.

Theory of Pathology Dysfunctional families may cause several problems, but it certainly is not the simple and single cause of all difficulties. Family therapy can no doubt help family members who need to learn how to communicate effectively with one another. It is not helpful for problems that are more directly related to individual choice and responsibility. If a person's problem is the dysfunction of the family system, if the family does not respond so that an individual's needs are met, that individual has no hope of having those needs met (see Jones and Butman, pp. 364-366).

Nature of Health Family therapy's concept of the nature of health is viewed from the context of the family system rather than from a more individual perspective. In family therapy, the issue is the well-being of the family.

A functioning family will no doubt facilitate the production of healthy individuals, but a definition of healthy individuals and healthy families is needed.

A functioning family may produce an individual as described above, but a healthy individual is more than these qualities (Jones and Butman, p. 368).

Method of Therapy Family therapy has not developed a theoretical basis for technique, nor has a standard approach been universally adopted among those practicing family therapy. Therapists have incorporated other theories and practices into their approach to family therapy. Thus, the connection between theory and technique is weak. There is no logical reason for choosing one intervention over another. Nevertheless, all approaches within the family therapy framework aim to improve communication, individuation, etc.

Enabling dysfunctional families to improve their communication with one another helps those families with that problem, but the movement needs a theoretical base for whatever techniques it uses and a rational explanation for choosing one intervention over another.

An approach that focuses on family dysfunction without addressing the other pathologies of the individual family members is incomplete. Family therapy has a depth of understanding concerning family dynamics but needs a wider understanding of pathology in general (Jones and Butman, p. 370).

Summary: Symptomatic behavior occurs because the family system does not meet family members' needs for closeness, self-expression, and meaning. In other words, pathology is the result of a dysfunctional family. Family therapy aims to improve communication, individuation, increased empathy, improved role agreement, reduced conflict, and individual symptom improvement.

From a biblical perspective, family therapy is too narrow because it is atheistic, humanistic, and only deals with the individual in the context of the family. God is not included, nor is God needed in the family system, not even to give meaning to the functional family. Family therapy is reductionistic, assuming that all symptoms are a result of a dysfunctional family and that for the dysfunctional family to become functional, all the needs of all the family members would be met.

However, family therapy calls attention to a neglected area.

1. Family therapy's focus on the family, instead of just the individual, is a refreshing contribution to psychotherapy (Eph. 5:22-6:4).
2. Family therapy's explanation of family dynamics, like the characteristics of A dysfunctional family, the subsystems, etc., is helpful. This is a case where the additional information is compatible with the Scripture.

Chapter 18

NOUTHETIC COUNSELING

Jay Edward Adams (born January 30, 1929), a Presbyterian minister, is the originator of Nouthetic counseling, a Christian approach to counseling. Later, it was renamed "biblical counseling." Adams is a "thoroughgoing Calvinist" (Powlison, p. 11), that is, a five-point Calvinist (Powlison, p. 12, 29). According to him, "The Bible, as interpreted by Reformed Protestants" [Calvinism], taught pastors all that is "necessary to counsel competently." (Powlison, p. xvi). In short, he applied "Reformed Protestantism to counseling" (Powlison, p. 3); he "extended the scope of his Calvinistic presuppositions to cover the task of personal counseling" (Powlison, p. 98; Powlison stresses this point over and over; see pp. 5, 11, 36, 37, 97, 98, 100, 101, 102, 107, 111, 115, 123, 125, 126, etc.).

Background

Jay Adams Jay Edward Adams (1929-2020) was born in Baltimore and was converted at age 15 due to reading a New Testament that a friend had given him. He received a Bachelor of Divinity degree from Reformed Episcopal Seminary (finished in 1947; granted the degree in 1951 after receiving a BA), a Bachelor of Arts in Greek from Johns Hopkins University (1951), and completed most of the coursework for a Masters in Theology, but quit before writing a thesis at Pittsburgh-Xenia Seminary (1953-54), a Masters in Sacred Theology from Temple University (1958) and a Ph.D. in speech from the University of Missouri (1963). He was ordained in the United Presbyterian Church in 1952. He pastored churches in Pennsylvania and New Jersey, served as a professor at Westminster Theological Seminary in Philadelphia (1970), was the director of the Doctoral program at Westminster Theological Seminary in California, and then worked as a church planting pastor in South Carolina. He was the founder of the Christian Counseling and Educational Center (1966; reincorporated as the Christian Counseling and Educational Foundation, the CCEF in 1968), the National

Association of Nouthetic Counselors (1975), and the Institute for Nouthetic Studies. Adams has written over 100 books, including *Competent to Counsel (1970) and The Christian Counselor's Manual (1988)*.

In *Competent to Counsel*, Adams explains how Nouthetic (from the Greek *noutheteo*, to admonish) counseling began. Having learned little about counseling in seminary, early in his first pastorate, a man in his congregation tried to talk to him but broke into tears and could not speak. Adams did not know what to do. He writes, "I was helpless." Less than a month later, the man died. As a result of that experience, Adams asked the Lord to help him become an effective counselor (Adams, *Competent*, p. xi).

To improve his counseling skills, Adams began reading the current counseling volumes. He says he found little help in them and almost all either commended non-directive Rogerian methods or advocated Freudian principles. As he attempted to put what he found into practice, he kept wondering how he could re-translate what seemed to be sin as "sickness" (Adams, *Competent*, p. xi).

Disillusioned with what he found in the standard books on counseling, he began referring people with serious problems to psychiatrists or state mental institutions with the result that they returned worse off or no better. He also had a problem with the non-Christian counsel given by an unconverted psychiatrist. In a footnote, he cites the *Living Bible* translation of Psalm 37:30-31 and Psalm 1:1, which says the blessed man does not walk in the counsel of the ungodly (Adams, *Competent*, p. xii).

Doing graduate work in practical theology, Adams took a course in pastoral counseling taught by a practicing psychiatrist on the staff of a large university hospital. He says the teacher had a thorough knowledge of Freudian doctrine, which he zealously taught. In Adams's opinion, the teacher's insight mostly proved to be wrong and when his best advice was put into practice, it simply didn't work (Adams, *Competent*, pp. xii-xiii).

After that, Adams said he drifted into a hit-and-miss pattern of counseling, "growing out of the on-the-spot application of scriptural exhortations." To his surprise, he became a more successful counselor than ever. He concluded that the more directive he became ("simply telling counselees what God required of them"), the more people were helped. It was repentance for sin and commitment to biblical behavior patterns that relieved people (Adams, *Competent*, p. xiii).

Then Adams was asked to teach practical theology at Westminster Theological Seminary. He was expected to teach a course on the shepherding work of a pastor and that part of that course covered the basic theory of pastoral counseling. He had less than a year "to think through the problem and prepare" his lectures. In studying the Bible to prepare his lectures, he concluded, "James 5:14-16 seem to confirm the importance of confession of sin, as well as the use of medicine, in the healing of some physical illnesses." He says he began to ask himself, "If, as James teaches, one sinful behavior is at least sometimes responsible for physical illness, what about the possibility of a similar responsibility from mental illness?" Later, he began to ask himself if much of what is called "mental illness" is an illness at all. For example, the Bible calls homosexuality and drunkenness sins, but most medical health literature calls them "sickness" or "disease." Then he asked himself if those books were also wrong in misclassifying problems like depression, neurosis, and psychosis as sickness (Adams, *Competent*, pp. xiii-xiv).

In reading Mowrer's *The Crisis in Psychiatry and Religion*, and *The New Group Therapy*, Adams was "astounded" to discover that Mowrer had gone beyond his own thinking. Mowrer challenges the very existence of institutional psychiatry, stating outrightly that he believed the current psychiatric dogma was false. As a result of corresponding with Mowrer, Adams ended up working under him at the University of Illinois for two months during the summer of 1965. During that time, Adams worked in two state mental institutions where he participated in group therapy with Mowrer for seven hours a day. (Adams later concluded that "group activity is unscriptural and, therefore, harmful.") People labeled neurotic, psychoneurotic, and psychotic were helped by confessing their deviant behavior (not to God, but to others whom they had wronged and making restitution whenever possible) and assuming personal responsibility for it. During those two months, Adams also studied the principal biblical data on counseling with special reference to what the Scripture says about conscience (Adams, *Competent*, pp. xiv-xvi).

As a result of his experience with Mowrer, Adams concluded: 1) The people in those mental institutions were there because of their own failure to meet life's problems; they were there because of their unforgiven and unaltered sinful behavior. 2) What does the Bible say about such people and the solution to their problems? (Adams, *Competent*, p. xvi).

From Mowrer's book *The Crisis in Psychiatry and Religion*, Adams learned that the Medical Model of mental illness removed responsibility from the counselee and, as a result, psychotherapy became a search into the past ("parents, the church, society, grandmother") to find others on whom to place the blame. "Therapy consists of sliding against the too-strict Super-ego (conscience) which these culprits have socialized into the poor sick victim" (Adams, *Competent*, p. xvii). Mowrer proposed a Moral Model of responsibility. "He said that the 'patient's problems are moral, not medical. He suffers from real guilt, not guilt feelings (false guilt). The basic irregularity is not emotional but behavioral. He is not a victim of his conscience but a violator of it. He must stop blaming others and accept responsibility for his own poor behavior. Problems may be solved, not by ventilation of feelings, but by confessing sin." Adams concluded that people were in those mental institutions not because they were sick but because they were sinful. Many had fled to these institutions to escape the consequences of their wrongdoing (Adams, *Competent*, pp. xvi-xviii).

In his Ph.D. dissertation in the history of science and medicine at the University of Pennsylvania (1996) entitled *Competent to Counsel?: The History of a Conservative Protestant Anti-Psychiatry Movement,* David Powlison, who describes himself as a "passionate participant" in Nouthetic counseling, says, "Adams's intellectual system contains six main parts. 1). His epistemology arose from Reformed Protestantism [Calvinism]. 2) He defined problems in living morally as expressions of sin. 3) He treated physiological and social constraints in the context of personal problems, not their causes. 4). He proclaimed the grace of Christ as the comprehensive solution to life's problems. 5). He defined counseling as pastoral and church-based. 6). He subjected secular counseling to a program of suspicion, debunking their intellectual and professional claims" (Powlison, p. xvii).

In 1970, Adams wrote *Competent to Counsel*. Before it was published in March 1969, several leading evangelical psychologists met at the International Airport Motel in Philadelphia to evaluate it. Representatives from the Narramore Christian Foundation (Rosemead, CA), the Evangelical Counseling Center (Atlanta), Fuller Theological Seminary (Pasadena, CA), and Conservative Baptist Theological Seminary (Denver) presented critiques of the book. Adams was commended for his attempt to anchor counseling in Scripture, but he was also criticized, at times sharply. His model was said to be superficial and simplistic. His critics said Adams had failed to recognize the extent of Mowrer's heritage implicit in Nouthetic counseling; that in the interest of stressing behavioral change, he neglected motivational issues; that his ideal counselor projected an aggressive, impatient, and businesslike stance toward counselees, rather than communicating caring and patience. Adams disagreed; he went home to "sharpen it up more" (Powlison, p. 43).

Nouthetic Counseling

In March 1979, the Christian Counseling and Educational Foundation (CCEF), originally founded by Adams, sponsored a two-day symposium at a Philadelphia Presbyterian retreat center called Krisheim. The purpose of the meeting was to debate the question, "What is Biblical Counseling?" Other questions to be debated included the relationship between psychotherapy and sin, between secular psychology and biblical theology, between psychotherapists and pastors as counselors, and between supportive and directive counseling relationships. The participants were Adams, Henry Brandt (Ph.D. in Marriage and Family Relations from Cornell University, 1952; he has been called "the father of modern biblical counseling"), Bruce Narramore, John Carter (Narramore's colleague at Rosemead), and clinical psychologists Gary Collins and Larry Crabb (Powlison, p. 66).

John Bettler, a friend and partner of Adams, moderated the meeting. "Bettler frequently voiced to his best friend, Adams, his objection to how Adams treated opposing views. Bettler thought that Adams was unfair, creating and attacking caricatures. On one occasion, Bettler put these concerns in print" (Powlison, p. 74; see John Bettler, "Biblical Counseling: The Next Generation," *Journal of Pastoral Practice)*. 8. no. 4, pp. 3-10, 1987). In the Krisheim meeting, Bettler "hope[d] to bridge the rift between Nouthetic counselors and evangelical psychotherapists for the sake of mutual constructive dialogue" (Powlison, p. 67).

Each participant presented a paper, followed by a discussion and debate. Three topics reoccurred. The first issue was the nature of sin. As one participant put it, the issue concerned the relationship between "sins" (discrete behaviors) and "sin" (complex intrapsychic distortions of belief and motive). The participants seem to have reached a consensus on this issue.

The second issue was the relationship between secular psychology and the Bible. All participants affirmed the final authority of the Scripture over psychology and that there was something to be gained from studying secular psychologists, but what the exact contribution of each source looked like in practice proved highly controversial and difficult to articulate. There was disagreement on this issue. Narramore, Carter, and Collins gave psychology far greater weight than Adams, Brandt, and Crabb.

The third issue was the nature of the counseling relationship. Narramore and Carter criticized Crabb for overemphasizing cognitive change at the expense of the counselor-counselee relationship (Powlison, pp. 67-68).

Adams questioned Narramore's indebtedness to Freudian analysis: lengthy therapy without concretely defining moral goals, and they sparred over whether Adams was equally indebted to Mowrer for his short-term counseling model. When Brandt, who had been mostly silent, commented that Jesus spent three years intensely working with his twelve disciples, an observation that supported Narramore, Adams turned to Brandt and said, "Henry, I think you've had the wool pulled over your eyes." He attempted to argue. Initially, Crabb and Adams lined up against Carter and Narramore, while Collins tried to synthesize the positions, and Brandt just listened. Crabb challenged Narramore and Carter's view that the psychotherapeutic relationship was more important than the content of counseling. Narramore and Carter argued with Crabb for the validity of their psychoanalytic style: long-term psychotherapy from one to three years, several times per week, whose goal was more relationship building than directive. They identified themselves as heavily influenced by psychoanalytic thought, which was greatly misunderstood, and argued that most clients needed relationships more than new scriptural insight. Narramore felt that his choice of long-term psychoanalytic relationships rather than direct, didactic problem-solving was ultimately a matter of personal preference, not a biblical mandate. He declared, "This is one of the single largest weaknesses in the evangelical church; we have somehow made spiritual growth a cognitive and willful process much more than an interpersonal one." Crabb argued that the care was not the cure, asking whether the relationship is corrective or provides a vehicle for correction. Collins seemed to think that each side had made a valid point (Powlison, p. 68).

Brandt backed his side, but he ardently affirmed that there were many different possible counseling configurations. He considered his choice of relatively brief counseling as a matter of personal preference. Brandt was satisfied with Narramore's use of the Bible, saying, "What I like about [Narramore's] presentation, he's finally telling me how he uses the Word rather than me and him arguing over whether to use extra-biblical stuff or not." Adams's only ally among the participants had dramatically switched allegiance. Adams sat silent as Brandt, Narramore, and Collins discussed a newfound consensus regarding the legitimacy of variety in counseling models. "Distinctively pastoral, church base, 'anti-Freudian' counseling had come up short in the exchange" (Powlison, p. 69).

Bettler's hopes were dashed. As a result of this meeting, Adams would never again dialogue with evangelical psychologists. The others gave up on Adams as irascible and sectarian. Narramore said that he was willing to talk again with Bettler, but he did not care to interact with Adams. In the years to come, Crabb, who had always denounced Nouthetic counseling, wrote even more sharply against Adams. Brandt, who had been more favorable to Adams in the 1979 airport meeting, had little to do with Adams and the Nouthetic counseling movement. Adams was convinced that the evangelical psychologists were false teachers who had persuasively twisted Bible words to mean unbiblical things, and the others were convinced that Adams was too cantankerous and intransigent to be worth talking to (Powlison, pp. 69-70).

David Powlison In 1988, David Powlison, who describes himself as a "sympathetic critic" of Nouthetic counseling, wrote an article entitled "Critical Issues in Contemporary Biblical Counseling," in which he outlined his assessment of "the balances and imbalances in Jay Adams's model" (Powlison, p. xii). In that article, Powlison said the biblical counseling movement faces six critical issues (see Powlison, pp. 241-259):

1. Counseling in the Christian church is significantly compromised by secular assumptions. "Under the 'all truth is God's truth' slogan, with its notion that both Science and the Bible were revelational, carloads of undiluted sectarianism were hauled into the church."

2. Motivation must be more explored and integrated within our theory and practice. The goal of counseling should be nothing less than visible obedience to the Lord. One danger is that speculative psychological systems are used to analyze insight into the motivations of the human heart. "'Self-esteem or 'needs' become the magic crucible from which all human life flows. My 'self-talk' is invested with supreme power to determine the course of my life." Another danger is that we depart from the Bible if we ignore motives and drift toward an existentialistic view of people. "The caricature that we are behavioristic may indeed be true more than we would like to admit." Behavior flows from within, and our theory and practice have not given this attention. "Motivational issues play a far more prominent role than we realize." "We become incipiently moralistic." Biblical counselors should be dealing with expectations, fears, and beliefs that control people's responses to their situations. Biblical counselors must look for "false gods." Powlison wrote, "It seems to me that critics of Nouthetic counseling have been right in discerning a gap, or at least relative inattention, in our treatment of motivation.... I propose that we hear their criticism."

3. The relationship between human responsibility and human suffering needs much clarification. We need to rethink how we understand people. Nouthetic counseling has strongly affirmed human responsibility and the role of the flesh, but it has not discussed the impact of the world and the devil as fully. There is a biblical view of people as sufferers; there is a biblical view of people as victims. "People are sinned against, abused, criticized, tempted, or rejected. What about the impact of other

general hardships of life: poverty, injustice, physical disabilities, allergies, sickness, and bereavement?" People are responsible and suffer; they are guilty and victims. "I suspect that, at times, we simply have been deficient in our counseling worldview; we have been sub-biblical in the name of being biblical. Would anyone deny that 'Nouthetic' counseling practice often has been less than biblical in its sensitivities of suffering people? ... Do we move quickly past physical or emotional pain to immediately tackle the counselor's responsibility for his reaction? Are we patient? Do counselees know we understand how they experience life?"

4. The biblical data concerning the counselor-counselee relationship needs further understanding. "The authoritative shepherd who decisively intervenes is only one of the modes of biblical counseling. It is not even the primary mode. It is the backup mode when the primary mode fails. The most characteristic biblical counseling relationship is a long-term friendship consisting of mutually invited counsel, generating dependency on God and a constructive interdependency on one another. The authoritative, short-term intervention is the emergency, life-saving measure." Is our relatively impersonal and objective counseling biblical, or are we simply mirroring the professional detachment of psychotherapy? "The vast bulk of biblical counseling will not look authoritative. In fact, a pastor should aim to deemphasize the authoritative, formal, confronting, and unilateral elements in his counseling as much as is appropriate to the case at hand.... How many counselees have been needlessly confronted—perhaps even put on the defensive—when they would have confronted themselves had probing questions been asked? Biblical counseling, like helping in family life, has minimal confrontational and disciplinary events."

5. Biblical counseling needs to interact with a wider audience for our own edification. Generally, we have been shut out of intellectual and educational centers. We are shut up in a fairly narrow sector of believing Christendom. We need to speak with Christian academics.

6. The relationship between biblical counseling and secular psychology needs to be publicly clarified. From the beginning, Adams spoke of a legitimate role of psychology. He said, "I do not wish to disregard science, but rather I welcome it as a useful adjunct for the purposes of illustrating, filling in generalizations with specifics, and challenging wronged human interpretations of Scripture, thereby forcing the student to restudy the Scripture." The question is not, "What can we learn from secular psychologists?" The question is, "How can we speak into their world and turn their world upside down?"

Later, Powlison wrote that Nouthetic counselors "supplemented, developed, and even altered aspects of Adams's initial model." They paid "a great deal of attention to (1) interpersonal dynamics, such as motivation theory, self-evaluation, belief, and self-deception; (2) the impact of and response to varieties of suffering and socialization; (3) the compassionate, flexible, probing, and patient aspect of counseling methodology; (4) nuances in the interaction between Christian faith and modern psychologies; (5) the particulars of marital and familial communication; and (6) the cause and treatment of so-called addictions" (Powlison, p. 275).

Heath Lambert Still later (2012), Heath Lambert wrote *The Biblical Counseling Movement after Adams*, a popular version of his doctoral dissertation. Lambert is currently the Executive Director of the Association of Certified Biblical Counselors and Associate Pastor of First Baptist Church in Jacksonville, Florida. [He has since become pastor of First Baptist.] He wrote, "Counseling is ministry.... The two are equivalent terms.... If counseling is equivalent to ministry, it means that it must be informed by the Bible and that those who do it for theologians.... Counseling is, therefore, by definition, a theological task" (Lambert, p. 21).

He goes on to observe, "People who wrote during the first twenty years of the movement often sounded different from those who have been writing in the last twenty years of the movement." Lambert calls the differences "improvements" (Lambert, p. 24). He analyzes the improvements, which he also calls "advancements," in the biblical counseling movement.

Lambert starts with a brief overview of counseling, beginning with the Puritans. Then psychology took over helping people with their problems. "The next book after the Puritans that would offer unique biblical insight into helping people with their problems was Jay Adams's *Competent to Counsel*, more than one hundred years later" (1970; Lambert, p. 26).

By the late 1980s and early 1990s, new leadership arose consisting of such men as Ed Welch, Paul Tripp, and David Powlison, who was the clear leader. After majoring in psychology at Harvard and working for several years in private psychiatric hospitals, Powlison became disillusioned with the mental health system, which was a significant catalyst for his spiritual conversion to Christianity. After his conversion, he entered Westminster Theological Seminary to study biblical counseling. He earned a Ph.D. in the history of science and medicine from the University of Pennsylvania (Lambert, p. 44).

Taking their cues from Powlison, new leaders advanced the Nouthetic counseling movement in several different ways: 1) conceptual advancements include how to do ministry to people who are suffering as well as to people who are sinning and how to understand motivational issues, 2) methodological advancement from Adams's formal and authoritative way to a loving, brother, one another relationship, 3) theological advancement in defending the approach of Nouthetic counseling, that is, talking to advocates of other models in a tone that is kind and gracious and less bombastic than Adams's. The movement has grown and matured since the initial leadership of Adams, who has been one of the most consequential men in church history in the last 150 years, and yet his work was "imperfect" (Lambert, pp. 45-47).

"Every great man in church history had imperfections in his work, whether it be Athanasius, Augustine, Calvin, or Edwards.... All biblical counselors are united around core principles of the sufficiency of Scripture, the necessity of the power of the gospel to bring about true and lasting change, progressive sanctification, the importance of the church, and concern over secular psychology.... Contemporary Biblical counselors have attempted to advance his [Adams] thought" (Lambert, p. 47). Lambert refers to the leadership of Adams as the "first generation" of biblical counseling and the leadership of Powlison and those who followed him in improving Adams's thought as the "second generation" (Lambert, p. 47).

After his brief account of the history of counseling, Lambert describes in detail areas of "advancement" within the movement.

1. The View of People. "The model that Adams developed included a heavy emphasis on confronting sin patterns observed in counseling. While the second generation has not abandoned the need to confront sin, it is sought to advance the movement in seeing the counselee in a more nuanced way as both a sinner and a sufferer" (Lambert, p. 50). "Adams did acknowledge suffering.... [The issue is] *the degree to which* Adams addressed the issue and how his thought *stood in need of development*" (Lambert, p. 52, italics his). "Adams moves straight to the discussion of the benefits of suffering without considering—in dynamic and detailed ways—personal pain and turmoil of those experiencing difficulty" (Lambert, p. 54). "Adams referred to those struggling under the weight of pain as 'whiners' and 'complainers.' ... This talk represents a nonbiblical harshness and insensitivity that the critics have been right to condemn and the second generation of biblical counselors have sought to correct" (Lambert, p. 55).

"In Adams's model, habit is critical to understanding because it is behavioral habits that condition sinners to sin" (Lambert, p. 67). "There is little discussion of what stands behind this behavior. There is hardly any focus given to asking the question of 'why'" (Lambert, p. 69). "For Powlison, the key that unlocks the door of motivation is worship. It is worship that motivates human activity.... According to Powlison, there are two options: the living God in Christ or a substitute. To articulate what the substitute may be, Powlison describes heart idols" (Lambert, p. 75). "Over the last 20 years, the movement has been defined by the usage of Powlison's metaphor" [the metaphor is "idols of the heart"] (Lambert, p. 76). "The movement has advanced from Adams's outward focus on behavior term or inward focus on motivation" (Lambert, p. 80).

2. The View of Counseling. "God's Word provides us with resources needed to construct the theology of the counseling process. It is not necessary for Christians to listen to secular psychology to learn how to do counseling. Additionally, where counselors land regarding the counseling process is the acid test of whether they are truly biblical" (Lambert, p. 81). The biblical counseling movement has remained consistent (from Adams to the present) in three areas: 1) information gathering (listening and learning together good information), 2) the importance of instruction (in contrast to Rogers, who believed that counselors should never advise, teach, or direct), 3) counseling implementation (counseling is not just talk, or even insight; it always involves the counselee doing something, (Lambert, pp. 82-87).

Where Adams's methodology needed advancement was in his understanding of the counseling relationship. His approach was relatively "formal and authoritative in nature. Adams said that pastors should "endeavor to restrict all intensive counseling to formal sessions in the study," but "there is no evidence that any such approach is commanded in Scripture" (Lambert, p. 87). Furthermore, "Adams's emphasis on pastoral authority tended to obscure the importance of building loving relationships with the counselee.... [It] "does not seem to take seriously the plight of the struggling counselee" (Lambert, p. 88).

"The authoritative shepherd who decisively intervenes is only one of the modes of biblical counseling. It's not even the primary mode. It is the backup mode when the primary mode fails. The most characteristic biblical counseling relationship is a long-term friendship, consisting of mutually invited counseling and generating dependency on God as well as constructive interdependency on one another. The authoritative, short-term intervention is the emergency, life-saving measure…. Adams tells me I need compassion, identification, and mutuality, but he teaches and models rebuke, proclamation, and authority" (Powlison, cited by Lambert, p. 90).

In this aspect of counseling, the biblical counseling movement has developed in six areas: 1) Counseling that is familial. Powlison grounded his approach in 1 Thessalonians 5:14. Mack, another leader in the biblical counseling movement, grounded his approach in 1 Timothy 5:1-2. 2) Counseling that demonstrates affection. The counselee needs to know that the counselor cares and understands. The cliché "people don't care how much you know until they know how much you care" captures a biblical point. 3) Counseling that is sacrificial. Tripp says, "Relationships between sinners are messy, difficult, labor-intensive, and demanding. These ideas of being affectionately desirous and willing to share one's self [see 1 Thessalonians 2:7-8] was simply not addressed by Adams." 4) Counseling that is person-oriented. Adams's approach was sometimes cruel and ultimately harsh. 5) Counseling that sees the counselor or as a fellow sinner and sufferer. Powlison said, "Adams rarely adopts the stance of a fellow sufferer and fellow sinner in need of identical mercy and grace." (See Galatians 6:1, 6.) Counseling that addresses suffering before sin. Counseling should engage the sufferings of counselees before engaging their sin. "In sum, the second generation of biblical counselors urge those who practice personal ministry to avoid the error of Job's counselors who had a monolithic view of Job as a sinner" (a summary of Lambert, pp. 90-99).

3. Defending Nouthetic counseling. Lambert defines eight apologetic moments in the biblical counseling movement: 1) The 1969 "airport meeting" (as noted above) of Adams, Narramore, Tweedie, and others to review the manuscript of *Competent to Counsel*. His critics charged Adams with failure in various tests of both Scripture and science. They said his model was superficial and simplistic and he made unsubstantiated claims concerning the success of Nouthetic counseling. 2) At the 1979 "Krisheim symposium" (also noted above), Adams received more criticism from his peers; some even expressed their total unwillingness to speak to Adams again because of his "irascible and sectarian" tone. 3) In 1988, Gary Collins arranged for the gathering of thousands of integrationists (those who integrate the Bible and psychology) in Atlanta (The Congress on Christian Counseling). When they presented Adams with a plaque for his "pioneering" work in Christian counseling, in his acceptance speech, Adams said that in his writings, he was not trying to refute Christian professionals; he was trying "to expose pastors to the futility and dangers of attempting to integrate pagan thought and biblical truth.... [Then he said] I urge you [the Christian professionals listening to him!] to give up the fruitless task to which I alluded: the attempt to integrate pagan thought

with biblical truth.... Counseling has to do with changing people. But, you see, that's God's business.... Pagan thought and ways are at odds with God's. God proposes to produce fruit (love, joy, peace, self-control, etc.) by means of His Spirit through the Word. Then others came along and claimed they could produce love, joy, and peace apart from the Spirit and the Word. The two proposals and the methods that go with them or essentially competitive. That's why they can't be integrated. If the Old Testament teaches anything, it's this: God doesn't bless His competition. That's why integration won't work. I invite you to abandon this useless endeavor." Adams never again interacted with integrationists. 4). In 1976. Adams contributed to a book, *The Construction of Madness: Emerging Concepts and Interventions into the Psychic Process.* In this secular book on schizophrenia, Adams was asked to present the Christian understanding of schizophrenia. He said the schizophrenic "is a sinner, who, according to the Bible, has been subjected by God to vanity because of his rebellion against his Creator." The counselor needs to confront the sinner with his sin. This time, "the brisk edginess that characterized his engagement with integrationists was not present. Adams's tone was much more patient and winsome." 5). In 1977, Adams was invited to address the faculty and students at the University Psychiatric Clinic in Vienna, Austria. Adams told them that secular approaches to psychotherapy needed a standard and that standard is Jesus Christ. He told them that his model included the responsibility of counselees, the verbal confrontation necessary to engage them, and the counselor's concern for the counselee's well-being. Again, his tone was milder than with the integrationists (a summary of Lambert, pp. 102-111).

The second generation of biblical counselors added three other apologetic moments. 6) In 1995, *The Journal of Biblical Counseling* published Edward Welch's address to the doctoral students in clinical psychology at Hahnemann University. He spoke respectfully to the audience, but in many ways was more stringent and confrontational than Adams's remarks in a similar context. 7) In 2000, Eric Johnson and Stanton Jones edited *Psychology and Christianity*, which was an examination of four Christian approaches to psychology: the levels-of-explanation approach, integration, Christian psychology, and the biblical counseling movement. Powlison wrote the biblical counseling chapter insisting on the sufficiency of Scripture and the fallacy of secular models. 8) In 2001, Powlison contributed to *Care for the Soul*, an attempt to explore integration. In this book, for the first time, a biblical counselor defined the value of psychology. He outlined three guidelines for using secular psychology: to develop a systematic theology for the care of the soul, to expose, debunk, and reinterpret alternative models, and to learn what we can from other models. He acknowledged that because of the doctrine of common grace, even the most incorrect secular theories can correctly understand some things (a summary of Lambert, pp. 111-116).

Lambert concludes that there is still room for more apologetic development, that is, more ways to engage other counseling positions. Not only Westminster Theological Seminary but The Master's Seminary, Southeastern Baptist Theological Seminary, Southwestern Baptist Theological Seminary, and Southern Baptist Theological Seminary now all have full-time faculty teaching biblical counseling courses. Lambert concedes that biblical counselors do not have everything figured out. Engagements with other models can provoke biblical counselors to consider areas they have overlooked. He even says that those who are called and gifted with sufficient skills in biblical counseling can pursue secular education and credentials provided they are under the spiritual direction of pastors in their local church, thus making them "counseling missionaries" in secular mental health facilities. He adds that there is an inherent danger in purely secular education, so counselors must be accountable to spiritual leadership that will help them stay oriented to biblical principles (Lambert, pp. 116-120).

At this point, Lambert discusses an issue he feels needs clarification. In his book, *The Foundation of Soul Care: a Christian Psychological Proposal* [2007], Eric Johnson [Ph.D., Michigan State University] critiques the biblical counseling movement. He makes a distinction between two schools of thought: traditional biblical counseling (TBC), which closely adheres to Adams's views and dominates the movement and progressive biblical counseling (PBC; Powlison; et al.), which is willing to go beyond Adams in certain respects, such as a focus on being rather than doing, a more balanced perspective on sin and suffering, relationships in counseling, and more irenic nature of discourse. The firm line between the two groups is the issue of the sufficiency of Scripture. He calls the TBC view "absolute sufficiency," "extreme sufficiency," and "Bible only," while the PBC position recognizes the inadequacy of the extreme sufficiency position, "allowing other sources of information to contribute to the Bible's teaching." Lambert believes, however, that such a division is unwarranted, insisting PBC (Powlison) believes in the sufficiency of Scripture and TBC (Adams) affirms the scientific value of secular psychology (Lambert, pp. 122-137).

Next, Lambert says there is an area that still needs advancement. In 1995, in an article in the *Journal of Biblical Counseling* entitled "Idols of the Heart and Vanity Fair," Powlison introduced the concept of "idols of the heart." Lambert insists, however, that instead of idolatry being the problem, it "is a secondary problem flowing out of the primary problem, which is the sinful, selfish-exalting heart" (Lambert, p. 139). The examination of several Old Testament passages indicates that idols were worshiped purely and exclusively for the benefit the people believed they would gain (Lambert, pp. 139-142). "Idol worship, then, was a secondary problem flowing out of the primary problem of the worship of self.... The problem of the Israelites was not idolatry *per se* but their effort to decide—unilaterally—what they wanted and how they would go about getting it. They worshiped themselves, focusing on their own desires" (Lambert, p. 143).

The New Testament presents the same underlying heart problem as the Old Testament. "Just as it is true that every sin has its roots in a failure to love God and neighbor, so it is true that every sin has its root in a pursuit of one's own desire above all other considerations" (Lambert, p. 144). "Mankind's most fundamental problem is the desire to grasp after divine status. All sinful people desire to manipulate others into service instead of seeking selfishly to serve them. The problem with sinners is that instead of seeking to love God, they seek to put themselves in the place of God" (Lambert, p. 145). Whether it is called "pride," "self-sufficiency," or "a desire to be like God," the issue is sinners exalt themselves above the true God (Lambert, p. 146).

Some sinners exalt themselves in ways they learned from the world (upbringing, role models, exposure to different cultures). "Each sinner has his own set of lusts that are uniquely appealing to his flesh.... Working in and through each of these is the dark power of the devil." The world, the flesh, and the devil place objects of desire before the sinful heart to stroke its love of self. Such idols include not only idols of stone and wood but also sex, relationships, power, and a million other things. "Idols are extreme elements that the world, the flesh, and the devil use to influence people to feed the lust of their self-exalting heart. Idols, then, are those outward things that the sinful heart fixates upon to fulfill its desires in its exercise of attempted self-sufficiency" (Lambert, p. 147).

Lambert concludes that a fuller articulation of motivation and idolatry includes:
- A better understanding of pride (the root of idolatry is pride).
- A better understanding of people. The second generation of biblical counselors looked at behavior, asked why, and concluded there are idols of the heart. The third generation looked at idols, asked why, and concluded there was a heart that longs for the glory of God.
- A better understanding of sin. "When sinners think they might not get the glory due to God alone, they fret and plot about how to get it (anxiety);

when they are denied that glory, they punish themselves by recoiling in dependency (anguish), punish others with raffle outburst or slow, plotting revenge (anger); or they slink off to our garden of secret delights where they are in control (avoidance)" (Lambert, p. 151).
- A better understanding of repentance. Repentance is not just repentance of one specific idol; it is repenting of the desire for the glory that is due to God.
- Compassionate counseling. Counselors can identify and help counselees who struggle with things they have not because a common theme runs through all wrong behavior: living for the worship, honor, and glorification of themselves. "The sinful, self-seeking heart seeks to get the universe to orbit around itself: all sentiments—counselees and counselors alike—have this in common, though they seek different methods to forget about" (Lambert, p. 153).
- Protection against "idle haunts."
- Protection against introspection (a summary of Lambert, pp. 150-151).

Lambert's concluding chapter includes the observation that the advancements made in the biblical counseling movement have made it more thoughtful, more caring, and is learning to speak more wisely and lovingly to outsiders, as well as making the movement more biblical (Lambert, p. 159).

Understanding the history of the so-called "biblical counseling movement," one cannot help but conclude that if the second generation made advancements over the first and the third generation made advancements over the second, hopefully, the fourth generation will become even more biblical.

The Theory

View of People According to Nouthetic counseling, a person consists of a body and a spirit; people are physical and spiritual beings ("heart" in the Bible). The theology of embodied souls is that the body has strengths and weaknesses and the heart is obedient and disobedient (Walch, p. 51). According to the Scripture, there are organically based problems stemming from sinful attitudes and behavior (Adams, *Competent*, p. 28). His view "assumes that problems stem from sin" (Powlison, p. 101). Powlison explains that Adams's view of sin includes "specific wrong behavior, distorted thinking, bad attitudes, whether conscious or unconscious, all organized around a compulsion to live for one's own desires" (Powlison, p. 101). As was pointed out in the section on "background," the "second generation" of biblical counselors have broadened the view of people to include suffering as well as sinning (Lambert, p. 50).

Theory of Pathology Nouthetic counseling "assumes that problems stem from sin.... [Sin includes] specific wrong behavior, distorted thinking, and bad attitudes, whether conscious or unconscious, all organized around a compulsion to live for one's own desires—the pervasive depravity captured in an Augustinian-Calvinistic view of human nature" (Powlison, p. 102).

According to Adams, the three levels of problems are: 1) presenting problems, 2) performing problems, and 3) preconditioning problems (Adams, *Competent*, p. 148). Habit patterns develop over many years and must be replaced by new biblical patterns (Adams, *Competent*, p. 149). Going back into the past is sometimes unnecessary, but there are at least two reasons for doing so: 1) to establish that nonbiblical response patterns are the root of one's immediate problems (Adams, *Competent*, p. 151). For example, unloving parents may have been the prime instructors in such behavioral pattern, but the critical issue is how the client learned to respond to such treatment (Adams, *Competent*, p. 151 fn.) and 2) to discover and confess any "perfect tense" sins (the Greek perfect tense is an action in the past that has present effects versus the aorist tense which is a completed action of the past, that is, sins that have been dealt with; Adams, *Competent*, p. 152). Because of "perfect tense" sins, the past may truly be the present (2 Cor. 12:21; Adams, *Competent*, p. 152).

Sin (wrong behavior, thinking, and attitudes) →habits →personal problems

"Adams considered the diagnosis 'sin' appropriate for the gamut of normal problems in living: interpersonal conflict, unhappy emotions, bad behavior, faulty beliefs, and typical reactions to suffering. He also believed that applied to the most extreme problems in living: 'schizophrenia' and other forms of bizarre behavior.... He believed that most 'mental illnesses' could be unmasked as instances of things the Bible treated under the category of sin.... Adams's fundamental thesis about bizarre behavior was: 'apart from organically generated difficulties, the 'mentally ill' are really *people with unresolved personal problems*'" (Powlison, p. 105-106, italics his). In other words, to not have their sin detected, people resort to bizarre behavior, which becomes a habit (Adams, p. 30). It is like the grammar school child who feigns illness when he doesn't want to take a test for which he has not prepared adequately (Adams,

p. 32). People with so-called "mental illness" are not mentally ill; their problem is guilt, shame, and fear (Adams, p. 32).

"Depressed persons whose symptoms failed to show any sign of a biochemical root should be counseled on the assumption that they are depressed by guilt (Adams, *Competent*, p. 126). "Even in suffering, sin was the major problem" (Powlison, p. 105). Adams rarely talked about "hurting people," believing that sin and misery appeared together and suffering was an opportunity to glorify God (Powlison, p. 116). Adams described three causes that contributed to psychiatric diagnoses: 1) cultural perception labeled certain behaviors as deviant, whether or not this merited definition as problems of sin; 2) chronic or acute biological malfunction, such as tumors, sleep loss, or drug effects; and 3) habitual sinful responses to life generated most of the behavior that led to a psychiatric label. Discernible sins in so-called schizophrenics include avoidance of responsibility or of suffering, resentment, fears, guilt, false beliefs, self-pity, adultery, grandiose, fantasizing, mishandling of disappointment, camouflage, manipulation, and so forth (Powlison, pp. 106-107). Adams thought that much sin occurred without awareness because it is both self-deceiving and habitual (Powlison, p. 107). According to Adams, each individual must bear personal responsibility for allowing others to influence his conduct (Powlison, p. 111).

Nature of Health According to Adams, people's greatest need is forgiveness. After that, people need the Holy Spirit to aid them in making concrete changes in belief and behavior (Powlison, p. 125). The purpose of Nouthetic counseling is to foster love toward God and toward one's neighbor. "God's authoritative instruction through the ministry of His Word, spoken publicly (from the pulpit) or privately (in counseling), is the Holy Spirit's means of producing love in the believer" (Adams, *Competent*, p. 54). "The goal of Nouthetic counseling is set forth plainly in the Scriptures: to bring man into loving conformity to the law of God" (Adams, *Competent*, p. 55).

A structured or disciplined life conforms to God's commandments; living a life of love is the goal. The goal is total structuring according to God's law (Adams, *Competent*, p. 155) in every area of life (Adams, *Competent*, p. 156). "Structure is the means of moral living. Lives structured according to the 10 Commandments are, by the very nature of the case, also structured according to the principles upon which God constituted the world" (Adams, *Competent*, p. 160). "Holy living, then, involves habit" (Adams, *Competent*, p. 162).

"Nouthetic counseling in its fullest sense, then, is simply *an application of the terms of sanctification*" (Adams, *Competent*, p. 73, italics his). The goal of counseling is the renewal of the image of God, which means being conformed to the image of Christ. In the power of the Spirit, the old patterns of life are to be put off, and new biblical patterns are to be put on. This demands personal change and responsibility. Throughout history, God turned Jacobs into Israels, Simons into Peters, and Sauls into Pauls (Adams, *Competent*, p. 74). Old patterns are learned, but what is learned can be unlearned. God's Word changes people's thinking, decisions, and behavior (Adams, *Competent*, p. 75).

Method of Therapy Nouthetic counseling is based on the Greek word *nouthesis*. Adams says there is no exact English equivalent for this Greek word (Adams, *Competent*, p. 44), but he concludes that it means "confrontation" (Adams, *Competent*, p. 41). He says that Nouthetic confrontation consists of at least three basic elements. 1) It always implies a problem and presupposes an obstacle that must be overcome; something is wrong in the life of the one who is confronted" (Adams, *Competent*, p. 44). 2) Problems are solved by verbal means. He says the concept behind this word is "person-to-person verbal confrontation" and he cites Nathan's confronting David, Christ restoring Peter, and Eli's failure (Adams, *Competent*, p. 46). 3) The verbal correction is intended to benefit the counselee (Adams, *Competent*, p. 49), that is, changing that in his life, which hurts the counselee (Adams, *Competent*, p. 50).

"Notice that Christian counseling involves the use of authoritative instruction. 'Authoritative instruction' requires the use of directive, nouthetic techniques.... Nouthetic counseling advocates the assumption of responsibility and blame, the admission of guilt, the confession of sin, and the seeking of forgiveness in Christ" (Adams, *Competent*, p. 55). Nouthetic counselors fail. "Failure is often complex and therefore difficult to analyze" (Adams, *Competent*, p. 56). Settling for something less than a totally re-orientation life is his failure (Adams, *Competent*, p. 57).

In the final analysis, counselors were to "repent, trust, and obey." Adams did not just tell people what to do; planning on it, he told them how to do it (Powlison, p. 127). The counselor is to be a coach who teaches, models, warns, and encourages others (Powlison, p. 128).

Evangelism is essential. People cannot be helped in any fundamental sense apart from the gospel of Jesus Christ (Adams, *Competent*, p. 68). Evangelism is "absolutely essential" to counseling (Adams, *Competent*, p. 69), but as a Calvinist who believes in limited atonement, that is, Christ died only for the elect, Adams says, "As a reformed Christian, the writer believes that counselors must not tell any unsaved counselee that Christ died for him, for they cannot say that. No man knows except Christ himself, who is his elect and for whom he died. But the counselor's task is to explain the gospel and to say very plainly that God commands all men to repent of their sin and believe in Jesus Christ" (Adams, *Competent*, p. 70). "While it may take several sessions to reach an appropriate point to present the gospel, nevertheless, all counseling should be done from within a Christian milieu" (Adams, *Competent*, p. 71). Powlison observes, "Adams's overt evangelistic thrust communicates how his counseling model was counseling for conservative Protestants and predominantly for the pastor commissioned to be a minister of the conservative Protestant gospel" (Powlison, p. 129).

Adams was so convinced that counseling was the application of sanctification that he called counseling an unbeliever "pre-counseling." This does not mean that he did not counsel unbelievers. He was "not averse to helping non-Christians make constructive changes in their lives, short of them becoming believers" (Powlison, p. 129). Adams wrote, "It is right to help unregenerate men to conform (even though it be such an outward conformity) to scriptural standards. Since he does good works from the wrong motives, an unregenerate man cannot please God (Romans 8:8). Yet the Confession rightly observes that for the unbeliever to neglect doing the right thing would be more displeasing to God. So that to help unbelievers solve their problems, to help them change habit patterns from less correct the more correct patterns, to get them to do formally what the Word of God says about certain aspects of their lives, is to honor God and to do that which is of good use, both to the unbeliever and to others. So there is a warrant, in conjunction with evangelism, to help unbelievers (all the while evangelizing) though evangelism be unsuccessful. Jesus cleansed ten lepers, but only one returned to give him thanks. Counselors too may sometimes ask, 'Where are the nine?'" (Adams, *Competent to Counsel*, pp. 72-73).

Given Adams's attitude toward the gospel, it is not surprising that for him. "counseling is fundamentally a pastoral activity and must be church-based.... He also believed that the Bible taught a distinctive counseling methodology and ordained the church as the community in which message and method would be implemented" (Powlison, p. 130). "Adams's counseling was first and foremost 'pastoral' counseling, in the strict sense: the work of the ordained pastor.... [It is] "church-based, pastor-led counseling.... Preaching, among other things, is preventative counseling" (Powlison, p. 132). He also "viewed church discipline as an essential component in the biblical counseling endeavor" (Powlison, p. 133).

"Adams was suspicious of counseling centers, even though he had founded one with a comprehensive charter" (Powlison, p. 134). "Adams clearly did not wish to define a counseling methodology that would be suitable for counselors operating autonomously of conservative Protestant doctrine and ecclesiastical contacts.... Similarly, he did not intend a counseling methodology suitable for counselors who had no interest in considering the implications of the Christian faith for explaining and addressing their problems" (Powlison, p. 135).

Adams describes his specific methodology in *Competent to Counsel*. For example, he says, "God's remedy for man's problems is confession" (Adams, *Competent*, p. 105). Giving hope is one of the important factors in counsel. "Man in misery needs hope" (*Competent*, p. 137). "The constant theme of nearly all of the prophets was judgment, but they also proclaim a message of hope" (Adams, *Competent*, p. 138). "Taking people seriously about their sins is an important way to give them hope" (Adams, *Competent*, p. 141). Restitution is biblical (Prov. 6:31; Lev. 6:1-7; Num. 5:5-8; Adams, *Competent*, p. 153). A person's problem may affect every aspect of his life, including his social life, married life, work, physical, and financial matters (Adams, *Competent*, p. 155). Modeling is part of problem-solving. In 2 Thessalonians 3, Paul discusses church discipline to deal with an "unruly" (disorderly) person. He told them they should follow his example (Adams, *Competent*, p. 177). "Role-play may also be one valid means of extending the principle that scriptural discipline be taught by example" (Adams, *Competent*, p. 178; where does the Bible teach role-play?).

Adams cites a study that says, "There is good reason to believe that the most powerful environment for the induction of certain kinds of behavior is to have that behavior exhibited by others.... The mood represented by the majority of social group influences the mood of all of its members." Adams adds, "The counselor's own attitude in counseling, then, is important" (Adams, *Competent*, p. 182).

Counseling experience has shown conclusively that explicit modeling is not essential to counseling. It may have grave dangers as a regular practice, such as the counseling session degenerating into story swapping (Adams, *Competent*, p. 181). Group therapy sessions have a dubious biblical warrant for existence. It is questionable whether confession should be encouraged apart from a reconciliation context (Adams, *Competent* p. 181 fn.).

Adams lists other methods. People must learn how to use Scripture on their own to solve problems, meaning the counselor must be ready to give at least elementary advice regarding Bible study methods. Have the clients draw up a list of problems, prioritize them, and give them homework to start solving them (Adams, *Competent*, pp. 194-196). Use a problem-solution form consisting of four columns (what happened, what I did, what I should've done, what I now must do), which means the counselor must spell out methods for getting things done, including long-range goals, short-range goals, scheduling, and planning (Adams, *Competent*, pp. 196-197).

Record progress. Have clients record the results of the work. Have them write out agreements. The covenantal structure of God's relationship implies this and the written tablets of the law serve such a purpose (Adams, *Competent*, p. 198).

Be specific. Solve specific problems first and then use the solutions to illustrate the general principles (Adams, *Competent*, p. 199).

Take one thing at a time. Since clients, like an iceberg, initially keep four-fifths of their problems underwater, counselors should use a *Personal Data Inventory* (Adams, *Competent*, pp. 271-274), which is calculated to dig out the roots of problems (Adams, *Competent*, p. 200). First, deal with the surface issue (Adams, *Competent*, p. 201).

Use team counseling. A counseling team consists of two or three but no more than four counselors. Jesus worked with the disciples, sent out 70 by twos, and Paul traveled with a team (Eccl. 4:9-12). Adams mentions the advantages (Adams, *Competent*, pp. 204-205), such as one counselor can take copious notes (Adams, *Competent*, p. 204), and the disadvantages (Adams, *Competent*, p. 206) of team counseling. It may be advisable to have the counselee's pastor be part of team counseling (Adams, *Competent*, pp. 207-208).

Interpret non-verbal communication. Counselors should learn to read faces, actions, and gestures as Paul did (Acts 14:8-9). "A good salesman knows when the customer is ready to buy" (Adams, *Competent*, p. 209).

Powlison lists other methods Adams used, including being "intentionally directed," worship (counselors singing with counselees), assigning homework, and enlisting a half-dozen people (friends, family members, employer) to write up a frank assessment of strengths and shortcomings (Powlison, pp. 137-138).

Adams's pamphlet *What Do You Do When Your Marriage Goes Sour?* contains an example of how he counseled people. It is the story of a Christian couple who decided to get a divorce but had no biblical grounds for it. Here is an edited summary of their story.

Emily said there was nothing left in their marriage. She didn't feel a thing for her husband, Phil. So, there was nothing left to build on. Phil agreed with his wife's assessment. He felt that every drop of love he once had for her had disappeared. The counselor told them he was sorry to hear about their difficulty and understood why they had come for help. He told them that if they didn't love each other anymore, the only thing they could do was to learn how to love one another. Both Phil and Emily reacted to that suggestion. Emily responded, "How can you learn it? You can't produce feelings out of thin air."

The counselor explained that love is not a feeling. It is a determination to do good for another person because God has told you to do so. So, love begins with the desire to please God. The couple was skeptical that love could be taught. The counselor then explained that God commands us to love. If love were feeling, it could not be commanded. The counselor told Phil that God commanded him to love his wife as Christ loved the church (Eph. 5:25), which means that Phil had to love his wife enough to be willing to die for her.

When Phil said forget it because he could not love his wife like that, the counselor said he could not forget it because God commands it and Phil could perhaps begin at a lesser level, such as loving his wife like his neighbor. When Phil objected to that, the counselor said he could love his wife at the lowest level, meaning loving her like he loved an enemy and that God provided power to enable us to do things He commanded. When Phil resisted this, the counselor informed him he could not rebel against God and expect things to go well. On the other hand, if Phil repented of his sin and learned to love his wife, he would experience peace and joy.

At this point, when the counselor asked Phil if he wanted to please God, Phil said that he did and that he knew the divorce was wrong, but the thought of putting his marriage back together again was unrealistic. The counselor promised Phil that if he meant business with God and did what He said, his marriage would sing within 6 to 8 weeks. Phil thought that was too good to be true.

The counselor assured Phil that he had seen it happen often and that there were concrete things that Phil could do, such as asking for God's forgiveness and forgiving each other. Phil said he was willing to give it a try. The counselor reiterated that love was not a feeling; it was giving, and he cited verses that demonstrate that.

Emily objected that they would be hypocrites if they did that without feeling it. The counselor reminded Emily she was thinking of a feeling-oriented view of life rather than a biblical one and that people should do whatever God tells them to do, whether they like it or not. He explained that we do many things we don't feel like doing. When she said she didn't feel like forgiving Phil, the counselor explained that forgiveness was not a feeling. Forgiveness promises to do three things: 1) not use it against the person in the future, 2) not talk to others about them, and 3) not dwell on them myself. He also reminded her that this was not something she could do in her own strength.

When they agreed to do what the counselor said, he gave them homework, namely reminding Phil that as the head of his home, it was his responsibility to see to it that there was love in the home. He told Emily she was to submit to her husband.

Evaluation

Philosophical Assumptions Like all methods of therapy, Nouthetic counseling is based on philosophical assumptions, except in this case, the philosophical assumptions are theological.

    1. Theistic. Nouthetic counseling is theistic. Adams insists that he is not a disciple of Mowrer or William Glasser, an author in the Mowrer tradition. Adams says he is far from them because "their systems begin and end with man. Mowrer and Glasser failed to consider man's basic relationship to God through Christ, neglected God's law, and know nothing of the power of the Holy Spirit in regeneration and sanctification" (Adams, *Competent*, p. xviii).

    2. Theological. Nouthetic counseling claims to be based *solely* on the Bible. Adams states the Scripture "is the basis and contains the criteria by which I have sought to make every judgment" (Adams, *Competent*, p. xxi). He declares, "There is a biblical solution to every problem" (Adams, *Competent*, p. 130). Powlison agrees, "Biblical counseling has rightly stressed that wisdom, lying open on the pages of Scripture, is the sole criteria for counseling" (Powlison, p. 253). It would be more accurate to say that Nouthetic is theological.

Actually, Nouthetic counseling claims to be based *solely* on the Bible, but Adams, its founder, was so heavily influenced by Mower that he saw Mowrer's concepts in the Bible and concluded that was what the Bible taught about counseling. (He did not start with the Bible to see *everything* it says about counseling. Had he done that, he would have come up with different conclusions. For example, he would not have concluded that confession is *the* aim of counseling.) Just look at what Mowrer said and compare it with what Adams said.

When Mowrer was 13, his father died, and a year later, he suffered his first major depression. At the University of Missouri, he majored in psychology and adopted behaviorism. While working on his Ph.D. at Johns Hopkins, because of another episode of depression, he underwent psychoanalysis for the first time. As an Assistant Professor at the Harvard Graduate School of Education, when his depression returned, he underwent a second, much lengthier analysis and felt that he was much improved. His symptoms soon returned, however, leading him to question Freud's premises. Despite his doubts, he underwent a third analysis. As a result of the failure of psychoanalysis, he gave up on it.

Attending a seminar led by Harry Stack Sullivan persuaded Mowrer that the key to mental health was in scrupulously honest human relationships, not in intrapsychic factors. As a result, Mowrer confessed to his wife his adolescent sexual behavior and his affair during their marriage. She was upset, but she and Mowrer were convinced that those secrets might explain his bouts of depression. The depression went into remission for eight years. Then he suffered his worst psychological collapse, was hospitalized for three and a half months, and was successfully treated, for a while, with one of the first antidepressants.

Reading the novel *Magnificent Obsession* by Lloyd C. Douglas impacted Mowrer's thinking. In the novel, good deeds done in secret endow the characters with almost magical power. Mowrer applied that concept to misdeeds kept secret. He concluded, "You *are* your secrets," sometimes reworded as "You are as sick as your secrets." When Mowrer counseled someone who would not confess anything of significance, he would "model" confession for them by disclosing something from his own life. Mowrer also advocated the idea that mental illness has a substantial biological and genetic basis. He set out to restore the consciousness of personal sin and guilt to churches. He taught a program in morality and mental health, which Jay Adams attended.

Is it not apparent that Mowrer heavily influenced Adams? Powlison says Adams was "radicalized by contact with Mowrer" (Powlison, p. 24), Mowrer gave him "the contours of a counseling method" (Powlison, p. 37), and "Nouthetic counseling was only conceived in mind and practice of its founder [Adams] during the summer of 1965" (Powlison, p. 13). That is the summer Adams spent with Mowrer! Powlison readily admits that "During 1965-66, Adams began to implement what he had discovered from Mowrer and what he was discovering in the Bible" (Powlison, p. 37).

Powlison names some of the specific items: Mowrer attacked dominant psychotherapies for "ineffectiveness and for neglecting the moral dimension inherent in problems in the living" (Powlison, p. 24), challenged Freudian theory, described people as morally responsible, and called troubled human behavior "sin" (Powlison, p.

35). "Adams concluded from his time with Mowrer and his own counseling experience that most people diagnosed as mentally ill and, consequently, subject to psychiatric care were chiefly suffering from a 'failure to meet life's problems. To put it simply, they were there because of their unforgiven and unaltered sinful behavior'" (Powlison, p. 109) and "One characteristic Nouthetic phrase was 'the put off and put on.' Sinful problem behaviors would be 'put off' and godly behaviors 'put on.' Adams described this process, borrowing language from Mowrer, as a process of 'dehabituation' and 'rehabituation'" (Powlison, p. 103).

Powlison says four aspects of Mowrer's view profoundly impacted Adams: 1). People's guilt was real, not false. They were violators of conscience and not victims of an overactive conscience. 2). People needed to confess their failings and make restitution. 3) The method of counseling was direct and directive. 4) Freudianism failed. The responsible ethics woven into the medical model of neurosis and psychosis was bankrupt (Powlison, pp. 35-36). The moral model replaced the medical model.

Powlison points out that "to critics who read Mowrer and Adams side-by-side, it was evident that the entire structure of Adams's theory was Mowrerian." More specifically, he learned from Mowrer, "an authoritative style that minimizes the counseling relationship, a short-term, intervention model of practice that employed standard directive techniques such as role-playing, modeling, group pressure, and homework. He learned all of these from Mowrer, not the Bible. He had then read the Bible in their light." He brought secular principles "through the back door." He who criticized integrationists was himself an integrationist. Critics "notice conceptual and methodological similarities between Adams and B. F. Skinner, William Glasser, Alfred Adler, and Albert Ellis, again correspondences Adams would not acknowledge" (Powlison, p. 185).

Which came first, the chicken or the egg? Did Adams, as he claims, study the Bible and come up with Nouthetic counseling, or was he exposed to Mowrer and then saw some of Mowrer's concepts in the Scripture? The similarities between Mowrer and Nouthetic counseling are so extensive it is hard to avoid the conclusion that Mowrer influenced Adams so much that he saw Mowrer's concepts reflected in the Bible. Adams studied counseling in the Bible like a reporter who researches a story by starting with a point of view. As Mowrer made confession his fundamental methodology, so Adams says he studied the Bible and, lo and behold, instead of coming away with the conclusion that the Bible contains *many* methods of "counseling" (1 Thess. 5:14), he lands on one of the few passages that mention confession (Jas. 5:16) and makes confession the be-all and end-all of counseling!

Adams himself says, "Mowrer was involved in very deep personal problems and came to his theories of confession and responsibility by trial and error. In the process, he stumbled upon modeling" (Adams, *Competent*, p. 180). Powlison states, "O. Hobart Mowrer, William Glasser, and Perry London provide the most significant resources for Adams" (Powlison, p. 148) and "He [Adams] acknowledged the influence of Mowrer, Glasser, Szasz, and others had had on him and he recognized strands of insight even in theories less to his taste " (Powlison, p. 153).

3. Optimistic. "Biblical counseling has resisted seeing people as determined—whether by heredity, the sins of others, organic imbalances, poor models, unmet needs, mental forces imposed on us as 'illnesses,' or demonic inhabitants" (Powlison, p. 247). "Adams was optimistic that counselees could develop different ways of handling life if they only would rely on God's truth (the Bible), power (the Holy Spirit), and people (those who had become 'competent to counsel')" (Powlison, p. 125).

4. Anti-secular psychotherapies. When Adams began grappling with counseling in the 1960s, the dominant secular theories were Freudianism and Rogerianism. He said, "All that can be said of Freud is that his view has encouraged irresponsible people to persist in and expand their irresponsibility" (Adams, *Competent*, p. 17) and Rogerian counseling consists of a philosophy of the autonomy of man and a method of listening to counselees and reflecting what they say back to them without giving advice to them (see esp. Adams, *Competent* p. 80). In other words, the solution to people's problems lies within them and can be tapped into by nondirective techniques (Adams, *Competent* p. 81). God is unnecessary (Adams, *Competent*, p. 82).

Adams insists, "Destroying the foundation and preserving the superstructure is impossible. Because nonbiblical systems rest upon nonbiblical presuppositions, it is impossible to reject presuppositions and adopt the techniques that go out of and are appropriate to those presuppositions" (Adams, *Competent*, p. 102). Rogerianism "must be rejected *in toto*. Every remnant of this humanistic system exalting man as autonomous must be eradicated. The basic premise leads to the methodology. Reject one and you reject the other" (Adams, *Competent*, p. 103).

Adams wrote, "Psychology should be a legitimate and very useful neighbor to the pastor. Psychologists may make many helpful studies of man (e.g., on the effects of sleep loss). But psychologist ... should get out of the business of trying to change persons" (Adams, cited by Powlison, p. 150). As far as Adams is concerned, the functional troubles of the soul belong to the pastor by divine right (Powlison, p. 151).

Powlison says explanations that involve heredity, hormones, or temperament drew Adams' fire (Powlison, p. 115). Adams opposed psychiatric theories of grief, including the stage theories of Elizabeth Kubler-Ross. "He thought the stage theories converted descriptions—what sometimes happened to some people in some cultures—into a normative theory" (Powlison, p. 116). Adams disassociated himself from other goals of psychotherapies, such as exploration of one's inner world, behavioral engineering to accomplish the will of either client or therapist, emotional healing, self-actualization, learning to get psychological or social needs met, producing cathartic relief from the feelings attached to repressive memories, building ego strength, cultivating self-confidence, releasing inner forces of health, breaking undesirable habits, getting in touch with inner divine energies, learning to cope with the disease of addiction, becoming better adjusted socially, constructing a personal myth, learning to assert one's own will, and so forth" (Powlison, p. 126).

Adams proposes a parable of the tack. A fellow sitting on a tack is suffering from severe pain. One counselor immediately prescribes tranquilizers or painkillers. A do-it-yourselfer, not having any pills in his medicine cabinet, may resort to his chemical solution by anesthetizing his brain with alcohol. A surgeon may suggest that the nerves that are activated may be severed, which would be like slashing the flashing red light on the dashboard with a hammer. A Freudian analyst would point out the pain was located in the sexual area. Looking back into the patient's childhood experiences to learn about some of his early sexual experiences would alleviate his pain. If he asks a Rogerian counselor how to get rid of his pain, the therapist would reply, "I'm not going to advise anything. I'm sure that you have all the resources within yourself to solve the difficulty. I will reflect your question back to you and help you clarify and gain insight." A biblical counselor would say, "Get off the tack. Sit down on the chair over here and let's talk about how to avoid sitting on a tack in the future" (Adams, *Competent*, pp. 103-104).

Yet when asked if we can learn something from psychologists, Adams answered, "Yes, we can learn a lot: I certainly have.... I do not object to psychology or psychologists, as such.... I deplore psychology's venture into the realm of value, behavior, and attitude change because it is an intrusion upon the work of the minister" (Adams, cited by Powlison, p. 152). He even admitted that "there is an element of truth reflected by every false position" (Powlison, p. 153), because "in the common grace of God, unbelievers stumble over aspects of truth in God's creation" (Adams, cited by Powlison, p. 154).

For example, Adams says, "Frankl is correct in observing that meaning (or perhaps a better word would be 'purpose') is fundamental not only to a full and productive life, but also to the wellbeing and, in some instances, the continued existence of a human being.... Frankl rightly has observed that man cannot live without at least such day-to-day goals and purposes." Adams said, "Frankl and other existential psychiatrists can offer nothing....; For them, the future is but a long dark tunnel. Apart from meaning related to God, the apparent meaning that one finds in the pleasures of this life soon evaporate" (Adams, cited by Powlison, p. 154). Adams also said that the Frankl system was "fundamentally non-Christian" because it refused to adopt normative Christian values and meaning and failed to introduce these is essential in the counseling process" (Powlison, p. 154).

In the final analysis, Adams acknowledges some truth in psychology, but he rejects the use of secular psychology! Powlison says that although Adams agreed it had something to offer, he "spent little time studying psychology" (Powlison, p. 172) and although Adams said Christians could reclaim the truth dimly reflected, "in practice, very little, such appropriation took place within nouthetic circles" (Powlison, p. 155). Adams explains why when he says, "All counseling by its very nature ... implies a theological commitment by the counselor. He simply cannot become involved in the attempt to change beliefs, values, attitudes, relationships, and behavior without waiting to make it deep into theological waters" (Adams, cited by (Powlison, p. 156). Adams went so far as to say that "The church ... either has been deceived by Satan's counsel or has found itself in conflict with it. There is no neutral ground, *compromise* or *conflict* are the only two alternatives" (Adams, italics his, cited by Powlison, p. 158).

Thus, Adams rejected the use of secular psychotherapies, even when practiced by evangelical Christians. He felt that even though an evangelical psychotherapist might have personal beliefs and ethics that are orthodox, "such a practitioner was in a highly irregular and dangerous position. Such counselors were uneducated in the things that mattered most and educated in the things that were dubious" (Powlison, p. 159). Adams says, "Typically, the self-appointed Christian 'professional' has spent years studying psychology at the graduate level but has little more than a Sunday School (or, at best, a Bible school) knowledge of the Bible" (Adams, cited by Powlison, p. 159). By "self-appointed," Adams means that they are "unaccountable to those same ordaining and overseeing presbyteries, bishops, pastors, or elders that keep the Nouthetic counselor within the fences of orthodoxy" (Powlison, p. 159).

For Adams, Christians who practice secular psychotherapies are "compromisers who undermined the pastorate and orthodox theology" (Powlison, p. 159). Adams was highly critical of Bruce Narramore, Larry Crabb, and others. He "credited them with good intentions but little else" (Powlison, p. 161). Adams thought that Crabb's notion of human nature was reprehensible and "the dead hand of Ellis, Adler, and Rogers lay all over Crabb's theory of human personality," that "Bruce Narramore's view of guilt was Freudianized," and that James Dobson's view of child-rearing was a "near total capitulation to behaviorism" (Powlison, pp. 161-162).

Adams wrote, "In my opinion, advocating, allowing, and practicing psychiatric and psychoanalytic dogmas within the church is every bit as pagan and heretical (and therefore perilous) as propagating the teaching of some of the most bizarre cults. The only vital difference is that the cults are less dangerous because their error is more identifiable since they are controversial by existing creedal statements" (Adams, cited by Powlison, p. 161). In Adam's view, Scripture and the church are the only legitimate actors in the counseling field (Powlison, p. 162).

Although a staunch Calvinist, Adams rejects Calvin's view of truth discovered by non-Christians. Calvin said, "In man's perverted and degenerate nature, some sparks still gleam.... The mind of man, though fallen and perverted from its wholeness, is nonetheless clothed and ornamented with God's excellent gifts.... We shall neither reject the truth itself, nor despise it wherever it shall appear" (John Calvin, *Institutes of the Christian Religion*, pp. 12, 15; cited by Powlison, p. 164).

The Bible is not against all secular thought. All truth is God's truth, but not all truth is in the Bible, a truth the Bible recognizes. Paul argues that nature teaches us (1 Cor. 11:14; Rom. 1:26). He even quotes pagan sources to prove his point (Titus 1:12), which demonstrates that it would be biblical to use "secular" material to prove a point. He also teaches that we are to do good to all men, especially those who are of the household of faith (Gal. 6: 10). In the parable of the Good Samaritan, a person's needs were met without addressing anything spiritual (Lk. 10:25-37). Are believers not to love everyone, including their enemies, which means doing what is best for them (Lk. 6:35)? The theological concept of "common grace" is that God blesses unbelievers and, therefore, believers ought to do good to unbelievers to be like their heavenly father (Lk. 6:35-36).

View of People Nouthetic counseling has a reductionistic view of people. It reduces people to physical and spiritual beings. They are either sinners or sufferers.

Should they not also be viewed as immature (1 Cor. 3:1), deceived (Jas. 1:22), struggling (Job), confused (Ps. 13), etc.? A more complete biblical concept sees people as spiritual, social, psychological, purposeful, and physical beings (see Chapter 2, "The Standard of Evaluation").

Theory of Pathology Adams says that according to the Scripture, organically based problems stem from sinful attitudes and behavior (Adams, *Competent*, p. 28). From a biblical point of view, there is no doubt that sin causes many problems, but the Bible also recognizes the impact and influence of people, especially parents, and events. Powlison says that Adams's treatment of the range of factors that significantly shape human behavior is unsystematic and uneven. Adams mentions physical factors, social events in which people were wronged by others, the role of the devil, but "he never discusses more general social factors that contribute to problems in living: socialization and enculturation, the impact of political, economic, racial, class, and gender issues. Adams gave somatic events a far more significant impact than social events" (Powlison, p. 110). While, on the one hand, Adams acknowledged the pervasiveness of socialization effects, his sole concern was to warn against excuse-making and exhort moral responsibility. Powlison quotes Adams as saying, "Each individual must bear personal responsibility for how he has allowed others to influence his conduct.... Since we may reshape ourselves, we are responsible for the shape we are in." According to Adams, "even the child 'who has been berated time and again by his parents; who has been told in a hundred ways that he is worthless; who is constantly criticized and condemned' was entirely responsible for the depression or rebellion that typically followed: 'if he believes what he is told, then, that is what he is—a weak person dependent upon others for self-evaluation'" (Powlison, p. 111).

The Bible teaches that people are ultimately responsible for their attitudes and actions, but it does not present a simplistic view that all people need to do is acknowledge their sins and repent. The problem may be immaturity, a lack of knowledge (Heb. 5:12), a lack of support (1 Thess. 5:14), etc.

Nature of Health From a biblical point of view, it is difficult, if not impossible, to argue with Adams that health is salvation and progressive sanctification, especially when sanctification is defined as love for God and neighbor. However, whereas he defines progressive sanctification as conformity to Christ, because of his Reformed theology (Calvinism), he emphasizes conformity to the Law. A more balanced view of conformity to Christ would include being gracious as well as being righteous. Jesus was full of grace and truth (Jn. 1:14; for a detailed description of Christ-like spiritual maturity, see G. Michael Cocoris, *The Spiritual Life: Clarifying the Confusion*, available at Amazon.com).

Method of Therapy Adams bases his method of counseling on the Greek word *nouthesis* (nouthetic), which he says means "person-to-person verbal confrontation" (Adams, *Competent*, p. 46). The Greek word *nouthesis*, however, conveys the idea of admonishing rather than confronting. It comes from two Greek words ("mind" and "to place;" hence, the root meaning is "to put in mind") and means "admonish, exhort" (Abbot-Smith lexicon; Acts 20:31; Rom. 15:14; 1 Cor. 4:14; Col. 1:28; 3:16; 1 Thess. 5:12, 5:14; 2 Thess. 3:15). Strong says it means "to put in mind, that is, (by implication) to caution, to reprove gently, admonish, warn" The Arndt, Gingrich lexicon says it means "admonition, warn" (they say the noun form means "admonition, instruction, warning"). No major modern translation renders it "confrontation" (on Rom. 15:14, see "admonish" in the KJV; NKJV; NASB and "instruct" in the NIV; ESV).

Richard Trench, who authored the classic book on Greek synonyms in the New Testament, says it means "admonition." He adds, "It is training by word—by the word of encouragement when this is sufficient, but also by that of the remote remonstrance of reproof, of blame, where these may be required." He says it "continually, if not always, has the sense of admonishing with blame" (Trent, pp. 112-113). As Adams points out, Trench also argues that the compound nature of the word affirms the idea of rebuke, but not all agree with Trench. Although the Latin Vulgate translated the Greek word *nouthesis* by the Latin word *correptio*, which means "seizure, attack, reproof, rebuke, censure," Jerome wanted to get rid of *correptio* on the ground that in *nouthesis* no rebuke is implied (see Trench, p. 113). In his comments on Colossians 1:28, Eadie translates *nouthesis* as "reminding." He adds, "There is no warrant in the context for translating this first term [*nouthesis*] by the Latin *correptio*—as in the Vulgate; as if the apostle meant to say ... that men in sin needed to be rebuked."

The way the Greek word *nouthesis* is translated conveys a significantly different tone than confront. The word "admonish" conveys a much milder meaning than does the word "confront." The English word "admonish" means "1. to caution, advise, or counsel against something. 2. to reprove or scold, especially in a mild and good-willed manner: *The teacher admonished him about excessive noise.* 3. to urge to a duty; remind." The English word "confront" means "1. to face in hostility or defiance; oppose: *The feuding factions confronted one another. 2.* to present for acknowledgment, contradiction, etc.; set face to face: *They confronted him with evidence of his crime.* 3. to stand or come in front of; stand or meet facing: *The two long-separated brothers confronted each other speechlessly.* 4. to be in one's way: *the numerous obstacles that still confronted him.* 5. to bring together for examination or comparison."

The misinterpretation of the Greek word *nouthesis* as "confrontation" instead of the milder "admonition" has tainted the entire Nouthetic counseling movement with a non-biblical tone. The "second generation" has noted the tone's fallacy (without correcting its basis), but according to Johnson, the majority still follow Adams.

Furthermore, there is more than one way to counsel. Paul says, "Now we exhort you, brethren, warn those who are unruly, comfort the fainthearted, uphold the weak, be patient with all" (1 Thess. 5:14; Powlison made this observation). The unruly need to be warned (*nouthesis*, admonished), but not all who need counseling are unruly. The fainthearted need comfort, not confrontation. The Greek word translated fainthearted" means "small souled." It is a reference to the discouraged and despondent. There are two words in the New Testament translated "comfort." One is directed more or less to the will, and the other more or less toward the emotions. The one here is the latter. It means "to comfort, console." It is addressed especially to the feelings. There is a difference between warning and consoling. Warning implies blame; consoling does not.

The weak need to be supported ("uphold the weak"). This probably refers to some who are buckling under the pressure from persecution (1 Thess. 3:3, 5). When anyone does not have the strength to cope with the pressure and stress they are under, they need support from others, not confrontation. The Greek word translated "uphold" means to "lay hold of." It was used of a servant laying hold of his master in the sense of being devoted to him (Mt. 6:24). Here, it means to lay hold, to support. We are to hold on to them, cling to them, and be devoted to them. People need somebody who will stand by them and with them, understand them, and teach them. Just knowing that somebody is there, somebody who cares, gives them strength. The therapy is having someone—someone to talk to—someone who understands and cares. By listening, the counselor is the therapy. From a biblical point of view, people change because they respond to relationships and truths.

To determine what the Bible teaches about counseling, instead of making "confrontation" and "confession" the be-all and end-all, would it not be more biblical to study the way the members of the Trinity counseled people? For example, God the Father did not "confront" Elijah and make him "confess" when he was depressed. The Lord fed him (1 Kings 19:5-8) because he was physically exhausted (1 Kings 19:7), began the "counseling session" by asking a question concerning the situation, letting Elijah express how he felt (1 Kings 19:9-10), and instead of "confronting him" and having him "confess," the Lord "educated him" (1 Kings 19:11-12). When Elijah did not exactly get the point the Lord was making (1 Kings 19:13-14; when asked the same question a second time, Elijah's response was identical to his first response), the Lord did not "confront him" or "make him confess," but instead gave him a new commission (1 Kings 19:15)! The Lord "counseled" Jonah in a similar fashion (Jonah 4:1-11). When Jonah was angry and suicidal (Jonah 4:1-3), the Lord again began with a question and gently reasoned with him by teaching him (Jonah 4: 4-11).

Jesus Himself is the ultimate example of a "counselor" (Isa. 9:6). While He was confrontational, He is most pictured as being compassionate. His main method was teaching. He asked questions. He told stories. He did not deal with everyone the same way; He didn't even heal blind people all the same way!

When Jesus told the disciples that He was leaving and sending them the Holy Spirit, He referred to the Holy Spirit as "another Helper" (Jn. 14:16, 26; 15:26; 16:7). The Greek word translated "another" means "another of the same kind." In other words, Jesus was a Helper and when He left, He would send another like Him. The Greek word translated "helper" is *paraclete*, a Greek word that means "called to one's side, especially called to one's aid, hence, an advocate, a pleader, an intercessor." It was used of a friend of the accused person called to speak to his character or otherwise enlist sympathy in his favor (A-S). The word is secondary to counseling, supporting, or aiding that individual. This Helper would help by teaching (Jn. 14:26).

If any word in the Bible should be used to describe the overall biblical approach to counseling, it should be the word *paraclete*, not the word *nouthetic*; that is, helper, not confronter.

Summary: Except for physically based problems and suffering, problems of daily living are a result of sin and, therefore, people must be confronted with their sin so that they may come to know Jesus Christ and become spiritually mature.

From a totally Biblical perspective, Nouthetic counseling is limited because its views are too narrow. The problem with so-called "biblical" counseling is that it is not biblical enough. It has a reductionistic view of people and the method of therapy and a restricted view of secular psychology, which is a denial of their own doctrine of common grace. If you see all problems as a nail, the only tool you need is a hammer. If you see all problems as sin, confrontation is the only tool you need. If you broaden

Nouthetic Counseling

the view to see all problems as either suffering and sinning, you will add compassion before confrontation, but you will still ultimately use confrontation as the method of therapy.

Powlison, a defender of Adams, lists criticisms against Adams given by fellow evangelicals: 1) Adams misused the Bible. 2) Adams's view of human nature was superficial, too shallow, and too narrow, and his view of sin was naïve. 3) Adams ignored the effects of suffering. He acknowledged but paid little attention to being sinned against [the second generation has tried to correct this]. He was often charged with being one of "Job's counselors," who passed over the suffering to confront Job with his sin. 4) Adams's approach to change was legalistic, not gracious (change her behavior and you'll be right with God). His approach was "joyless moralism." It ran the danger of a "pharisaical self-righteousness." 5) Adams's insistence on the primacy of the preacher as an authoritative counselor was problematic. Counseling was reduced to "private preaching." Confrontation is sometimes appropriate, but Adams did not confront the right way or use other appropriate methods. Adams magnified the Greek word *noutheteo* (admonish, which he used to justify confrontation) when he should have landed on *parakaleo*, which means "called alongside to help." Crabb noted the lack of emphasis on love, support, compassion, and patience. As Carter and Narramore pointed out, "change takes place when truth is presented in relationship" (Carter and Narramore, *The Integration of Psychology and Theology,* p. 133). 6) Adams's interaction with secular psychology was uninformed. His attack on psychology was ignorant, unfair, and unreflective. He misunderstood the theories and he was indebted to Mowrer far more profoundly than he acknowledged. 7) Adams's manner escalated controversy into hostility. He described psychotherapy as a pseudo-profession, and his peers described him as belligerent, brash, abrasive, bombastic, argumentative, divisive, and arrogant. In addition to criticisms leveled against Adams by his fellow evangelicals, mainstream Protestants also criticized Adams's understanding of human nature, his grotesque overemphasis on behavior, and his counseling as pervasively superficial. Secular psychotherapists rarely hear of Jay Adams and Nouthetic counseling (Powlison, pp. 167-193). "Though Adams claimed that thousands of pastors agreed with him, it appears that tens of thousands disagree" (Powlison, p. 205). Professors from leading Reformed seminaries opposed Adams (Powlison, p. 212). Even Bettler, a friend and partner of Adams, criticized Adams's "misuse of the Bible, externalism, neglect of social factors, overtly directive methodology, unfairness to the real views of psychologists" (Powlison, p. 212).

One other issue needs to be mentioned. What about Christians counseling non-Christians? Although the purpose of the Bible is to bring people to faith in Christ and to bring believers to Christ-like spiritual maturity (2 Tim. 3:15-17), it acknowledges that believers should help people whether they are believers or not. In the Old Testament, the Lord told the Jews who were taken captive to Babylon to: "Seek the peace of the city where I have caused you to be carried away captive and pray to the LORD for it; for in its peace you will have peace" (Jer. 29:7). Jesus taught "love your enemies, bless those who curse you, do good to those who hate you, and pray for those who spitefully use you and persecute you, that you may be sons of your Father in heaven; for He makes His sun rise on the evil and on the good, and sends rain on the just and on the unjust" (Mt 5:44-45). Paul echoed Christ when he said, "As we have opportunity, let us do good to all" (Gal. 6:10).

As was pointed out earlier, even Adams himself was "not averse to helping non-Christians make constructive changes in their lives, short of them becoming believers" (Powlison, p. 129). Adams wrote, "It is right to help unregenerate men to conform (even though it be such an outward conformity) to scriptural standards. Since he does good works from the wrong motives, an unregenerate man cannot please God (Romans 8:8). Yet the Confession rightly observes that for the unbeliever to neglect doing the right thing would be more displeasing to God. So that to help unbelievers solve their problems, to help them change habit patterns from less correct to more correct patterns, to get them to do formally what the Word of God says about certain aspects of their lives, is to honor God and to do that which is of good use, both to the unbeliever and to others. So there is a warrant, in conjunction with evangelism, to help unbelievers (all the while evangelizing), though evangelism is unsuccessful. Jesus cleansed ten lepers, but only one returned to give him thanks. Counselors too may sometimes ask, 'Where are the nine?'" (Adams, *Competent to Counsel*, pp. 72-73).

Nevertheless, several concepts in Nouthetic counseling are needed.

1.   People are spiritually separated from God; their most fundamental need is to know Him by trusting His son Jesus Christ, who died for their sins and rose from the dead (Jn. 3:16).

2.   People need to grow to Christ-like spiritual maturity (Col. 1:28).

Chapter 19

OTHER CHRISTIAN RESPONSES

Besides Jay Adams, other Christians have responded to "psychology" and "psychotherapy." Here is a sample of some past Christian responses to "psychology" and more recent Christian responses to psychotherapy.

"Augustine is widely recognized as the first great Christian 'psychologist.' Augustine unified the best of Augustinian and Aristotelian tradition and produced an influential body of psychological thought, covering the appetites, the will, habits, the virtues and vices, the emotions, memory, and intellect" (Johnson, p. 12).

In the fourth century, John Chrysostom (347-407) wrote a short treatise entitled "On the Priesthood: A Treatise in Six Books," which has been called "the first really great pastoral work." He exalts being a priest over being king, saying, "The priesthood far excels royal dignity as the soul excels the body." In emphasizing the importance of preaching, he states, "There is but one method and way of healing appointed after we have gone wrong, and that is the powerful application of the Word." In other words, the "healing" of souls is by preaching the Word.

"Possibly the most significant Christian psychology author since the Middle Ages was Soren Kierkegaard, who used the word *psychology* to describe some of his works, and who wrote some profound psychological works" (Johnson, p. 13).

Eventually, psychology also became about helping people. "As the impetus to turn psychology into a natural science grew across the West, biblical study and philosophical reflection were systematically excluded as sources of knowledge about human nature in favor of the empirical investigation of the structure and processes of the senses, mind, memory, and behavior" (Johnson, p. 19). In the meantime, as the field of psychology grew, conservative Christians generally moved away "from intellectual engagement with the wider culture." "The bulk of fundamentalist literature focused on doctrinal beliefs (like end-time prophecy), moral issues, and evangelism. The state of one's soul—apart from whether one was born again—was largely neglected. As a result, for decades, the most sophisticated pastoral care literature was written by more liberal Christians" (Johnson, p. 29).

Then, Bible-believing Christians began to interact with the field of psychology. Henry Brandt (Ph.D. in Marriage and Family Relations from Cornell University, 1952) has been called "The Father of Modern-Day Biblical Counseling." For decades, he counseled individuals to evaluate their heart attitudes and behavior in the light of biblical teaching.

In 1954, Clyde Narramore began a radio program called "Psychology for Living" that eventually played on over 200 Christian stations nationally (Johnson, p. 30). "In the late 1950s, Clyde Narramore became the first well-known author, speaker, and counseling practitioner who was certifiably both a psychologist and conservative Protestant" (Powlison, p. 27). Powlison says Narramore "packaged a popularized Freudianism with evangelical terminology and morality" (Powlison, p. 27), but Johnson claims that Narramore wrote an influential book (1960) "outlining a Christian approach to therapy that incorporated a high view of Scripture along with a Christianized form of the person-centered counseling of Carl Rogers" (Johnson, p. 30). In 1958, he founded Narramore Christian Foundation, the first international Christian counseling and training ministry.

Fuller's School of Psychology opened in 1965. Johnson says, "Fuller Theological Seminary was the first evangelical school to begin a doctoral program in clinical psychology (1964)" (Johnson, p. 31).

In 1968, the Narramore Christian Foundation began to explore the possibility of starting a graduate school of psychology, offering a doctoral degree that was more theologically conservative than Fuller Seminary and that emphasized practitioners rather than theoreticians. Clyde Narramore was president and Bruce Narramore, Clyde's nephew, became the founding Dean of the Rosemead Graduate School of Professional Psychology, which opened in 1970. In 1973, the graduate school began publishing the scholarly *Journal of Psychology and Theology*, a journal that aimed to "serve as a forum for the integration and application of psychological and biblical formation." Bruce Narramore was the founding editor. In 1977, Rosemead merged with Biola University.

Gary Collins (Ph.D. in psychology, Purdue University, 1963) was influenced by Paul Tournier. He was one of the first psychologists to teach at an Evangelical seminary. In 1969, Trinity Evangelical Divinity School (Deerfield, Illinois) hired him as its first psychologist, Professor of Pastoral Psychology. In 1977, Collins wrote *Rebuilding Psychology*.

Other Christians Responses

In 1970, James Dobson (Ph.D. in child development from USC) wrote *Dare to Discipline*. It combined common sense, behavioral psychology's positive rewards, a stress on self-esteem, carefully applied spankings, and an evangelical faith. He was critical of Watson, Freud, and Dr. Benjamin Spock. He drew on Thorndike, Glasser, and self-esteem theory (Powlison, p. 53).

In 1970, Jay Adams published *Competent to Counsel*.

Norm Wright graduated from Westmont College, Fuller Theological Seminary (MRE), and Pepperdine University (MA). He received two honorary doctorates, DD and D.Lit. from the Western Conservative Baptist Seminary and Biola University, respectively. In 2015, he graduated with a D.Min. from Phoenix School of Theology. In 1988, at the First International Congress on Christian Counseling, Adams, Clyde Narramore, and H. Norman Wright were each honored as a "father of Christian counseling" (Powlison, p. 44).

Larry Crabb (Ph.D. in clinical psychology, University of Illinois) offered a "psychodynamic model, grafting familiar evangelical themes—sin, love of Jesus, practical obedience, church friendships—onto an acknowledgment of the darker feelings and drives in the human heart." He targeted the problems of daily life, including anxiety, irritability, mild depression, and even major problems such as eating disorders, marital breakdowns, sexual perversions, and recovery from abuse (Powlison, pp. 53-54).

In 1975, Dallas Theological Seminary hired two psychiatrists, Frank Minirth and Paul Meier to teach counseling in the practical theology department. They combined an impeccable profession of evangelical faith with professional conventions. "This hiring signaled a significant institutional defeat for Adams, as he had presented a major lecture series at Dallas Seminary in 1973 entitled 'The Use of the Scripture in Counseling'" (Powlison, p. 54).

In 1982, *The Journal of Psychology and Christianity*, the second integrationist journal, was founded.

Over the years, evangelical Christians have had different reactions to psychology from "summarily dismissed" to "uncritically embraced" (Jones and Butman, p. 18). In 2000, Eric L Johnson and Stanton L Jones edited *Psychology and Christianity*, a book that presented four models of the relationship between psychology and Christianity. The contributors were Gary R. Collins (an integration view), David G. Myers (a levels-of-explanation view), David Powlison (a Biblical counseling view), and Robert C. Roberts (a Christian psychology view). In 2010, Eric L Johnson edited the second edition, *Psychology and Christianity: Five Views*. The contributors were David G. Myers (the level-of-explanation view), Stanton L Jones (an integration view), Robert C. Roberts and P. J. Watson (a Christian psychology view), John H. Coe and Todd W. Hall (a Transformational psychology view), and David Powlison (a Biblical counseling view). Neither of these books dealt with the total rejection view.

Here is a brief explanation of Christians's six (so far) reactions to psychology. Any Christian reaction to psychology has two parts: 1) their view of the place of Scripture and 2) their view of psychology.

The Bible Only and Rejection of Psychology

The Bible Only Christians who hold this position claim that the Scripture contains all that is needed to deal with the issues of daily living. Bobgan and Bobgan contend: "Numerous passages extol the sufficiency, power, and excellency of God's Word. For instance, 2 Peter 1:2-4 says: 'Grace and peace be multiplied unto you through the knowledge of God, and of Jesus, our Lord, according as his divine power hath given unto us all things that pertain unto life and godliness, through the knowledge of him that hath called us to glory and virtue: Whereby are given unto us exceeding great and precious promises: that by these ye might be partakers of the divine nature, having escaped the corruption that is in the world through lust'" and "We believe in the absolute sufficiency of Scripture in all matters of life and conduct." (Bobgan and Bobgan, pp. 5-8, 12). This is a Bible-only position. Bobgan and Bobgan say, "For Christians, there are no psychotherapies that should be used instead of the Bible or as an adjunct to the Bible" (Bobgan and Bobgan, p. 18).

Psychology All psychology is to be rejected. All counseling should "depend solely upon the truth of God's Word, without incorporating the unproven and unscientific psychological opinions of men" (Bobgan and Bobgan, p. 8). Bobgan and Bobgan argue: "If someone is improved or delivered from his problems, competent biblical ministry could have done better. Psychological explanations about life and psychological solutions to life's problems are not only unnecessary for Christians but spiritually detrimental" (Bobgan and Bobgan, p. 20). "Psychological systems with their explanations of the nature of man and how he should change" should be "rejected as an alien religion" (Bobgan and Bobgan, p. 7). "People who attempt to integrate psychology with Christianity are like the Israelites adding idols to their worship of God. (Jer. 2:11:13; Ezek. 6:6; 14:6- 8; 20:31, 39.)" (Bobgan and Bobgan, p. 18). "Witchdoctors and psychotherapists have common roots for their work" (Bobgan and Bobgan, p. 20).

According to Jones and Butman, some advocates of this view describe psychotherapy as "Satanic" or "completely secularized" and "unredeemable" (Jones and Butman, p. 18).

Sufficiency of Scripture and the Contribution of Psychology

The Bible Nouthetic counseling, later called "biblical counseling," believes in "the sufficiency, superiority, and practicality of Scripture for dealing with all of the issues of life" (MacArthur Jr. and Mack, p. ix). In short, its slogan is "the sufficiency of Scripture." This position is almost identical to the "Bible only" position (it has even been called that), but the two are not exactly the same because the sufficiency of the Scripture view at least allows psychology to contribute.

Psychology Adams says, "I do not wish to disregard science, but rather I welcome it as a useful adjunct for the purpose of illustrating, filling in generalizations with specifics, and challenging wronged human interpretations of Scripture, thereby forcing the student to re-study the Scriptures" (Adams, p. xxi). Powlison puts it like this: "Empirical research will contribute to better understanding people ... but it is an auxiliary discipline, a flying buttress attached to the Cathedral wall, not the sanctuary, in which the community lives" (Powlison, p. 198).

To explain the biblical counseling view of psychology, Powlison divides the psychological pie into six pieces (see Powlison, pp. 249-262).

"Psych-1 is the stuff of life. It simply describes how we operate in the world we inhabit.... Human beings operate psychologically. The torrent of experiences, thoughts, feelings, motives, attitudes, memories, volitions, beliefs, assumptions, schemata, perceptions, and so on is what I mean by Psych-1" (Powlison, pp. 249-250).

"Psych-2 is most like what we think of as *science*, the intentional pursuit of organized knowledge" (Powlison, p. 255, italics his). It "refers to the organized knowledge, to close observation and systematic descriptions of human functioning. Psych-2 is the thing about psychological books and psychologists in person that makes them so interesting." ... "This observational-descriptive aspect of psychology helps us get to know the myriad, significant psychological factors" (Powlison, pp. 253-254).

"We must place Psych-2 in the context of many other sources of significant knowledge," including the Bible, knowing yourself, knowing other people, drinking deeply in good novels, poetry, drama, film, music, visual arts that capture experience, and reading history, biography, cultural studies, cultural anthropology, reading thoughtfully writers in psychology and psychiatry, who noticed things you never notice and are both informative and provocative. "I particularly appreciate the humanistic tradition within psychology and psychiatry—Peter Kramer, Robert Coles, Ann Freud, Harry Stack Sullivan, Armand Nicholi, Irwin Yalom, and others. They demonstrate an admirable curiosity and a tenderness that humanizes strugglers. They wore theoretical commitments relatively lightly. In their thoughtful humanity, you can discern the rough shape of realities—truth and love—that biblical wisdom brings into bright daylight" (Powlison, pp. 254-255).

As biblical counselors, "We can learn, should learn, and do learn from anyone and everyone. But we do seek to be aware of the blinkering and distorting effects of faulty assumptions and explanations (including our own failures to apprehend the Christian gaze and to express wise love). John Calvin's interactions with the Greek philosophers provide a good historical parallel to how biblical counseling interacts with the modern psychologist. On a superficial reading, he seems almost contradictory. He applauds the Greek's brilliant insights and, in the next breath, dismisses them as blind and wrongheaded. But this is exactly the way that a God-centered gaze interprets other gazes, simultaneously appreciative and contrary. Using a mid-twentieth century metaphor, secular psychologists have 'neurotic insights,' simultaneously brilliant and distorted" (Powlison, p. 255).

Psych-3 is "an interpretive and explanatory model that organizes and weighs the torrent of Psych-1 and Psych-2 information.... Theory and worldview provide the interpretive center of the psychological enterprise" (Powlison, p. 256). "Personality theories systematically differ from the Christian gaze. Secular Psych-3s diverge home from the Christian Psych-3.... They offer faults and shallow views of humanness and we must better account for the human experience and offer better answers" (Powlison, p. 257).

"Psych-4 refers to various psychotherapeutic models and skills aiming to redress problems in the living.... Counseling is a fundamental task of Christian wisdom.... Psychotherapy is not a neutral, technical enterprise. Counseling practices and strategies are designed to facilitate change in beliefs, behaviors, feelings, attitudes, values and relationships.... One cannot intend to help another change without some ideal for human functioning, usually explicit, and easy to tease out when implicit. Ideals assert criteria of good and evil, true and false, significance and irrelevance" (Powlison, p. 257).

"We are glad when they [secular psychotherapists] accomplish common-grace goals—restraining a suicide, sweetening a marriage, sobering a drunk, walking through a rough patch with a troubled person—just as we are glad when an imam, a self-help guru or more willpower accomplishes good things. But these other 'pastorates' heal lightly the woes and wrongs of the human condition. The competencies of other psychotherapies will stimulate and challenge us, but our calling is to build distinctively Christian counseling ministry that fulfills the mission God has given his people" (Powlison, p. 258).

Psych-5 refers to institutional and professional arrangements.... "Psychology as Psych-5 is a mental health *system*.... Psychotherapeutic activity occurs in clinics, hospitals, and offices. Board exams, accreditation, and supervision legislate both education and practice (and explicitly delegitimize other contacts). Licensing laws and courts reinforce (or destabilize) the social structure of professional practice.... If you need to talk to someone, the pathways are in place that lead you to a mental health professional. Health insurance companies reimburse the conversations of only certain kinds of practitioners.... The attempt to change people is qualitatively different from scientific study and the efforts to understand what is" (Powlison, pp. 259-260, italics his).

"We commend the common-grace good, for example, when social institutions provide a safety net in a sheltered timeout for troubled people. We're glad that a suicidal person can be cocooned out of harm's way. We commend the research intended. But we find the vision of personhood seriously deficient" (Powlison, p. 260).

"Psych-6 refers to the ethos pervading popular culture.... A psychological way of thinking pervades the popular mindset in the West.... The ethos of dependency on a Savior and speaking truth in love offers a startling contrast to the ethos that dominates the popular mind and media" (Powlison, pp. 261-262).

This view has been criticized as having "little need for science" (Myers, in Johnson, p. 274). Coe and Hall say, "In Powlison's case study, "no psychological theories regarding the formation of personality and presenting problems are utilized, nor is the change process articulated.... Relational psychotherapies, for example, have proven enormously helpful in bringing about such change" (Coe and Hall, in Johnson, p. 289). In other words, this view allows for psychology to make a contribution, but it has been criticized for not incorporating the contributions of psychology into its system.

Christian Psychology and Supplementation of Psychology

The Bible The "Christian psychology" view of Roberts and Watson (Baylor University) proposes the development of "a psychology that accurately describes the psychological nature of human beings as understood according to historic Christianity" (Roberts and Watson, in Johnson, p. 155). They claim the Bible contains a psychology. They begin by examining the Sermon on the Mount, which they contend is not about ethics (rules for action and social policies) but character. The Sermon on the Mount is not thought of as psychology because when we think of psychology, we expect certain terms such as behavior, personality, dysfunction, emotion, therapy, drive, defense mechanisms, etc. Human actions, thoughts, and emotions are explained and evaluated in psychology. The Sermon on the Mount speaks of being blessed, poor in spirit, sorrowful, gentle, comforted, pure in heart, peacemaker, righteousness, anger, adultery, lust, love, forgiveness, etc. In other words, it offers its concept of human nature, an ideal of people functioning, an explanation and evaluation of actions, thoughts, and emotions, and recommendations and strategies for change (Roberts and Watson, in Johnson, pp. 156-157).

"The Sermon conceptualizes *psychopathology*. It is a disposition to anger, grudge-bearing, and revenge; to lust, adultery, and divorce, to hatred of enemies, or to manifest itself as greed, and acquisitiveness are being mastered by management; as hypocrisy and ostentatious (both public and private); as arrogance and disrespect for what is great; as anxiety about necessities; as judgmentalism of others, and blindness to one's faults. A person who is given to or mired in such dispositions will be functioning poorly as a human being, and he or she will not be mature, happy, or solidly grounded" (Roberts and Watson, in Johnson, p. 157, italics theirs).

"The Sermon conceptualizes *personal well-being* as compromising of the following character traits and their implied actions and attitudes: gentleness, desire for righteousness, mercy, purity of heart, being a peacemaker, being a lover of enemies, being disposed to forgive offenses, poverty of spirit, willingness to be persecuted for Jesus' sake, mourning, penitence, humility, respect for great things, self-unawareness (the opposite of private ostentation was), treasuring the kingdom of God, expecting good things from God, enduring through difficulties. A person who had these traits or was disposed to these actions and emotions would, according to the psychology of the Sermon, be 'mature,' 'perfect' or 'blessed' or solidly founded like a house built on a rock (Mt. 7:24)" (Roberts and Watson, in Johnson, p. 157, italics theirs).

"While the *psychological explanation* is not as patent in the Sermon as are the pictures of personal well-being and pathology, some patterns of explanation are explicit and others can be inferred. Inwardness (e, g., lust, anger) explains actions (adultery, revenge). Certain blindnesses are explained by the inverted patterns of 'treasuring,' that is, caring about things. Shades of personality ('hearts') are explained by 'treasuring.' Seeing God is explained by purity of heart. Hatred of God is explained by reference to being mastered by mammon" (Roberts and Watson, in Johnson, pp. 157-158, italics theirs).

"A number of *therapeutic interventions* (or avenues by which a person might move from pathological to healthy patterns of thought, passions, and actions) are rather explicit in the Sermon: be poor in spirit, mourning, behave gently, hunger for righteousness, be merciful and pure in heart, make peace, allow yourself to be persecuted for the sake of Jesus, let your light shine before people, keep the commandments, take responsibility for your own anger, take responsibility for other people's anger when you have caused offense, control your lustful eye, do not seek revenge on those who offend you, do not ostentatious in your piety, do not fret about daily needs, but seek the kingdom, focus chiefly on your own shortcomings rather than on those of others, do not hold others in contempt because of their shortcomings" (Roberts and Watson, in Johnson, p. 158, italics theirs).

These "interventions" are commandments, but some people may be at a loss as to how to do what is commanded. "What is needed, and what contemporary psychotherapies tend to provide, is some facilitation of the therapeutic action, some discipline by which, perhaps stepwise, a person can implement the commanded change. Here, post-biblical psychological tradition—the desert fathers, Gregory the Great, the sixteenth-century mystics and others—has responded by devising disciplines and helps that can be provided by advisors. Contemporary psychological research might add to the resources of the Christian tradition new strategies for inculcating the biblical virtues" (Roberts and Watson, in Johnson, p. 158).

Psychology There also needs to be empirical research within the Christian tradition. "The often-implied goal of the psychological establishment is to be as 'objective' as possible. Historically, this typically meant that any ideal of proper functioning must emerge inductively from an unbiased assessment of empirical data. But one important insight of 'postmodern' thought is that the pursuit of a contestable, worldview-neutral norms of human functioning is quixotic and necessarily beyond the reach of purely empirical methods. Psychology is essentially a normative discipline, and norms are never derived from data alone. A Christian empirical psychology will begin unapologetically with an explicit normative understanding of human beings and will thus be more methodologically obvious than any clinical or personality psychology that ever implicitly purported to be 'unprejudiced' but which, in fact, must orient itself by contestable ideal of proper functioning" (Roberts and Watson, in Johnson, p. 165).

"Christian psychology will need to use well-established, social-scientific methods to examine hypotheses about persons that reflect the teleological assumptions [people-as-they-should-be] of the worldview" (Robert and Watson, p. 165). For example, "newly developed scales demonstrate even more clearly that Christian beliefs about sin and about grace broadly predict better psychological adjustment" (Roberts and Watson, in Johnson, p. 167). "Christian psychologists will also need to examine issues in a comparative psychological perspective that brings the Christian worldview into explicit dialogue with the worldviews and often hidden metaphysical assumptions of established psychology" (Roberts and Watson, in Johnson, p. 167).

Stanton Jones said that he had trouble distinguishing the Christian psychology view from the core of the integrationist approach (Jones, in Johnson, p. 183). Nevertheless, he argues that the "key difference is how much we claim we can construct a complete psychology from the Scripture and Christian tradition and resources" (Jones, in Johnson, p. 185)

Jones adds that he remains "unconvinced that Roberts and Watson have clearly articulated a concise summary of what it is that constitutes their Christian psychology.... I find the discussion of the 'psychology' of the Sermon on the Mount to be edifying yet unsatisfying. Clearly, there are clusters of psychological insight offered there that must be formulated with a Christian thinker; there are, after all, the very words of our Lord and Savior. But is what is offered here a systematic psychology? ... They have not systematized these teachings [from the Sermon on the Mount] with the other teachings from the whole of Scripture. Nor have they systematized these teachings with all of Scripture with psychologies that develop throughout church history" (Jones, in Johnson, pp. 185-186).

Coe and Hall criticize this approach for not going "far enough in its critique of science" (Coe and Hall, in Johnson, p. 188). [It] "does not emphasize the rich knowledge that can be gained from less qualitative sources, such as observation and reflection on life, relational experience in doing psychotherapy and in counseling, in-depth interviews" (Coe and Hall, in Johnson, p. 190).

Other Christians Responses

Biblical Transformation and the Extension of Psychology

The Bible The "transformational psychology" of John Coe and Todd Hall (Biola University) proposes that the core tenants of Christianity, such as the existence of God, people being made in the image of God, salvation by grace through faith, etc., should *shape the entire process, product and person* doing psychology (Coe and Hall, in Johnson, p. 205).

The person's spiritual and emotional development and the psychologist's transformation are fundamental to the process (Coe and Hall, p. 205). "*Spiritual disciplines that foster union with God and good character in Christ are essential to doing good psychology.*... Spiritual disciplines develop character and, thus, "are linked to the *transformation of the person doing psychology*, the *process* of doing good psychology and to the end theoretical *product* of psychology." The disciplines and psychological insights work together (Cole and Hall, in Johnson, p. 219, italics theirs). In the process of doing psychology, transformed psychologists must strive to be open to studying themselves, God, others, reality, and traditions. The goal is to allow *reality* and *faith* to shape the work of psychology (Coe and Hall, in Johnson, p. 203). "The Old Testament wise man provides a biblical precedent, justification and even mandate that the task of doing transformational psychology, for discerning wisdom for living observation and reflection on creation and Scripture in the fear and love of God" (Cole and Hall, in Johnson, p. 211).

The ultimate product of transformational psychology is conformity to Christ, the love of God and neighbor, and glorifying God (Coe and Hall, in Johnson, p. 212).

"Transformational psychology is not primarily written for unbelievers" (Coe and Hall, in Johnson, p. 204).

Psychology Christians need to rethink "the very nature of science itself" (Coe and Hall, in Johnson, p. 199). Modern science is "a method of measuring, repeating, and observing, which pre-determines the kinds of objects that are possible to discover and investigate. The classic-realist approach reverses the process: the object of investigation determines the methodology.... According to the ancients, one cannot know what is the best way to study what exists until one is adequately acquainted with what exists" (Coe and Hall, in Johnson, p. 140). "The modernist approach to science insists that facts are divorced from values and that science has nothing to do with providing ethical prescriptions for living. Transitional psychology discerns wisdom for living from observation and reflection on creation and Scripture" (Coe and Hall, in Johnson, pp. 210-211).

"The scientific method of qualification is purely *descriptive* and no longer addresses *prescriptive* realities—such as morality (right and wrong), values (good and bad) and character (virtue and vice)—which are grounded in ancient classical realistic science and natural law theories going back to the ancient Greeks. But psychotherapy depends on understanding values, such as psychological health and pathology" (Coe and Hall, in Johnson, p. 93).

Powlison says Coe and Hall stumble because of their reliance on the monastic tradition. "The form of Christianity that they bring to the table in engaging psychology expresses problematic distinctive of the 'spiritual formation' tradition; for example, contemplative prayer's wordless interiority; pursuit of the beatific vision in contemplation of God and creation; pursuit of the ineffable experience of the divine being; pursuit of the mystical union of the self with God ('beyond rationality'); transmitting the spiritual disciplines to serve contemplative purposes" (Powlison, pp. 242-243). "Contemplative spirituality does not track with the troubles and struggles of everyday people.... The Bible everywhere treats everyday human experience, and it never gestures toward monastic super spirituality" (Powlison, p. 243). "Privatized spirituality of desert monks and medieval monastics moves in a different direction from the community-oriented pastoral care and cure of souls" (Powlison, p. 244). He adds that evangelicals have grown weary of moralism, doctrinalism, and experientialism.

Framework of Theology and the Integration of Psychology

The Bible This view claims that the Bible reveals everything necessary for a full life in Christ, but it does not provide a full understanding of human beings (Jones, in Johnson, p. 101, Wheaton College), for example, child development or personality (Jones, in Johnson, p. 110). The Bible reveals information about God, people, and the world, but the Bible does not reveal everything about God (great is the mystery of godliness), people (e.g., the age of accountability), or the world. Paul did not know everything about himself (1 Cor. 4:4); he did not even understand himself (Rom. 7:15)! The Bible provides a framework; psychology can be integrated into that framework. "To claim that *the Bible is true in everything it teaches is not the same thing as claiming that it teaches the truth about everything in every area* (nor that we perfectly grasp the truth that it teaches)" (Jones, in Johnson, p. 278, italics his).

Psychology Science is limited. It does not deal with values or morals and is not always as objective as people suppose, especially when it comes to studying human beings. Science determines facts, but more than one theory can explain the facts. In other words, facts are often interpreted through a personal or cultural grid, including such concepts as functional and dysfunctional, competent and incompetent, mature and immature.

Science determines the age of rocks and Christianity depends on the Rock of Ages; science studies how the heavens go and Christianity tells us how to go to heaven. Carl Rogers, Abraham Maslow, and others believe "that human beings are basically good, that dysfunction is the result of the socializing environment and not of the person, and that the core human motivation is that of seeking self-actualization" (Jones, in Johnson, p. 103).

Nevertheless, the Bible and psychology can be integrated by utilizing the biblical framework for understanding people. Data gained from the scientific study of people can be integrated into that framework. Jones argues that the "integrationists understand that our commitment to a biblical view of persons provides a presumptive framework" (Jones, in Johnson, p. 185). Carter and Narramore put it like this: "The dual facts of humanity created in the image of God and the human race as fallen constitutes the framework for our [Christian] view of people (Carter and Narramore, p. 56). Some psychological views of humans dehumanized them. Hamlet exclaimed, "How like a god!" In essence, Pavlov, a behaviorist, explains, "How like a dog!"

The biblical framework for integration insists that people are made in the image of God and need a relationship with Him. They are responsible for their actions.

Coe and Hall responded: Integration lacks a clear methodology and does not have an adequate model for the science of the person (Coe and Hall, in Johnson, p. 137). "Purely descriptive science can no longer provide a science of values or the understanding of prescriptive realities—such as morality (right and wrong), values (good and bad) and character (value advice)—which were grounded in natural-law theories going back to the ancient Greeks.... [Integration is an] "artificial, nonscientific, and secondary process" (Coe and Hall, in Johnson, p. 139).

Biblical Distinction and Psychology Distinction

The Bible The proponents of this position "share a common Christian faith" with other evangelical points of view (Myers, in Johnson, p. 50). They believe that Jesus is the son of God and the Bible is the Word of God.

Psychology This approach contends that there is a sharp distinction between psychology and theology, that the boundaries should not be blurred, and that to confuse them would be to distort both (see Johnson, p. 33). "Better to respect religion as religion and science as science, and then build a bridge in between them" (Myers, in Johnson, p. 228).

"Clyde Narramore's *Psychology of Counseling* (1960) is an early evangelical example of this approach. The first portion of the book is essentially a discussion of Rogerian principles of counseling.... There is a discussion of specific problems pastoral counsel is likely to encounter and a listing of relevant Scripture references.... But there is no real integration at a conceptual level" (Carter and Narramore, p. 96).

Carter and Narramore call this the parallels model. They explain that according to this model, both psychology and Christianity have their rightful place and that there are two versions of it, the isolation version (the two are separate and there is little or no significant overlap) and the correlation version (some aspects are correlated, for example, the superego is equivalent to the conscience) (Carter and Narramore, pp. 91-92). David G. Myers calls his approach "levels-of-explanation." He defines psychology as the science of behavior and mental processes (Myers, in Johnson, p. 49). His levels of explanation consist of theology, philosophy, sociology, psychology, biology, chemistry, and physics (Myers, in Johnson, p. 53). Coe and Hall say this understanding of the person is incomplete (Coe and Hall, in Johnson, p, 91), naturalistic, reductionistic (Coe and Hall, in Johnson, p. 92), and omits spiritual realities and nonphysical phenomena as well as ethics (Coe and Hall, in Johnson, p. 93). Powlison agrees, saying it does not go deep enough because Myers does not think "Christianly" about people (Powlison p. 97).

Summary: Various Christians have totally rejected all psychotherapies, totally accepted one or more explanations of psychotherapies, or tried to integrate the Scripture and the psychotherapies.

Other Christians Responses

Name	View of the Bible	View of Psychology
Bible Only	Bible is all that is needed	Psychology not needed at all
Biblical Counseling	The Bible is sufficient	Psychology can contribute
Christian Psychology	The Bible contains a psychology	Psychology can supplement
Transformational Psychology	The Bible transforms it all	Psychology needs to be extended
Integration	The Bible provides the framework but is limited concerning therapy	Psychology needs to be incorporated

Concerning the Christian psychology view, Jones, the proponent of integration, says, "The chief impetus behind the Christian psychology model is that we cannot, in faith, simply leave our psychological thinking to be done by non-Christians or even done by Christians according to the canons and methods of the establishment.... The argument is a good one, one that I have trouble distinguishing from the core of the integrationist approach" (Jones, p. 183). Jones adds, however, "The key difference is how much we claim we can construct a complete psychology from the Scripture and Christian tradition and resources" (Jones, in Johnson, p. 185) ... "I argue that what Scripture and tradition give us is fundamental but incomplete" (Jones, in Johnson, p. 187).

Concerning the transformational psychology view, Jones said, "When I finished reading the description of the transformational view, I was uncertain of what distinguishes this approach from the family of integration views properly understood.... They embodied the core commitments I have always associated with an integration view" (Jones, in Johnson, p. 231).

Concerning the biblical counseling view, Jones says, "If Powlison really does believe in substantive engagement with and learning from psychology, how does his view differ substantially from the integration view?" (Jones, in Johnson, p. 277).

The "levels-of-explanation" view, of course, accepts the findings of psychology. So, except for the "rejection" view, all Christian reactions to psychology accept some data from psychology. The question becomes, "What data from the various modern psychotherapies is compatible with Scripture?"

The relationship between the Scripture and psychology has been called "integration," but as the explanations of the various Christian reactions to psychology indicate, there are levels of integration. From a biblical point of view, what level of integration is acceptable? The differences and the debate are in the details. What do the details of integration look like? There are several different ways to integrate. For a detailed discussion of attempts at integration, see Crabb, *Effective Biblical Counseling*, pp. 31-56, Carter and Narramore, *The Integration of Psychology and Theology*, and Fleck and Carter, *Psychology and Christianity: Integrative Readings*.

To answer the question posed in the previous paragraph, the next chapter will summarize the various theories of psychotherapy, and the final chapter will delineate what in those theories is compatible with the Scripture.

Chapter 20

SUMMARY

A succinct summary of what each of the psychotherapies says concerning the five therapy categories provides an overview and highlights the differences between them (also see chart in the appendix).

Philosophical Assumptions

"Every psychological theory makes assumptions that relate to biblical revelation" (Carter and Narramore, p. 19). Philosophical assumptions include several subjects, two of which are particularly relevant to a biblical evaluation of psychotherapies; specifically, the relevant issues are the question of God and the matter of determinism.

God Some psychotherapies explain God away. For Freud, an atheist, religion is an illusion. Jung, for whom God is a mystery, described himself as a "Christian-minded agnostic." He rejected the historicity of Jesus Christ. According to him, religion represents nothing more than archetypes. Adler, a liberal Protestant, regarded the idea of God as "a concretization of the idea of perfection, greatness, and superiority." God is seen as a projection of our own psyche, which is the same as Freud's view, except Adler saw no serious conflict between his psychology and Christianity. (Today, Adlerians usually say, "religion is health-promoting insofar as it alleviates an individual's own self-bounded concern with his demise and encourages him to contribute to the usefulness of the ongoing social order.") As for behaviorism, statements such as "God exists" are not merely false; they are meaningless. Skinner explained religion away, saying it was nothing more than reinforcement. Ellis was an unabashed atheist whose atheism dramatically shaped some of his positions. Although Ellis allowed for the possibility that individuals with some religious faith can be emotionally healthy as long as they do not go overboard, he claims that devout belief tends to foster human dependency and increase emotional disturbance. Hence, too much religion is bad. For Ellis, ultimately, God is irrelevant and unnecessary. Cognitive therapy is materialistic, which denies the existence of the spiritual.

Some psychotherapies ignore God. In the psychodynamic approaches, the subject of God is never addressed as such. God is a non-issue. Reality therapy does not address the issue of God (Glasser was a Jewish atheist). Multimodal therapy pays no attention to God. People-centered therapy leaves God completely out of the process. Gestalt therapy does not need God. While claiming to be a complete system, transactional analysis excludes any reference to spiritual reality inside or outside the individual. God is never mentioned in family therapy.

Some parts of *some* psychotherapy theories are compatible with Christianity. While nonreligious existentialists regard an answer to authenticity that relies on God and His Word as inauthentic, or at least incomplete, because it relies on something outside the self. Kierkegaard, "the Father of Existentialism," said, "The self in being itself and is willing to be itself rests transparently in God." In other words, for him, to be a true self is to be a self-grounded in Self, that is, the Creator-God. Rollo May said, "Psychotherapy needs theology." He goes on to say, "The deeper one's thought penetrates in the field of psychotherapy, the closer one comes to the realm of theology," and "the fundamental questions with which psychotherapy ends can be answered only in the field of theology" (May, p. 218).

No psychotherapy holds to the existence of a personal God who has revealed Himself through nature and His Word.

Determinism Determinism, the pessimistic view, declares that all human behavior is determined by something other than choice. "Hard" determinism contends that psychological causation and human freedom are incompatible. Psychoanalysis declares that unconscious, unresolved internal conflicts in early childhood determine all human behavior. According to behaviorism, all behaviors are the inevitable results of relevant conditions. Human choice is an illusion. To a great degree, family therapy assumes that individuals have limited resources to directly and responsibly control their lives. The individuals do not directly confront their issues; the family must change for the individuals in it to change.

Freud says, "Humanity has in the course of time had to endure from the hands of science two great outrages upon its naive self-love. The first was when it realized that our earth was not the center of the universe.... The second was when biological research robbed man of his peculiar privilege of having been specially created, and relegated him to a descent from the animal world.... But man's craving for grandiosity is now suffering the third and most bitter blow from present-day psychological research, which is endeavoring to prove to the 'ego' of each one of us that he is not even

Summary

master in his own house but that he must remain content with the various scraps of information about what is going on unconsciously in his own mind...This is the kernel of the universal revolt against our science" (Freud, *A General Introduction to Psychoanalysis*, Eighteenth Lecture).

Moderate determinism ("soft" determinism), an optimistic view, redefines freedom to make it compatible with psychological determinism. Past relationships *influence* people, but their history does not *force* them to behave in a predetermined way. Their past only provides "probabilities" of how someone will act. Within boundaries, they have freedom and are, therefore, still accountable for their actions. According to Jung, people are shaped not only by their immediate and inherited past but also by their aspirations for the future (see also psychodynamic theories). Adler rejected hard determinism in favor a limited libertarianism. With an appreciation for the formative impact of the family and a person's "lifestyle," Adler emphasized choice and responsibility. This is a balance between determinism and the radical freedom of humanistic psychologies. On the one hand, Lazarus says that we are products of the interplay between our genetic endowment, physical environment, and social learning theory. At the same time, he acknowledges that we "deliberately" imitate models. He also says, "People are capable of 'overriding' the best-laid plans of contiguity, reinforcements, and example by their idiosyncratic perceptions."

Within the cognitive-behavioral school of thought, Bandura developed the notion of reciprocal determinism and other cognitive-behaviorists usually endorse it. According to Bandura, the environment determines people to a limited degree. People are also the determiners of their environment. For example, they may be affected by what they watch on TV, but they choose what they watch. The soft determinism of cognitive-behavioral therapy is a more balanced position than other theories. Jones and Butman go so far as to say that even though Bandura's view is faulty, it comes the closest to a Christian view of freedom. They say it avoids the "suffocating determinism" of classic psychoanalysis and behavior modification. It also avoids the radical suggestion about freedom embraced by humanistic psychotherapies (Jones and Butman, p. 209).

Human freedom, another optimistic view, proclaims humans are free to make choices and change their behavior. It is the opposite of determinism. According to rational-emotive therapy, to change, people must simply change their beliefs. Glasser rejects determinism. Humans are not passive, determined responders but actors pursuing desired ends. Existential therapy also rejects the notion that our acts are determined. It accepts the premise that external circumstances limit our choices, but it is based on the assumption that we are free and responsible for our choices and actions. We are the author or architect of our life and, therefore, we are always more than a victim of our circumstances. Person-centered therapy sees people as having the potential to act and make decisions *despite* their situations, histories, and limitations. Gestalt therapy insists that people are responsible for meeting their needs and behavior. Full responsibility is a key element of Gestalt therapy. Transactional analysis acknowledges the human tendency to be shaped by their past and insists that people can make decisions that will change the direction of their lives. In a sense, this is a view of limited freedom. In another sense, as with all humanistic approaches, TA attests that humans have a boundless capacity to change. In TA, freedom is the capacity to act autonomously.

From a biblical point of view, soft determinism is more accurate than the alternatives. Behavior is not totally determined; people are responsible for their choices, indicating that there is, at least, limited freedom. On the other hand, people are not totally free. They are influenced and impacted by many factors, but ultimately, they make a choice for which they are responsible.

Collins illustrates. "Let us assume that a high school graduate finds himself in a situation where he must choose between a number of alternatives for the future. Perhaps he is deciding whether to attend university, enlist in the Navy, enter his father's business, join a commune, accept a job in the community, or spend a year thumbing his way around the world. We can assume that he is free to choose between these alternatives, but it does not necessarily follow that he is equally disposed to each of these possibilities. His genetic endowment, experiences, unconscious fears, future expectations, social pressures—like his girlfriend's desire to get married and even direct supernatural influences may all have a bearing on his choice, thus making some alternatives much more likely than others. He may, in the end, decide 'by his own free will' to join the navy. Yet his decision was in large measure limited or determined by influences in his past and present life" (Collins, p. 148).

As was pointed out, psychotherapies are also naturalistic versus super-naturalistic (Freud; behaviorism; cognitive therapy; multimodal therapy), subjective (Freud; Jung; existential therapy; Rogers; Gestalt), humanistic (Adler; psychodynamic; Ellis; Rogers; Gestalt), and relativistic (Adler; reality therapy; TA; family therapy). Being basically atheistic, it is not surprising that psychotherapies are naturalistic, humanistic, relativistic, and subjective. Thus, when it comes to spiritual things, psychotherapies are the blind leading the blind. Spiritually speaking, psychotherapies contain the wisdom of the world. "There is a way that seems right to man" (Prov. 16:25). As Narramore says, "the non-Christian psychologist has a limited vision of the condition of man" (Narramore, p. 39).

View of People

With Freud and Jung, modern psychotherapies began with elaborate theories of people, but as the field developed, theories of people became less and less of a focus. Their goal became to develop well-articulated, small-scale theories about specific problems (for example, depression), not about people as a whole being (Jones and Butman, p. 198). Nevertheless, while not all psychopathologies formulate a theory of people, all make assumptions about them. Therefore, all have a theory of people, even though they are not explicit about those assumptions. Here is a short review of the theories of people in the four categories of psychotherapy: the psychodynamic, the cognitive/behavioral, the humanistic, and the relational.

The psychodynamic theories concentrate on early childhood experience. Freud had detailed concepts concerning people. People consist of an *id* (sexual and aggressive drives), an *ego* (the executive that governs the personality), and a *superego* (the internalization of the standards of parents and society). The ego has repressed material into the unconscious and that unconscious material, which consists of unresolved issues from the formative years of childhood, affects current behavior. A *conflict* exists between the id, ego, and superego. The id strives to express its drives. The superego seeks to inhibit the impulses of the id by persuading the ego to substitute moralistic goals for realistic ones and strive for perfection. Neurotic anxiety is the fear that the drives will get out of hand and cause one to do something for which one will be punished. Ideally, the ego controls anxiety through rational means. When the ego cannot control anxiety by direct and rational methods, it relies on ego defense mechanisms. These defense mechanisms (a form of self-deception) transform the threatening anxiety into some alternate form the person can handle. Everyone goes through stages of development: the *oral* stage, the *anal* stage, the *phallic* stage, and the *genital* stage, which is from ages twelve to eighteen.

Like Freud, Jung had an elaborate view of people. The *psyche* is the whole individual. The sub-systems of the *psyche* are the *ego*, *personal unconsciousness*, and *collective unconsciousness*. Two "attitudes" determine the orientation of the conscious mind, namely, extraversion and introversion. Within the broad "attitudes" of extroversion and introversion are four types: 1) the thinking type (logical, objective), 2) the feeling type (subjective experience), 3) the sensation type (stimuli from the senses), and 4) the intuitive type (creative, imaginative, and integrative). The *personal unconsciousness* includes everything repressed. Within the personal unconsciousness, groups of things might clump together to form a cluster or constellation. Jung called these cluster experiences "complexes," which are defined as emotionally toned ideas and behavioral impulses. The *collective unconscious* is not dependent upon personal experience. It is a reservoir of latent images, which people inherit from their ancestral past, including all human ancestors and pre-human and animal ancestors. The contents of the collective unconscious are called *archetypes*, patterns of behavior corresponding to the innate way a bird builds its nest. Archetypes can form complexes. Some archetypes are important in shaping personality and behavior. These include the animus and anima, persona, the shadow, and the self. These archetypes are innate psychic predispositions to perception, emotion, and behavior. The hand submerged in water with just the fingertips protruding above the surface of the water illustrates Jung's view. The fingertips above the water are *conscious* experiences. The submerged shafts of the fingers symbolize the *personal unconscious* and the body of the hand represents the *collective unconscious*, which all people share in common.

    According to Jung, the psyche is a self-regulating system that perpetually strives to maintain a balance between opposing propensities and, simultaneously seeks its own growth and development. People are born with a drive to achieve individuation, that is, wholeness. The personality of an individual is destined to individuate as the body is destined to grow.

    Jung recognized four basic stages of life. The childhood stage begins at birth and lasts until puberty or sexual maturity. The children live enclosed in the psychic atmosphere of their parents. Later, the ego begins to form. The youth and young adulthood stage begins during puberty. The psyche begins to take its own shape. The individual has to make his or her place in the world. Hence, the strengthening of the will is of the utmost importance.

    The middle age stage starts between the ages of 35 and 40. The main task is to re-center life around a new set of values. The old age stage is the period of extreme old age. As people pass from one stage to the next, new aspects of the Self demand expression. In the first half of life, the primary concerns are biological and social. In the second half, the concerns are cultural and spiritual. In the first half, the natural aim is to have children, protect them, and acquire money and social position. The transition from

Summary

one stage to another is a time of potential crisis. Jung acknowledged that environmental factors enormously influence people's psychological development. Nevertheless, he maintained that these influences act by bringing out the "subjective aptitudes" with which all are born. For Jung, these aptitudes include gender awareness, psychological type, and archetypes.

Psychodynamic theories, in general, claim that each individual has an internal world that is affected by the past and which, in turn, affects one's functioning in the present. The way the past affects the individual is variously explained. We relate to people through our internalized representations of past relations. In short, we transfer parts of past images of people onto others. If the past images are strong enough and we do not sort out the distortions, we may feel and act in unrealistic ways toward others. We also have an internal representation of ourselves, which we formed during our earliest interactions with others. If treated with adequate nurturing, we developed a whole and integrated sense of self, which included a realistic awareness of both good and bad qualities. If our needs were not met, an integrated sense of self is not developed. The development of an integrated or mature self takes place in stages through the first few years of life. For the child to complete a stage adequately, parents must meet the needs of the child.

The cognitive-behavioral theories (Adler, Ellis, Beck, Glasser, Lazarus) emphasized present perception. (The concept that a person's subjective worldview is a basic factor in explaining behavior is also incorporated in existential therapy, person-centered therapy, Gestalt therapy, and transactional analysis.)

Adler insisted on a holistic approach. Out of feelings of inferiority, the drive to feel significant emerges. All people crave a sense of mastery, meaning, and significance. The unique way we develop a style of striving for competence is what constitutes individuality. Consciousness, not the unconscious, is the center of personality. People are motivated primarily by social urges rather than sexual urges. Behavior is purposeful and goal-directed. Adler stressed choice, responsibility, meaning in life, and striving for success and purpose. Thus, the cornerstone of Adler's view of people is that people are decision-making, social beings with a unified purpose.

According to Adler, several factors influence people's development, including birth order, subjective perception, purposeful behavior, and lifestyle (an individual's basic orientation to life). Although it is not exactly another "factor" in personality development, a critical issue in understanding people is the concept of *life task*. Life presents challenges in the form of life tasks. Adler originally proposed three life tasks: living in a society with others, work or occupation, and sex and marriage. Others added two more. Thus, everyone must master five life tasks: 1) self-acceptance (getting along with ourselves), 2) friendship (relating to others), 3) love and family relations (achieving intimacy), 4) work (making a contribution), 5) religion (developing our spiritual dimension, including values, meaning, life goals, and our relationship to the universe or cosmos).

Behaviorism claims that there is nothing special about humans. Needs, drives, motives, and conflicts are disregarded. People are a bundle of behavior patterns, reflexes, perceptions, and impressions. People are understood by looking at the "atoms" of their behavior patterns and how these atoms are arranged and related. These atoms are not "held together by or emanating from a comprehensive core, which might be called a 'self.'" Classical conditioning and operant learning processes explain all behavior.

Ellis views the self as merely a collection of empirical characteristics; therefore, he is much like the traditional behaviorist. There really is not a *self* at a person's core. The core assertion of rational-emotive therapy (RET) is that a person's thoughts are central to understanding that person. At the same time, RET recognizes that people are feeling and doing creatures. The basic concepts of the RET's view of people are: 1) "People are born with a potential to be rational as well as irrational." 2) "People's tendency to irrational thinking, self-damaging habitations, wishful thinking, and intolerance is frequently exacerbated by their culture and family group." 3) "Humans tend to perceive, think, emote, and behave simultaneously." As for personality development, RET recognizes but does not explore the fact that the family and the culture impact the individual. For RET, the issue in the development of personality and emotional disturbance is *beliefs*.

Cognitive therapy focuses on micro theories of specific pathologies. It does not have a grand postulate about personality. Personality is shaped by cognitive beliefs and assumptions, which develop early in life from personal experiences and identification with significant others. People form concepts about themselves, others, and how the world operates. This view of people is atomistic; it virtually focuses solely on the cognitive. People are thinking machines. Emotions are cognitively caused and, hence, incidental. Other people are seen as "stimuli" in an environment. They are resources of reinforcement, punishment, or modeling. The more human and "warm" concepts, such as love, wisdom, and compassion, are missing.

Summary

Glasser does not have a formal theory of personality. He views people holistically. Humans are teleological and phenomenological beings who work to meet their needs as they perceive them. People are responsible for their choices. All humans have five basic psychological needs: 1) *belonging* (to love and be loved), 2) *power* (to define and establish one's sense of personal worth, power, and purpose, which is strikingly parallel to Adler), 3) *freedom*, 4) *fun*, and 5) *survival*. What gives people different personalities is that their needs differ in strength.

According to Glasser, people picture a "quality world," which he describes as mental pictures that fall into three categories: 1) The people we most want to be with, 2) the things we most want to own or experience, and 3) the ideas and systems of belief that govern much of our behavior. People want to feel as good as possible. Therefore, they choose to put particular pictures in their personal world of the people, things, and beliefs that make them feel much better than they do with other people, things and beliefs. Happy people have at least one person in their quality world. Total behavior consists of four inseparable components: *activity* (walking, talking, eating), *thinking*, *feeling*, and *physiology* (the heart pumping blood, etc.). All four components work simultaneously. Thus, the concept of "total behavior." People are responsible for fulfilling their needs and doing so in a way that does not deprive others of their ability to fulfill their needs. When we want good relationships and are not able to get them, we create self-destructive total behaviors. "Depressing" is the most common, but there are also "anointing," "headaching," "back aching," etc. Human behavior is purposeful and originates from within rather than from external forces. We are completely motivated internally and all of our behavior attempts to get what we want and, in so doing, form effective control of our lives. To be more specific, Glasser suggests that our brain systems compare their pictures of our needs with their pictures of available behavioral responses and, thus, choose ways of dealing with perceived reality. In other words, we choose the world we want (that is, goals) and then choose the behavior that is our attempt to move the real world closer to the "in-the-head" quality world we want. Actions, thoughts, and even emotions are actively chosen ways of responding to the perceived world and, therefore, we are responsible for all aspects of our reality.

The closest Lazarus comes to a theory of personality is to postulate the premise that human beings are complex creatures that can be divided into seven areas of functioning. Lazarus explains, "In the final analysis, we are biochemical-neurophysiological entities. Human life and conduct are products of ongoing behaviors, affective processes, sensations, images, cognitions, interpersonal relationships, and biological functions" (Lazarus, p. 504). The first letter of each of these "modalities" spells BASIC IB." The final B was changed to D for drugs/biology because one of the most common biological interventions is the use of medication; hence his "Basic ID." At the same time, Lazarus says it is essential to include factors that fall outside the BASIC ID, such as socio-cultural, political, and other macro-environmental events. People are products of the interplay of their genetic environment, physical environment, and social learning history.

Humanistic theories focus on the future in the sense that people are to be all they are meant to be (Yalom; Rogers; Perls). The Existential view of people is also holistic. Although it is difficult to describe a particular personality theory as definitively and distinctly "existential," most theoreticians talk about three levels of existence: the "world around" is the biological world, including biological needs, drives, and instincts, and the "with world," the world of fellow human beings, and "own world," the personal existential world of meaning. Humans are capable of self-awareness. They can reflect and make choices, thereby increasing their possibilities for freedom. Humans are alone, isolated, alienated, and have no meaning. With awareness of our responsibility for choices and of the consequences of these choices comes anxiety.

The Person-centered view of people is holistic. The core assertion of Rogers' personality theory is that there is only one motivational force for all humanity: the tendency toward self-actualization. Even though children are given a drive toward actualization and an inerrant organismic valuing process to guide them, they still need their parents' acceptance and positive regard.

Gestalt therapy lacks a clearly articulated theory of people. Gestalt therapy is holistic. It is a hybrid that draws freely on psychodynamic and phenomenological formulations while stressing the unity of mind, body, and feelings. Humans are biological organisms with strong needs such as breathing, hunger, thirst, sex, shelter, and survival. They are fully responsible for meeting their needs constructively, creatively, and healthily. Self-actualization is a biologically based drive for fulfillment, as opposed to the Rogerian perspective of "optimization of personal potential."

Furthermore, people can deal effectively with their problems provided they make full use of awareness of what is happening in and around them. They are responsible (response-able), meaning they are the primary agents in determining their behavior. A detailed, developed concept of the development of people is also missing in Gestalt therapy. Instead of using our energies to meet our biological needs in more adaptive ways, we spend our energy in social roles and symptoms. As a result, the full range of

Summary

our emotional and sensory-perceptual processes become constricted and we develop increasingly distorted views of our environment and ourselves.

The Relational theories stress relationships (Berne; family therapy). Transactional analysis (TA) assures that humans have needs ("strokes"). Positive strokes take the form of affection or appreciation. There is a need for stability and structure in relationships and we need to have our basic assumptions about our position in life confirmed or supported by others. Personality structure is composed of three conscious or pre-conscious ego states. Each ego state is an organized psychological system of feelings, thoughts, and behaviors that are distinct and mutually exclusive. The three are the parent (P), the adult (A), and the child (C). The Parent ego state contains "shoulds" and "oughts." It expresses a value system, morals, and beliefs. The Adult ego state processes the data received from the external world and the information from the other two ego states. This part of the people is not emotional, passionate, or judgmental. It is realistic, objective, and logical. The child ego consists of the feelings, impulses, and thoughts within and spontaneous acts. The child within us never grows up, regardless of how old we are.

While there are seeming similarities between Freud's psychic structure and TA ego states, there are major differences. For Freud, only the ego was deemed conscious. In TA, all three structures are part of the ego, and all are conscious or potentially conscious. More importantly, Freud thought psychological experience is the result of the interaction of all three structures of the person, the id, the ego, and the superego, but in TA, personality is largely the function of one ego state at a time. These ego states are essentially mutually exclusive.

The development of the people involves *scripts*, *transactions*, and *games*. Children are "scripted" very early in life, usually by parents. A transaction is a stimulus and a related response between two ego states. Thus, when two people are relating, six ego states are present. Moreover, this transaction can occur on one of two levels, either on a social (overt) level or a psychological (covert) level. Games are transactions (at both social and psychological levels) designed to prevent intimacy, result in specific bad feelings for at least one player, and advance scripts. The unpleasant feelings after the game are called "rackets." Rather than allowing unpredictable intimacy, people play games, that is, they engage in ulterior and cross transactions to make a predictable outcome occur.

Family therapy does not have a theory of people as such. The focus is on the family, not on individuals. Thus, it is not possible to summarize a consistent theory of people.

Nevertheless, some observations can be made. People are viewed holistically and in relationship to their environment. People are the product of social interaction, which means they are the result of their family of origin. Since family therapy sees people in the context of the family, it is helpful to understand their view of family. A family is a social unit in which people attempt to meet their needs for intimacy, power, and meaning by mutual choice. The psychological development of an individual results from the family system.

Theory of Pathology

Psychoanalysis (Freud) claims that unconscious, unresolved internal conflicts between the id and the superego during the first six years of life overwhelm the ego, which creates anxiety and neurotic symptoms. In short, the problem is childhood conflicts that are unconscious and unresolved.

Drives → internal conflict → anxiety → defense mechanisms → neurotic symptoms

Analytical Psychotherapy (Jung) says that not paying attention to the unconscious and attempting to compensate for the lack of balance causes symptoms.

Archetypes → activation → anxiety → complex

Psychodynamic therapy insists that the lack of necessary nurture in early childhood results in the formation of an immature personality, one in which the internal sense of self and others is distorted.

No nurture → immaturity → problems

Adlerian therapy teaches that in the context of the family, having formed a "lifestyle" (non-conscious cognitive concepts about self and the world) based on subjective experience, people get discouraged. When they lose the courage to face life's demands directly and achieve significance, they move from having inferior feelings to having an inferiority complex.

Inferior feelings → lifestyle → loss of courage → inferiority complex

Summary

Behavior therapy claims that people learn conditioned responses when motivated by survival and the drive to adapt to a challenging environment.

Environment → conditioned response → problem (anxiety; depression; etc.)

Rational-emotive therapy (Ellis) argues that irrational beliefs produce emotional upsets.

Irrational beliefs → emotional consequences

Cognitive therapy (Beck, et al.) contends that cognitive distortions produce psychological distress.

Distorted thinking → emotional disturbance

Reality therapy (Glasser) maintains that based on personal perception, people's attempts to meet their needs produce ineffective behaviors.

Needs → quality world (my happy world) → choice → ineffective behaviors

Multimodal therapy believes that while people are troubled by a multitude of specific problems, most problems arise from deficient or faulty social learning processes.

Insufficient social learning → emotional problems and disorders

Existential therapy proclaims that in response to the issues of death, freedom, isolation, and meaninglessness, people adopt defenses and strategies that are inauthentic and self-deceptive in that they evade freedom and responsibility.

Awareness of ultimate concern → anxiety → defense mechanism

Person-centered therapy asserts that people develop an ideal self dictated by others as a result of acting according to the rules and judgments of authority figures. This does not fit who they really are. There is an incongruence between the self-concept and one's experience. The distorted self-concept results in an impaired perception of oneself, one's world, and of the choices one can make.

Distorted self-concept (incongruence) → impaired perception of self, choices, etc.

Gestalt therapy declares that people are fragmented and unaware because they do not fully express emotions. That individual can be brought to awareness and responsibility through existential contact with another person.

Unexpressed emotions → deception → irresponsibility

Transactional analysis (TA) states that, as a result of being scripted (or scripting themselves) in early childhood, adults play games to manipulate people to give them strokes, but the stroke results in bad feelings.

Needs → confused ego states → games

Family therapy affirms that symptomatic behavior occurs because family members' needs for closeness, self-expression, and meaning are not met in the family system.

Needs → dysfunctional family → symptomatic behavior

Nouthetic counseling assumes that problems stem from sin, that is, wrong behavior, distorted thinking, and bad attitudes, whether conscious or unconscious, which become habits that produce personal problems.

Sin (wrong behavior, thinking, and attitudes) → habits → personal problems

So, what is the problem (pathology)? In Adlerian therapy, it is "lifestyle" (non-conscious cognitive concepts about self and the world). In rational-emotive therapy, it is irrational beliefs. In cognitive therapy, it is distorted thinking. In reality therapy, it is "quality world" (one's perception of "my happy world"). In multimodal therapy, it is "imagery" (a picture of oneself) and "cognition" (which includes insights, philosophies, ideas, and judgments that constitute one's fundamental values, attitudes, and beliefs). In existential therapy, it is awareness of ultimate concerns. In person-centered therapy, it is incongruence (a distorted self-concept).

Summary

In Gestalt therapy, it is deception about unexpressed emotions). In transactional analysis, it is being scripted (a confused ego state). Nine out of fourteen secular psychotherapies, one way or another, say pathology involves personal perception.

Nature of Health

According to Freud, healthy individuals have "worked through" their childhood conflicts. They have enough conscious awareness of their drives to have self-control over them, good ego strength, and are growing toward maturity. They have socially acceptable behavior.

For Jung, the nature of health is *individuation* defined as a biological process by which every living creature becomes what it was destined to become from the beginning. What people are meant to be is in their subconscious. Healthy people, therefore, follow the urgings of their unconscious. The ideal Self is actualized by becoming what one was meant to become, which is done by experiencing all of the archetypes in their proper balance. There are several archetypes, and they must be in balance. The goal of complete balance and unity is rarely if ever, reached, except in a Jesus or a Buddha.

In the Psychodynamic school of thought, healthy people are mature people, defined as people who realize their full potential as a person in personal relationships. More specifically, mature adults see themselves and others realistically, meaning viewing themselves and others as having both good and bad qualities without having to either idealize or reject them by passing moods or pressing needs. Mature individuals see the world and others accurately and, therefore, do not need exaggerated psychological defenses.

According to Adler, a healthy person is likely to have grown up in a family where the parents modeled how to choose attainable goals and effective, flexible ways of solving problems. They are likely to have a functional or productive lifestyle. When persons are functioning well, they will naturally embrace the highest value, namely, social interest, which is a concern for the welfare of others.

In Behaviorism, health is simply the modification of a particular behavior, such as an anxiety disorder, depression, cigarette smoking, or overeating. Indirectly, Behaviorism suggests that optimal human well-being is the development of competencies.

As for Ellis, the goal is to think more rationally, feel more appropriately, and to act more functionally to achieve the goals of living longer and more happily. Healthy people are those who have developed an effective rational philosophy. Such people will feel appropriately and act functionally. Ellis believes that people should strive to acquire and internalize specific values, many of which can be considered rational attitudes. These values are self-interest, social interest, self-direction, high frustration tolerance, flexibility, acceptance of uncertainty, commitment to creature pursuits, scientific thinking, self-acceptance, risk-taking, long-range hedonism, non-utopianism, and responsibility for our own emotional disturbances. Healthy people are emotionally flexible, adaptable, and relatively content regardless of what happens. Nothing is of ultimate value. So, there is nothing to be upset about; only one's happiness is highly valued.

The Cognitive school of thought focuses on specific pathologies and does not have a well-defined view of health other than solving the immediate issues such as depression or a phobia. Healthy people are competent people, that is, they are effective at accomplishing a specific task or getting what they want.

The goal of reality therapy is to help people reconnect. This reconnection almost always starts with the counselor/teacher first connecting with the individual and then using this connection as a model for how the disconnected person can begin to connect with the people he or she needs. Healthy people act responsibly and in accord with reality; they will be able to meet all of their basic needs to some degree.

Multimodal therapy does not propose an idealized model for humans. At best, it seems to be saying that healthy people are untroubled functioning individuals. To a great degree, what that means is left up to the client. Like its "father" behaviorism, multimodal therapy lacks a definitive description of psychological health.

When it comes to Existentialism, healthy individuals are *authentic individuals*, that is, as they develop a clear sense of identity. They can increasingly make conscious and deliberate choices to be a "self in truth." Such individuals have a definite commitment to *becoming*, which includes seeing themselves as increasingly capable of identifying and removing blocks that thwart their maturing process and having a well-formulated philosophy of life that will guide their current and future actions. Healthy relationships with others are built by clearly established identities, not by trying to be or becoming something other than who we are.

Rogers (person-centered therapy) claimed that healthy individuals have congruence between what they want to become, what they perceive their self to be, and what they actually experience they are. The chief Rogerian virtues are to be fully alive to the

Summary

moment, completely self-accepting, and strongly committed to an ongoing process of personal growth.

Perls (Gestalt) contended that for people to grow, they must lose their mind and come to their senses, meaning they need to stop thinking too much in self-defeating ways and become fully aware of what they are experiencing, especially emotionally, in any given moment. Healthy individuals are mature in that they have an integrated personality and integrity and are responsible, growing people. They are truthful with themselves and are not buried under layers of deceit. They are also in touch with their feelings and are living in the moment. They are self-sufficient. Indeed, self-sufficiency is a pre-eminent virtue in Gestalt therapy.

Transactional analysis says healthy individuals are *unscripted*. They have abandoned the programming of their parents (or their early decisions) and have decided to be spontaneous and intimate. They can function out of each one of the three ego states but will spend most of their time in the Adult, Natural Child, and Nurturing Parent. The influence of the Adapted Child and Critical Parent will be minimized.

The Family therapy concept of health is the well-being of the family. The qualities of a strong family include: 1) Responding positively to challenges and crises rather than denying or distorting reality. 2) They have a clearly articulated worldview, often expressed in religious terms. 3) They communicate well, meaning that they actively listen, affirm and support, express their thoughts and feelings, and manage their differences. 4) They spend time together in a variety of planned and spontaneous tasks. 5) They make and honor promises to one another as well as take tasks and responsibilities seriously. As a result, there is a sense of belonging and respect for individual differences. 6) They know how to express their love and appreciation for one another.

So what is the solution to people's problems? What is health? Again, it depends on who is answering the question. In psychoanalysis, it is having enough conscious awareness of one's drives so that one has self-control over them, good ego strength, and are growing toward maturity. In analytical psychotherapy, it is individuation, experiencing all of the archetypes in their proper balance. In Psychodynamic therapy, it is maturity, that is, accurately seeing self, the world, and others. In Adlerian therapy, it is functioning well and naturally embraces the highest value, namely, social interest, which is a concern for the welfare of others. In Behaviorism, it is modification of a particular behavior. In rational-emotive therapy, it is to think more rationally, feel more appropriately, and to act more functionally to achieve the goals of living longer and more happily. In cognitive therapy, it is being competent, that is, being effective at accomplishing a specific task or getting what one wants. In reality therapy, it is acting responsibly and in accord with reality to meet all of one's basic needs. In multimodal therapy, it is being untroubled, functioning individuals. In Existentialism, it is being an authentic individual, that is, having a clear sense of identity. In People-centered therapy, it is congruence being fully alive to the moment, completely self-accepting, and strongly committed to an ongoing process of personal growth. In Gestalt, it is ceasing thinking too much in self-defeating ways and becoming fully aware of what they are experiencing, especially emotionally, in any given moment, that is, being mature in that one has an integrated personality, integrity, and is a responsible, growing person. In transactional analysis, it is being unscripted, so one can be spontaneous and intimate. In Family therapies, it is being in a functional family. In all secular psychotherapies, health is all about the individual, the individual having self-control, being balanced, being mature, modifying a particular behavior, thinking rationally, being competent, acting responsibly, being functional, having a clear sense of identity, being fully alive in the moment, being fully aware of what one is experiencing, or being spontaneous and intimate. In a few cases, health involves other people, meaning being in a functional family or having social interest.

Method of Therapy

Classic psychoanalysis uses free association and interpretation of resistance, transference, and dreams to make the unconscious conscious and thereby gain insight (a re-living of painful childhood experiences) so that behavior is based more on reality and less on drives. The ultimate aim is the total reconstruction of the personality.

Jung said that when it came to individual cases, he had no method at all. He used a variety of methods, including having people dance, act, sing, play musical instruments, paint, etc. Techniques are to be adjusted or modified depending on the psychological type of the client. Jung's biographer points out that despite his many inconsistencies in therapy, there was one major constant, namely, the first stage in therapy was for his clients to have doubt about their personality type and function. Jung divided analysis into four stages: 1) Confession. 2) Elucidation. 3) Education. 4) Transformation. Dreamwork is the core of Jungian therapy because it is one of the most fruitful ways to understand a person's unconscious. The therapist affirms whatever direction the

Summary

therapy process. Modification procedures are then implemented. Continuing assessment is done throughout and after the intervention period to verify that change is occurring as expected. The basic idea is that people develop problems in response to stimuli; the solution is to retrain the response with different stimuli.

Ellis says RET aims at one major goal: "minimizing the client's central self-defeating outlook and acquiring a more realistic, tolerant philosophy of life." He adds, "Rational-emotive practitioners often employ a fairly rapid-fire active-directive-persuasive-unconscious provides, especially through the self-archetype. Since archetypes are deeply buried in the collective consciousness, unknown and unknowable to the individual, they can only express themselves in symbols. Jung taught that every appointment was a social occasion as well as a clinical interview. Jung thought psychoanalysts did not need to see patients intensively for a long period. As a rule, he met with patients twice a week. Then, he broke off the treatment every ten weeks or so to throw the patient back into his normal milieu.

In the Psychodynamic approach, because humans are fundamentally relational beings, healing can only come through relationships. Healthy relationships have therapeutic potential. The therapist cannot lead the patient to a greater level of maturity than the therapist has himself attained. Through a relationship with the therapist, a client strives to develop the ability to relate to self and others in healthy ways, unencumbered by painful relationships from the past.

For Adler, therapy is a process of encouraging and changing one's lifestyle. The process contains four phases that are not linear and do not progress in rigid steps. They are 1) *Relationship.* The first phase is establishing and maintaining a friendly relationship between equals. Therapeutic progress is possible only when the goals of counseling are clearly defined and when there is an alignment of goals between the therapist and the client. 2) *Analysis.* Interview techniques are used to understand how clients see themselves, their world, and their goals. The client's family constellation is explored to ascertain prevailing conditions when the child was forming lifestyle connections. The summary of one's life story permits the determination of the patient's "basic mistakes." Other forms of analysis are also used, including dreams, which are seen as rehearsals of possible future courses of action. 3) *Insight.* Adlerians challenge clients to develop insights into mistaken goals and self-defeating behaviors by offering suggestions in the form of questions or qualified statements. An intellectual insight is the patient's desire to play the game of therapy rather than the game of life. Real insight is understanding translated into constructive action. 4) *Reorientation.* The action-oriented phase involves reeducation or putting insights into practice. Clients must be willing to do something specific about their problems. A number of techniques are employed.

Behavior therapy begins with assessing the "controlling" conditions influencing the problematic behavior. It is not the person that is assessed; it is the behavior. The therapist proceeds to foster a collaborative relationship with the client by showing as much of the conceptualization with the client as is feasible, modifying the conceptualization as needed and enlisting the client as a collaborator in the philosophic methodology. In most instances, they quickly pin the client down to a few basic irrational ideas." He calls this *cognitive-persuasive aspect* of RET its "most distinguishing characteristic." In other words, after ABC comes "D," that is, *disputing*. Disputing is the application of the scientific method to help clients challenge their irrational beliefs. The three components of disputing are detecting, debating, and discriminating. Eventually, the client arrives at "E," an *effective philosophy*. A new and effective rational philosophy consists of replacing inappropriate thoughts with appropriate ones. Finally, the client comes to "F," a new set of *feelings*. Corey summarizes the RET therapeutic process in four steps: 1) Show the clients that they have incorporated many irrational "shoulds," "oughts," and "musts." 2) Demonstrate that the clients keep their emotional disturbances active by thinking illogically and repeating self-defeating meanings and philosophies. 3) Help them modify their thinking and abandon their irrational ideas. 4) Challenge clients to develop a rational philosophy of life so that they can avoid other irrational beliefs in the future. Ellis says, "Rational-emotive therapists do not believe a warm relationship between counselee and counselor is a necessary or sufficient condition for effective personality change. They believe therapists should accept clients fully but criticize and point out the deficiencies of their behavior." RET also uses a number of techniques, including homework, imagery, role-playing, shame-attacking exercises, etc.

In cognitive therapies, cognitive and behavioral methods are used to challenge dysfunctional beliefs and promote more realistic adaptive thinking. The therapist asks questions to elicit the meaning, function, usefulness, and consequences of the patient's beliefs. The patient ultimately decides whether to reject, modify, or maintain all personal beliefs, being well aware of their emotional and behavioral consequences. Beck believes successful counseling rests on genuine warmth, accurate empathy, nonjudgmental acceptance, and the ability to establish trust and rapport. He emphasizes Socratic dialogue. He places more stress on helping the clients discover their misconceptions for themselves, using persistent but gentle logic and persuasion

Summary

to change the client's thinking. It has been suggested that there are three major types of cognitive-behavioral therapy interventions: 1) *cognitive restructuring*, where the focus is on the direct form of modification of maladaptive thought patterns, 2) *coping skills training*, where clients are assisted in developing cognitive and behavioral skills for dealing with challenging situations, 3) *problem-solving training*, where clients expand their general capacity for understanding and facing challenging problems.

Glasser teaches that people must be involved with other people to learn how to meet their needs in a realistic way. Therapy guides irresponsible people toward more responsibility. In *Reality Therapy*, Glasser says that reality therapy is made up of three separate but intimately interwoven procedures. First is involvement, meaning that the therapist must become so involved with the patient that the patient begins to face reality and see how his behavior is unrealistic. Second, the therapist must reject the unrealistic behavior while still accepting the patient and maintaining his involvement with him. Third, in varying degrees, depending upon the patient, the therapist must teach the patient better ways to fulfill his needs within the confines of reality. Glasser listed the eight major steps in conducting reality therapy. 1) Make friends and ask clients what they want. 2) Ask, "What are you doing now?" 3) The therapist helps the client realize that what he or she is currently doing is ineffectual. 4) Make a plan to do better. 5) Get a commitment to follow the plan worked out in step number 4. 6) No excuses. 7). No punishment. 8). Never give up.

In multimodal therapy, the emphasis is on the uniqueness of each individual. Hence, there is no typical treatment format. A basic premise is that patients are usually troubled by a multitude of specific problems and that a multitude of particular treatments should deal with these problems. Multimodal therapists practice "technical eclecticism." They borrow techniques from other therapy systems. Most of the techniques listed by Lazarus are standard behavioral procedures, but these techniques are never used in a shotgun manner. Multimodal therapists ask, "What works, for whom, and under what conditions?" Two specific procedures seem to enhance treatment effects, namely bridging and tracking. Bridging is the procedure in which the therapist deliberately tunes into the client's preferred modality before branching off into other dimensions that seem likely to be more productive. Tracking is the firing order of the different modalities.

The Existential approach does not have a well-defined set of techniques. It is more of an *approach* or *attitude* about how best to help others grow than a set of theories and techniques. Hence, few specific techniques flow from existential therapy. The basic goal is to enable clients to realize that they are free to make choices about the direction of their lives and to help them make commitments that will assist them in becoming more *authentic*. This is not done through mechanistic techniques but rather through a highly personal encounter between therapist and client. The essential task of the therapist is to understand the client's subjective world, clarify that subjective world, challenge or confront the client with the need for choice, and assume full responsibility for his or her actions, insights, and relationships. Corey claims that there are three phases in existential therapy. In the initial phase, the therapist assists clients in identifying and clarifying their assumptions about the world. During the next phase, clients are encouraged to examine the source and authority of their value system more fully. The final phase focuses on helping clients put what they have learned about themselves into action.

Person-centered therapy does not consist of techniques. Rogers's approach never involves advice-giving, interpretations, teaching, or other interactions. These, it is argued, are based on a fundamental disrespect for others; they foster dependency and thwart the development of any meaningful sense of autonomy. Formal assessment of the presenting concerns or underlying dynamics in the form of psychological testing or psychiatric diagnosis are seen as inappropriate and unnecessary. Such a diagnosis may, more often than not, interfere with effective therapy. In person-centered therapy, the therapeutic relationship is of the utmost importance. Active listening, clarification and reflection of feelings, personal presence, and "co-participation" are the only necessary "tools" coupled with a profound respect for the process and inner directness.

According to Rogers, the following six conditions are necessary and sufficient for personality change to occur: 1) Two persons are in psychological contact. 2) The first, whom we shall term the *client*, is experiencing incongruency. 3) The second person, whom we shall term the *therapist*, is congruent or integrated into the relationship. 4) The therapist experiences unconditional positive regard or real caring for the client. 5) The therapist experiences an empathetic understanding of the client's internal frame of reference and endeavors to communicate this experience to the client. 6) The communication of the therapist's empathetic understanding and unconditional positive regard to the client is, to a minimal degree, achieved. No other conditions are necessary. Constructive personality change will occur if these six conditions exist over some period. These conditions do not vary according to client type, are sufficient for all approaches to therapy, and apply to all personal relationships, not just to psychotherapy.

Summary

In Gestalt therapy, confrontational contact and being brought to awareness are the tools of therapy. The therapist is to facilitate the client's process of self-discovery and learning and not teach. The immediate aim is the attaining of awareness. Increased awareness by itself is viewed as curative. This encounter with another person is not to gain insight. For Perls, insight is not just a waste of time; it can reinforce the client's defenses against awareness. Growth is through confrontation and encounter. Gestalt therapy is the most directive and confronting approach to therapy. The "rules" of Gestalt therapy include: clients must communicate entirely in the present tense, using only "I" language, no talking about others ("no gossiping") is permitted, and asking questions is discouraged. Clients are to focus on the affective and bodily sensations of their immediate experience. These rules are designed to intensify the direct experience and to integrate conflicting feelings within the individual. Other techniques are used, including dream analysis.

Transactional analysis utilizes a contract between the client and therapist. The contract contains specific goals and the criteria to determine whether goals are reached. When the contract terms are completed, the therapeutic relationship is terminated, unless a new contract is established. TA is usually done in group therapy; individual counseling is used as an adjunct. It is highly educational. More than any other therapy, TA teaches the theory itself. First, the client is helped to understand the ego states, be enabled to experience blocked states, and make choices about what to experience at what time. Then, transactions are analyzed, followed by confrontation concerning games and rackets. The script is examined and the client is challenged to make a deliberate decision about a new life position. Finally, clients are encouraged to change their life scripts at least or, even better, to give up scripts entirely and live spontaneously and intimately.

As for family therapy, a theoretical base for family techniques has not been firmly established nor is there a standard treatment. While techniques differ, family therapists agree that treatment goals are improved communication, individuation, increased empathy, improved role agreement, more flexible leadership styles, reduced conflict, and individual symptomatic improvement.

So, what do therapists do to help people solve their problems? What are the methods of therapy? Once more, it depends on who is answering the question. In psychoanalysis, it is free association and the interpretation of resistance, transference, and dreams; in analytical psychotherapy, there is no method except always determining one's personality type. In Adlerian therapy, it is a process of encouragement. In behaviorism, it is modification of behavior. In rational-emotive therapy, it is a fairly rapid-fire active-directive-persuasion. In cognitive therapies, it is having a warm, empathetic, nonjudgmental acceptance to establish trust and rapport and using persistent but gentle logic and persuasion to change the client's thinking. In reality therapy, it is establishing a relationship (being friends) and teaching the person to face reality. In multimodal therapy, there is no typical treatment format; there is a multitude of specific treatments, except for always using bridging and tracking. In Existentialism, there is no well-defined set of techniques except a highly personal encounter between therapist and client. In person-centered therapy, there are no consistent techniques except developing a relationship and never giving advice or interpretations or teaching. In Gestalt therapy, it is confrontational (it is the most directive and confrontive approach). In transactional analysis, it is a contract between client and therapist that contains specific goals and the criteria to determine whether goals are reached, group therapy, and teaching the theory itself. In family therapy, there is no standard treatment.

Five of the fourteen secular psychotherapies have no specific method of therapy. Six start with establishing a relationship (analytical psychotherapy; Adlerian therapy; cognitive therapies; reality therapy; existentialism; and person-centered therapy). A few are directive (rational-emotive and Gestalt). One way or another, virtually all teach (ok, interpret). Some go so far as to say the therapist is therapy.

Summary: The various views of psychotherapy are not monolithic. To say that they widely differ from each other is to put it mildly (from direct confrontation to never giving advice). From a biblical perspective, no theory of psychotherapy is complete or comprehensive.

Many of the theories of psychoanalysis are the results of self-analysis (Freud; Jung; Erikson; Adler; Ellis; Frankl; Rogers). Jung wrote, "Philosophical criticism has helped me to see that every psychology—my own included—has the character of a subjective confession. Even when I am dealing with empirical data, I am necessarily speaking about myself" (Jung's *Collective Writings*, vol. IV, para. 774).

In his book *The Interpretation of Dreams*, Freud related his self-analysis. He explored his dreams and examined his childhood sexuality. Between 1913 and 1917, Jung explored his own unconscious by analyzing his dreams and visions. Erikson, the American school of thought originator in the psychodynamic approach to psychotherapy, coined the phrase "identity crisis." He had a personal identity crisis. Ellis developed his

Summary

approach around the way he dealt with his own problems. Glasser's interest in psychology stems from his eagerness to deal with his own intensely shy nature. The essentials of Roger's person-centered therapy evolved predominantly out of his own experience.

Virtually all of the theories of psychotherapy are reductionistic. None of them are as comprehensive as the Bible, which views human beings as spiritual, social, psychological, purposeful, and physical creatures. All theories of psychotherapy do not include the essential issue of trusting Jesus Christ, who died for the sins of the world and rose from the dead for the gift of eternal life (Jn. 3:16). Nor do they include the absolutely indispensable item of depending upon the grace of God to make it through life (Heb. 4:16). Many of the psychotherapies do not include the critical issues of human beings being social, purposeful, and physical creatures.

Chapter 21

CONCLUSION

Some of the concepts in psychotherapy are compatible with the Bible and some are not. After a brief review of the biblical perspective of the five categories of therapy (for a more detailed explanation, see Chapter 2, "The Standard of Evaluation"), the concepts of psychotherapies in each area compatible with the Scripture are listed. Admittedly, this includes repetition.

Biblical Perspective

Philosophical Assumptions From a biblical perspective, the truth about people is obtained from a study of the Scripture, observation, experience, including the experience of others (see Proverbs), etc. The Bible contains all the truth necessary for salvation and spiritual maturity (2 Tim. 3:15-17). That does not mean, however, that all truth about people is in the Bible. The truth about people can also be obtained from other sources. The truth about people from outside the Bible is not necessary for spiritual maturity, but can be useful for understanding people and helping them physically, emotionally, etc.

View of People Scripture teaches that *people are physical, psychological, purposeful, social, and spiritual beings.* They are a persona (self) in a body. They have the capacity to think, feel, and act. Because of Adam's disobedience, sin and death (separation) entered the world. Sin has separated people from God, from each other, and within themselves. It has affected every part of every person. The body is diseased. The mind is deceived. The emotions are degraded. The will is depraved. The conscience is deranged. Relationships are dysfunctional. The spirit is dead.

Development of Personality Without delving into detail, the Bible recognizes the factors that *influence* and *impact* people in forming personality in general and thoughts, choices, feelings, purposes, and speech in particular. These include heredity, gender, family of origin, age, class, nationality, and individual choice.

Psychotherapies, A Simple Explanation and Biblical Evaluation

The Bible does not explain, in the modern psychological sense of the term, how the formation of a people takes place. Nevertheless, the Scripture would support the idea that the persona needs to experience love to learn to love (1 Jn. 4:10-11). As people are loved, they develop trust in response to love and distrust in response to not being loved. Furthermore, as people are loved and as they develop love and trust, they also develop a self-concept and a worldview that determines, to a great degree, what they do and do not do.

Theory of Pathology In a sense, the cause of all problems is sin. Sin has affected the whole creation, people's relationship to God, and people's relationship to each other, and has fragmented people within themselves. Thus, there can be, and often are, spiritual, social, natural (meaning from nature), and personal dimensions to a problem. The Scripture teaches that the sources of difficulty are the world, the flesh, and the devil. While it is true that people are *influenced* by heredity, environment, early experiences, and so on, God holds people accountable for their choices. Heredity makes a person *predisposed* to something. Environment, early experiences, perceptions, assumptions, past and present relationships, and expectations are all factors that influence people's *choices*, but in the final analysis, people are responsible for the choices they make.

Nature of Health For people to be "healthy," they must know Jesus Christ by trusting Him for the gift of eternal life and grow to Christ-like spiritual maturity. Believers in Jesus Christ should love God, believe Him, obey Him, and depend on His grace for strength. Socially, they should know how to relate lovingly to others and when and how to submit. Emotionally, the Scripture teaches that people should be able to feel and express their emotions without negative, destructive emotions getting out of control. Rationally, people should be reasonable and sensible. Volitionally, people should make the right, wise choices. The Scripture does not describe in detail what physical health is or how to get it, but it does recognize that sleep is important and that exercise is profitable.

Method of Therapy There is no "method of therapy" (as such) in the Bible. Nevertheless, God's method of ministry (counseling) is *people*. Therefore, the first and foremost issue is the relationship between the counselor and the counselee. The counselor must be a mature individual who helps people by praying, modeling, loving, comforting, teaching, exhorting, correcting, rebuking, and even excommunicating. The counselor must be patient. The counselee must assume personal responsibility for his or her attitudes and actions.

Conclusion

Philosophical Assumptions

The Bible "The first essential attitude for effective integration is respect for the complete inspiration and authority of the Scriptures" (Narramore, p. 42). At the same time, recognizing the concept of general revelation, integration is nothing more than integrating special revelation (the Bible) and general revelation (nature) (Carter and Mohline, p. 97). The two main philosophical issues are theism versus atheism and determinism versus freedom.

God A biblical approach assumes there is a God. Biblical Christianity teaches that God created human beings in His own image and desires to be personally involved in their lives. The Bible is His Word designed to bring believers in Jesus Christ to spiritual maturity (2 Tim. 3:15-17).

People are judged to be "abnormal" if their behavior is at odds with society's expectations. Psychotherapists frequently define pathology regarding psychological functioning. In other words, people may behave normally but are still assumed to be disturbed if they experience internal conflicts leading to intense and prolonged feelings of insecurity, guilt, anxiety, or unhappiness. In addition to the social, psychological, and physical criteria, a biblical approach to counseling proposes that people are abnormal if they are not rightly related to God (Collins, pp. 182-183).

That does not mean that a Christian therapist *must* always aim at bringing every client to spiritual maturity. Christians can serve people apart from attempting to bring them to spiritual maturity. Christians minister to people physically (for example, feeding the hungry) and medically without "preaching" to them so they can help people with their mental, emotional, and social problems. At the same time, Christians believe that people have a spiritual problem that needs to be addressed if people are going to be all God intended them to be. They need to trust Jesus Christ for the gift of eternal life and grow to Christ-like spiritual maturity.

Determinism vs Free will Determinism does not explain the fact that human behavior is often unpredictable and beyond external control. Moreover, it has profound implications concerning the concepts of sin, crime, responsibility, guilt, and punishment. Besides, in the final analysis, even those who believe in biological or social determinism teach that people should exercise self-control. Freud assumed that if people acquired insight (rational understanding) into why they think, feel, and behave as they do, it would enable them to change their behavior.

Psychotherapies, A Simple Explanation and Biblical Evaluation

In an article in *Breakpoint*, Chuck Colson wrote, "This denial of free will is known as determinism. Determinists insist that their explanations neither justify wrongdoing nor weaken people's resolve to do the right thing. A recent study shows just how wrong they are. Researchers recently published the results of experiments testing the link between the belief in free will—that is, the ability to choose right and wrong—and honesty. Kathleen Vohls of the University of Minnesota and Jonathan Schooler of the University of British Columbia gave college students a math exam in which students would be paid for each correct answer. They told the students that "a computer glitch would cause the answers to appear on the screen" and that they should press a key to keep from seeing the answers. Students were told that failure to press the key was cheating, although no one would know who had cheated. Before taking the exam, some of the students were asked to read a piece that said that "most educated people do not believe in free will." Another group read a piece affirming free will and the third read about sugar.

"You can probably guess what happened: The "no free will" group was "more likely to let the answer appear—that is, to cheat. This pattern held up in another test involving self-grading: Students in the "no free will" group were, again, significantly more likely to cheat.

"Vohls told *Mercatornet Magazine* that these findings tie 'in with evidence that cheating is on the increase' among college students. While there 'are many possible reasons for this,' the erosion in our belief in free will and conscience is almost certainly one of them.

"Thus, according to Vohls, it is important to understand the 'dangers' posed by the 'links between determinism and unethical behavior.'

"She (Vohls) is right, and what is more troubling is that one piece was all it took to alter students' behavior. Imagine what a lifetime of this kind of indoctrination can do."

On the other hand, the notion of human freedom is difficult. People who want to change find it is not as simple or easy as making a decision. The debate over determinism and free will reminds us how limited our understanding of behavior and our ability to predict and control it really is.

From a biblical point of view, people are *influenced* by their environment and events. At the same time, they are endowed with reason and will, which means they can use their rationality to apprehend what is good and do what is right. People can reason, weigh options, and anticipate the consequences of actions. People are responsible for their choices.

Conclusion

This is not exactly the view of cognitive therapy, which is close to the biblical view. According to cognitive therapy, people have limited freedom but always do what they must do. In practice, however, cognitive-behavioral therapy acknowledges a person's capacity for change through "self-control" and related processes.

Only a theistic view of people that asserts they are created with moral accountability is an adequate grounding for a full concept of limited freedom (Jones and Butman, p. 209).

View of People

The Nature of People From a biblical point of view, people are spiritual, social, psychological, purposeful, and physical beings. Their persona (self) is united to a body. They have the capacity to think, feel, and choose. Sin has alienated people from God, separated people from each other, and fragmented people from within themselves.

For the most part, the Bible presents people holistically, but it also speaks of people as thinking, feeling, and choosing individuals. Glasser's concept of "total behavior" combines both concepts. As he points out, behavior consists of four inseparable components: activity (walking, talking, eating), thinking, feeling, and physiology (the heart pumping blood). A person walking down the street is described as walking. Yet that person is also thinking and feeling and has a beating heart. There are thinking, feeling, and choosing components to human activity, all of which make up the person together.

Most psychotherapies focus on only one aspect of what it means to be human. On the one hand, in doing so, they have made observations that are useful in understanding people. On the other hand, in so doing, many are guilty of focusing on one aspect to the exclusion of the others (reductionism) or seeing one element out of balance to the others. For example, psychoanalysis analyzes emotions and ignores the mental aspects of human behavior. Cognitive-behavioral advocates concentrate on thoughts and downplay emotions. Virtually all schools of thought leave the spiritual out of their classroom. A more comprehensive view of people is needed, which includes the spiritual and social as well as the psychological (mind, emotions, and will) dimensions of people. Carter and Narramore say that what is needed is an understanding of people that is as comprehensive as possible (Carter and Narramore, p. 16). Collins says, "Our helping will be more effective if we do not lose sight of the holistic nature of man" (Collins, p. 184).

Development of Personality From a biblical point of view, a number of factors influence and impact who people are.

Spiritually, people are born separated from God with a sinful nature (Isa. 53:6; Eph. 2:1). They are under the influence of the world, the flesh, and ultimately, the devil. At the core of their being is pride, selfishness, and rebellion. Their attitude is "I want it. I want all of it, and I want it now." Being alienated from God, they react to life emotionally and have a skewed perception. For example, "With a sense of isolation comes a perception of the *lacking*—either not *having* enough or not *being* good enough" (Ornish, p. 90).

Socially, people grow up within a family ("family of origin"). Apples *usually* land near the tree trunk (Deut. 6:4-9). In the context of the family, children should learn the most important lessons of life, love, trust, obedience, submission, etc., and the process starts early. David says, "You *are* He Who took me out of the womb; You made me trust *while* on my mother's breasts" (Ps. 22:9). David reminds God that it was He who took him out of the womb and He taught him to trust. In poetic terms, David says, God taught him to trust while on his mother's breasts. Most commentators interpret this to mean that God taught David to trust from a very early age. Is it possible that the meaning is that God taught David to trust by giving him the experience to trust his mother's breast for food?

The Family therapy movement has described the qualities of a strong family as: 1) They respond positively to challenges and crises. 2) They have a clearly articulated worldview. 3) They communicate well. 4) They spend time together. 5) They make and honor promises to one another. 6) They know how to express their love and appreciation for one another. The family, even the extended family, is important in the development of the people. "To reform a man, you must begin with his grandmother" (Victor Hugo). The social element includes neighbors, peers, community, organizations, and church. Since all humans have the same selfish nature, as they develop, they experience conflicts, broken relationships, and deep hurts. As Tennyson says, we are part of all we have met.

Psychologically, people are born with a temperament; they are born with a "bent." Jung is the only major psychotherapist to address this issue. People are born either male or female and it is as if they not born on the same planet. People are born with needs. They are born with an academic aptitude, athletic ability, artistic talent, etc. They also arrive with a mind, emotions, and a will. In addition, events have an impact on the development of people.

Conclusion

The cognitive function includes things such as personal perception. People have a self-concept and a "worldview," a way in which they view the world. The concept that a person's subjective worldview is a basic factor in explaining behavior in Adler, the cognitive-behavioral therapies, rational-emotive therapy, reality therapy, existential therapy, person-centered therapy, and Gestalt therapy (see Corey, p. 138).

The cognitive function also consists of expectations. Adler spoke about "lifestyle," a psychological map or guide that includes a self-ideal (Mosak). Glasser had things to say about a person's "quality world," or mental pictures, which fall into three categories: 1) The people we most want to be with, 2) the things we most want to own or experience, and 3) the ideas and systems of belief that govern much of our behavior. The cognitive function involves a value system. People embrace the value system of those they trusted and admired as they were growing up, or they adopt a different value system. In other words, the apple does not *always* fall next to the tree. It falls next to the tree unless the tree is on a hill, in which case, the apples roll away from the tree. There is an internal conflict between one's sinful nature and value system.

People are emotional beings. The three primary emotions are guilt, fear, and anger. Like Adam, being afraid of exposure, people hide (Gen. 3:9). To stop *feeling* the pain or to prevent experiencing more pain, they develop defense systems (denial, avoidance, projection, etc.).

Narramore points out some Christians tend to downplay emotions. They say that the Christian life is like a train: facts are the engine, faith is the next car, and feelings are the caboose (Narramore, p. 36). In a conversation I had with him, he illustrated that view in contrast to his view. He held his hand so that his four fingers were one on top of the other. He explained that the little finger (feeling) was last under all the other fingers. Then, to illustrate his view, he turned his fingers so that they were all parallel to each other and said we should give mind, emotions, and will equal consideration.

People are volitional creatures. Granted, people are influenced by our biological predisposition (Gen. 25:23-27), childhood experiences (Prov. 22:6), and environment (Rom 12:2), but ultimately, they are personally responsible and accountable for their thoughts, emotions, words, and actions. "Crime, in the final analysis, remains inexplicable in as much as it cannot be fully traced to biological, psychological, and/or sociological factors. Totally explaining one's crime would be tantamount to explaining away his or her guilt and to seeing him or her not as a free responsible human being but a machine to be repaired" (Frankl, p. 173). "Life is built on character, and characters is built on decisions. The decisions are based on values, and values must be accepted by faith" (Wiersbe on Lk. p. 68).

As people grow up, they have experiences that become defining moments for them emotionally and/or mentally.

Physically, the body affects the mind and emotions, and the mind and emotions affect the body. People are born with predispositions toward a particular disease and can also be born with a predisposition toward an emotional problem. Our experiences and our emotional reactions to them ("significant emotional events") impact our bodies (the emotions cause biochemical changes in the organs of our body and, over time, affect our immune system, resulting in disease), mold our thinking, and affect our behavior.

Viktor Frankl, a medical doctor who was imprisoned in a concentration camp during World War II, wrote, "Those who know how close the connection is between the state of mind of a man—his courage and hope or lack of them—and the state of immunity of his body will understand that the sudden loss of hope and courage can have a deadly effect. The sudden cause of my friend's death was the expected liberation that did not come and he was severely disappointed. This suddenly lowered his body's resistance against the latent typhus infection. His faith in the future and his will to live had become paralyzed and his body fell victim to his illness—and thus the voice of his dreams was right after all" (Frankl, pp. 96-97).

In the final analysis, people are like trees. They have one trunk and many roots. All the roots contribute to the tree, but the tree is not any one root (see the illustration of the sinking of the Titanic, chapter 2, The Standard of Evaluation).

Theory of Pathology

There is a spiritual dimension to pathology. In a sense, the cause of all problems is sin. In their book *The Integration of Psychology and Theology*, two Christian psychology professors say that in the ultimate sense, all psychopathology is traceable to sin, but, they quickly add, that does not mean that all problems are caused by conscious, willful, or personal sin. It means all problems are traceable to the first sin (Carter and Narramore, p. 109).

Sin has affected the whole creation, people's relationship to God, their relationship to others, and fragmented people within themselves. Thus, sin has affected every part of every person. The spirit is dead. The mind is deceived. The emotions are degraded. The will is depraved. The conscience is devoid. The body is diseased. Relationships are

Conclusion

dysfunctional. The Scripture teaches that the sources of difficulty are the world, the flesh, and the devil. While it is no doubt true that people are *influenced* by their heredity, environment, early experiences, etc., at the same time, God holds people *accountable* for their choices. Heredity makes a person *predisposed* to something. Environment, early experiences, perceptions, assumptions, past and present relationships, and expectations are all factors that influence people's *choices*, although, in the final analysis, people are responsible for the choices they make. Pride is often at the bottom of wrong choices.

To avoid facing personal responsibility, people often practice blame-shifting. A sick joke tells the tale. A woman's husband had been slipping in and out of a coma for several months, yet she stayed by his bedside every single day. When he came to, he motioned for her to come nearer. As she sat by him, he said, "You have been with me all through the bad times. When I got fired, you were there to support me. When my business failed, you were there. When I got shot, you were by my side. When we lost the house, you gave me support. When my health started failing, you were still by my side. You know what?" When she said, "No," he replied, "I think you bring me bad luck."

There are social dimensions to many problems. The psychodynamic approach traces the cause of problems to the lack of necessary nurture in early childhood, resulting in an immature person. Adler teaches that people develop an inferiority complex because of concepts about self and the world ("lifestyle") formed in the context of the family. Multimodal therapy believes most problems arise from deficient or faulty social learning processes. Family therapy affirms symptomatic behavior occurs because family members' needs for closeness, self-expression, and meaning are not met in the family system. Transactional analysis states that as a result of being scripted (or scripting themselves) in early childhood, adults play games to manipulate people to give them strokes, but the stroke itself results in bad feelings.

There are psychological elements to pathology, that is, mental, emotional, and volitional components. Several psychotherapies point to a mental aspect. For example, although he acknowledged the impact of the family, for Adler, the problem is perception. Ellis says irrational beliefs produce emotional upsets. Beck contends that cognitive distortions produce psychological distress. Glasser maintains that based on personal perception, people's attempts to meet their needs produce ineffective behaviors.

Some psychotherapies emphasize the emotional component. Gestalt therapy declares people are fragmented and unaware because they are not fully expressing their emotions.

Still others focus on the volitional component. Existential therapy proclaims that in response to the issues of death, freedom, isolation, and meaninglessness, people adopt defenses and strategies that are inauthentic and self-deceptive in that they evade freedom and responsibility. Person-centered therapy asserts that due to acting according to rules and judgments of authority figures, people develop an ideal self-dictated by others, which does not fit who they really are. A distorted self-concept results in impaired perception of one's self, one's world, and the choices one can make.

In other words, most psychotherapies trace the root problem to *one* primary function of a human being. On the one hand, there is truth in what many of them say. On the other hand, virtually all practice reductionism. What is missing in the biblical framework is any suggestion that the problem is in the unconscious mind, which is only accessible through such techniques as the interpretation of dreams (Freud and Jung) and the claim that people's problems are a result of conditioned responses (behaviorism). A more biblical view insists that in their separation from God, people are proud and deceived (unaware); thus, they act irresponsibly and enter into conflicts with others.

Alienation → pride → deceived mind, degraded emotions, depraved will → conflicts

Note: Aside from being separated from God, pride is the root problem. Our pride makes us fearful of exposure and our fear makes us defensive.

Pride (selfishness) → fear of exposure → defense

Nature of Health

The situation is so bad that to make people what God intended them to be, He has to start all over by giving people a new nature. Our part is to abandon all self-righteousness to trust Christ, who died for our sins and rose from the dead to be declared righteous.

In a biblical worldview, the nature of health is Christ-like spiritual maturity, which involves a long, slow process. God develops godly characteristics in believers who respond to Him and His Word. Pride needs to be replaced with humility. Humility is the

Conclusion

will to trust God and love others.

$$\text{Humility (openness)} \rightarrow \text{faith (trust, relax)} \rightarrow \text{love}$$

To grow spiritually, people must humbly assume responsibility for themselves and respond appropriately to the people and trials in their lives by depending on God's grace. It is a process of putting off old attitudes and habits and putting on Christ-like attitudes, speech, and behavior. As that is done, a Christ-like character is formed. Christ-likeness is being full of grace and truth. It is being holy, righteous, and just on the one hand and being loving, gracious, and merciful on the other. It is loving God and others.

Several psychotherapies say that health is maturity, but they define maturity differently than the Bible does. Even Freud says healthy individuals have worked through their childhood conflicts so that they have enough conscious awareness of their drives and, in turn, to have self-control over them. Healthy people have good ego strength, are growing toward maturity, and have socially acceptable behavior, but his concept of maturity is not what the Scripture teaches. For example, Krishnamurti says, "It is no measure of health to be well adjusted to a profoundly sick society." Nevertheless, his view of maturity includes self-control, which is part of spiritual maturity (Gal. 5:23).

The Psychodynamic approach says healthy people are mature people, that is, people who realize their full potential in personal relationships. More specifically, mature adults see themselves and others realistically, meaning viewing themselves and others as having good and bad qualities without having to either idealize or reject them based on passing moods or pressing needs.

For Adler, healthy people have the courage to do their best to accomplish life's tasks, take risks, and be content to do "good enough" rather than perfectly, and thus to face life squarely without evasion or excuse. They are coping with courage and growing in their concern for others. Certainly, personal responsibility and concern for others are part of maturity.

Glasser scantily defines health as the result of responsibly and effectively meeting one's needs. If people act responsibly and in accord with reality, they can meet their basic needs to some degree.

According to Perls, healthy individuals are mature in that they have an integrated personality and integrity, and are responsible, growing people. They are truthful with themselves and are not buried under layers of deceit. They are also in touch with their feelings and are living in the moment. They are self-sufficient. Indeed, self-sufficiency is a pre-imminent virtue in Gestalt therapy. Much of that is biblical; self-sufficiency is not.

The concept of health in family therapy is viewed from the context of the family system rather than from a more individual perspective. A strong family responds positively to challenges and crises, has a clearly articulated worldview often expressed in religious terms, communicates well, spends time together in various planned and spontaneous tasks, makes and honors promises to one another, and takes tasks and responsibilities seriously. They also know how to express their love and appreciation for one another.

Method of Therapy

As the chapter on "The Standard of Evaluation" points out, there is no one and only therapy, counseling, or ministry method in the Bible. Jesus did not deal with any two people the same way. He did not even heal all blind people the same way! It takes all kinds of gifts and ministries to bring believers to spiritual maturity (Eph. 4:11-16). Different types of problems call for different approaches. Paul wrote, "Now we exhort you, brethren, warn those who are unruly, comfort the fainthearted, uphold the weak, be patient with all" (1 Thess. 5:14).

From a practical point of view, different methods work in different situations. Carter and Narramore put it like this: "Short-term, directive counseling is ready-made for a variety of situational problems and certain personalities. Long-term therapy may be very helpful for others. Behavioral methods are clearly successful in relieving a variety of symptoms. And many people respond well to non-directive counseling. The variety of effective therapeutic styles suggests that no one counseling methodology will serve all purposes" (Carter and Narramore, pp. 113-114).

Some people only need direction for their future. Others need an explanation to clarify how their perception(s) is distorted. Still others need help to deal with their dysfunction. In other words, depending on the situation, people need redirection, reeducation, and/or reconstruction.

Conclusion

Past	emotional conflict (emotions)	needs insight/reconstruction
Present	distorted thinking (mind)	needs new perception/reeducation
Future	lack of goal (will)	needs choices, purpose/redirection

God's primary method of ministry (counseling) is *people*. God uses people to help people. He uses parents (Prov. 22:6), elders, who, if nothing else, are to serve as models (1 Pet. 5:3), gifted believers (Eph. 4:11-16), and fellow believers (see "exhort one another" in Heb. 10:25). It is in a community of believers that individual believers grow (Col. 2:2). Since that is the case, the first and foremost issue in counseling is the relationship between the counselor and the counselee.

Those who would help others must be mature individuals themselves (see "spiritual" in Gal. 6:1; see also Rom. 15:14). People helpers can pray, model, love (see esp. 2 Tim. 2:24-26), comfort, teach, exhort, correct, rebuke, excommunicate, etc. Much could and should be written on each of these characteristics. The counselor must also be patient (1 Thess. 5:14). There are rarely any quick fixes. Problems usually take time to develop and usually take time to solve. Therefore, patience is imperative.

Some psychotherapies have emphasized the relationship between the counselor and the counselee. Jung believed in treating human beings rather than "patients" and taught that every appointment was a social occasion as well as a clinical interview. Adler's fourfold method of therapy begins with the relationship between the counselor and counselee. Even behaviorism establishes a collaborative relationship with the client by showing as much of the conceptualization with the client as is feasible, modifying the conceptualization as needed, and enlisting the client as a collaborator in the therapeutic process. The psychodynamic approach insists that since humans are relational beings, healing can only come through relationships ("the therapist is the therapy"). Glasser teaches that people must be involved with other people to learn how to meet their needs in a realistic way. In contrast to a highly personal approach, Freud sat out of sight behind the couch! Ellis did not believe that a warm relationship between counselee and counselor was a necessary or sufficient condition for effective personality change.

Beyond establishing a loving relationship, much of what the Bible says about counseling could fit under the broad umbrella of teaching, including encouragement, exhortation, and correction. The third stage in Jung's fourfold approach to therapy was education. Glasser teaches that the therapist must teach patients better ways to fulfill their needs within the confines of reality. Transactional analysis is highly educational. More than any other therapy, it teaches the theory itself. In contrast, according to Gestalt therapy, the therapist is not to *teach*.

Many techniques have been developed that have no relationship to anything mentioned in the Scripture but have proven successful in understanding and helping people. One outstanding example is teaching people about their personality type (temperament). Although Jung used many different techniques, the one thing he consistently did was see to it that, in the first stage of therapy, his clients understood their personality type. He insisted that techniques be adjusted or modified depending on the psychological type of the client. For more information on temperaments, see my brother's website on temperament (fourtemperaments.com).

Another helpful technique is teaching gender characteristics. Rejecting the idea that people are born with a blank slate and, therefore, gender differences are due entirely to culture, Jung taught gender differences were biological or were from archetypes. The masculine archetype is driving, penetrating, aggressive, and disciplined, while the feminine is yielding, containing, nurturing, concrete, and intuitive. In Jungian thought, every man has an anima (a feminine element) and all women have an animus (a masculine element), but these archetypes are often underdeveloped. Whole individuals embrace both of these dimensions. For a popular treatment of gender differences, see *Men Are from Mars, Women Are from Venus* by John Gray; see also *He Says, She Says* by Lillian Glass.

Many other techniques have proven helpful, including helping people become aware of their defense mechanisms (denial, projection, repression, etc.) and helping people get in touch with suppressed emotions. Behaviorism has been useful in dealing with autism, classroom discipline, assertiveness training, and, especially, phobias. Gestalt insistence on being *in the present* has a place. People focused on the past or the future cannot enjoy the present. As someone has said, "Many are crucified between two thieves, the regrets of yesterday and the anxieties of tomorrow."

Summary: The Bible has a more comprehensive view than any of the psychotherapies, but while all theories of psychoanalysis leave something to be desired, all contain insights that are compatible with the Bible and those insights can be used to supplement what the Bible has to say about people.

"Theology is more comprehensive and forms a backdrop in which psychology may be integrated" (Carter and Moline, p. 103). By embracing the spiritual, social, psychological (mind, emotions, will), purposeful, and physical aspects of people, the

Conclusion

Bible offers a more comprehensive view of people's makeup, the development of people, the explanation of pathology, and the nature of health. The Bible also includes the past, the present, and the future. For people to be all that they were designed to be, they must be reconciled to God, restored to a functional relationship with other people, reestablished in a purposeful life, and renewed mentally, emotionally, and volitionally.

Some psychotherapies offer detailed explanations and a wide range of methods for helping people that are compatible with the Bible. So, start with the biblical framework and "spoil the Egyptians" (Crabb, p. 47), that is, take from unbelievers that which is useful. In short, the Bible provides a framework; psychotherapies can fill in some details.

APPENDIX: PSYCHOTHEAPIES

Originator	Pathology	Therapy	Health
Sigmund Freud 1896/1923	unconscious, unresolved internal conflicts	free association and interpretation of resistance, transference, and dreams to make the unconscious conscious and thereby gain insight	conscious awareness of their drives so that they have self-control over them, good ego strength, and are growing
Carl G. Jung 1907/1911	not paying attention to the unconscious and attempting to compensate for the lack of balance	know personality type and dream work	becoming what one was meant to be by experiencing all of the archetypes in their proper balance.
Erik Erikson 1902	lack of nurture in childhood results in immature people	through a relationship with the therapist, a client strives to develop the ability to relate to self and others in healthy ways	mature people, i.e. seeing self and others realistically
Alfred Adler 1908/1912	having formed a "lifestyle" (non-conscious cognitive concepts about self and the world) based on subjective experience, people get discouraged	by encouragement and changing their lifestyle. Four steps: relationship, analysis, insight, and reorientation	have a functional or productive lifestyle. When persons are functioning well, they will embrace social interest, which is a concern for the welfare of others
B. F. Skinner 1953	motivated by survival and the drive to adapt to a challenging environment, people learn conditioned responses	focus on behavior to get a response to different stimuli.	modification of a particular behavior
Albert Ellis 1962	irrational beliefs produce emotional upsets	disputing to help clients challenge their irrational beliefs	to think rationally, feel appropriately, act functionally
Aaron T. Beck early 1960	distortions produce psychological distress	challenge dysfunctional beliefs and promote more realistic thinking	competency, that is, effective at a specific task or getting what one wants
William Glasser 1961/1965	based on personal perception, people's attempts to meet their needs produce ineffective behaviors	involvement, reject unrealistic behavior and teach better ways to fulfill needs	act responsibly and in accord with reality
Arnold A. Lazarus 1958	most problems arise from deficient or faulty social learning processes.	use what works, for whom, and under what conditions	untroubled functioning individuals

Psychotherapies, A Simple Explanation and Biblical Evaluation

Originator	Pathology	Therapy	Health
Rollo May 1953 Viktor Frankl 1959	in response to the issues of death, freedom, isolation, and meaninglessness, people adopt defenses and strategies that are inauthentic and self-deceptive in that they evade freedom and responsibility	a highly personal encounter between therapist and client	authentic individuals, that is, they have developed a clear sense of identity
Carl Rogers 1940	people develop an ideal self dictated by others as a result of acting according to rules and judgments of authority figures	therapeutic relationship	congruence between what they want to be, what they perceive are, and what they experience or are
Frederick S. Perls 1946	people are fragmented and unaware because they do not fully express their emotions	confrontational contact and awareness	of being truthful with themselves, not buried under layers of deceit. Also, in touch with their feelings and living in the moment
Eric Berne 1964	as a result of being scripted (or scripting themselves) in early childhood, adults play games to manipulate people to give them strokes	a contract between the client and the therapist	unscripted, having abandoned the programming of their parents (or their early decisions), and have decided to be spontaneous and intimate
Family Therapy 1956	symptomatic behavior occurs because family members' needs for closeness, self-expression, and meaning are not met in the family system	no standard treatment	a strong family includes 1) responding positively to challenges, 2) having a clearly articulated worldview, 3) communicating well, 4) spending time together, 5) making and honoring promises to one another as well as taking tasks and responsibilities seriously. As a result, there is a sense of belonging and respect for individual differences. 6) knowing how to express their love and appreciation for one another.
Jay Adams 1970	Sin in thinking and behavior	confrontation and confession	salvation and sanctification

BIBLIOGRAPHY

Adams, Jay. *Competent to Counsel.* Nutley, New Jersey: Presbyterian and Reformed Publishing Company, 1970.

_____. *What about Nouthetic Counseling?* Grand Rapids: Baker Book House, 1976.

Arlow, Jacob A. "Psychoanalysis" in *Current Psychotherapies*, edited by Corsini and Wedding, 4th ed. Itasca, IL: F. E. Peacock Publishers, Inc., 1989. Jacob A. Arlow is The Clinical Professor of Psychiatry at the New York University College of Medicine.

Bair, Deirdre. *Jung. A Biography.* Boston: Little, Brown and Company, 2003. Bair did extensive research in Zurich.

Bayly, Joseph. *What About Horoscopes?* Elgin, IL: David C. Cook Publishing Co., 1970.

Beck, Aaron T. and Weishaar, Majorie E. "Cognitive Therapy" in *Current Psychotherapies*, 4th ed., Raymond J. Corsini and Danny Wedding, 4th ed., Itasca, IL: F. E. Peacock Publishers. Inc., 1989.

Berne, Eric. *Games People Play.* New York, Grove Press, Inc., 1967.

Bobgan, Martin and Deidre. *The Psychological Way/The Spiritual Way.* Minneapolis: Bethany Fellowship, Inc., 1979.

Berkhof, L. *Systematic Theology.* Grand Rapids: Wm. B. Eerdmans Publishing, 1961.

Carter, John D. and Mohline, Richard. "The Nature and Scope of Integration: A Proposal," *The Integration of Psychology and Theology.* Grand Rapids: Zondervan Publishing House, 1979.

Carter, John D., and Narramore, Bruce. *The Integration of Psychology and Theology.* Grand Rapids: Zondervan Publishing House, 1979.

Cocoris, G. Michael. *Evangelism: A Biblical Approach.* Insights from the Word, Santa Monica, CA, 2018.

_____. *The Spiritual Life: Clarifying the Confusion.* Insights from the Word, Santa Monica, CA, 2018.

Cocoris, John T. *Born with a Creative Temperament.* McKinney, TX: Profile Dynamics, 2014.

_____. *The Temperament Model of Behavior.* McKinney, TX: Profile Dynamics, 2014.

Collins, Gary R. *The Rebuilding of Psychology,* Wheaton: Tyndale House, 1977.

Comer, Ronald J. *Fundamentals of Abnormal Psychology*, New York: W. H. Freeman and Company, 1996. Ronald J. Comer is a professor at Princeton University. *Fundamentals of Abnormal Psychology* is a college textbook.

Corey, Gerald. *Theory and Practice of Counseling and Psychotherapy*, 4th ed. Pacific Grove, CA: Brooks/Cole Publishing Company, 1991. Gerald Corey is a Professor of Counseling at California State University Fullerton. He received a doctorate in counseling from the University of Southern California.

Corsini, Raymond J. and Wedding, Danny, editors. *Current Psychotherapies*, 4th ed. Itasca, IL: F. E. Peacock Publishers, Inc., 1989.

Cousins, Norman. "The Mysterious Placebo: How the Mind helps Medicine Work," *Saturday Review*, Oct. 1, 1977.

Crabb Jr., Lawrence J. *Effective Biblical Counseling*, Zondervan Publishing House, 1977.

Douglas, Claire. "The Roots of Analytical Psychology," a lecture given at the C. G. Jung Institute of Los Angeles, January 14, 2003. Claire Douglas is a Jungian analyst.

Dusay, John M. and Dusay, Catherine Mulholland. "Transactional Analysis" in *Current Psychotherapies*, edited by Corsini and Wedding, 4th ed. Itasca, IL: F. E. Peacock Publishers, Inc., 1989.

Erickson, Millard J., *Christian Theology*. Grand Rapids: Baker Book House, 1990.

Ellis, Albert. "Rational-Emotive Therapy" in *Current Psychotherapies* (4th ed.), Raymond J. Corsini and Danny Wedding, 4th ed. Itasca, IL: F. E. Peacock Publishers. Inc., 1989.

Fiebert, Martin S. "Sex, Lies and Letters: A Sample of the Significant Deception in the Freud/Jung Relationship." www.csulb.edu. Martin S. Fiebert is a professor at California State University at Long Beach.

Foley, Vincent D. "Family Therapy," in *Current Psychotherapies*, edited by Corsini and Wedding, 4th ed. Itasca, IL: F. E. Peacock Publishers, Inc., 1989.

Fleck, J. Roland and Carter, John D. Carter. *Psychology and Christianity: Integrative Reading*. Nashville: Abington, 1981.

Frankl, Viktor, E. *Man's Search for Meaning*. New York: Washington Square Press, 1984.

Galipeau, Steven. "The Shadow: The Dark Side of the Self," a lecture at the C. G. Jung Institute of Los Angeles, March 3, 2003. Steven Galipeau is a Jungian analyst, lecturer, and author.

Grubin, David. "Young Dr. Freud," a PBS documentary.

Bibliogaphy

Hall, Calvin, S. and Nordby, Vernon, J., *A Primer of Jungian Psychology*. New York: Times Mirror, 1973.

Hallesby, O. *Temperament and the Christian Faith*. Minneapolis: Augsburg Publishing House, 1962.

and Theories (1902-1935)." www.cgyungpage.org.Hartman, Gary V. "A Time Line of the History and Development of Jung's Works."

Johnson, Eric. *Psychology and Christianity: Five Views*, edited by Eric L. Johnson. Downer Grove, Il, InterVarsity Press, 2010.

Jones, Stanton L. and Butman, Richard E. *Modern Psychotherapies*. Dowers Grove, IL: InterVarsity Press, 1991.

Jung, Carl Gustav. *Collected Works*. ed. Herbert Read, Michael Fordham, and Gerhard Adler. London: Routledge, 1953-78.

_____. *Man and His Symbols*. London: Aldus Books, 1964.

_____. *Memories, Dreams, Reflections*. London: Routledge, 1963.

Kreisman, Jerold J. and Straus, Hal. *I Hate You – Don't Leave Me*. New York: Avon Books, 1989.

Kaufmann, Yoram. "Analytical Psychotherapy" in *Current Psychotherapies*, edited by Corsini and Wedding, 4th ed. Itasca, IL: F. E. Peacock Publishers, Inc., 1989. Yoram Kaufmann is a psychiatrist in private practice.

Lauzun, Gerard. *Sigmund Freud: The Man and His Theories*, translated by Patrick Evans. Greenwich, Conn: Fawcett Publications, Inc., 1962.

Lazarus, Arnold A. "Multimodal Therapy" in *Current Psychotherapies*, edited by Corsini and Wedding, 4th ed. Itasca, IL: F. E. Peacock Publishers, Inc., 1989.

MacArthur Jr., John F. and Wayne A. Mack. *An Introduction to Biblical Counseling*. Santa Clarita, CA: The Master's College, 1994.

MacGregor, Geddes. *Dictionary of Religion and Philosophy*. New York: Paragon House, 1991.

May, Rollo. *The Art of Counseling*. New York: Abingdon Press, 1939.

May, Rollo and Irvin Yalom. "Existential Psychotherapy" in *Current Psychotherapies*, edited by Corsini and Wedding, 4th ed. Itasca, IL: F. E. Peacock Publishers, Inc., 1989.

Miller, Barry. "Archetypes of the Collective Unconscious," a lecture given at the C. G. Jung Institute of Los Angeles, January 21, 2003. Barry Miller is a Jungian analyst.

Mosak, Harold, H. "Adlerian Psychotherapy" in *Current Psychotherapies* (4th ed.), Raymond J. Corsini and Danny Wedding, 4th ed. Itasca, IL: F. E. Peacock Publishers. Inc., 1989.

Narramore, S. Bruce. "Perspectives on the Integration of Psychology and Theology" in *Psychology and Christianity: Integrative Readings*, J. Roland Fleck and John D. Carter, editors, Nashville: Abington, 1981.

Pelletier, Kenneth R. "Mind as Healer, Mind as Slayer." *Psychology Today*, February 1977.

Raskin, Nathaniel J. and Carl R. Rogers. "Person-Centered Therapy" in *Current Psychotherapies*, edited by Corsini and Wedding, 4th ed. Itasca, IL: F. E. Peacock Publishers, Inc., 1989.

Ross, Colin and Pam, Alvin. *Pseudoscience in Biological Psychiatry, Blaming the Body*. New York: John Wiley & Sons, 1995.

Smith-Marder, Paula. "Complexes," a lecture given at the C. G. Jung Institute of Los Angeles, February 4, 2003. Paula Smith-Marder is a Jungian analyst.

Stevens, Anthony. *Jung*. Oxford: Oxford University Press, 1996. Anthony Stevens is a graduate of Oxford University, a Jungian analyst, and an author.

Sweeney, Joan. "Is Psychoanalysis Flawed by Freud's Own Failing?" *The Los Angeles Times* Feb. 14, 1984.

Time Magazine, "Is Freud Dead?" November 29, 1993.

White, Robert W. *The Abnormal Personality*, 3rd ed. New York: The Ronald Press Company, 1964. White was a Professor of Clinical Psychology at Harvard University. He received his degree from Harvard.

Wilson, G. Terrence. "Behavior Therapy" in *Current Psychotherapies* (4th ed.), Raymond J. Corsini and Danny Wedding, 4th ed. Itasca, IL: F. E. Peacock Publishers. Inc., 1989.

Yalom, Irvin D. *Love's Executioner*. New York: HarperCollins Publishers Inc., 2000.

Yontef, Gary M., and James, S. Simkin. "Gestalt Therapy" in *Current Psychotherapies*, 4th ed. Raymond J. Corsini and Danny Wedding (4th ed.), Itasca, IL: F. E. Peacock Publishers. Inc., 19

About The Author

G. Michael Cocoris is a gifted communicator. He can make even complicated subjects simple, clear, and practical. His breadth of experience has allowed him to relate to a wide range of audiences.

Michael received a Bachelor of Arts degree from Tennessee Temple University, a Master of Theology degree from Dallas Seminary, and a Doctorate of Divinity from Biola University. He traveled the United States for over a dozen years as a speaker. He has also been a seminary professor, visiting lecturer, and world traveler, including hosting tours to Israel and China.

Michael has pastored three churches, including a rural church when he was in seminary, an urban church, the historic Church of the Open Door, first in downtown Los Angeles and later in Glendora, California, and a suburban church, the Lindley Church in Tarzana California, a suburb of Los Angeles. While at the Church of Open Door, he had a daily radio broadcast.

Michael has written numerous magazine articles, mainly for *Biblical Research Monthly*. He has authored a number of books, including *Seventy Years on Hope Street, A History of the Church of the Open Door*; *The Spiritual Life, Clarifying the Confusion*; *Repentance, The Most Misunderstood Word in the Bible*; *Evangelism: A Biblical Approach*; *The Salvation Controversy*; *Lordship Salvation: Is It Biblical?*; *The Books of the Bible, the Subject, Structure, Situation, and Significant Verses of Each Book*; *Psalms, A Song for Every Situation, Each Summarized on One Page*; and *Psychotherapies: A Simple Explanation and Biblical Evaluation*. In addition, he was a contributor to *The NKJV Study Bible* and *Nelson's New Illustrated Bible Commentary*.

Michael is the pastor of the Lindley Church in Tarzana, California. He and his wife, Patricia, lived in Santa Monica, California.

www.ingramcontent.com/pod-product-compliance
Lightning Source LLC
Chambersburg PA
CBHW081438070526
44586CB00019B/2166